Shakespeare's
Letters

Shakespeare's Letters

~

ALAN STEWART

OXFORD

UNIVERSITY PRESS

OXFORD

UNIVERSITY PRESS

Great Clarendon Street, Oxford OX2 6DP

Oxford University Press is a department of the University of Oxford.
It furthers the University's objective of excellence in research, scholarship,
and education by publishing worldwide in

Oxford New York

Auckland Cape Town Dar es Salaam Hong Kong Karachi
Kuala Lumpur Madrid Melbourne Mexico City Nairobi
New Delhi Shanghai Taipei Toronto

With offices in

Argentina Austria Brazil Chile Czech Republic France Greece
Guatemala Hungary Italy Japan Poland Portugal Singapore
South Korea Switzerland Thailand Turkey Ukraine Vietnam

Oxford is a registered trade mark of Oxford University Press
in the UK and in certain other countries

Published in the United States
by Oxford University Press Inc., New York

British Library Cataloguing in Publication Data

Data available

Library of Congress Cataloging in Publication Data

Data available

Typeset by SPI Publisher Services, Pondicherry, India
Printed in Great Britain
on acid-free paper by
CPI Antony Rowe, Chippenham, Wiltshire

ISBN 978-0-19-954927-6

1 3 5 7 9 10 8 6 4 2

For

Daniel Ebalo

ACKNOWLEDGEMENTS

This book started out having nothing to do with Shakespeare. My original interest was in how early modern letters worked, an issue that became crucial when I was working on the correspondence of Francis Bacon in 2000–2 at Birkbeck, University of London, with Patricia Brewerton and Andrew Gordon. Virtually every day the three of us would abandon our dark basement office for an equally dark basement coffee bar and ponder the strange and wonderful quirks of the materials we were dealing with. What initially seemed to be a straightforward subject—surely letters are just letters?—became increasingly complex the closer we looked, and, to me, increasingly fascinating.

That conversation has continued since, and led naturally to further, inspiring collaborations. Lisa Jardine and I worked on the founding in 2002 of a Centre for Editing Lives and Letters in London, where I had the opportunity to teach a graduate course on 'writing lives from letters'. Patricia Brewerton and I convened the *unFamiliar Letters* conference at Birkbeck in July 2002, which brought together forty scholars all working on early modern epistles. Heather Wolfe and I curated the Folger Shakespeare Library's 2004 exhibition *Letterwriting in Renaissance England*, and edited its accompanying catalogue, during which time Heather taught me much about the physical materials of letters. Lynne Magnusson and I led a seminar on letter-writing at the 2007 Shakespeare Association of America meeting, which furthered our discussion of all things epistolary. These experiences, and these colleagues, were invaluable in helping me think about letters. But it was Barbara Mowat who informed me that my vague ideas for a book on letters would be better put to use on the plays of William Shakespeare, and I realised instantly that, quite characteristically, she was right. And so I spent the summer of 2005 in Paris re-reading Shakespeare, and the summer of 2006 in London researching Shakespeare's use of letters. *Shakespeare's Letters* is the result.

I have been incredibly fortunate to write this book at Columbia, in the everyday company of a remarkable set of colleagues, all of whom have read, listened to, debated and flayed various parts of this project: Julie Crawford, Kathy Eden, Jean Howard, David Scott Kastan, Molly Murray, and Anne Lake Prescott. I am particularly indebted to Jim Shapiro who has done more than anyone else to encourage, cajole, and provoke me into writing about Shakespeare's letters. Among an inspiring graduate cohort, I am especially indebted to András Kiséry and Adam Hooks, who commented on drafts, and to Rebecca Calcagno, who tried to correct my ignorance of the plays of Shakespeare's contemporaries with a stream of helpful references. Friends and colleagues further afield read drafts of chapters, answered queries, or allowed me to read their unpublished research: I thank Amanda Bailey, Diana Barnes, David Bergeron, Paul Cannan, Christopher Ebert, David Kathman, Jerry Passannante, Chris Ross, Adam Smyth, Goran Stanivukovic, and Matthew Steggle. I am particularly grateful to James Daybell, whose own work has opened up the field of early modern letters, and who has remained a generous and supportive fellow traveller. I thank Rob Blackshaw and Hilary Fraser for making their homes available to me; and especially Richard Schoch who has been a gracious host and good company on the many occasions when I returned to London.

Ideas were tried out on audiences at Queen Mary and Birkbeck, both University of London; the Columbia Early Modern Seminar; the Columbia University Shakespeare Seminar; the University of North Carolina at Charlotte; the University of Southern

California's Early Modern Studies Institute at the Huntington; the annual meetings of the Renaissance Society of America (2006) and the Shakespeare Association of America (2006, 2008); and a Folger Institute faculty seminar on *The English Grammar School*. For invitations to speak, and for questions and challenges, I'm grateful to Corey Abate, Michael Baron, Anston Bosman, Warren Boutcher, Bianca Calabresi, Maurice Charney, Joanna Cheetham, Cyndia Clegg, Stephen Clucas, Lynn Enterline, Gina Fitzmaurice, Cora Fox, Elizabeth Goodland, Elizabeth Hanson, Deb Harkness, Andrew Hartley, Tom Healy, Heather James, Jeffrey Kahan, Yvette Khoury, Mary Ellen Lamb, Rebecca Lemon, Naomi Liebler, Zoltan Markus, Kirk Melnikoff, Margaret Mikesell, Jen Munroe, Curtis Perry, June Schlueter, Bruce Smith, Tiffany Werth, Sue Wiseman, Suzanne Woofford, and many others.

Valuable help was supplied by the Folger Shakespeare Library in the form of a short-term fellowship to work on 'the materiality of early modern letters' (2000), and by the UK's Arts and Humanities Research Council for postdoctoral research support on the Bacon letters project (2000–2). I am grateful once again to the collections and staff of the British Library, the Folger Shakespeare Library, Columbia University's Butler Library, and the Shakespeare Birthplace Trust Record Office, especially Robert Bearman and Mairi MacDonald. For their help in providing images I am indebted to Jo Wong (Shakespeare Birthplace Trust), Wendy Zieger (Bridgeman Art Library), Stephen Tabor (Huntington Library), Bettina Smith (Folger), Camille Lynch (National Gallery of Ireland), and Anna van Lingen (Rijksmuseum Amsterdam).

Part of Chapter 1 of this book has appeared in *Shakespeare Studies*; a version of Chapter 3 was published in *Shakespeare Quarterly*; some passages from the Introduction will appear in a different guise in *Textual Practice*. I am grateful to these publications for the permission to re-use material, and to their editors for comments on drafts of the work: Garrett Sullivan and Susan Zimmerman; Jonathan Gil Harris, Gail Kern Paster, and Bill Sherman; and Andrew Hadfield.

At Oxford University Press, my editor Andrew McNeillie has been a welcome supporter of this project from the outset. I am grateful to him for his confidence, and for the entire team at OUP, especially Jacqueline Baker and Fiona Smith, for their enthusiasm and expertise. For their wonderfully full, generous, and supportive readers' reports, and the example of their own work on letters, I am indebted to Lynne Magnusson and Gary Schneider. For their careful proofreading and copy-editing, I thank Camasin Middour, Susan Beer, and Carolyn McAndrew.

I dedicate this book to Daniel Ebalo, with my love and gratitude.

CONTENTS

ILLUSTRATIONS

ABBREVIATIONS

For ease of reference, quotations from Shakespeare's plays and verse have been taken from the modernized texts in the most recent individual Arden volumes (either 2nd or 3rd series), using the Arden edition's abbreviations for each work (see below). The relevant editions are listed at the head of the Bibliography (pp. 362–3). Any readings dependent on specific Quarto or Folio printings have been noted in the text.

AC	*Antony and Cleopatra*
AW	*All's Well That Ends Well*
AYL	*As You Like It*
CE	*The Comedy of Errors*
Cor	*Coriolanus*
Cym	*Cymbeline*
Ham	*Hamlet*
1H4	*King Henry IV Part I*
2H4	*King Henry IV Part 2*
H5	*King Henry V*
1H6	*King Henry VI Part 1*
2H6	*King Henry VI Part 2*
3H6	*King Henry VI Part 3*
H8	*King Henry VIII (All is True)*
JC	*Julius Caesar*

KJ	*King John*
KL	*King Lear*
LC	*A Lover's Complaint* in *Shakespeare's Sonnets*
LLL	*Love's Labour's Lost*
Luc	*Lucrece* in *The Poems*
MA	*Much Ado About Nothing*
Mac	*Macbeth*
MM	*Measure for Measure*
MND	*A Midsummer Night's Dream*
MV	*The Merchant of Venice*
MW	*The Merry Wives of Windsor*
Oth	*Othello*
Per	*Pericles*
R2	*King Richard II*
R3	*King Richard III*
RJ	*Romeo and Juliet*
Son	*Shakespeare's Sonnets*
TC	*Troilus and Cressida*
Tem	*The Tempest*
TGV	*The Two Gentlemen of Verona*
Tim	*Timon of Athens*
Tit	*Titus Andronicus*
TN	*Twelfth Night*
TNK	*The Two Noble Kinsmen*
TS	*The Taming of the Shrew*
VA	*Venus and Adonis* in *The Poems*
WT	*The Winter's Tale*

Introduction: Searching for Shakespeare's Letters

In February 1795, a select group of London society's great and good converged on 8 Norfolk Street, off the Strand, to view, by invitation only, a set of manuscripts described by their host Samuel Ireland as 'the Shakespeare Papers',[1] an assortment of personal correspondence, contracts, legal instruments, and manuscript drafts of *King Lear*, a portion of *Hamlet*, and the hitherto unknown play *Vortigern and Rowena*.[2] Subscriptions for a print edition at four guineas a throw were snapped up, and a high-quality folio volume entitled *Miscellaneous Papers and Legal Instruments under the hand and seal of William Shakspeare* was issued on 24 December 1795.[3] Interest was so intense that Ireland was able to negotiate with Richard Brinsley Sheridan for a production of *Vortigern* at the Drury Lane Theatre to open on 2 April. But by the time the curtain rose on *Vortigern*, the Shakespeare Papers had lost their lustre. Simmering suspicions of foul play[4] had culminated in the publication of *An Inquiry into the Authenticity of certain Miscellaneous Papers and Legal Instruments*, a 435-page critique by the leading Shakespeare scholar of the day, Edmond Malone, who released his tome to devastating effect just two days before the first performance.[5] By the time leading man John Philip Kemble pronounced the deathly fifth-act line 'And when this solemn mockery is o'er', the audience was in hysterics;[6] *Vortigern* closed on its opening night. Although Ireland continued to defend his edition,[7] his son William Henry soon confessed that he had forged all the documents in a misguided attempt to please his father,[8] and the Ireland Shakespeare papers were fated to become a by-word for the gullibility of those who search for Shakespearean relics.[9]

Forgeries they may be but the Ireland papers are intriguing because they tell us what readers were thought to want from Shakespeare papers in 1795.[10] Although the single performance of *Vortigern*, a suitably theatrical icon of hubris and bathos, has been a focal point for later tellings of the story, top of the wish-list at the time were the letters. From the first advertisement of the papers' existence the emphasis was laid, not on the newly discovered plays, but on the letters; the *Miscellaneous Papers* opened with the letters; and Malone (perforce, since he had not seen the play-text) spent his energies demolishing the letters.[11] The centrality of the letters is not surprising: in the 1790s, great figures, both dead and still living, were read through multiple-volume editions of their collected correspondence. After half a century of consuming fiction dominated by the epistolary novel, British readers expected letters to provide insight not only into events of the letter-writer's life, but also into emotions and self-reflection, producing a kind of ongoing autobiography with narrative vigour. And these are the letters that Ireland knew his readers wanted: letters to Anne Hathaway (complete with verses and a lock of his hair) providing proof that the Bard was in love with his wife-to-be; a letter to fellow actor Richard Cowley, the first Verges in *Much Ado About Nothing*, proof that he was a hands-on player immersed in the colourful theatrical world of his day; correspondence between Shakespeare and the earl of Southampton, proof that he was a poet blessed with the personalized patronage of the aristocracy; and, in pride of place opening the collection, a letter from the Virgin Queen herself addressed 'For Master William / Shakspeare / atte the Globe bye / Thames', and docketed by the playwright, 'Thys Letterre I dydde receive fromme / mye most gracyouse Ladye

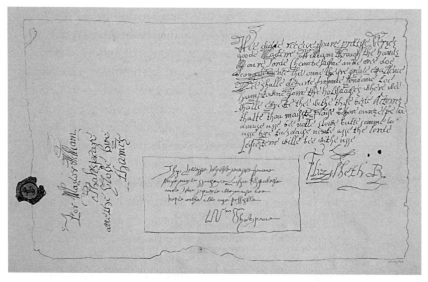

1. Queen Elizabeth's letter to William Shakespeare, as published by Samuel Ireland. Samuel Ireland ed., *Miscellaneous Papers and Legal Instruments under the hand and seal of William Shakspeare* (London: Egerton *et al.*, 1796), unnumbered plate.

Elyzabethe/ande I doe requeste itt maye bee/kepte with alle care possyble/Wm Shakspeare' (see illustration 1).[12] As the biographer, playwright, and Ireland paper 'believer' James Boaden put it, with these papers 'it will be clearly proved that all the degrading nonsense, of his holding horses, &c., will be found utterly fictitious, and that this great man was the Garrick of his age'.[13]

Although Malone was merciless in his ridicule of Ireland's papers on grounds of their dubious orthography, language, phraseology, handwriting, and paper,[14] he was by no means opposed to the idea of 'Shakespeare papers'. Quite the contrary: he absolutely shared the Irelands' mania for such documentary evidence. Indeed, his attack on Samuel Ireland was in part defensive: having spent years trawling through county records offices looking for the poet's hand to little effect, Malone was evidently shaken by Ireland's announcement of his impressive findings, and promptly issued an urgent call for similar documents in *The Gentleman's Magazine*, in which he expressed the hope that 'persons possessed of ancient papers would take the trouble to examine them, or permit others to peruse them'—these persons, he believed, would be descendants of the executors of Shakespeare's last descendants.[15] The Shakespeare Malone wanted to find was a sturdier, more practical man than Ireland's: a successful commercial playwright who dealt in property, a family man whose papers would pass properly through familial and legal channels. But letters, he too believed, would be where he would find the man.

In this book, I too am searching for Shakespeare's letters. But I believe Malone and Ireland were on a wild goosechase, on the trail of the kind of letters that would make sense to the 1790s reader. Not only were they looking for the wrong letters, they were looking in the wrong place. For Shakespeare's letters survive in abundance—in his plays, or, more precisely, on his stage. At a conservative estimate, one hundred and eleven letters appear on stage in the course of Shakespeare's plays, and his characters allude to many more, running through all the genres and his entire career—early plays and late plays, comedies, tragedies, tragicomedies, and histories all contain letters.[16] In fact, Shakespeare depicts letters in all but five of the First Folio plays, so that their very absence in itself becomes telling. *The Comedy of Errors* follows its Plautine source *Menechmi*, which does not contain letters though other Plautus plays notably do. There is nothing named a letter in the semi-magical world of *A Midsummer Night's Dream*, nor in the play-world of *The Taming of the Shrew*, nor in *The Tempest* where Gonzalo (channelling Montaigne) dreams of a land where 'Letters should not be known' (*Tem* 2.1.151).[17] Alone among the English history plays, which are usually riddled with letters, *Henry V* dispenses with strictly epistolary communications, despite the fact that the chronicles insist on that king's especial facility with the letter form: instead, Shakespeare's *Henry V* is obsessed with the spoken word, whether it be the rousing oratory of the king's speeches, the conversations heard by the king in disguise, or the scenes of multiple, often conflicting tongues that point the play's intra-national and international focus.

But in every other play, Shakespeare physically places letters on stage. To some extent, Shakespeare is contributing to a tradition of stage letters that stretches back as far as Euripides and was exploited masterfully by Plautus.[18] While Shakespeare undoubtedly draws on classical theatrical models for plot devices involving letters, *Shakespeare's Letters* will insist however on the historical specificity of what I shall call his 'grammar of letters': a vocabulary and a set of images that originate in the material practices of the letter-writing culture of early modern England. In other words, although Shakespeare conjures settings from the Trojan wars, through Rome and ancient Britain, to the Wars of the Roses, to sixteenth-century Venice, the letter-writing culture he represents is emphatically that of late Elizabethan and Jacobean England, with one halfhearted exception, *Titus Andronicus*, to prove the rule. It is these letters that are at the heart of my study of *Shakespeare's Letters*.

Early Modern English Letters

Letters were vital to the early modern world. In any situation where face-to-face oral communication was impossible, letters became the conduit through which news was relayed, orders were conveyed, plans were laid, and trade was transacted. They were the social glue that held firm friendships, alliances, and kinship ties between individuals at a distance. Despite its social importance, however, the epistolary system was far from foolproof. Letters were routinely delayed, misdelivered, lost, and intercepted. Letters could be the clinching proof in a legal case but they could equally be forged and doctored. For every normative statement I could make about early modern letters, there is evidence aplenty to contradict it in practice.

In recent years, early modern English letters have been the subject of considerable critical scrutiny.[19] The social functions of letters have been examined by Susan Whyman and James Daybell,[20] while the burgeoning realm of vernacular letters has been highlighted by Roger Chartier and Gary Schneider.[21] The rhetoric of English letters has been explored by Frank Whigham and Peter Mack;[22] the role played by letters in constituting and maintaining friendly relations between men has been analysed by Jonathan Goldberg, David Bergeron, Alan Bray, and Jeffrey Masten;[23] the possibilities that letters bring to women's history have been explored by Daybell and Sara Jayne Steen;[24] and the various postal systems have been documented by Philip Beale and Mark Brayshay.[25] A series of exhibitions, conferences, seminars, and special editions of journals has opened up the field impressively.[26] Most pertinently to this project, Lynne Magnusson's important study *Shakespeare and Social Dialogue* has analysed Shakespeare's plays against the prescriptions and examples of early modern English letter-writing manuals to demonstrate that the rhetorics of these two apparently disparate genres draw on a set of shared assumptions about personal interactions.[27] Despite the valuable insights generated by all this work, however, it is still tempting for us to see letters as providing an unmediated glimpse into the past—and even more tempting for audiences of Shakespeare plays to glimpse a letter on stage and believe that what they're seeing is something similar to what arrives in their mail boxes each morning. But these stage letters are radically unfamiliar to us.

Since the stage is a realm of speech and action, not of writing and reading, we might not expect the early modern theatre to reflect letters in the real world. As Frederick Kiefer writes, 'Shakespeare and his contemporaries knew that reading and writing, in themselves, do not necessarily exert a theatrical appeal. The sight of an actor perusing a book or composing a letter is not likely to engage an audience for long since these are essentially solitary activities and typically require a certain self-absorption on the part of reader or writer.'[28] Other critics have been more scathing. Muriel Bradbrook complains that 'whenever Shakespeare can think of nothing else to do, he puts in a misdirected letter';[29] Ann Pasternak Slater has attacked as 'painful' Shakespeare's apparent 'readiness to pull explanatory letters out of the air in the hurried conclusions of both comedy and tragedy'.[30] To many critics, Shakespeare's letters are 'plot devices', designed only to further the narrative.

But this cannot be the whole story. For, as Stephen Orgel notes, 'Renaissance plays seem compulsively to turn to scenes of writing, to letters and documents, to written discourse as the mode of action', to the extent that 'the writing of documents is endemic to Renaissance drama'.[31] Indeed, Orgel's point is especially well taken with regards to Shakespeare, whose drama is notably riddled with examples of written discourse: notes, books, petitions, proclamations, challenges, maps, scrolls, bonds, deeds, papers, verses, schedules, treaties, riddles, commissions, rolls, messages, articles, packets, warrants, depositions, inventories, supplications, resolutions, sonnets, wills, indictments, oracles, ballads, lists (from market lists to lists of entertainments), almanacs, play parts, prophecies, characters, gamuts, inscriptions, speeches, calendars; plus a few heavier items of writing paraphernalia: tablebooks, wax tablets, non-wax tablets, and the odd tombstone.[32] Jonas Barish goes further, claiming that 'Shakespeare places a quite extraordinary reliance on *writings* in his plays, even where it almost seems as though he is dragging them in, looking for excuses to insert them. He weaves them deeply and inextricably into the verbal texture of the plays, whether in documents we actually see or those we only hear about, whether they are read out word for word or merely paraphrased, so that graphic communication becomes as natural and inevitable and indispensable a part of the verbal medium as its vocal counterpart'.[33] But while Orgel and Barish draw attention to writings or *documents* in a general sense, it is letters that are most frequently seen on stage in Shakespeare's plays, and it is to letters that this study turns.

I have deliberately chosen 'letters' as my working category rather than the class of 'documents' or the practices of 'reading and writing'. Several critics, notably David Bergeron, Frederick Kiefer, and Frances Teague, have studied the documents in Shakespeare's drama, and others, led by Jonathan Goldberg, have analysed the acts of reading and writing in the plays.[34] Some have considered letters among the mass of paperwork to be read or written, or pondered

the use of letters in an individual play, but Shakespeare's stage letters as a whole have attracted less sustained critical interest.[35] At
first glance 'letters' may appear narrow in its specificity, but it is
intended to be expansive in its scope, encompassing activities, sites,
and social relationships not usually associated with the category of
'documents' nor with the textual practices of reading and writing.
My understanding of 'letters' ranges from the still raw materials
of writing implements—the gall in ink, the goose from which the
quill is plucked—through the manual processes of folding the paper,
writing, dusting and sealing the letter, its bearing and (hopefully)
delivery by messenger, its reception—a complex performance of
which reading of the text is only one part—and its ultimate retention, whether filed in the archive, talismanically pressed to the heart,
or committed to the flames.

It is the working assumption of this book that only by paying
attention to this wider culture of letters can we understand the part
the letters played in early modern England, and on the early modern
English stage. The implications of this are twofold. First, the period
in which Shakespeare is writing is importantly removed from our
modern understanding of letters, fixated on notions of privacy and
personal subjectivity, and anonymous postal systems. Second, what
happens to letters when they are placed on a stage is specific to that
cultural institution, and is further removed than has been previously
assumed from the ideologies that permeate the letter-writing textbooks of the early modern England. *Shakespeare's Letters*, then, is an
attempt to excavate both of these pasts—historical and theatrical—
in order to capture the particular nature of the letters on Shakespeare's stage.

unFamiliar Letters: Privacy Before the Post Office

The assumption of modernity is that letters circulate between
private individuals by means of an anonymous and impersonal

postal service. Such an understanding underpins the most influential recent theorization of letters and letter-writing in European
contexts by Jacques Derrida and Bernhard Siegert.[36] But it is an
assumption that will not bear scrutiny in relation to the England
of Shakespeare's day. First, not all letters derive from an individual:
a good many letters were written by someone other than the signa-
tory, either a household secretary or amanuensis, or a commercial
scrivener paid for his services. The role of the secretary has been
well explored by Jonathan Goldberg, Richard Rambuss, and others;[37]
and our understanding of early modern scribal culture has been
enhanced by Harold Love and Peter Beal.[38] We see the personal
secretarial relationship at work in several Shakespeare plays, with
male secretaries serving both men and women. When Enobarbus
leaves, Antony orders Eros to 'Write to him—| I will subscribe—
gentle adieus and greetings. | Say that I wish he never find more
cause | To change a master!' (AC 4.5.13–16). Antony expects Eros
to draft the letter, according to his general instructions and he will
provide the subscription and superscription. Goneril instructs her
steward Oswald to write a letter to Regan—'How now Oswald? |
What, have you writ that letter to my sister?' (KL 1.4.329–30)—and
then clearly tells him that he may add to the letter: 'Inform her
full of my particular fear, | And thereto add such reasons of your
own, | As may compact it more'(1.4.332–5). While Goneril's relation-
ship with Oswald is often seen as suspect (see Chapter 5), we meet
precisely the same phenomenon, rendered quite innocuously, in *All's
Well That Ends Well*, where the Countess of Rousillon instructs her
steward to write an emotionally powerful letter to her son:

> Write, write, Rynaldo,
> To this unworthy husband of his wife;
> Let every word weigh heavy of her worth
> That he does weigh too light; my greatest grief,
> Though little he do feel it, set down sharply.
> Dispatch the most convenient messenger.
>
> (*AW* 3.4.29–34)

The fact that she moves directly from instructions for the letter's composition to instructions for its delivery suggests that the Countess may not even wish to subscribe the letter herself: the entire process is in the hands of her trusted steward. This habit of allowing servants to write personal letters was especially the case for elite letter-writers (as in all the above instances) and, it has been argued, for female letter-writers, if we accept that rates of literacy were lower in women than in men.[39] Moreover, the reception of letters was by no means a private affair. As we shall see, letters are usually delivered in public, and often read silently in public, or aloud in gatherings of various sizes. These habits necessarily challenge our casual linking of letter-writing and individual privacy.

Similarly, there is a tendency in work on early modern letters to look for the germ of what Siegert has dubbed the 'Epoche der Post' ('age of the postal system'). In Siegert's analysis, postal systems were '*instrumenta regni*': in the medieval period as the state systems promoted the exercise of empire while courier services formed closed systems facilitating the specialist worlds of the university, the law courts, and merchants. Siegert traces the rise of the modern postal system from the early seventeenth century, when Cardinal Duke Albrecht VII, viceroy of the Netherlands, gave formal permission in 1600 to the Taxis family to charge postage for private letters, effectively allowing the state to regulate all postal exchange.[40] While Siegert's study is based in continental Europe, one might track a similar shift in seventeenth-century England. In 1635, Charles I issued a proclamation that permitted his subjects to use the royal post for private mail—although his motives were primarily financial, the new charges (from 2d to 8d per letter depending on the length of journey) being an easy means to raise funds. While there were moments over the following decades when the government took the service back into their own hands, the long-term viability of the service was assured by Oliver Cromwell's 1657 act 'for settling the Postage of England, Scotland and Ireland', which lowered the rates for hiring horses and permitted government officials to use the post without charge. At the Restoration, Charles II reiterated Cromwell's move by passing another act 'for erecting and establishing a Post Office' (1660); in 1661, postmarks were introduced to help account-ability; and in 1680, cut-price intra-London and Westminster cor-respondence became possible, thanks to William Dockwra's penny post.[41]

Our assumption that such a postal service exists has ramifica-tions beyond the history of the mail. Ian Watt famously insisted that the development of the epistolary novel, culminating in the masterpieces of Fielding and Richardson, was 'materially assisted by a very great improvement of postal facilities', starting with the establishment of the penny post.[42] He writes that, as a result, 'Their drama unrolls in a flow of letters from one lonely closet to another', producing the effect that he names 'private experience'.[43] Before this shift, the convention of the dedicatory epistle had been exploited to various ends in such literary works as Thomas More's *Utopia* (1516); and George Gascoigne's 'The aduentures of Master F.I' (1573),[44] and letters become the whole story as early as 1602, when Nicholas Breton's popular *A poste with a madde packet of letters*, a primitive 'intercepted letters' publication, made its first appearance.[45] But the later epistolary novels, with their assumed nexus of letter-writing, privacy, and subjectivity are qualitatively different, precisely because of the new possibilities of the mail system, and we should be wary of projecting this understanding of the private letter back onto the early modern stage.

What Shakespeare's audience recognized in his plays was a far older postal set-up, one that did not always reach the status of a 'sys-tem'. Although a private Royal Post was in existence, Shakespeare's plays never depict it. Instead, they are concerned with a messy, *ad hoc* arrangement of messengers sent between individuals, some-times members of a personal retinue, sometimes not. The only official messenger that is portrayed is the carrier, part of a slower system that carried not only letters but goods and people (see Chapter 3). In Shakespeare's understanding of letters, then, we find not the first glimmers of the *Epoche der Post*, but a long-established model still in robust form, in many ways a traditional system of highly personalized epistolary communication, where virtually every letter transaction involved a bearer, messenger, or carrier whose identity one knew. It is the aim of *Shakespeare's Letters* to recapture this lost culture of letters, with the aim of throwing new light on the dozens of letters that cross Shakespeare's stage.

How Shakespeare Didn't Read his Erasmus

Early modern English letter-writers did not have to look far for advice on how to construct their letters. Many Neo-Latin writers, including Desiderius Erasmus and Juan Luis Vives, produced letter-writing manuals or epistolographies, which have been well studied by Judith Rice Henderson, Charles Fantazzi and Lisa Jardine.[46] As the sixteenth century progressed, vernacular manuals came onto the market, led by William Fulwood's *The Enimie of Idelnesse* (1568)[47] and Abraham Fleming's Ciceronian *A Panoplie of Epistles* (1576),[48] and others aimed at increasingly specialized markets: servingmen in Walter Darell's 1578 *A short discourse of the life of seruingmen ... With certeine letters verie necessarie for seruingmen, and other persons to peruse;*[49] secretaries in Angel Day's *The English Secretorie* (1586)[50] and Thomas Gainsford's 1616 *The Secretaries Studie;*[51] merchants and factors in John Browne's *The Marchants Avizo* (1588);[52] and, later, women.[53] These too have been studied illuminatingly by Lynne Magnusson and Gary Schneider.[54]

Most of these manuals, and the critics who study them, rehearse a standard historiography of Renaissance letter-writing that runs something like this. In the medieval period, letters were written according to the *ars dictaminis*, whose birth has been traced back at least as far as the late-eleventh-century writings of the monk Alberic of Monte Casino. The *ars dictaminis* understood letter-writing as a rhetorical art and elaborated a protocol which prescribed forms and formulae for writing.[55] The rise of humanism in trecento Italy, however, saw a revival of interest in the classical period's familiar letter, sparked by Francesco Petrarca's 1345 rediscovery in Verona's cathedral library of a manuscript of Cicero's familiar letters to Atticus, Quintus, and Brutus, a revelation that reportedly moved him to tears. Petrarch was inspired by Cicero to develop a new critical theory of letter-writing, and to write and collect his own prose letters, a habit that became popular with such prominent quattrocento Florentine humanists as Giovanni Boccaccio, Coluccio Salutati, Leonardo Bruni, and Poggio Bracciolini, the last two of whom edited and disseminated collections of their own letters. By the time the printing press appeared in Europe, letter-writing was a fashionable academic movement, ripe for development, and in 1495 Marsilio Ficino became the first living writer to disseminate his personal correspondence in print.

It was the Dutch humanist Erasmus of Rotterdam, however, who most fully realized the possibilities of the letter form. He not only published many of his letters, but used them to create the image, and subsequently the reality, of a pan-European network of like-minded humanist scholars, whose printed letters not only disseminated their ideas but also promoted their careers. As Lisa Jardine has compellingly demonstrated, Erasmus forged his lasting reputation through a manipulation of the familiar letter in print, simultaneously ensuring that letters were central to his pedagogical programme.[56] Erasmus himself dictated that any edition of his works 'that concern literature and education' should contain four key works, of which the first was *De conscribendis epistolis*, his most sustained work on letter-writing.[57] More subtly, but equally effectively, Erasmus's exemplars and techniques constantly drew on letter-writing: in his *De copia*, to give only the most prominent example, the first practical demonstration Erasmus gives of copious writing is on the phrase 'tuae litterae me magnopere delectarunt' ('your letter pleased me mightily')—he comes up with some two hundred variants.[58] In this way, Erasmus promulgated his definition of the letter (sometimes citing as authority the Greek sophist Libanius, sometimes Terence's contemporary Turpilius): 'A letter is a conversation between two absent persons', arguing that 'the letter differs hardly at all from the ordinary speech of everyday conversation'.[59]

Since Erasmus had an effective near-monopoly of the textbooks used in English schools,[60] so the story continues, his ideas about letter-writing were instilled into generations of schoolboys, including, at Stratford-upon-Avon's grammar school, the young William Shakespeare; in his reconstruction of Shakespeare's possible grammar school education, T.W. Baldwin devotes an entire chapter to 'Shakspere's epistles'.[61] As the sixteenth century progressed, moreover, these Erasmian ideas, thus far confined to a Latin-reading elite, were adapted and translated into the vernacular for use by an increasingly wider constituency: for those literate men who could not read Latin, for merchants, for professional secretaries, for women. It would follow that a boy such as William Shakespeare, schooled in an Erasmian grammar school programme and a reader, as Lynne Magnusson has persuasively argued, of letter-writing manuals, must have inherited an Erasmian understanding of letters.

There are several problems with this neat narrative. First, there's the fact that 'real' extant early modern letters are perversely ignorant of anything approaching the epistolary theory that was supposed to dictate them. Then as now, it seems that experts vigorously dispensed 'how-to' advice in an attempt to bring some order to an activity that was, in reality, wonderfully miscellaneous, even chaotic. Thus, while letter-writing manuals can tell us something about the practice they seek to regulate, they signally fail to explain or contain the myriad forms of letter-writing in the period. But Shakespeare's letters take us beyond a simple ignoring of Erasmian protocols. More crucially, as I shall argue more fully, Shakespeare's understanding of letters is radically different from Erasmus's—indeed, one could go so far as to say that his portrayal of letters on stage comprises a wholesale rejection of Erasmian theories of letter-writing. Despite Erasmus' influence on the grammar school curriculum and on the English letter-writing manuals, I shall argue, his was not a model that Shakespeare found helpful in conceiving his stage letters.

To pursue this, I turn to the single Shakespearean letter episode that has been claimed as definitively Erasmian. In an important essay, Lisa Jardine shows how the rhetorical affect produced in the Erasmian familiar letter was used by Shakespeare to produce feeling in the scene in *King Lear* where a gentleman recounts to Kent how he brought letters to Cordelia.[62] Asked by Kent 'Did your letters pierce the queen to any demonstration of grief?' the Gentleman recounts how Cordelia 'took them, read them in my presence, | And now and then an ample tear trilled down | Her delicate cheek. It seemed she was a queen | Over her passion, who, most rebel-like, | Sought to be king o'er her' (*KL* 4.3.9–15). At Kent's prompting, he goes on to explain how 'smiles and tears' were in competition in her reaction, but how she made 'no verbal question' beyond 'once or twice .. heav[ing] the name of father,' and crying 'Sisters, sisters, shame of ladies, sisters! | Kent, father, sisters! What, i'the storm, i'the night? | Let pity not be believed!' before running off 'To deal with grief alone' (4.3.16–33).

Critics have not been kind to this scene. Marvin Rosenberg notes that 'the sweetness of [the Gentleman's] tone is so cloying that some critics have wished the scene banished, and some producers have banished it'[63]—as indeed did the playwright, the play's revisers or its editors in the Folio (it appears only in the Quarto edition). The scene fascinates Jardine precisely because we have such trouble reading it. Arguing that we have 'lost touch' with a particular 'historicized version of letter writing', Jardine proposes that the scene is 'a text-book example of the production at a distance of intense emotion and passionate feeling', drawing on the model of familiar epistle promulgated so influentially by Erasmus. Jardine notes 'the importance for Erasmus of the affective dimension in epistolary writing—shared feeling, textually transmitted, substitutes for the individual who cannot be present, whose absence is a cause for regret and longing on the part of both parties in the textual transaction'.[64]

Jardine's reading of the passage seems to me absolutely accurate: Cordelia's face, as reported by the Gentleman, clearly expresses the emotion provoked by the letter. But despite the success of this scene, Jardine notes that *Lear* as a whole is hardly the best vehicle for an Erasmian argument, since 'most of the many epistolary transactions in *Lear* are not so securely morally admirable', tending 'not to connote the bonds of intense personal communication, but rather to mislead and distort'—Edmund forges a letter to implicate Edgar in treachery; Goneril's adulterous letter to Edmund brings about their downfall; letters from France lead to Gloucester's blinding. 'Clearly something un-Erasmian, or possibly anti-Erasmian is at stake here', Jardine concludes.[65] Indeed, this letter is an oddity not just in *King Lear*, but in Shakespeare's drama as a whole, precisely because, uniquely among his letters, it does pay homage to the Erasmian tradition of letter-writing. But, significantly, although the emotion is produced by the receipt and reading of a letter, the letter itself is missing: we do not see that letter on stage, nor hear its words. Shakespeare produces a moment of perfect Erasmian epistolarity by dispensing with the stage letter. This uniqueness of this Erasmian scene thus perversely confirms that Shakespeare's characteristic use of letters is indeed 'un-Erasmian' or even 'anti-Erasmian'—as we'll see, it instead regards letters not primarily as rhetorical or textual, but also, and crucially, as material objects.

Stage Traditions

Where, then, did Shakespeare find the model for his letters if not in the dominant letter-writing ideology promulgated by Erasmus? One obvious answer is the existing, albeit fragmentary stage tradition, both classical and vernacular. In the fifth century BCE, Euripides famously embedded letters in his plays *Iphigenia in Tauris*, *Iphigenia in Aulis*, and *Hippolytus*, and also in the lost *Sthenoboia* and *Palamedes*.[66] Even if entire Euripides plays in Greek might have been beyond most grammar school boys, the works were available in a parallel, annotated Greek and Latin edition.[67] From Euripidean drama, Shakespeare may have learned of 'The incriminating letter, the letter malevolent, the letter counterfeit, the letter intercepted and the letter substituted', as James Svendsen dubs them, all motifs he reworked in his own plays.[68]

Euripidean letters can convey emotional states. In *Iphigenia in Aulis*, Agamemnon is 'all but raving mad', a state conveyed by the way he is writing a letter: 'The words you have written you erase again, you seal the tablet and then break the seal, you throw the pine frame upon the ground, and weep copious tears.'[69] The letter in question is a countermand to an earlier letter that gives orders to bring his daughter Iphigenia to Aulis, so that Agamemnon may sacrifice her; this second letter will be intercepted by Menelaus. Often, letters seem to serve as evidence, only to be undermined in some way. In *Hippolytus*, Phaedra's corpse holds an inscribed tablet claiming that Hippolytus raped her, and her husband Theseus is convinced of its authenticity because of its 'gold-chased seal'.[70] But it turns out that Phaedra was lying—the letter is genuine, but its contents are false. In *Iphigenia in Tauris*, Iphigenia, disguised as an executioner, gives Pylades the chance to escape death by carrying a letter to Greece. When he worries that he might be shipwrecked, she tells Pylades the contents of the letter so that he can memorize it, and in so doing, reveals the identity of the writer as herself, Iphigenia. The audience is made aware that, without this doubling of written and oral message, Iphigenia's identity would have remained unknown to Pylades and his friend Orestes.[71]

Here we have letters intercepted, letters that tell lies, letters that are never sent—all forms that Shakespeare will later exploit. In particular, Euripides' letters all share a vexed relationship to speech. Hippolytus argues that the dead Phaedra cannot bear witness against him, while Theseus claims that she can through her letter, but Hippolytus is right, since the letter is false, and Phaedra cannot be interrogated about it. Agamemnon reveals his change of heart in speech, but his letter does its work despite this. Iphigenia's letter would take months to bring to light her location and identity, but she reveals this in a few minutes in speech, and the letter is never sent. In all of these instances, the letter form is shown to have, if anything, negative powers—the ability to tell the wrong story or to command the wrong orders—while interrogation and debate strengthen the positive power of speech. It is also hinted that a letter by itself is not an adequate proof: Phaedra's letter is a clear example of this, while Agamemnon tells the old man not to break the seal: it is a token by which the letter might be known as authentic.

More accessible to Shakespeare were the letters in Plautus' plays *Pseudolus*, *Trinummus*, *Curculio*, and *Bacchides*.[72] In the labyrinthine plots of Plautine comedy, the forging of letters is a constant theme. In *Curculio*, the eponymous parasite steals a ring from Captain Therapontigonus, the rival of his friend Phaedromus, writes a letter and seals it. The sealed letter is then used to procure money from a banker to pay a pimp to release Phaedromus' sweetheart Planesium.[73] In *Pseudolus*, the soldier Polymachaeroplagides leaves his seal as a token, and sixty *libri* in cash with a pimp named Ballio, instructing him to give Phoenicium to the person who brings him a similar token and the balance of the money he owes. Calidorus' servant Pseudolus manages to fool the soldier's henchman Harpax into handing over the token, claiming to be Ballio's servant Syrus. Charinus's slave Simia then goes to the pimp, pretending to be Harpax, and claims the girl. In both these plots, what is really being toyed with is the authentification of identity, achieved not through letters *per se* but by the ring that an individual uses to seal letters and formalize contracts. The one character who does write a letter in *Pseudolus*, significantly, is a character without such rights: the courtesan Phoenicium, whose letter to Calidorus is read aloud by Pseudolus, rendering her sexually available: 'I judge these characters are after children, the way they climb on top of each other... Oh, I see your girl friend, sir... Look! At full length on the tablets, lying in wax.'[74]

In *Trinummus*, the ease of these plots is ferociously challenged. In a ploy to prevent his friend Charmides from discovering that in his absence his estate has been decimated, Callicles seeks advice from his friend Megaronides. He comes up with a plan to hire some foreign-looking man, dressed in exotic clothes, to come to Lesbonicus, claiming to have been sent from his father Charmides in Seleucia. The hired man will have two letters, one for Lesbonicus, one for Callicles. Callicles spies a problem: 'But when he brings those letters all sealed, don't you suppose the lad knows his father's signet ring? [paterni signum]' Megaronides pooh-poohs the idea. 'Hundreds of explanations can be evolved—he lost the one he had, and then got himself a new one. In fact, even if they aren't brought sealed, he can say they were unsealed and examined at the custom-house.' In the event, however, unforeseen complications arise. The hired man encounters Charmides, who has returned home, and crumbles under the pressure of Charmides' interrogation.[75] Here we find another motif that will repeat through Shakespeare's works— no matter how solid the material detail of the letter, it is the bearer on whom its successful transaction depends.

Letters also appear prominently in several late medieval and Tudor dramas. On occasion, they function as the present sign of absent authority, as in the late fixteenth-century *The Digby Play of the Conversion of Saint Paul*, when Saul asks Caiaphas and Annas for 'Your letters and epistles of most sovereignty | To subdue rebellious that will, of forwardness, | Against our laws rebel or transgress.' They agree, and Annas presents Saul with the required epistolary signs of that sovereignty: 'And by these letters, that be most reverent, | Take them in hand, full agree thereto!'[76] Letters are used to convey news, as in Thomas Sackville and Thomas Norton's *Gorboduc*,[77] or as part of a courtship, as in Nicholas Udall's Terentian *Ralph Roister Doister* (discussed in Chapter 6).[78] But more often in Tudor drama, letters signal disruption: they are stolen, lost, forged, opened without permission, read by the wrong person. In John Skelton's *Magnificence*, Fancy, posing as Largesse, delivers from Sad Circumspection

to Magnificence 'this wrytynge closed vnder sele', which he claims
was delivered to him at Pointoise. But the letter was in fact written by Counterfeit Countenance, who uses, along with counterfeit
kindness, counterfeit weight, and counterfeit language, 'Counterfet
letters by the way of sleyght'.[79] In Robert Wilson's *Three Ladies of
London* (1581?) the evil Lady Lucre uses letters to urge Mercadorus to
'cosen' the Jew Gerontus; Lady Love and Lady Conscience put their
hands to pre-written letters of recommendation to Lucre for Sincerity to get him a benefice; a letter placed by Lucre in Conscience's
bosom 'Willing me to keep secret our lascivious living' is the means
by which Lucre is exposed.[80]

So when Shakespeare starts to write in the late 1580s, he has a
stock of stage letters with which to play, and he does not hesitate to
exploit them. Most frequently, letters are used to convey news and
intelligence from remote locations. Letters confirm the identity of
an abandoned baby in *The Winter's Tale*. Sealed letters of conspiracy
are evidence of Aumerle's guilt in *Richard II*. But more often than
not, Shakespeare uses these letters with a sophisticated twist, which
usually tends to undermine stability. News letters come thick and
fast, often in groups of three, carrying news that changes by the
minute, or intelligence reports that contradict each other. Letters
are used to assert authority by the disguised Duke in *Measure for
Measure*—but also to disguise his whereabouts. As discussed earlier,
letters that appear to be from an individual are in fact written by
subordinates; and letters are deliberately forged, as Edmund forges
a letter from Edgar (*KL* 1.2), Maria creates a letter that Malvolio will
believe is from their mistress Olivia (*TN* 2.5), and Hamlet substitutes a letter to the king of England (*Ham* 5.2). Letter delivery is
particularly vexed. Friar John fails to deliver a letter from Romeo
on time because of the plague—with fatal consequences (*RJ* 5.2).
Letters are put into the hands of illiterates for delivery: given a party
invitation list, Capulet's servant laments that he 'can never find what
names the writing person hath here writ' (*RJ* 1.2.34–44); Costard
manages to mix up a letter from Armado to Jacquenetta with one

from Berowne to Rosaline (*LLL* 3.1.4.2). Letters are vulnerable to interception: Goneril's adulterous letter to Edmund is seized by Edgar and passed to her husband Albany.

It would be possible to fill a book simply by detailing all these myriad uses of letters in Shakespeare's drama. But I want here to suggest something more. What Shakespeare does in his plays is to take these time-honoured letter motifs and turn them into something that is at once much more complex and emotionally compelling, and he does so, I shall argue, through focusing not on the affective rhetoric of letters, as Erasmus does, but—taking his cue rather from Euripides and Plautus—on the letter as a material object.

Social Life and Stage Life

A stage letter is also, of course, a stage property. Letters are in fact the most common stage property in Shakespeare's plays, appearing more frequently than any other object except costumes and 'prosthetic' props such as swords, crowns, handkerchiefs, beards, and hairpieces.[81] Despite a rash of recent scholarship on stage properties,[82] however, stage letter-props have remained for the most part overlooked.[83] Their invisibility may in part relate to the nature of the archive mined recently by playhouse historians: the physical stuff of which letters are made—paper, ink, wax and seals—do not figure in account books, perhaps because they would be part and parcel of the everyday working stock of each playing company. Whatever the reason, stage letters have a habit of slipping through precisely those categories and methodologies that might explain them.

Over the past two decades, literary critics working in the early modern period have paid new attention to the *object* as opposed to the human *subject* that had previously been the obsession of a field intent on a self-fashioning Renaissance.[84] The work of these critics, drawing on the anthropological examination of the 'social life of things' by Arjan Appadurai,[85] or the 'cultural biography' of things by

Igor Kopytoff,[86] has allowed us to see anew the role of the material object in the literature and the culture of the period. But sometimes the move to understanding the theatrical representation of such objects has been difficult, leading some scholars to feel the need to choose between an anthropological and a theatrical approach. Lena Cowen Orlin, for example, in an important early attempt to track 'the performance of things' in *The Taming of the Shrew*, usefully draws on Pierre Bourdieu's notion of 'cultural consecration', which confers on persons and situations it touches, and also on objects 'a sort of ontological promotion akin to a transubstantiation'. Despite dealing centrally with a stage play, she concludes that 'the cultural consecration in which I am interested is fundamentally anthropological rather than specifically theatrical'.[87] At the other end of the scale, Andrew Sofer, in his *The Stage Life of Props* is interested only in the theatrical: he notes how 'Enlivened by the actor's touch, charged by the playwright's dialogue, and quickened in the spectator's imagination, [objects] take on a life of their own as they weave in and out of the stage action.'[88] Thus, in Sofer's account, the appearance of a skull on stage is tracked only to *Hamlet* and not, for example, to other sites where the skull alludes to something else: medicine, say, or grave-robbing, or even the *memento mori* tradition.

Stage letters—as the staged representation of an everyday cultural practice—have both a social life and a stage life. The social life of letters could lead us towards an historicist study of letter-writing in early modern English society. The stage life of letters could lead us towards a study of the theatrical traditions into which Shakespeare inserted his plays by including the device of the letter. It is my aim in this study to attempt both: to show that Shakespeare's use of letters draws on the prevalent cultural understanding of letters, but also to show that they have a stage life that is specifically theatrical. In turn, that stage life has implications for our understanding of the early modern letter's social life. Conceiving of letters as material objects draws our attention to the stuff of which they are made, the form they take, the format their components follow. This is certainly part of Shakespeare's design, as we shall see in Chapter 1. However, much of this detail, though sometimes referred to in speech, is not visible to the audience. In understanding the stage letter as a stage property, this book proposes that Shakespeare's plays see letters as a theatre audience sees letters: not primarily as texts, but as material objects that move between individual characters. These objects contain text, certainly, but the message they convey is not primarily about that text, but about from whom they come, to whom they go, and how they make that journey. Indeed, as will become increasingly clear, Shakespeare revels in contradicting the text of a letter with its physical journey.

The visual impact of a stage letter can be read in its purest form in *Pericles*. In the dumb-show preceding Act 2, Pericles and Cleon enter from one door talking, and are met by 'a Gentleman with a letter to Pericles' entering at another door. Pericles 'shows the letter to Cleon', 'gives the Messenger a reward and knights him'. Pericles and his train exeunt through one door, and Cleon through another (*Per* 2.0.17 SD). Here the letter tells us that news from elsewhere has been sent to Pericles; that he is grateful for it, to the point where he rewards the messenger with a knighthood; and that it leads to his departure from Cleon. The next dumb-show has Pericles with Simonides, again encountering a Messenger who 'kneels, and gives Pericles a letter'. Pericles shows the letter to Simonides, and 'the Lords kneel to him'. Thaisa and her child enter, and the King 'shows her the letter; she rejoices', and she and Pericles depart (3.0.14 SD). Letters signal news from elsewhere that has an impact on the present scene; expressions of joy or anxiety, and subsequent actions imply the effect of their contents on the reader. In each case, the Chorus then explains what the letters contained—but the audience does not need that information to understand what is happening.

A more complex understanding of letters seen can be found in the narrative poem *A Lover's Complaint*, printed with Shakespeare's *Sonnets* in 1609.[89] *A Lover's Complaint* is wilfully theatrical in its construction, turning its reader into an audience member. In a pastoral setting, the poem's speaker hears and sees 'a fickle maid full pale' (5) perched on a riverbank. She is depicted emotionally 'Tearing of papers, breaking rings a-twain' (6), weeping into a 'napkin' (15) sown with 'conceited characters' (16), and throwing into the river 'A thousand favours [drawn] from a maund' (36), 'folded schedules' (43), and 'yet moe letters, sadly penned in blood' (47). The speaker, and therefore we, observe her voyeuristically from a distance, with no access to the history motivating this emotion-filled destruction. At length, a herdsman enquires what she is doing, and the woman recounts her story. She was the object of the attentions of a young man, who had himself been wooed by a series of female admirers. These women had presented him with 'tributes' (197), 'talons' (204), and 'trophies of affections hot' (218), but now, he claimed to the young woman, they 'of force must your oblations be; | Since I their altar, you empatron me' (223–4).

The most obvious interpretation, following John Kerrigan's reading, would be that it is these secondhand, 'emotionally traded', tokens that the woman is now tearing and throwing into the river.[90] But it is also possible, as Colin Burrow suggests, that 'they are a little less transparent than that', since 'the specific significance of these things in the lives of those we observe is withheld from us',[91] while Patrick Cheney goes so far as to suggest the 'possibility that the young courtier might well have composed the "papers" himself', given his 'notorious falsehood'.[92] The confusion registered by these critics is deliberately engendered by the poet. Although we see them, we cannot know what is in the objects, so we are invited to speculate and to draw our conclusions. But the young man lays bare the tricks that these objects play on those who see them. In telling the woman why the tokens given by his admirers mean nothing to him, he reveals the fallacy in the imagination of their senders: they sent him 'pallid pearls and rubies red as blood, | Figuring that they their passions likewise lent me | Of grief and blushes, aptly understood, | In bloodless white and the encrimsoned mood, | Effects of terror and dear modesty, | Encamped in hearts, but fighting outwardly' (198–203). The material objects are designed to serve as metaphors for their senders' emotions: sometimes the relationship is made explicit by the addition of 'deep-brained sonnets, that did amplify' the 'dear nature, worth, and quality' of the gift (209–10). So when he hands these objects to the woman, he exhorts her to 'Take all these similes to your own command, | Hallowed with sighs that burning lungs did raise' (227–8). The gifts are only 'similes', meaningless unless embued with the figurative life that their senders intended; now he claims they are 'Hallowed with sighs that burning lungs did raise' (228), but in their double circulation, are the sighs the man's, or those of his female admirers?

What the *Complaint* presents is an explicit understanding that letters can be classed not only alongside other written texts, but also with other material objects such as rings and handkerchiefs.[93] It also demonstrates how material objects can say one thing in their text—the posies in the rings, the sonnets accompanying the jewels, the blood-written letters—but that those texts can be nuanced, ignored, or outright contradicted by the transactions made by their containing materials. What takes on importance in this spied-on scenario are not the texts contained within the objects nor even necessarily the objects themselves—although the response they provoke is clearly depicted—but the interpersonal transactions that they enable and to which they bear witness. A study of Shakespeare's letters, it follows, will be an examination not of their texts, but of interpersonal transactions, including some of the most emotionally heightened transactions in his drama.

Letters and Characters: Stage Traces on the Page

Having claimed that the stage letter is first a stage property, and only second a text, I must however confront the fact that our evidence for the nature of stage letters lies in the form of printed playtexts. Recent studies have focused attention back on the printed form of playtexts, without arriving at a critical consensus: for many scholars, the early printed Shakespearean play-texts are compromised traces of stage performances lacking either authorial input or even particular care on the part of the printer;[94] for others, it is equally clear that Shakespeare wrote expressly for the printed page.[95] In its dual capacities as text and stage property, the letter provides an interesting tool for furthering these debates.

The texts of letters obviously appear in Shakespeare's printed plays, some thirty-one of them. But what can we tell about them from their appearance in print? Letters in printed drama of the period usually present the texts of letters formatted distinctly as a letter, rather than merely part of a character's speech—and indeed, virtually every edition of Shakespeare since has done the same. In this, they follow what had by the 1590s become a print convention of typesetting letters to resemble the standardized layout of hand-written letters, most obviously with the placing of the (printed) 'signature' at the bottom right of the epistle.[96] Important work by Leah Marcus and Jonathan Goldberg has drawn attention to the anomalies of these printed play-letters. Marcus has pondered why some speech prefixes for printed letter-texts are either missing or 'repeated' (that is, a character who is already speaking is re-cued to read out the letter).[97] Goldberg has examined how some letters are printed in italic, and suggested how print fonts might correlate, and not correlate, to the various hands (and especially the signatures) used in manuscript letters.[98]

To give just one example: in Act 4, Scene 6 of *Hamlet* a sailor enters to Horatio and tells him 'There's a letter for you, sir—it came from th'ambassador that was bound for England—if your name be Horatio, as I am let to know it is' (*Ham* 4.6.9–12). The letter is then read out. In F (illustration 2), the letter is prefixed by the instruction '*Reads the Letter*' with no speech prefix to denote the speaker; taken literally, this would imply that the preceding speaker, the sailor, 'reads the letter'. This assumption would then be supported by

the fact that the lines immediately following the letter are prefixed
'*Hor.*', suggesting that Horatio starts to speak only here. But this
is evidently wrong: it would be against all known protocol for the
sailor to open and read out a letter addressed to a social superior,
unless asked to. In Q2, by contrast, the letter-text is marked by the
speech prefix '*Hor.*' making it clear that Horatio indeed reads out
the letter. However, even in Q2, the lines following the letter are
marked '*Hor.*' as if Horatio were not already speaking. Why should
there be a missing speech prefix in F, or a 'double' speech prefix in

> *Say.* Hee shall Sir, and't please him. There's a Letter
> for you Sir : It comes from th'Ambassadours that was
> bound for England, if your name be *Horatio*, as I am let
> to know it is.
>
> *Reads the Letter.*
>
> HOratio, *When thou shalt haue ouerlook'd this, giue these*
> *Fellowes some meanes to the King: They haue Letters*
> *for him. Ere we were two dayes old at Sea, a Pyrate of very*
> *Warlicke appointment gaue vs Chace. Finding our selues too*
> *slow of Saile, we put on a compelled Valour. In the Grapple, I*
> *boorded them: On the instant they got cleare of our Shippe, so*
> *I alone became their Prisoner. They haue dealt with mee, like*
> *Theeues of Mercy, but they knew what they did. I am to doe*
> *a good turne for them. Let the King haue the Letters I haue*
> *sent, and repaire thou to me with as much hast as thou wouldest*
> *flye death. I haue words to speake in your eare, will make thee*
> *dumbe, yet are they much too light for the bore of the Matter.*
> *These good Fellowes will bring thee where I am.* Rosincrance
> *and* Guildensterne, *hold their course for England. Of them*
> *I haue much to tell thee, Farewell.*
>
> *He that thou knowest thine,*
> Hamlet.
>
> Come, I will giue you way for these your Letters,
> And do't the speedier, that you may direct me
> To him from whom you brought them. *Exit.*

2. Hamlet's letter to Horatio in *Hamlet Prince of Denmark*, First
Folio (F) edition. *Mr. William Shakespeares comedies, histories, &*
tragedies Published according to the true originall copies (London:
Isaac Iaggard, and Ed. Blount, 1623).

Q2? Moreover, as Goldberg notes, in F the letter is separated out by being printed in italic, prompting him to ask 'Do italics therefore mark the letter as *not* part of the play?'[99]

Recently, the performance-oriented researches of Tiffany Stern have suggested a possible solution. Some eighty years ago, W.W. Greg made an important discovery about the way in which players learned their parts—and indeed, as I shall suggest, about what comprised their 'character'. Greg prepared an edition of a manuscript at Dulwich College, a roll comprised of several pieces of paper which contained the lines for the part of Orlando in Robert Greene's play *Orlando Furioso* (a part thought to have been played by Edward Alleyn).[100] Printing the manuscript (A) in parallel with the 1594 printed edition (Q) of the play,[101] Greg revealed many discrepancies between the two versions, including some that 'prove on examination to be not additions in Q but omissions in A'. These included verses hung up by Sacrapant in the grove: although clearly to be read out by Orlando, and indeed commented on in his roll-lines, the verses did not appear in the roll.[102] Greg proposed that the absence of these essential verses 'proves that they were written on scrolls hung upon the stage to be read at performance'. Since players performed in multiple plays, 'it was desirable so far as possible to lessen the burden on the actors' memories, and we may presume that such devices as this were frequent'.[103] Greg's observations have been resurrected by Stern, who is equally struck by the elements that fail to sit comfortably in a player's role in early printed Shakespeare texts. Prologues, epilogues, songs, and letters, she notes, 'tend to be visibly separated from the body of the text' by differentiated typefaces or even by titles, belying the homogeneous typography of modern editions: 'it is as though prologue, epilogue, song and letter are not entirely part of the texts to which they are attached'.[104]

The lack of speech prefixes for printed stage letters, it follows, may result from the letter-text not being part of any player's roll: Horatio's roll would have his own non-letter lines, and then '*Reads the Letter*', and the Horatio-player would indeed read out the letter

Say. A fhall fir and pleafe him, there's a Letter for you fir, it came fiõ th'Embaffador that was bound for *England*, if your name be *Horatio*, as I am let to know it is.

Hor. Horatio, when thou fhalt haue ouer-lookt this, giue thefe fellowes fome meanes to the King, they haue Letters for him : Ere wee were two daies old at Sea, a Pyrat of very warlike appointment gaue vs chafe, finding our felues too flow of faile, wee put on a compelled valour, and in the grapple I boorded them, on the inftant they got cleere of our fhyp, fo I alone became theyr prifoner, they haue dealt with me like thieues of mercie, but they knew what they did, I am to doe a turne for them, let the King haue the Letters I haue fent, and repayre thou to me with as much fpeede as thou wouldeft flie death, I haue wordes to fpeake in thine eare will make thee dumbe, yet are
            they
they much too light for the bord of the matter, thefe good fellowes will bring thee where I am, *Rofencraus* and *Guyldenfterne* hold theyr courfe for *England*, of them I haue much to tell thee, farewell.
            So that thou knoweft thine Hamlet,

Hor. Come I will you way for thefe your letters,
And doo't the fpeedier that you may direct me
To him from whom you brought them.   *Exeunt.*

---

3. Hamlet's letter to Horatio in *Hamlet Prince of Denmark*, Second Quarto (Q2) edition. *The tragicall historie of Hamlet, Prince of Denmarke* (London: N[icholas] L[ing], 1604).

on stage. The second speech prefix (for his lines to the sailors) would not be necessary, because he continues to speak. The printer's use of italics would then, as Stern suggests, merely register the fact that the (italic) letter stands distinct from the (roman) players' parts. The Quarto lacks an instruction to read the letter, but again is short on speech-prefixes: it is not specified that Horatio reads the letter, although the speech prefix 'Hor.' is given before his lines following the letter. This again would suggest that the letter has a different status from Horatio's non-letter lines that follow.

This anomaly, however, speaks to more than the player's need to memorize as little as possible. It also indicates a particular understanding of the relationship of a character to the letters she or he reads on stage. Stern quotes a telling anecdote related by the dancer and actor Edward Cape Everard, who died around 1818. Stepping in at the last moment for John Palmer in the role of the miller's son Richard in a Theatre Royal Haymarket production of *The Miller of Mansfield* in 1775, Everard recalls how 'when I had to read a long letter in the first scene, on opening it, I found it a mere blank!' Evidently, Everard expected letter-props to contain their text on stage. 'I cannot suppose that this negligence was designed', he writes, without conviction, 'but I'll be bold to say, that if Mr Palmer had played the part', this circumstance would not have arisen. But, as he continues, 'Luckily for me, I had always made it a rule to study my Letters, as well as my character; it was well I did.'[105] Everard here does something intriguing: he separates out his 'Letters' from his 'character'. His use of 'character' might simply suggest the definition of 'the personality or "part" assumed by an actor on the stage' (*OED* 17a.). But in his contrasting of 'character' and 'letters,' it is clear that, for Everard, preparing for a play, a 'character' means the script-roll that contains his 'character' (a definition not entered in the *OED*), which is separate from the 'Letters' that his stage-character will read out. The conflation of modern printed editions of 'character' and 'letter' into a single speech (as Hamlet's letter to Horatio is conflated with Horatio's subsequent speech to the sailors) is at least partially resisted by the early editions through the use of differentiated typographies and double speech prefixes, mediated reflections of stage practice.

But this rather crudely materialist explanation does not tell the whole story. Shakespeare goes much further in his presentation of letters read out on stage, wreaking havoc with the notion that a letter could be separated from a character. In this book, I suggest that Shakespeare takes full advantage of this radical unmooredness of the staged letter to interrogate its multiple relationships to its author, its writer, its recipient, its speaker, its readers, its hearers. Shakespeare complicates the possibilities of a speaker responding to a letter, by having nine of his letters read out by someone other than their intended recipient. This permits the exposure of the writer's secret intents to a third party and allows for that third party to comment on the letter, as when Gloucester reads out Burgundy's letter to Henry VI (*1H6* 4.1); when Polonius provides a running critique of Hamlet's love-letter writing skills in reading out his letter to Ophelia (*Ham* 2.2), and Bertram reads out the letter that Parolles sends to Diana, excoriating Bertram himself (*AW* 4.3); or when Boyet reads out the love-letter from Don Adriano to Jacquenetta (*LLL* 4.1). Sometimes this device is deployed to graver effect. In *The Two Gentlemen of Verona*, the Duke exposes the plans of his daughter Sylvia to elope, by reading Valentine's letter to her (*TGV* 3.1). The fact that Olivia orders Fabian to read out Malvolio's angry letter signals her refusal to give proper attention to the real injuries done to her steward (*TN* 5.1). And in some cases, letters can be fatal: Imogen reads out her own death sentence, in Posthumus's instructions to Pisanio to kill her (*Cym* 3.4). Perhaps the most complex variation of this theme comes in *King Lear* when Edgar reads out the adulterous letter from Goneril to Edmund (*KL* 4.6). This is a letter he has inherited after killing its bearer, Oswald, and whose intended recipient, his own brother Edmund, he will also bring to his death—and indeed, the reading of this letter is in some ways a fitting revenge. Edgar, after all, was the fictional writer of a letter 'to Edmund', which Edmund then allowed their father to read out (*KL* 1.2), although in reality, that letter was from Edmund and designed for his father's eyes: Edmund merely confected the situation where Gloucester believed he was reading someone else's correspondence, as Edgar is now.

The complications do not stop here. Of the thirty-one letters read out on the Shakespearean stage, eleven are interrupted by commentary and interjections, sometimes from the speaker (who is, of course, not the 'writer' of the letter), sometimes from other characters. Some of the most memorable moments in Shakespearean drama arise from a character reading, and responding to a letter alone (or believing himself alone): Hotspur's angry rejection of Worcester's urging him to caution (*1H4* 2.3.1–15); Brutus' betraying of his secret ambition in interpreting and completing the letter sent anonymously from Cassius (*JC* 2.1.46–58); 'Ganymede''s perverse reading of Phoebe's letter to 'him' (*AYL*, 4.3.40–63); and the most sustained example, Malvolio's willful self-delusion as he reads the letter dropped in his path by Maria (*TN* 2.5.82–179). In these instances, a letter, supposedly the voice of its sender, becomes instead a dialogue between sender and recipient.

Shakespeare has only one character read out his own letter, again to dramatic effect. In *Julius Caesar* Artemidorus reads out his letter urging Caesar to beware the ides of March. But within the conventions of stage letters, the sight of a man reading out his own letter should alert us that something is awry. This is a letter that will physically reach its intended recipient but is never read by him. The letter that is voiced by its writer by its very nature goes nowhere. Artemidorus is the anomaly that demonstrates, by contrast, how stage letters usually work. For the element I have thus far ignored is perhaps, in dramatic terms, the most important: the means by which the letter travels from its sender to its recipient. Often invisible on the printed playtext page, the letter-bearer was totally visible on the early modern stage. It is not by accident that in the bizarrely over-annotated manuscript playbook of Philip Massinger's *Believe as You List*, the zealous bookkeeper Edward King not only appends a list of the six letters that must be taken on stage but also records *by which player* they must be taken on.[106] In both the Q2 and F versions of *Hamlet*, it is the letter-bearer, the sailor, who speaks directly before the letter is read: it is wholly appropriate that we include not only the writer Hamlet and the recipient Horatio but also the bearer sailor in our consideration of the unspecified speaker of that letter, for it takes all three of them to bring about that reading of the letter. In a very real sense, the stage direction should read: *[Hamlet Writes— Sailor Bears—Horatio Reads] the Letter.*

Shakespeare's staging of letters thus necessarily draws attention to the relationships that are forged and maintained by the transaction of letters, and the mechanisms by which those transactions take place. But beyond that, in several of his plays, Shakespeare can be seen to be developing something far more complex through his deployment of letters: to suggest analogies and resonances that are not necessarily visible through any other means. In my extended readings of plays such as *The Merchant of Venice* (Chapter 4), *King Lear* (Chapter 5), and *Hamlet* (Chapter 7) we shall see this dramaturgy at work, but one example here will suffice to make the point. We are first introduced to Lady Macbeth as she is reading aloud a letter ('*Enter Macbeths Wife alone with a Letter*', according to the Folio). That letter is, of course, from Macbeth, but its double status on stage—in its physical state, written in Macbeth's hand, and in its textual content, uttered in Lady Macbeth's voice—presents the two characters as one, even though the characters have not yet occupied the same stage. Beyond its spatial figuring of the Macbeths as singular (a representation not possible by any other means), the letter plays with time, collapsing present and future: as Lady Macbeth exclaims ecstatically to her absent husband, 'Thy letters have transported me beyond | This ignorant present, and I feel now | The future in the instant' (*Mac*, 1.5.56–8). It is the *letters* that produce this two-in-one effect: Macbeth never has to explain to her in person, on stage, what must happen for the witches' prophecy to come true.

This letter is then echoed by the only other letter in the play, but this time we do not see it. Before they observe Lady Macbeth sleepwalking, her waiting gentlewoman tells her doctor how 'I have seen her rise from her bed, throw her night-gown upon her, unlock her closet, take forth paper, fold it, write upon't, read it, afterwards seal it, and again return to bed; yet all this while in a most fast sleep' (5.1.4–8). It has been suggested that Lady Macbeth is here writing her will and testament, or a confession, both readings that foreground the role of conscience in the scene.[107] But the reference to folding and sealing strongly implies that she is writing a letter, a reference to the letter that she is first seen reading aloud. It is only fitting that by the fifth act, the letter is the stuff of nightmare, as Lady Macbeth takes on herself the terrible signs of guilt, conscience and remorse that Macbeth now lacks, as she folds, writes, reads, and seals the letter that once was his, but has to return it to her closet, never able to send on her guilt. And what was once Macbeth's writing, spoken in her voice, now becomes her writing, utterable to nobody.

The two opening chapters of *Shakespeare's Letters* present its key theses. In Chapter 1, 'The Materiality of Shakespeare's Letters', I show that Shakespeare is at pains to draw on the material conditions of letters in his own day. This stretches from the materials that the letter-writer must use (paper, ink, quill, knife, sandbox, desk, seal, wax, ribbon) and the imagery to which they give rise; the protocols of letter-writing, including the use of prescribed layouts, formats for valedictions, subscriptions and superscriptions, as well as etiquettes of folding and sealing. Shakespeare constantly plays on these traditions, presenting his audiences with a series of assumptions about early modern letter-writing that we must assume they understood—even if, as was likely the case, many of them were not (by modern standards) 'literate'—and that we nowadays miss. While these protocols pervade the language of the plays in metaphorical terms, however, puns about superscriptions and folding do not necessarily make for great theatre, so Shakespeare evolves a new, theatrical method for conveying these ideas. I highlight how Shakespeare's dramatic practice differs from the cues given in his source materials by exploring how the letter torn up in a fit of passion then reassembled—a common motif of prose romances—necessarily changes in character when taken onto the theatrical stage in *The Two Gentlemen of Verona*. Another change is seen in the adaptation of the chronicle histories in *Henry VI Part One*, when the king receives a letter from Burgundy whose 'churlish superscription' (an address that fails to demonstrate the proper respect) betrays his change of allegiance. In Shakespeare's dramatization, although this superscription is commented on, the lack of decorum is already signalled by the more visible sign of an inappropriate letter-bearer, Sir John Fastolfe.

Chapter 2, 'Shakespeare's Roman Letters', takes the second strand of the thesis: that Shakespeare's theatre poses a challenge to the historiography that assumes the primacy of the Erasmian familiar epistle in early modern England. While Erasmus carefully abstracts his letters from the messy and historically specific material conditions of their production, fellow humanist Juan Luis Vives provides a thoroughgoing historicist account of letter-writing in the classical era, a critical approach whose influence one can see in Ben Jonson's *Sejanus*. Shakespeare follows neither of these approaches. In his Roman plays, by contrast, letters are presented with striking anachronism, suggesting that the playwright thought it best to rely on immediate identification rather than historical accuracy. In his treatment of Plutarch's account of *Antony and Cleopatra*, in particular, Shakespeare systematically explores the role played by letters in Antony's vexed negotiation between Rome and Egypt, insisting on their importance to the play's action—but finally he undermines the role of letters in the foundation of Roman historiography, deliberately pitting their ineffectiveness against Cleopatra's theatrical potency. Shakespeare's letters are about transaction now, not history in the future.

The two next chapters take their cue from the one manuscript letter connected to Shakespeare that has survived: a letter written to him by Richard Quiney, a Stratford-upon-Avon man, in October 1598. Discovered by Edmond Malone in 1793, it remained unpublished and unpublicized until after Malone's death, perhaps because it implies that Shakespeare was a moneylender, an identification Malone was keen to avoid. Chapter 3, 'Shakespeare and the Carriers', argues that what appears to be a reference to Quiney's lodging-house, the Bell Inn in Carter Street, is in fact a reference to the carrier system between London and Stratford. By reading Quiney's fortuitously preserved letters, we can find a way into

understanding what Shakespeare's own correspondence with Stratford might have resembled at a time when the carriers provided
the lifeline between capital and provinces. This chapter analyses
the sole Shakespearean scene in which carriers appear—*Henry
IV Part One*, Act 2, Scene 1—and suggests that this scene, often
cut in performance, sets up the crucial connections between the
carriers, the inn system, and the highway robbery that Falstaff,
Hal, and the others carry out. In adapting materials from his
source play *The Famous Victories of Henry the Fifth*, Shakespeare
deliberately extricates Hal from the attack on the carriers, setting up a moral distinction between Falstaff and Hal from the
outset.

Chapter 4, 'Shakespeare is Shylock: Letters of Credit in *The
Merchant of Venice*', takes the interpretation of the Quiney letter in
a different direction, building on the work of economic historian
Craig Muldrew to argue that it points to an attempt by Quiney and
his partners to place Shakespeare in a series of credit relationships
that would benefit Stratford. I then re-read *The Merchant of Venice*
in the light of such credit relationships transacted through letters,
demonstrating how the play is structured through the transacting
of sealed bonds of various kinds. Letters are essential to the long-
distance trade dealings of a merchant like Antonio; a specific sort of
letter, the sealed bill of obligation, constitutes the crux of Antonio's
deal with Shylock, and of Shylock's encounter with Venetian law;
a letter enforces Bassanio's return to Venice, while another allows
Bellario to accredit Portia in Venice; and letters provide the proofs
that will bring the play to its ostensibly happy end. The letters, bearing credit either financially or legally, or both, force us to reconsider
the lazy assumption that the relationships between Antonio and
Bassanio, or Jessica and Lorenzo, are fundamentally different to the
relationship forced between Antonio and Shylock.

In Chapter 5, I move on to deal with the question of delivery
of early modern letters, what I call 'the matter of messengers'. In
King Lear we see Shakespeare's most complex use of stage letters,

one that has baffled and angered critics from Bradley to Goldberg. Building on Richard Halpern's argument that the central conflict in the play is not between Edmund and Kent, but between Kent and Oswald, Goneril's steward, I argue that this opposition is played out through their differing version of what constitutes a proper messenger. While the play's sympathies may seem to be with Kent, he is, compared with Oswald, a pretty useless messenger. Having complicated the question of what or who makes a good messenger, *King Lear* goes on to explore the dilemma of letters without messengers—Erasmian letters, perhaps. We are led to see the dangers of letters without adequate messengers, from the letter supposedly thrown in at Edmund's window to Goneril's letter to Edmund that never reaches him, but which does reach Oswald, Edgar, and Albany.

In the final two chapters, I turn to *Hamlet*, the only Shakespeare play in which the title character is an inveterate letter-writer, penning letters during the course of the play to Ophelia, his mother, his uncle, Horatio and, fatally, to the king of England. Chapter 6, 'Lovers' lines: letters to Ophelia', argues that Hamlet's epistolary courtship of Ophelia is distinctly presented as a legally binding courtship leading to marriage. Clandestine marriage was a hotly debated topic in the England of 1600: the social signs of what legally constituted a marriage were well known. This chapter argues that the theatre had developed its own codes for what constituted a marriage between characters, and that the giving and receiving of letters was one of the well-known stage signs. Ophelia's enforced attempt to return Hamlet's letters reads clearly as a cutting off of their marriage plans—which leaves her compromised, and leads directly to her madness and suicide.

Chapter 7, 'Rewriting Hamlet,' focuses on the letter that Hamlet forges to the king of England, to replace the letter Claudius has written to ensure Hamlet's murder. The substitution of these two Bellerophontic letters can be traced to Shakespeare's Danish source by Saxo Grammaticus and its French language derivative by François de Belleforest, but with an important difference: in the sources, the letters are carved in wood, and the Hamlet character merely erases and re-razes the relevant names in the instructions. In Shakespeare's play, by contrast, the letter has to be written in all its sixteenth-century, paper, ink, wax and seal fiddliness. I argue that this episode has explicit resonances for the play's central theme: Hamlet's need to remember, which is famously figured as the writing on wipeable 'tables'. Whereas Hamlet puts his trust in the power of his rewritten letter to explain his story to posterity, his reliance on supplemental technologies of knowledge (whether they be tables or letters) is shown to be disastrous.

Taken as a whole, *Shakespeare's Letters* seeks to force critical attention back onto the letters that populate, perhaps even over-populate the Shakespearean stage, and suggest that we do not yet understand what is happening there. Letters look so familiar, and yet the culture of letters Shakespeare puts on stage needs to be made unfamiliar to us. Although the methodological impulse may seem largely historicist, it should soon become apparent that the resulting insights are simultaneously dramaturgical. We need to rethink what it means for Ophelia to return Hamlet's letters; for Falstaff to ambush carriers; for Kent to fail to deliver letters; for Maria's handwriting to be misread for Olivia's. Shakespeare's plays do not merely register the cultural presence of an ideology of letters. Instead, they work to produce something new, something that is not mirrored in the work of any of his theatrical contemporaries, and something that is resolutely theatrical. While readers may not find the letters we are all hoping to find, the letters that will bring them to the private life of the man from Stratford, they hopefully will find here the letters that will bring them closer to the ways in which that man approached his craft.

I

The Materiality of Shakespeare's Letters

Given the abundance of letters on the Shakespearean stage, it is striking how rarely we see them being written. Characters frequently commission the writing of letters, or announce that they have written a letter, or that they're going to write a letter. Some go so far as to make practical arrangements: Suffolk calls for 'pen and ink' (*1H6* 5.2.87), Romeo orders his man Balthasar to 'Get me ink and paper' (*RJ* 5.1.25), Cleopatra and Pericles call for 'ink and paper' (*AC* 1.5.68, 79; *Per* 3.1.65), and Malvolio pleads four times for 'a candle, and pen, ink, and paper' (*TN* 4.2.80–1, 105–6, 110–11) but we never see them write their letters.[1] The only two instances of characters who write on stage are Titus Andronicus hastily penning a supplication to be delivered by the Clown (*Tit* 4.3.105); and Richard III chaotically drawing his military plans in his tent (*R3* 5.3.41, 50).[2] Both Titus and Richard are by this point men on the edge, their acts of writing not signs of mastery, but evidence that they're losing control. Indeed, it could be argued that all those that call for pen and ink are emotionally disturbed: Suffolk dangerously in love with a future queen; Cleopatra intent on winning back her errant lover; Pericles facing the sudden death of his beloved wife; and Malvolio locked in darkness. The stage letter-writer is routinely depicted as slightly crazed, and with good reason: it's well nigh impossible to write a letter on stage.

The banal challenges posed by writing are neatly conveyed in an exchange between schoolboys from Claude Holiband's 1583 *Campo di Fior or else The Flovrie Field of Fovre Langvages* (based on Juan Luis Vives' 1538 dialogues, *Linguae Latinae exercitatio*):

MEN. Truely one cannot write with this penne and inke. . . .

MAU. Why not? / Why so?

MEN. Seest thou not how the penne spreadeth the inke about the paper?

MAU. My inke is so t[h]icke, | That thou wouldest say it were claye . . . | Marke I praye thee how it sticketh on the nibbe of the penne: | And will not fall out to writte. | I will put water into mine inke-horne, | . . . That the inke may come the better out of the penne. / . . .

MAU. This is the best writing paper. / The inke spreadeth not on this paper. / The inke runneth not through this paper.[3]

Pen, ink, paper: even the most basic materials are flawed. Those who spent their lives writing complained bitterly of the toll it took on their physical and mental health: indeed, the monks of the medieval scriptoria developed an entire literature on the subject.[4] But only once in Shakespeare's drama do we catch a glimpse of the real labour of writing, when it is used to highlight the failure of due process. In *Richard III*, a scrivener enters, carrying the indictment against Lord Hastings which 'in a set hand fairly is engross'd' to be read publicly at Paul's. 'Eleven hours I have spent to write it over', explains the scrivener, 'For yesternight by Catesby was it sent me', and the 'precedent' (the preamble) 'was full as long a-doing'. By the time he'd finished writing, the indictment was irrelevant because Hastings' head was already off (*R3* 3.6.1–9).

The raw materials of letter-writing in the early modern world were multiple and specific; their effective use took time, skill and labour. While a handful of other playwrights did put letter-writing on stage, generally to comic effect, Shakespeare chose not to, or at least not in a literal sense. In this chapter, I argue that Shakespeare instead embues his plays with the language and experience of the material letter-writing process—what we might call the grammar of early modern letter-writing—and turns it into something richly theatrical.

The Lamb and the Bee: the Raw Stuff of Letters

Is not this a lamentable thing, that of the skin of an innocent lamb should be made parchment; that parchment, being scribbled o'er, should undo a man. Some say the bee stings, but I say, 'tis the bee's wax: for I did but seal once to a thing, and I was never mine own man since.

(*2H6*, 4.2.80–2)

For Shakespeare's Jack Cade, parchment is still the skin of a lamb while wax comes from a bee, and contains the bee's sting. Imogen eulogizes the makers of the 'Good wax' she breaks open on Posthumus' letter: 'blest be | You bees that make these locks of counsel!' (*Cym* 3.2.35–6); Hamlet and Horatio recall that parchment is 'made of sheepskins ... | ... and of calves' skins too' (*Ham* 5.1.107–8). Elsewhere, as we'll see, pens are goose quills, ink is gall. The raw materials of writing possessed vivid associations for their early modern users, in part no doubt because they often prepared them themselves. And as Cade reminds us, they go far beyond ink and paper.

In an inventory of his household possessions in 1556, Sir William More of Loseley Hall in Essex listed the contents of 'myne owne closette'. Besides the books, maps, chairs, desks, boxes, pictures, weights and balances, touchstones, a globe, and a counterboard, he provides a rather alarming list of the materials which he needed in order to be able to write:

> Itm. a standyshe of pewter ... xvj d. ....
> Itm. a dust boxe of bone ... viij d.
> Itm. a payre of sesers ... ij d.
> Itm. too whetstones ... j d.
> Itm. a haere of bone to be made a sele vj d.
> Itm. a penne of bone to wryte with iiij d.

Itm. a payre of compasses . . . ij d.
Itm. a Sele of many Seles . . . ij d.
Itm. a hamere . . . ij d.
Itm. a penknyf . . . j d.
Itm. a foote rule . . . j d.
Itm. a pene of yron . . . j d..[5]

While it might not be immediately clear to the modern reader why an early modern writer might need a dustbox or whetstones to write a letter, a survey of sixteenth-century pedagogical handbooks proves that Sir William was by no means excessive in his demands. The calligraphy manual *A Booke Containing Divers Sortes of handes* by Jean de Beau Chesne and John Baildon (1570) insists that the writer needed a good supply of materials beyond pen and paper:

> Ynke always good stoore on right hand to stand,
> Browne Paper for great hast, elles box with sand: . . .
> Wax quilles and penneknyfe see always ye beare:[6]

In his *Positions* of 1581, Richard Mulcaster advises that 'penne and penknife, incke & paper, compasse & ruler, a deske & a dustboxe will set [children] vp'.[7] Francis Clement's *Petie School* (1587) agrees that 'The writer must prouide him these seuen: *paper, incke, pen, penknife, ruler, deske,* and *dustbox,* of these the three first are most necessarie, the foure latter very requisite.'[8] So when one of the interlocutors in John Florio's 1591 Italian instruction manual, *Florios Second Frvtes,* decides to write a letter, he demands: 'Give me my deske, and som pen and ynke, and paper . . . | Giue me my penknife, to make a pen . . . | Giue me some wax, some sealing thrid, my dust box, & my seale.'[9]

First came the writing surface. The early modern desk, as Lena Orlin reminds us, was not a flat table, but 'what we would generally call a portable desk, a box with a slanting top . . . Desks were placed on top of tables'.[10] Sometimes doubling as a lockable storage space—Antipholus of Ephesus has secreted 'a purse of ducats' in 'the desk | That's cover'd o'er with Turkish tapestry'

(*CE* 4.1.104–6)—the desk's sloping top was used for writing letters. In his 1590 *The Writing Schoolemaster*, professional calligrapher Peter Bales recommends a desk for its beneficial effects on posture: 'The best and easiest writing is vppon a Deske, for the better auoyding of too much stooping, whereby your health may be impaired.' The body, he claims, should be placed 'right forward . . . tourne not your head too much aside, nor bend it downe too lowe, for auoyding of weariness and paine: and for such as haue occasion to sit long, I would wish them to sit soft, for their better enduring to write'. Bales even considered the well-being of the eyes: 'for comforting of the sight, it is verie good to couer their deske with greene, & to vse all other helpes that may be procured, for the preseruation of your eyes'.[11] In short, the necessity of the desk meant that letter-writing was ideally an activity to be undertaken sedentary—so even when Hamlet is writing a letter in a situation of intense pressure, the first thing he does, he claims, is 'I sat me down' (*Ham* 5.2.31).

The materials of writing did not come cheap or easily. Francis Clement advises that 'The whitest, finest, and smothest paper is best',[12] and when Lorenzo sees a letter from Jessica, his conceit moves from identifying her handwriting to her hand to the paper, the latter two emphatically white, and therefore precious—'I know the hand. In faith, 'tis a fair hand, | And whiter than the paper it writ on | Is the fair hand that writ' (*MV* 2.4.12–14).

But for the English, who produced mainly brown or wrapping paper, the whitest, finest and smoothest paper was a relatively expensive commodity, the vast majority imported from France.[13] Most surviving household account books of the period contain multiple entries for paper expenses, whether bought in a quire (twenty-five sheets), a ream (twenty quires), or in bulk, in a bale (ten reams). Good quality paper was important. Peter Bales advised against paper that was too rough or too smooth: 'for being too rough, it marreth your pen; and being too smoothe, it will be too slipperie, that you cannot write steadily thereon'. Unfinished sheets of paper also needed to be cut to size, for which purpose Sir William More has a pair of scissors, as Holibrand's schoolboys note: when one complains that 'The brimmes of this paper are not euen', the other suggests he should 'Cut awaye some of the margen with a paire of scissers, | . . . For by this meane the leafe is the fairer'.[14] Parchment, the writing surface for many legal documents, posed its own problems: chalky parchment could be remedied by 'tak[ing] the chaulke off with a knife and a pumice stone', but even Bales was stumped by greasy parchment: 'If it be greasie, then knowe I no helpe for it at all, but to leaue it for some other vse.'[15]

An exchange in *Florios Second Frvtes* captures both the expense and the necessity of suitable paper to the would-be letter-writer:

> *L.* I haue no paper: neither is there any in the house.
> *S.* Goe buie some, here is monie.
> *L.* How much shall I buye?
> *S.* A quire: but let it be good, and that it doo not sinke.
> *L.* It is very deare of late.
> *S.* Let it cost what it will, I must needes haue some.[16]

S's concern that the paper 'doo not sinke' refers to a potential problem with paper: its irritating ability to absorb ink, causing it to spread or 'run'.[17] According to Hugh Platte, writing in 1594, it was a major problem for students who needed to 'note in the margentes of their bookes if their paper should happen to sinke, which is an especiall fault in many of our late yeere bookes of the Law'. To remedy this, Platte recommended rubbing the guilty paper 'wel ouer with the fine powder or dust of Rosen and Sandrach [red arsenic sulphide] mingled in equall parts before you write therwith', making sure the powder was tied hard 'in a rag of Laune or thin Cambrick', and rubbing 'the paper thoroughly well'.[18] An alternative was 'stanchgrain', for which du Beau Chesne and Baildon provide a recipe: 'Make stanche graine of allome, beaten full smalle, | And twise as muche rosen [resin] beaten with all | With that in a faire cloute knit verye thinne, | Rubb paper or parchment, or [before] ye begyn.'[19]

While paper was a bought commodity, pens were homemade, crafted from birds' feathers. The quill should be well chosen: both de Beau Chesne and Baildon, and Clement specify the third or fourth in a goose's wing, 'some what rownde', and failing that, '[t]ake pynyon [the last feathers] as next, when Rauens quille is skante'.[20] The quill had to be prepared, using a pen-knife. De Beau Chesne and Baildon advise that the writer should 'Make clyft without teeth your penne good, and hard: | Thinner, and shorter on right hand regarde: | The clyfte somewhat long, the nebb not to shorte.'[21] This was evidently easier said than done: in *The Petie School*, Clement's instructions on pen-making run onto three pages, and are accompanied by measurements reproduced on the printed page for reference.[22] One of Holibrand's boys has an unpalatable trick for smoothing down the feather: 'My maister taught me to make my penne softe with spitell, and rubbing it against the inside of my cote.' 'A pretie secret', says his master, approvingly.[23] Above all, pen needed to have a sharp nib, and indeed the sharpness of a pen was almost proverbial: 'pick out mine eyes with a ballad-maker's pen', protests Benedick (*MA* 1.1.234–5). This was achieved by the penknife, which for calligrapher Peter Bales was of prime importance: in his step-by-step guide to 'faire writing', 'the choice of your penknife' occupies the first chapter. He advises that 'a right *Sheffeild* knife is best: a good Razor is next, being not too thicke or too thinne grounded'; others exist but they are only 'indifferent good'.[24] The necessity of the penknife was given dramatic force in *The Spanish Tragedie*, when the mute Hieronimo 'makes signes for a knife to mend his pen', a perfectly understandable gesture for a man who has been told to write ('O he would haue a knife to mend his Pen')—but then he uses the knife to stab the Duke and himself to death.[25]

The penknife, it should be noted, was not simply employed in the preliminary operation to produce the perfect pen, then discarded. Writing was an ongoing two-handed operation: as de Beau Chesne and Baildon put it, 'Your Peneknife as staye in leaft hand lett rest.' The pen in the right hand needed constantly to be kept in good shape by the metal penknife held in the left hand—kept neither 'to softe nor to hard is best', we are advised—hence the need for the two whetstones in Sir William More's closet. Moreover, not just any whetstone will do for Bales: 'for the better keeping of your knife in good edge, it is verie conuenient and necessary, that you be furnished with the finest whetstone, called a hoane'—'hone', hence the modern verb 'to hone'—'the white hoane is the best, the blacke is next, and slate will serue for a shifte; refusing vtterly the hard whetstone, except your knife be verie blunt'. The pen needs a knife, a knife needs a whetstone, and a whetstone predictably has its own demands: 'after you haue well whetted your knife on the hoane or slate, it is verie good to smooth the same vpon the vpper drie leather of a shwe, which will make it to cut the more kindly'.[26] So dry shoe-leather joins the unlikely tools of the study.

Next on the list was ink, which more often than not was also homemade. De Beau Chesne and Baildon's calligraphy primer devotes a rhyme to the making of ink:

> To make common yncke of wyne take a quarte,
> Two ounces of gomme, let that be a parte,
> Fyue ounces of Galles of copres take three,
> Large standing dooth make it better to be:
> Yf wyne ye do want, rayne water is best,
> And asmuch stuffe as aboue at the least:
> Yf yncke be to thicke, put vinegre in:
> For water dooth make the colour more dymme.[27]

The authors then go on to specify how 'To make yncke inhast', how 'To keepe yncke longe', and how 'To make special black yncke' ('lampblacke thereto with gome water grinde' to make it thicker).[28] Clement's *Petie School* provides another recipe;[29] printed household companions often contained some pertinent advice on the subject;[30] and it seems that virtually every household manu-script miscellany contains at least one favoured recipe for ink.[31] Once concocted, ink was then poured from its storage bottle into an inkhorn. It was common to place some material inside the inkwell—Vives mentions cotton, silk-thread, linen, and silk—but the downside to that is that inevitably 'when thou dippest the penne in cotton, | There will alwayes remaine some heare [hair] in the cliffe [cleft] of the penne', which then had to be drawn out, 'Or if thou takest it not awaye, | Thou shouldest make blottes sooner then letters.'[32]

Pens and ink were often housed for convenience in either a stand known as a standish (as in Sir William More's office), or, for peripatetic writers, an inkhorn. The inkhorn was predominantly used by scriveners—Dogberry calls for Francis Seacoale to 'bid him bring his pen and inkhorn to the jail' (*MA* 3.5.54) to take down their examinations—and thus a symbol of literacy. For the rebels' leader Jack Cade, the inkhorn is enough to condemn the clerk of Chatham: 'Away with him, I say! Hang him with his pen and inkhorn about his neck' (*2H6* 4.2.100–1). As one might expect, mobile ink brings its own problems: when the inkhorn is carried about, Vives advises, a sponge should be placed in it.[33] Some carried their knife and pens in a 'penner' or 'pennard', a case of either metal or leather: in *Florios Second Frutes*, one student says 'Giue me my penknife, to make a pen', while the other retorts, 'It is in your penner.'[34] And a letter-writer's tool did not end with the contents of a standish, inkhorn, and penner. Once written, a letter's ink needed to be dried, usually by sprinkling fine sand or powder from a dustbox (Thomas Middleton's *Michaelmas Term* has a character named 'Dustbox the Scriuener').[35] Vives suggests more rudimentary materials: bran, or sand, or dust scraped from a wall.[36]

The colours of the writing table were instantly familiar to Shakespeare's audience, mapping easily onto love poetry clichés and moral evaluations. Against the white paper, ink is black. In *The Two Gentlemen of Verona*, Launce tells Speed that the news in his paper is 'The blackest news that ever thou heard'st.' 'Why, man? How black', asks Speed; 'Why', comes the answer, 'as black as ink' (*TGV* 3.1.280–2). Sonnet 63 refers to 'these black lines' (63.13); while Sonnet 65 looks to the paradoxical 'miracle' 'That in black ink my love may still shine bright'. (65:13–14). The white of the goose-quill contrasts with the black of the ink. Don Armado writes of the event 'that draweth from my snow-white pen the ebon-coloured ink' (*LLL* 1.1.235–6). Troilus enthuses of Cressida's 'hand, | In whose comparison all whites are ink | Writing their own reproach' (*TC* 1.1.52–4). But the contrast between white paper and black ink is more strikingly used in the negative. When Pisanio receives a letter ordering him to kill Imogen, he exclaims, 'O damn'd paper! | Black as the ink that's on thee! Senseless bauble, | Art thou a foedary for this act, and look'st | So virgin-like without?' (*Cym* 3.2.19–22). Or as Othello muses of Desdemona, 'Was this fair paper, this most goodly book | Made to write "whore" upon?' (*Oth* 4.2.72–3). As these uses suggest, there is implicit in the putting of black ink to white paper a violence which is literalized in *The Comedy of Errors* when Dromio of Ephesus claims to Antipholus of Ephesus, 'that you beat me at the mart I have your hand to show. | If the skin were parchment and the blows you gave were ink, | Your own hand-writing would tell you what I think' (*CE* 3.1.11–14).

Of all its ingredients, ink was most associated with galls, the excrescence produced by the friction of insects on oaks. But because this gall shares its name with the bile secreted by the liver, Shakespeare and his contemporaries could not resist conflating the two. Posthumus commands Imogen to write to him in his absence, 'And with mine eyes I'll drink the words you send, | Though ink be made of gall' (*Cym* 1.1.31–2). When Sir Toby Belch encourages Sir Andrew Aguecheek to challenge Sebastian to a duel in a letter, he urges, 'Let there be gall enough in thy ink; though thou write with a goose-pen, no matter' (*TN* 3.2.47–8)—Aguecheek's cowardice is neatly equated with the goose feathers he'll write with. Beyond being black gall, ink is also wet. 'Write till your ink be dry, and with your tears | Moist it again, and frame some feeling line | That may discover such integrity', Proteus advises the Duke (*TGV* 3.2.74–6). But that wetness means that ink can ultimately drown its subject: 'O', cries Leonato of his daughter Hero, 'she is fallen | Into a pit of

ink that the wide sea | Hath drops too few to wash her clean again'
(*MA* 4.1.139–41).

Ink is not always black. The use of blood as ink is familiar from
Bel-Imperia's letter written in blood ('For want of incke') in Thomas
Kyd's *The Spanish Tragedie*, where two stage directions specify 'A
Letter falleth' and 'Red incke'; and from Christopher Marlowe's
Doctor Faustus, where Faustus unforgettably signs the covenant with
the devil in his own blood, which dries up halfway through, forcing
him to pierce his skin again.[37] Shakespeare seems to play on the
image when Titus Andronicus, with one hand severed, is discovered
Faustus-like in his study and shows them in his remaining hand
what he has been writing in blood: 'See here in bloody lines I
have set down . . . witness these crimson lines' (*Tit* 5.2.14, 22). Unlike
with Faustus, we do not *see* Titus writing in blood. Consistently,
Shakespeare's depiction of the act of writing departs from any physical representation in favour of a complex cluster of images and ideas
based on the raw material stuff on which early modern writing is
made. But it is with the particular realm of letters that Shakespeare
is most acutely concerned.

Protocols

In recent studies A. R. Braunmuller and Jonathan Gibson, among
others, have drawn our attention to the layout of the early modern
manuscript letter.[38] As Gibson points out, 'Renaissance letter-writers
considered the physical appearance of a letter to be meaningful',
so that 'the disposition of blank space in a letter', which he dubs
'significant space', 'could carry important information about the
nature of the relationship between writer and addressee'.[39] Gibson's
argument is well taken, but he focuses our attention on the letter
when opened. In practice, the inside was the last feature of the letter
to be examined. On receiving the letter, a good deal of information
was gleaned instantly, even before scanning the text, from the letter's
outward physical appearance.

A complex letter-writing etiquette was firmly in place. First, letter-writers corresponding with their social betters should not skimp on paper. A letter usually comprised a single piece of paper: if the writer could afford it, a large bifolium sheet folded in half. As Antoine de Courtin wrote, 'To make use of large Paper rather than small, and a whole sheet (though we write but six lines in the first Page) rather than half a one, is no inconsiderable piece of Ceremony, one shewing reverence and esteem, the other familiarity or indifference.'[40] To use a scrap of paper to write a letter was considered insulting: surviving letters that were written on less than a sheet of paper invariably comment on and apologize for the fact.[41] When he is trying to convey Beatrice's love for Benedick, Leonato talks of how 'she'll be up twenty times a night, and there will she sit in her smock till she have writ a sheet of paper' (*MA* 2.3.131–3), the point being that to fill up an entire sheet of paper is truly excessive.

The text of the letter would be written on the 'front' page of this folded sheet, and continued inside, if necessary. The 'back' page, however, had to be kept blank. When the letter's text was completed, the letter would be folded up, with the 'back' page now forming the outside of the letter. The loose flaps would then be held in position with some melted wax, and perhaps some thread, and stamped with a seal. The writer had to remember to leave enough of the paper blank to ensure that the folding and sealing processes did not obscure what had been written. In *Love's Labour's Lost*, the Princess mocks a letter she has from her suitor, the king, that contained 'as much love in rhyme | As would be crammed up in a sheet of paper | Writ o'both sides the leaf, margin and all, | That he was fain [forced] to seal on Cupid's name' (5.2.6–9). In his passion, the king has filled the paper to the point that there is no margin, nowhere left to affix the seal, so the word 'Cupid' was obliterated by the wax.

The very folding of a piece of paper for letter-writing purposes contained important social signals. Sir Robert Cecil wrote to his son William, studying at Cambridge, to upbraid him for his incorrect folding: 'I have also sent you a piece of paper folded as gentlemen use to write their letters, whereas yours are like those that come out of a grammar school'.[42] The letter was usually folded up after it had been written: in his *Second Frvtes* one of Florio's interlocutors demands incredulously of his fast-writing companion, 'Haue you done alreadie? that you begin to fould?'[43] But it was also the case that some letters demanded folding *before* writing commenced. We find a rare theatrical trace of these decorous demands in a scene in *The First Part of Ieronimo*, the so-called 'prequel' to *The Spanish Tragedie*, as Jeronimo instructs Horatio in the writing of a letter. After pulling a table into position, he tells his companion 'Come write *horatio* write, | This speedy letter must away to night.' Horatio's immediate response is to fold the paper, the first step in letter-writing, but the printed stage direction indicates that '*horatio foulds the paper the contrary way*'. Jeronimo is horrified:

> What fold paper that way, to a noble man,
> to *Don andrea* Spaines embassador?
> Fie I am a shamed to see it,
> Hast thou worne gownes in the Uniuersity,
> Lost logick, suckt Philosophy,
> Eate Cues, drunke Cées, and cannot
> give A letter the right Courtiers crest:[44]

The preliminary folding of the paper provides the writer with guidelines for laying out the letter, the folds serving as rules for margins, so that Michel de Montaigne refers to 'a sheete without folding or margine' as a sign of a letter written 'in post-haste'.[45] A letter to an ambassador, like the one Horatio is writing, would need a large left-hand margin, or perhaps a large space between the salutation and the body of the letter, in order for the writer to show respect. Vives in his 1534 letter-writing manual *De conscribendis epistolis* points out that 'Nowadays it is customary to leave a blank space between the salutation and the letter itself, wider or narrower according to the rank of the person to whom it is written. One may call it, if you wish, the honorary margin'[46]—or, in Jeronimo's words, 'the right Courtiers crest'. Jeronimo's outburst expresses his shock that a man with a university education does not know how to do the one task for which that otherwise useless experience might prepare him: folding a piece of paper for letter-writing. As we'll see later (Chapter 7), that is precisely the kind of detail to which the Wittenberg-educated Hamlet attends when he is faking a letter from Claudius to the king of England: he '[f]olded the writ up in the form of th'other' (*Ham* 5.2.51), reproducing exactly the folding used by Claudius' secretaries. So, as Jeronimo and Hamlet suggest, folding the paper is the first step to writing a letter, which is why the sleepwalking Lady Macbeth is said to 'take forth paper, fold it' before writing upon it (*Mac* 5.1.6).

Whether guided by this folding or not, the writer should ensure that the relevant elements of a letter—salutation, valediction, sign manual (signature)—were properly placed and spaced on the paper. In his *Le grand et vrai art de pleine rhétorique* (1521), which influenced later English manuals, Pierre Fabri dictates a spatial layout that encodes social distinctions.[47] In translating Fabri's treatise in 1568, William Fulwood elaborates the proper local wording to accompany this accepted layout: 'to our superiours we must write at the right syde in the nether ende of the paper, saying: By your most humble and obedient sonne, or seruant, &c. And to our equalles we may write towards the midst of the paper saying: By your faythfull friende for euer. &c. To our inferiors we may write on high at the left hand saying: By yours &c.'[48] In *The English Secretorie* (1586) Angel Day also instructs his readers to position themselves on the page according to their relationship to the recipient. If the sender is much lowlier in rank, then his signature should appear at the very bottom of the page.

writing to anye personne of accompt, by how much the more excellent hee is in calling from him in whose behalfe the Letter is framed, by so muche the lower, shall the Subscription therevnto belonging, in any wise be placed. And if the state of honour of him to whome the Letter shall be directed doe require so much, the verye lowest margent of paper shall doe no more but beare it, so be it the space be seemelye for the name, and the roome fayre inough to comprehende it.[49]

Braunmuller argues that these writers posit 'a three-fold, two-dimensional social matrix: the position of the subscription left-to-right and top-to-bottom conveys the writer's sense of his social relation with the recipient—and possibly his suasive purposes in writing the letter'.[50] As Gibson notes, although the theorists do not necessarily agree, variously putting emphasis on the position of the first line of text, the position of signatures, and the left-hand margin, 'All of these regulations amount effectively to the same thing: the requirement that socially superior addressees be honoured with as much blank paper as possible', and the reason was obvious: '[p]aper was costly, so extravagant blanks in manuscript letters signified conspicuous expenditure'.[51]

The etiquette of signing off was well enough understood to be parodied on stage. In *The First Part of Hieronimo*, Jeronimo dictates the letter ending with the subscription 'I take my leaue', but in his penning, Horatio once again falls short. To convey the proper humility the subscription should be placed to the right of the letter, and near the bottom of the page. Jeronimo asks

> *Horatio* hast thou written leaue bending in the
> Hams: enough like a Gentleman vsher. Sfoote
> No *Horatio*, thou hast made him straddle too much,
> Like a Frenchman, for shame put his legs closer
> Though it be painefull.[52]

The subscription is personified as a bowing servant, but the trick is in achieving the correct degree of humility: like a gentleman usher, but not like an obscenely obsequious Frenchman. Shakespeare also mocks the polite conventions. In *Much Ado About Nothing*, Don Pedro asks Benedict to go to Leonato's house, 'commend me to him, and tell him I will not fail him at supper'. Benedick replies, 'I have almost matter enough in me for such an embassage. And so, I commit you—' (*MA* 1.1.256–61). The phrase 'And so, I commit you' is a standard epistolary valediction, and the other men instantly pick up on it, mocking Benedick:

CLAUDIO   'To the tuition of God. From my house'—if I had it—
DON PEDRO   'The sixth of July. Your loving friend, Benedick.'
BENEDICK   Nay, mock not, mock not...(1.1.262–6)

As Claire McEachern notes, in his mocking of epistolary closing formulae, Don Pedro even plays on the date, since 6 July was 'the quarter-day when rents were due, and hence a likely day for letter-writing'.[53]

For a letter to lack a proper subscription was shocking and rude—precisely the effect that Hamlet desires when he writes to Claudius:

High and mighty. You shall know I am set naked on your kingdom. Tomorrow shall I beg leave to see your kingly eyes. When I shall (first asking your pardon) thereunto recount the occasion of my sudden return.

(*Ham* 4.7.43–6)

While retaining the properly polite format of the petitionary letter, with its salutation encoding the relative positions of writer and recipient, Hamlet's chosen wording deliberately undermines the respectful genuflection. 'High and mighty' is a standard epithet of dignity for aristocracy, royalty and the divine—'A Prayer for the Queenes Maiestie' in Richard Day's *A booke of Christian prayers*, often bound with the *Book of Common Praier*, opens with an invocation to 'O Lord our heauenly father, high, and mighty king of kings, Lord of Lords, the only Ruler of Princes'.[54] Without the noun (king, prince, lord) to ground it, however, 'High and mighty' becomes an accusation of unwarranted superiority, as in its modern, always satirical usage. But if this were not clear enough, while the Folio version has the letter concluded with the simple sign manual 'Hamlet' (F, PP4^r), Q2 dispenses with the valediction and sign manual altogether (Q2, L3^v), stressing the rudeness of the missive.

The next step in preparing the letter was the sealing. Once folded up, the loose ends of the letter were sealed by the melting of wax onto the open edges, and the pressing of a seal into the molten wax. Wax is proverbially soft, malleable, able to take impressions, so the soldier in *Timon of Athens* uses it to take the 'character' of an inscription he cannot read (*Tim* 5.3.5–6; 5.4.67–9). But some references to wax in Shakespeare clearly draw on letter-writing culture. Sealing wax was usually red, a detail that is often evoked. Venus implores Adonis to 'Set thy seal-manual on my wax-red lips' (*VA* 516). Observing Lady Grey become increasingly flustered by the wooing of King Edward, Clarence whispers to Gloucester, 'As red as fire! nay, then her wax must melt' (*3H6* 3.2.51). Letters announcing or dealing with deaths or funerals, by contrast, would use black wax. On some letters, most notably love-letters, a sealing thread or ribbon was used, laced round the letter and then sealed with wax: the letters in *A Lover's Complaint* are 'With sleided silk, feat and affectedly | Enswathed and sealed to curious secrecy' (48–9), 'sleided silk' being silk that had been 'sleaved' or 'separated into loose threads' (*LC*, l. 48 n.) Other affectations might include the perfuming of letters dealing with love: as Gremio directs Lucentio, 'Take your paper, too, | And let me have them very well perfum'd, | For she is sweeter than perfume itself | To whom they go' (*TS* 1.2.149–52).

Once hardened, the wax created a hard seal that required some force to dislodge: that had to be broken apart or detached whole before the letter could be opened. Letters are therefore habitually 'broken open', 'broken up'. In *Love's Labour's Lost*, the Princess commands that the letter she believes to be from Biron should be opened with a particular brutal image: 'Break the neck of the wax, and everyone give ear' (*LLL* 4.1.60). Since the unbroken seal is a physical assurance that a document has not been tampered with, the seal was the guarantor of a contract, a notion Shakespeare exploits most fully in *The Merchant of Venice* (see Chapter 4). So in *The Winter's Tale*, much is made of 'the Oracle | . . . by Apollo's great divine seal'd up' (3.1.18–19), and brought by Cleomenes and Dion to Leontes. At the moment of revelation, an Officer prolongs the tension by insisting that the bearers swear that they have brought

> This seal'd-up oracle, by the hand deliver'd
> Of great Apollo's priest; and that since then
> You have not dared to break the holy seal,
> Nor read the secrets in 't.
>
> (*WT* 3.2.127–30)

The act of unsealing the oracle too becomes an act of heightened theatricality: 'Break up the seals and read', commands Leontes (3.2.131). As this scene implies, a seal should be broken only by the letter's intended recipient. In opening a letter destined for Edmund, the punctilious Edgar asks permission of the wax: 'Leave, gentle wax; and manners, blame us not. | To know our enemies' minds we rip their hearts, | Their papers is more lawful' (*KL* 4.6.254–6). His fretting about etiquette is darkly comic, given that Edgar has just killed the letter's bearer, Oswald. By contrast, Regan earlier wrongly demands of Oswald, 'Let me unseal the letter' (4.5.24).

The superscription of a letter was the last element to be added. Written on the 'outer' side of the folded letter, it indicated to whom the letter was to be delivered, and, if necessary, where that person would be found. Not simply an 'address' in the modern sense, it also needed to encode from the outset the relative social status of the sender and recipient. In their didactic dialogue in Abraham Fleming's *A Panoplie of Epistles*, the Maister and the Scholer come last to the question of superscriptions, since it is 'the last thing . . . required in an epistle': 'the superscription being (as it ought, and should be) finished, the epistle must needs be ended'.[55] Fleming gives a list of 'aptly agreeing' epithets for various ranks—'Most victorious King. Right puissant Prince. Most gratious Queene. Right renowmed Duke. Right honorable Earle. Right worshipfull Knight. And such like'[56]—but it is clear from other manuals of the period that his directions are woefully inadequate. As William Fulwood writes in the first English vernacular letter-writing manual, *The Enimie of Idelnesse*, 'the Superscription . . . must be vpon the back syde, the letter being closed, sealed, and packed vp after the finest fashion, whereupon must be written his name to whome the letters shold be addressed, & his dwelling place (if it be not notoriously knowne) placing therwith the name of his dignitie, Lordship, Office, Nobilitie, Science, or Parentage'.[57] In his popular *English Secretorie* (1586), Angel Day admitted that 'albeit few are the number that heerein shall be occasioned to occupy their penne', it was nonetheless useful to run through the titles 'that are or haue beene, latelye accustomed in our common-wealth' since 'it hath been parcell of a prescribed order so to doe'.[58]

The sense Day gives here of external pressure to formalize these titles is supported by later developments: by the mid-seventeenth century, protocols were highly elaborated and widely disseminated. Thomas Blount, in his 1656 *Academy of Eloquence*, appends a section on 'Superscriptions for Letters, to be addressed to all sorts of persons, according to the usage of the present times', moving from the proper address to a Duke ('To the most Noble (and some times) Excellent or illustrious Prince', down to the proper address for 'an ordinary Gentleman'. Shakespeare of course himself had to follow these conventions: both *Venus and Adonis* and *Lucrece* were printed with dedicatory epistles to the earl of Southampton. Blount prescribes,

> If to an Earle, Viscount or Baron
>> To the right honourable
> And to begin a Letter, we, either say
>> May it please your Honor or Lordship
>> Right honorable
>> My Lord.
> Which last is used only by Lords to Lords, or by Gentlemen of some
>> quality, otherwise it is held too familiar.[59]

Shakespeare properly begins with the superscription: 'TO THE RIGHT HONORABLE | Henrie Wriothesley, Earle of Southampton, | and Baron of Titchfield', and *Venus and Adonis* begins its letter, as Blount suggests for the non-lordly writer, 'Right honourable'.[60]

So the recipient had many signs to look for before dealing with the textual contents of a sealed letter. Johann Amos Comenius, writing on how to read a letter, advised 'the general characteristics of the letter, such as the address, the writer, and the date must be seen first (for unless these facts be known, the particular items of the letter cannot be properly understood).'[61] The seal might identify the sender. The subscription would encode the relative social status of the sender. Once broken open, the layout of the letter, the form of greeting and the placing of the signature would send its own message. These protocols were taken seriously—and they were equally ripe for parody. Holofernes, trying to gauge the provenance and intended destination of a letter, runs through the routine with beautiful pedantry:

I will overglance the superscript. *To the snow-white hand of the most beauteous Lady Rosaline.* I will look again on the intellect of the letter, for the nomination of the party written to the person written unto: *Your Ladyship's in all desired employment, Berowne.*

(LLL 4.2.130–4)

While Holofernes' pomposity is mocked in the use of the terms 'overglance', 'intellect', and 'nomination', his letter-reading technique is sound.

One of the most famous, and most commented letters in Shakespeare is the letter Maria writes for Malvolio to find. Malvolio's reading of the letter is staged in a manner that accentuates the theatrical aspect of letter-receiving: we watch him reading, commenting on and interpreting the letter, and we watch other characters watching him, commenting and interpreting his commentary and interpretation. Most critical work on Malvolio's reading of the letter focuses, with the literary critic's textual bias, on the letter's content, its words, and in particular the alphabetical characters on which he comes to obsess—*M O A I*—and those by which the supposed writer, Olivia, is betrayed sexually—*C U T* and *P*.[62] But this is to ignore his initial response to the letter, which is emphatically focused on the material letter, with its concerns of handwriting, superscription, and sealing:

What employment have we here?. . . .

By my life, this is my lady's hand: these be her very C's, her U's, and her
T's, and thus make she her great P's. It is in contempt of question her
hand . . .

To the unknowne beloved, this, and my good wishes.

Her very phrases! By your leave, wax. Soft! and the impressure her Lucrece,
with which she uses to seal: 'tis my lady! To whom should this be? . . .

(*TN* 2.5.82–96)

First Malvolio identifies what he believes to be his mistress's handwriting, the letter forms of her C, U, T, and capital P. Then he
reads the superscription, on the outside of the folded, sealed letter, and believes he recognizes her characteristic phrases. And then
he examines the wax seal, bearing the impression of a 'Lucrece',
matching the seal-ring Olivia uses. Despite, or perhaps because of,
his adherence to proper rules of identification, the deduction by
which Malvolio concludes that the letter is from Olivia and to him is
deeply flawed. The handwriting is very much like Olivia's—indeed,
later she will admit it is 'much like the character' (5.1.345)—but it
is in fact the work of her lady Maria. One might argue that to
the untrained male eye all women's handwriting might look similar: Olivia's writing will be in the italic hand routinely prescribed
for women, while a man like Malvolio would be used mainly to
a male secretary hand. But more importantly, Maria, as her lady-
cum-secretary Maria would know how to make her handwriting
resemble her mistress's—although Olivia can tell them apart: 'out
of question, 'tis Maria's hand' (5.1.346), she says, unwittingly echoing Malvolio's 'It is in contempt of question her hand' (2.5.89–90).
The phrases of the superscription are very much like those used by
Olivia, but they are absolutely standard for the day, and in any case,
Maria would know what Olivia's habitual phrases were. And of all
the seal-ring images available for a woman, the Lucrece was perhaps
the most clichéd—for convenience, Maria would probably have one
herself—and of course, as the ultimate icon of female chastity, not
least in Shakespeare's own writings, supremely inappropriate as the

image on a letter in which the female writer offers herself to her social inferior: '*She that would alter services with thee*' (2.5.157–8).

But there is one moment when Malvolio is spot-on. His exclamation of 'Soft!'—'By your leave, wax. Soft! and the impressure her Lucrece'—is usually glossed by editors as a self-instruction to proceed quietly or calmly.[63] But it is more likely, in the context of the line, to refer to the state of the seal, the 'soft' wax indicating that the letter has been sealed relatively recently, and its provenance is therefore local. The observation is therefore part of Malvolio's deductive process that leads him to believe that Olivia sealed the letter, although the true letter-sealer is even closer at hand.

Tearing Letters on Page and on Stage

It should be clear by this point that Shakespeare undeniably refers to and exploits notions of the early modern letter in its prescribed material forms. Certain features of 'real' letters are brought to bear in references to the layout of letters, to their superscriptions, to their folding and sealing. In the second half of this chapter, however, I shall suggest that this is only part of the story. While it borrows certain forms from its real-life counterpart, the Shakespearean stage letter is—because of the material conditions it has to negotiate—a different beast. The folded and sealed early modern letter was small, rarely bigger than four inches by two inches: therefore, only a very few features of a letter are visible on the stage. The breaking open of a seal is a vigorous enough act to be conveyed to an audience. The conceit of a letter penned in blood can be appreciated. One further action, perhaps the most visible and brutal, is also easily shown on stage: the tearing up of a letter. But, as I'll show, a stage-letter is different in substance from any other letter in fiction.

Letter-tearing is often adduced in narratives of all kinds to express heightened emotion, either anger or erotic passion. One such (entirely fictional) situation is described by Leonato in *Much*

Ado about Nothing: knowing that Benedict can overhear him, he depicts Beatrice's alleged love for him through her letter-writing and tearing: 'she'll be up twenty times a night, and there will she sit in her smock, till she have writ a sheet of paper' (2.3.130–3). The scene is erotically loaded: Beatrice writes at night, vulnerable 'in her smock'. The paper becomes sexualized, a bedsheet containing both her name and Benedict's: 'O, when she had writ it, and was reading it over, she found "Benedick" and "Beatrice" between the sheet' (2.3.136–8). The self-revelation throws her into a fury: 'O, she tore the letter into a thousand halfpence, railed at herself that she should be so immodest to write to one that she knew would flout her' (2.3.140–2).

The richest Shakespearean source for torn letters, however, is his early comedy, *The Two Gentlemen of Verona*. As editor William Carroll notes, 'The substantial traffic in letters in *Two Gentlemen*—six or possibly seven letters circulate—reflects issues of textuality and representation that spread throughout the entire play.'[64] It was of this play that Muriel Bradbrook proffered her more negative appraisal that, when at a loss for inspiration, Shakespeare invariably inserted 'a misdirected letter, of which there are a record number in this play.'[65] Letters criss-cross from Proteus to Julia, Julia to Proteus, Valentine for Silvia (to Valentine himself), Valentine to Silvia, Proteus to Silvia. Carroll suggests that 'These letters, variously delivered and read, or intercepted and torn up, become metonymies for sexual desire. Their errant and self-referential paths effectively reflect the confusions and failures of the main love plots',[66] a verdict that has been fruitfully elaborated by other critics.[67] But where Shakespeare most firmly revises his source materials is in the tearing of letters.[68]

In Act 1, Scene 3, Proteus sends a letter to Julia, via her maid Lucetta; Julia tears it up before attempting to reassemble it. Much of the play's plot is drawn from book two of Jorge de Montemayor's hugely popular 1559 Spanish romance *Diana*, and from Montemayor, Shakespeare takes the episode of a female servant who pressures her mistress to take her lover's letter; the mistress, initially reluctant, eventually capitulates.[69] But Shakespeare also turns to the story of Eurialus and Lucretia, a fifteenth-century erotic Latin novella by Enea Silvio Piccolomini (later Pope Pius II), familiar to sixteenth-century English readers in verse and prose adaptations, multiply printed from 1515 to 1596.[70] In Piccolomini's narrative, Lucretia falls in love with a visiting courtier named Eurialus. Eurialus sends a letter to her, using a hired woman with a reputation as a bawd, a means of address Lucretia finds insulting. At first, she rejects the letters, but then decides to have them so that she might 'caste them in the fyre'; therefore, 'snatchynge the paper from her, [she] tare it in peaces and trode vnder her fete, spyttynge at it, caste it in the asshes'.[71] But after the bawd leaves, Lucretia has a change of heart:

Truelye Lucres ... soughte vp the peeces of the lettre, and sette eche in theyre place, and ioyned soo the torne woordes that shee made it legeable whyche when shee hadde redde it a thousande tymes, a thousande tymes she kyssed it, and at the laste wrapped it in a fayre napkyn, and putte it amonge her Juels, and remembryng nowe thys woorde, nowe that woorde, continuallye she sooked in more loue, and determyned to wryte to Eurialus ... [72]

So Piccolomini's Lucretia, like Shakespeare's Julia, physically destroys the letter. In both prose tale and stage play, it is a powerful moment, when emotion leads to an outburst that destroys the object that represents her wooer. We are meant to see the tearing as in itself her response. This is made explicit in the *Tragœdia von Julio vnd Hyppolita*, a German-language variation of *Two Gentlemen of Verona* performed by English players around 1600: the messenger Grobianus asks Hyppolita, the Prince and Julius 'what answer shall I take to Romulus', and in turn each replies. 'That, that is my answer ... That is my answer too ... so and so do I answer him.' Although no stage direction is given, it is clear that each character tears her or his letter and throws it to the ground, and this action, performed publicly in front of the messenger, constitutes an 'answer'.[73]

But letter-tearing on stage differs from letter-tearing in a book. In Piccolomini's tale, the letter can be 'ioyned soo ... that shee made it legeable', that is, the pieces can be reassembled so that the letter can be read again, with less passion. This is a frequent trope in romantic fictions of the period. In George Gascoigne's 'The aduentures of Master F. I'. (1573), F. J. tears up a paper he believes to be his own letter, returned by his mistress Elinor, only to realize belatedly that 'it was not of his owne hande writing, and therewithall abashed, vppon better regard he perceyued in one péece therof written *(in Romaine)* these letters *S H E* : wherefore placing all the péeces therof, as orderly as he could, he found therin written, these fewe lynes hereafter followinge'.[74] In Robert Greene's *Philomela* (1592), when the eponymous heroine realizes that Lutesio has sent her a love letter, she 'rent the paper in a thousand péeces, ... vowing hir Lord should be reuenged vpon him for this intended villanie'. Realizing, however, that her case would be stronger, and 'that shée might aggrauate hir husbands displeasure the more against him' if she had the evidence, 'shée gathered vp the péeces, and laieng them together read them ouer' (on reflection, she decides against telling her husband).[75] Similarly in Emanuel Forde's *Ornatus and Artesia* (1599), Artesia, seeking to 'ouermaister her affections', refuses to read a letter from her lover Ornatus, and, to ensure she is not tempted, tears the letter into 'a thousand peeces'. Curiosity prevents her from sleeping, however, and she gets out of bed, pieces together the letter and reads it, secretly pleased by his attentions.[76]

In Shakespeare's play, by contrast, the letter must, perforce, remain in fragments—the stage prop has been destroyed. Julia immediately regrets the damage she has wrought on the papers: 'O hateful hands, to tear such loving words! ... I'll kiss each several paper for amends'. (1.2.105–08) Searching through the scraps, the text is splintered into phrases: '*kind Julia*', '*love- wounded Proteus*', 'But twice or thrice was *Proteus* written down' (1.2.109, 113, 117). Ultimately, she turns the scraps of paper on themselves so that the two names can consummate their passion: 'Thus will I fold them,

one vpon another; Now kiss, embrace, contend, do what you will'
(1.2.124–9).

While this is a cute conceit, it's a far cry from the wholesale
reconstruction of torn letters that the romance heroines contrive.
But the reason is clear. Julia has to appeal to the 'good wind' to
'[b]e calm' and 'blow not a word away' (1.2.118)—not simply an
expression here, since the player is contending with the conditions
of an outdoor stage like the Curtain or the Globe where protection
from the elements is by no means total. This possibility is played
on positively in the final act of *Troilus and Cressida* where Troilus's
tearing of a letter brought by Pandarus from Cressida is not signalled
in the stage directions, but in Troilus' words:

> PANDARUS ... What says she there?
> TROILUS Words, words, mere words, no matter from the heart;
> Th'effect doth operate another way.
> Go, wind, to wind! There turn and change together.
> My love with words and errors still she feeds,
> But edifies another with her deeds.
>
> (5.3.106–11)

Troilus calls on the papers to 'Go, wind to wind', fly from one
breeze to another, and like their inconstant writer, 'turn and change
together'. This is what Julia seeks to avoid, but her plea to the wind,
and the only partial salvaging of the torn letter brings home the
practical challenges of rendering material letters on the Elizabethan
stage.

Rather than avoid this problem, Shakespeare embraces it to comic
effect. Julia is later seen to carry Proteus' letters on her person.
When, disguised as Sebastian, she is employed by Proteus to carry
a letter to Silvia, she first hands over a letter that is not from her
employer—

> Madam, please you peruse this letter.
> Pardon me, madam, I have unadvised
> Delivered you a paper that I should not.
> This is the letter to your ladyship.
>
> (4.4.119–22)

As Carroll notes, some directors have decided that 'Julia still has Proteus' original torn letter, now conspicuously and comically taped back together'.[77] Quite how this might have been accomplished on the Elizabethan stage is not clear, but it is a tempting supposition. As Frederick Kiefer argues, 'Seeing this letter together with the letter to Sylvia, we cannot help reflecting on what they contain: equally ardent professions of love written by the same man to different women'.[78] This would also then explain Silvia's unexpected move: she asks to see the letter again, and when Julia refuses, says:

> There, hold.
> I will not look upon your master's lines:
> I know they are stuffed with protestations
> And full of new-found oaths, which he will break
> As easily as I do tear his paper.
>
> (4.4.125–9)

Does Silvia 'tear his paper' because she has just seen another, evidently torn paper? Has she recognized the handwriting on the two papers as being identical? It is at precisely this moment that she reveals to Sebastian/Julia her awareness of Proteus' other lover: as Sebastian announces, 'Madam, he sends your ladyship this ring' (4.4.130), Silvia refuses it, saying

> The more shame for him, that he sends it me,
> For I have heard him say a thousand times
> His Julia gave it him at his departure.
> Though his false finger have profaned the ring,
> Mine shall not do his Julia so much wrong.
>
> (4.4.131–5)

We move here from a letter that is nearly passed from Proteus to Julia to Silvia, to a ring that is nearly passed from Julia to Proteus (via Julia) to Silvia, pointing up the analogy between letter and ring as material objects to be exchanged. The play goes further, however, in pursuing the awkwardness of the letter transactions of the Julia-Proteus-Silvia triangle, through a parodic counterpoint in the efforts of Launce. Silvia's refusal to accept the letter from Proteus has been prefigured by her refusal of a previous missive from Proteus—the small dog that he sends, carried by Launce, a poor choice as bearer. *En route* to Silvia, the dog is stolen from Launce by 'the hangman's boys in the market-place', so he resourcefully 'offered her mine own'—the endearing but incontinent Crab—'who is a dog as big as ten of yours, and therefore the gift the greater' (4.4.53–6). Dogs-as-gifts, rings, and letters are thus presented as analogous; and just as Launce gives the wrong dog to Silvia, Sebastian will present the wrong letter to Silvia, provoking Silvia to rip up the letter from Proteus. All these parallels force us to consider the letter not as a text but as an object—analogous to a ring, or even to a dog—that moves between individuals.

This Churlish Superscription: The Letter and the Bearer

While Shakespeare's plays are clearly permeated by the grammar of letters and letter-writing, it would be wrong to assume that Shakespeare relies on a misplaced superscription or inappropriate folding for dramatic effect. These breaches of protocol might have had real impact in elite political worlds, but they make for poor theatre. Rather than shying away from these moments, however, Shakespeare developed a new, more theatrically effective way of rendering them. In so doing, he draws our attention to perhaps the single most important element of the early modern letter, which we are apt to forget: the letter's bearer. For the creation of a letter did not stop with its folding, writing, dusting, sealing, and superscription. In order for it to be successfully transacted, it had to be conveyed to the intended recipient, either by a personal messenger, or a bearer or carrier paid for the service. Future chapters will insist on the importance, and in some cases the supremacy of the bearer in Shakespeare's letter transactions, but for now, one example will suffice. It concerns what appears to be (and indeed is) a historically important failure to respect the epistolary protocols I have just outlined. But

in order to make this point theatrically, Shakespeare also dramatizes
the letter's delivery.

Shakespeare's source materials for *Henry VI Part One* gave him a
textbook example of a letter that failed to adhere to the protocols
linking proper superscription to relative social rank. As Hall reports
in his chronicles, the duke of Burgundy wrote to King Henry, but
something was awry with his superscription:

> This letter was not a litle loked on, nor smally regarded of the kynge of
> England, and his sage counsaill: not onely for the waightines of the matter,
> but also for the sodayn chaunge of the man, & for the strange superscrip-
> cion of the letter, whiche was: To the high & mighti prince, Henry, by *the*
> grace of God kyng of England, his wellbeloud cosyn: Neither naminge him
> kynge of Fraunce, nor hys soueraigne lorde, accordyng as, (euer before that
> tyme) he was accustomed to do.

Those present were 'sore moued with the craftye deed, & vntrue
demeanor of the Duke', and, unable to 'temper their passions, nor
yet moderate their yre, nor yet bridle their toungues, but openly
called hym traytour, deceiuer, and moste inconstante prynce'.[79] Passions, ire, and unbridled tongues—all provoked by the wording of
the superscription.

In Shakespeare's dramatizing of this scene, it is notable that the
King instructs Gloucester to 'view the letter | Sent from our uncle,
Duke of Burgundy' (1*H* 64.1.48–9)—an odd choice of verb, one
might think, but 'viewing' is precisely what Gloucester does first,
before he reads. He first views the superscription:

> What means his Grace, that he hath changed his style?
> No more but, plain and bluntly, 'To the King'.
> Hath he forgot he is his sovereign?
> Or doth this churlish superscription
> Pretend some alteration in good will?
>
> (4.1.50–4)

'Style' here is not Burgundy's manner, but the titles by which a
person (here, the King) is entitled to be addressed. Comprising a

list of the dominions over which she or he laid claim, the style of the sovereign had massive political import. Notably, in his 1586 discourse on titles, Angel Day does not dare suggest the proper address for the monarch: 'the soueraigne Maiesty excepted', he concedes parenthetically.[80] William Fulwood, however, does hazard an attempt: 'If wee write to our Superiour, wee must vse all honour and reuerence without embasing his name, or style, as, *To the King our Soueraigne Lord*.'[81] Whereas the historical letter from Burgundy to Henry VI boasted a more subtle difference—the omission of Henry's title of King of France—the stage letter's superscription is reduced to the simple 'To the King', which is adjudged plain, blunt and churlish. But they both lack the notion of '*Soueraigne Lord*', that Fulwood prescribes.

The letter itself is just six theatrical lines and thirty-seven words long:

> What's here? *I have upon especial cause,*
> *Moved with compassion of my country's wrack,*
> *Together with the pitiful complaints*
> *Of such as your oppression feeds upon,*
> *Forsaken your pernitious faction*
> *And joined with Charles, the rightful King of France.*

(4.1.55–60)

The king asks 'Is that the worst this letter doth contain?' and Gloucester affirms that 'It is the worst'—not least because it is 'all, my lord, he writes' (4.1.66–7). The letter ends abruptly, without the proper valediction, in itself a heinous lapse in courtesy. As Frederick Kiefer has argued: 'The curt salutation is matched by the letter's six-line length. The abrasive language makes the English court feel the sting of French arrogance.'[82] Significantly, although the content of the letter is absolutely damning, it is its presentation—the brusque superscription, the lack of valediction—that constitutes the primary offence to its audience.

It would be wrong to read this as a simple endorsement of title. Elsewhere in the play, titles are made a laughing stock, and again in relation to the titles of a letter's superscription. As he seeks out the English dead, Sir William Lucy asks the Dauphin Charles,

> But where's the great Alcides of the field?—
> Valiant Lord Talbot, Earl of Shrewsbury,
> Created for his rare success in arms,
> Great Earl of Washford, Waterford, and Valence,
> Lord Talbot of Goodrig and Urchinfield,
> Lord Strange of Blackmere, Lord Verdon of Alton,
> Lord Cromwell of Wingfield, Lord Furnival of Sheffeld,
> The thrice victorious Lord of Falconbridge,
> Knight of the noble order of Saint George,
> Worthy Saint Michael and the Golden Fleece,
> Great marshal to Henry the Sixth,
> Of all his wars within the realm of France.
>
> (4.4.172–83)

The titles are meant by Lucy to glorify Talbot, as indeed the probable source of Shakespeare's list, Roger Cotton's *Armor of Proofe* (1596), similarly meant to glorify not only Talbot but his descendant, the dedicatee of the book, who shared some of the titles: 'the right Honorable Gilbert Talbot, Earle of Shrewsburie, Lord Talbot, Furniuall, Strange of Blackmeare, Verdon, and Louetoft, Knight of the most noble order of the Garter'.[83] But to this roll-call of titles, Joan has a witty, and then devastating, rejoinder: 'Here's a silly stately style indeed: | The Turk, that two and fifty kingdoms hath, | Writes not so tedious a style as this' (4.4.184–6).

Editor Edward Burns suggests that Joan raises the Turk as an analogy because that 'Turkish rulers were proverbial for grandiloquence and pomposity', citing such theatrical avatars as Bajazet in Marlowe's *Tamburlaine the Great*.[84] I would argue that the allusion here is more specific, and takes us once again to superscriptions. In 1589, Richard Hakluyt had printed, in Latin and an English 'interpretation', 'the letters, or priuilege of the most mightie and *Musumanlike Emperour Zuldan Murad Chan, granted at the request* of Elizabeth by the grace of the most mightie God, and only Creator of heauen & earth, of England, France and ireland Queene, confirming a peace and league betwixt both the said princes and their subiects', issued in June 1580. This commenced with what formed a fairly standard solemn *intitulatio* to a 'ahdnāme' (treaty-letter), which gave the Murad III's 'style', his litany of titles; translated onto the pages of an English printed book, however, it appeared to be the most ridiculously overblown and self-serving superscription to a letter:

We most sacred Musulmanlike Emperor, by the infinite & exceeding great power, by the euerlasting and woonderfull clemencie, & by the vnspeakable helpe of the most mighty and most holy God, creator of all things, to be worshipped and feared with all purenesse of minde, and reuerence of speech, The prince of these present times, the onely Monarch of this age, able to giue scepters to the potentates of the whole world, the shadow of the diuine mercy and grace, the distributer of many kingdoms, prouinces, townes & cities, Prince, and most sacred Emperour of Mecca, that is to say, of Gods house, of Medina, of the most glorious and blessed Ierusalem, of the most fertile Egypt, Iemen, and Iouan, Eden & Chanaan, of Samos the peaceable, and of Hebes, of Iabza, and Pazra, of Zeruzub and Halepia, of Caramaria and Diabekiruan, of Dulkadiria, of Babylon, and of all the three Arabias, of the Euzians & Georgians, of Cyprus the rich, and of the kingdoms of Asia, of Ozakior, of the tracts of the White and Blacke Sea, of Grecia and Mesopotamia, of Affrica & Goleta, of Algeris, and of Tripolis in the West, of the most choise and principall Europe, of Buda and Temesuar, and of the kingdoms beyond the Alps, and many others such like, most mightie Murad Chan, the sonne of the Emperor Zelim Chan, which was the sonne of Zoleiman Chan, which was the sonne of Zelim Chan, which was the sonne of Paiizid Chan, which was the sonne of Mehemed Chan, &c.[85]

One can easily see how this might translate into the 'silly stately style' of 'The Turk, that two and fifty kingdoms hath', even if we don't quite reach forty here. While the Turk's style is a laughing stock, however, that of the king of England—including his claim to France—is the justified reason for the war, and for the play.

Yet, in what I shall show is a characteristic move, Shakespeare is not content to let the weight of Burgundy's insult lie in the wording of the letter. Instead, in his version, the letter causes offence before the superscription is viewed, through the choice of the man who carries it to the king. In Hall's chronicle, 'the duke of Burgoyne...sent Thoison Dor, his kyng at Armes [a chief herald], to kynge Henry with letters',[86] a properly respectful envoy to a sovereign. In Shakespeare's play however, the task is given to Sir John Fastolfe, who by this time has been emphatically vilified, although he has only spoken three lines. In the opening scene, the third messenger recounts Talbot's battle at Meux, claiming that victory would have 'fully been sealed up, | If Sir John Fastolfe had not played the coward', and 'Cowardly fled, not having struck one stroke', leading to 'the general wrack and massacre' (1*H*6 1.1.130–5); later, Talbot exclaims, 'But O, the treacherous Fastolfe wounds my heart, | Whom with my bare fists I would execute, | If now I had him brought into my power' (1.4.34–6). To reinforce these reports, we're later given a brief but vivid scene of remarkable cowardice, as Fastolfe retreats from the battlefield 'in such haste', 'To save myself by flight' (3.2.102–3). To labour the point, a Captain asks him, outraged, 'What? Will you fly, and leave Lord Talbot?' only to have Fastolfe reiterate 'Ay, all the Talbots in the world, to save my life' (3.2.105–6).

Introduced thus damningly as a '[c]owardly knight' (3.2.107), Fastolfe next appears carrying this letter, which he proffers to the king:

> My gracious sovereign, as I rode from Calais,
> To haste unto your coronation,
> A letter was delivered to my hands,
> Writ to your grace from the Duke of Burgundy.
>
> (4.1.9–12)

Talbot immediately intervenes, crying 'Shame to the Duke of Burgundy, and thee' (4.1.13)—Burgundy is already shamed before the contents of the letter are known, by his employment of this cowardly knight, who has been defined in contrast to Talbot's courage. But then Talbot goes further, ripping the Order of the Garter from Fastolfe's leg (4.1.13–16), detailing Fastolfe's cowardice at Patay, where the English lost twelve thousand men,[87] and lamenting the decay of the honour of the Garter (4.1.33–44). Heeding Talbot's word, the king banishes Fastolfe on pain of death without further ado (4.1.47) and turns immediately to the letter that Fastolfe brought: 'And now, my lord Protector, view the letter | Sent from our uncle, Duke of Burgundy' (4.1.48–9), the letter that will refuse to give him the proper respect and title. In making Fastolfe the letter-bearer, then, Shakespeare brings together Fastolfe's shameful performance in the field, his wrongful usurpation of the Garter, and Burgundy's rebellious lapse in letter-writing protocol, making them all of a piece, linked by cowardice, disloyalty, and unworthiness.

Fastolfe—now known as Falstaff—remains associated with letters in his remaining appearances in Shakespeare's plays. In *Henry IV Part Two*, there is a comic echo (or prefiguration) of the Burgundy letter. Bardolph brings greetings to Hal from his master, and Poins reads out the letter, providing a running commentary on the superscription: 'Sir John Falstaff, Knight, to the son of the King, nearest his father, Harry Prince of Wales, greeting' (2.2.112–14). Poins notes sardonically the 'Knight' epithet—'Every man must know that', he muses, 'as oft as he hath occasion to name himself' (2.2.104–5)—and on the construction that is more appropriate to official proclamations and licences than to personal letters—'Why this is a certificate!' (2.2.115).

I will imitate the honourable Romans in brevity . . . I commend me to thee, I commend thee, and I leave thee. Be not too familiar with Poins, for he misuses thy favours so much, that he swears thou art to marry his sister Nell. Repent at idle times as thou mayst, and so, farewell.

Thine, by yea and no—which is as much as to say, as thou usest him—
Jack Falstaff with my familiars, John with my brothers and sisters, and
Sir John with all Europe.

(2.2.116–27)

'My lord', says Poins angrily, 'I'll steep this letter in sack and make
him eat it', to which the prince replies, 'That's to make him eat
twenty of his words' (2.2.128–30). Once again, it is the form of the
superscription, the titles it contains, and the sheer brevity of the
letter that are offensive.

Falstaff's abuse of letters is evidenced again in *The Merry Wives
of Windsor*, where he unrepentantly woos both Mistress Page and
Mistress Ford using the same letter: 'They shall be my East and
West Indies, and I will trade to them both' (*MW* 1.3.67–9). When the
ladies discover his game, they assume that his letter-writing lacks all
sincerity—'I warrant he hath a thousand of these letters, writ with
blank space for different names'—and worse, that he has dragged
letter-writing down to a new low, the medium of print: 'sure, more,
and these are of the second edition. He will print them, out of doubt;
for he cares not what he puts into the press when he would put
us two' (2.1.66–70). Given his myriad letter-writing escapades, it is
no accident that when Falstaff dies, what's remembered of him is
that 'his nose was as sharp as a pen' (*H5* 2.3.16). Nor that when
the Ireland scandal broke in 1796, the next collection rushed to the
press was the *Original Leters, &c. of Sir John Falstaff and his friends;
now first made public by a gentleman, a decandant of Dame Quickly, from
genuine manuscripts which have been in the possession of the Quickly
family near four hundred years.*[88] The various improper uses he makes
of letters is a device by which Falstaff's amusing but ultimately
unforgivable lapses in decorum can be subtly, and consistently,
conveyed.

The influence on Shakespeare of the early modern letter, in
all its intricate materiality, is undeniable. Vocabulary and imagery
associated with the letter pervade his plays and verse. But generally speaking, the playwright can only invoke and gesture towards

a real-world epistolary system. Instead, Shakespeare develops a new grammar using stage letters, drawing on their materiality, but insisting that they must be understood through their participation in a performance—the performance not primarily of writing and reading, but of dispatching, carrying, receiving and archiving. In what follows, I shall argue that Shakespeare's development of the stage letter as theatrical rather than rhetorical is not accidental: rather, it poses a deliberate and consistent riposte to the dominant notion of letter-writing in early modern England.

2

Shakespeare's Roman Letters

Clock strikes. (JC, 2.1.190 SD)

~

Julius Caesar is infamous for the clock that strikes three times while the conspirators lay their plans in Brutus' house.[1] Whether a careless slip or a deliberate effect, the clock neatly highlights a material difference between classical Rome and early modern London while simultaneously illustrating the desire to make an historically distant scene resonant for a contemporary audience. It is a negotiation found constantly throughout Shakespeare's historical plays, although usually accomplished less jarringly. The setting of the Roman plays, in particular, distanced by time, geography and language from early modern England, presents particular problems for the representation of material practices that had fallen into disuse, or evolved beyond recognition. And yet this setting was felt to be strangely relevant to an educated early modern audience. Humanist scholarship insisted on, indeed relied upon, the immediacy of its key Roman authors whose works constituted the basic diet of sixteenth-century grammar-school boys. Humanist pedagogy had much invested in the supposed continuity of this classical curriculum which, it insisted, provided not merely historical but importantly contemporary *exempla*. When an Elizabethan clock strikes in Caesar's Rome, then, it might be heard as only natural, given the nearness of the two cultures—or it might serve to rupture their supposed harmony. In either case, as Phyllis Rackin has recognized, anachronism is 'double-edged', able simultaneously to achieve identification and alienation for its audience.[2]

The clock is not the only striking anachronism that night. Earlier in the scene, Brutus' servant announces that in his master's closet 'I found | This paper, thus sealed up' (2.1.36–7) a paper that the audience knows to have been thrown in at the casement on Cassius' orders. Not only is the material anachronistic—paper was not common in Europe for over another millennium—but the method by which the letter reaches Brutus owes far more to early modern London than to classical Rome. In Shakespeare's source for the incident, Thomas North's englishing of Jacques Amyot's French translation of Plutarch's *Lives*, 'bills' are published on public sites associated with Brutus; in the play, they are thrust into his private residence. In the negotiations made between a classical source and the demands of the contemporary stage, I shall argue, letters provide a telling case-study for the ways in which Shakespeare repeatedly turns to the contemporary over the historical, the emotionally compelling over the historically accurate: a striking Elizabethan clock and a thrown Elizabethan libel resonate far more effectively with Shakespeare's audience than would their Roman counterparts. And in choosing modern custom over ancient practice, Shakespeare takes sides in a quiet but steady debate among sixteenth-century scholars as to proper writing practices, and especially proper letter-writing practices.

When in Rome: Humanist Letters and Classical Epistles

Sixteenth-century humanism insisted that it was reviving, or even continuing, the classical tradition in its reading and writing practices.

Central to that project was the classical familiar letter, especially those of Cicero, read, analysed, and plundered for their language, ideas, and imagery. Theorists such as Desiderius Erasmus of Rotterdam placed letter-writing centrally in their pedagogical programmes, and the schools followed suit: Johann Sturm edited a selection of Cicero's letters, specifically designed to be used in the instruction of children, starting with simple short missives, and increasing in complexity.[3] In his reconstruction of Shakespeare's possible grammar-school education, T.W. Baldwin accordingly stresses the centrality of letters with an entire chapter devoted to 'Shakspere's epistles'. By the late sixteenth century, Baldwin concludes, boys were studying Erasmus' *De conscribendis epistolis* alongside Cicero's epistles, theory and practice, and were encouraged to imitate the Ciceronian ideal.[4]

Students were taught to work through imitation. Just how this might work in practice can be glimpsed in a 1549 Latin textbook by Antonio Schor. Schor prints a letter from Cicero to Aulus Trebonius; he then gives an example of an imitative letter that simply transposes the letter to a different recipient and occasion, repeating the form and much of the vocabulary; a second version then shows how the letter's form may be used with a very much changed vocabulary.[5] This was a standard exercise: William Kempe, who attended Eton in the 1570s, repeats it in his 1588 *The education of children in learning*, as does John Brinsley, master of Ashby School in Leicestershire, in his 1612 vernacular pedagogical manual *Ludus literarius*.[6] Both men give as their example 'the first Epistle of the first booke' of Sturm's edition, a letter from Cicero to his wife Terentia:

If you be in health, it is well: I am in health. I haue long looked for your Messengers. When they shall come, I shalbe more certaine what I am to do; and then I will forthwith certifie you of all things. See that you looke very carefully to your health. [Farewell. The Calends of September.][7]

The two theorists offer different approaches to the letter. Brinsley suggests that the following day, the student should 'make another Epistle, as being sent from their friend to whom they writ, in answere to that which they writ the former day: and in that to answere euery sentence from point to point, in as short manner as the former Epistle was, still reteyning the same phrases as much as they can'. His suggested response is 'I Reioyce greatly of your health. I am sory that you haue looked for the Carriers so long. They wil be with you very shortly, & then indeed you shalbe more certain what to do.'[8] Kempe suggests instead that the student should then write 'an Epistle in English of the like sentence, which he shall expresse in Latin with *Ciceroes* phrase'. So whereas '*Cicero* writeth to his wife, let vs imagin the Father to write to his Sonnes: he writeth of her messengers, of certaintie what to do, of care for her health: let the father write of their letters, of certaintie what to looke for, of care for their learning, in this wise:

> Peter Cole to Iohn and Charles his sonnes, sendeth greeting.
> If ye be in good health, it is well. I my selfe am in good health. Oftentimes I finde lack of your letters, the which being brought, verely I shall be more certayne what I am to looke for, and will certifie you thereof forthwith. Apply your Studye diligently. Farewell. The Ides of December.'

The student then translates this letter back into Latin.[9]

Both Kempe and Brinsley demonstrate the strong pull of humanist teaching ideals, and the practical influence of Sturm's edition of Cicero. But there is a problem here: the English letters produced by this exercise look nothing like English letters. Kempe's letter, for example, follows the Roman form of dating, increasingly obsolete by the late sixteenth century.[10] Its superscription ('Peter Cole to Iohn and Charles his sonnes, sendeth greeting') follows a Latin formula, not anything recognizable to an English letter-writer—it is the same phrasing that arouses mirth when Falstaff uses in his letter to Hal ('Sir John Falstaff, Knight, to the son of the King, nearest his father, Harry Prince of Wales, greeting' (*2H4* 2.2.112–14)) (see Chapter 1). As a result, the letter's valediction has no signature, which in an English letter would be considered odd—either invalid because unauthorized, or just plain rude. In short, this strategy may help a student's Latin, but the question still remains as to how this training leads to good letter-writing in English. As the failing schoolmaster Spoudeus complains to the successful schoolmaster Philoponus in Brinsley's *Ludus literarius*, 'As for inditing Letters in English, I haue not exercised my schollars in them at all; neyther haue I knowne them to be vsed in Schooles: although they cannot but bee exceeding necessary for scholars; being of perpetvall vse in all our whole life, and of very great commendation, when they are so performed.'[11]

A good deal of the blame for this *aporia* can be laid at Erasmus' feet. Erasmus saw his own epistolary practice in the model and tradition of Roman writers, especially Cicero, asserting a sustained continuity between the letter-writing Plato (recently brought into Latin by Marsilio Ficino) and the letter-writing Angelo Poliziano (his favourite modern writer) and, by extension, the letter-writing Erasmus of Rotterdam. So, in *De conscribendis epistolis*, teaching students how to write a letter, he constantly returns to the ancient world: 'The ancients always began a letter with the expression of a greeting. We note that in both Greek and Latin this was habitually done in the third person ...'; 'It is no departure from the practice of the ancients occasionally to append a name deriving from office, profession, or relationship by birth, or even by marriage, although this is contrary to the custom of most recent writers who out of respect put the names of rank first'; 'Immediately after "Farewell" the ancients add the place and date.'[12] When ancient and modern practices collide—for example, in the form of calendar to be used—Erasmus almost invariably sides with the ancient, his phrasing often implying that what is taken for granted by modern society is a mere aberration: detailing the Roman calendar with its 'ides' and 'calends', he reluctantly admits, 'It is only recently that some reckon from the beginning of the month'.[13]

To provide the illusion of continuity from the classical to the modern world, however, certain features of correspondence must be erased: Erasmus meticulously avoids discussion of material practices, insistently abstracting his letters from mundane concerns of paper, folding, writing, sealing, sending, bearing, receiving, and archiving—concerns that fill many extant letters of both ancient Rome and early modern Europe.[14] Dwelling on the material differences in letter-writing practices would betray the artificial nature of the continuity he desired. For the most part, he was successful: but despite 'the remarkable success of Erasmus' programme of education in the liberal arts in educational institutions, from the *gymnasia* and the grammar schools, to the Royal Colleges at Oxford and Cambridge',[15] his particular line on epistolography did not go unchallenged. Both before and after Erasmus, other scholars published letter-writing manuals. Many were published together in widely read anthologies: Erasmus' own short tract *Compendiaria conficiendarum epistolarum formula* was repackaged in 1537, for example, with Juan Luis Vives' *De conscribendis epistolis*, Conrad Celtis' *Methodus*, Christopher Hegendorph's *Methodus*, and Adrian Barland's *Compendiosæ institvtiones artis Oratoriæ*.[16] From 1576, Hegendorff's treatise was repeatedly printed together with George Macropedius' *Methodvs de conscribendis epistolis* (known as 'Macropedius'), including ten editions in London by Shakespeare's printer Richard Field,[17] although John Brinsley's Spoudeus claims that Macropedius is too difficult for schoolboys ('they will rather require an ancient learned Master to vnderstand, and make vse of them, then a younger Scholler').[18] While the vast majority of these writers shared Erasmus' focus on Cicero, there were some that also displayed a fascination for the widely divergent, even alien ways in which earlier cultures wrote, and especially how they corresponded with each other.[19]

The greatest challenge comes from the 1534 *De conscribendis epistolis* of the Spanish humanist Vives.[20] Like his friend and supporter Erasmus, Vives used the art of letter-writing to forge none too subtle links between his classical predecessors and his immediate circle of friends. In suggesting models for the letter's salutation, he slips, without acknowledgement, from 'Cicero to his Terentia, his Tullia, his Tiro', to 'Gonzalo Tamayo to his dearest friend Hugucionus; Idiáquez to Jerónimo Agustín, the other half of his soul; Stracelius to Crucius darling of his heart, and, as Aristotle said of a friend, to his other self'. As Charles Fantazzi points out, Tamayo, Hugucionus, and Stracelius were all students of Vives at Louvain; Crucius (Lieven van der Cruyce) an obscure teacher in Strazeele, Belle; while Alonso de Idiáquez, the only major figure named, secretary to the emperor Charles V, happened to be the dedicatee of the tract.[21] With this device of slipping without comment from Cicero's world to his own, Vives seems to display an adherence to an Erasmian agenda. But Vives was also acutely aware of, and keen to emphasize, the differences between classical and modern letters. His tract culminates in what he terms 'A miscellany taken from the epistolary usage of the ancient writers' ('Miscellanea de veterum consuetudine epistolari'), a fascinating slice of Renaissance historicist scholarship on the classical world; like all good historicism, it throws as much light on contemporary society as it does on the past. Vives describes the materials of classical letters, written on tablets or papyrus; interrogates the etymology of the terms for letter-bearers; analyses the nature of superscriptions in the ancient world—were they instructions for the bearer or part of the letter? (Vives believes the latter); and the means of closing a letter ('Once the letter was written, they folded it, tied it with linen or string and added wax'). While keen to assert continuity where possible, Vives is too much of an historian to erase difference where he finds it.

Vives' work on letters was followed by Justus Lipsius' *Epistolica institutio* (1590),[22] and more generally prefigured the antiquarian movement that reached its pre-eminence at the turn of the seventeenth century. Europe's Roman past played a central part in these researches, and some English authors attempted to incorporate the antiquarians' findings into their fictions. In Ben Jonson's *Seianvs his fall* (1605), for example, the long, climactic letter from Tiberius Caesar read out to the Senate in the fifth act, although (for obvious reasons) in English, is couched with several touches, linguistic and

typographical, that render it more 'Roman'. The letter opens with
the superscription 'TIBERIVS CAESAR TO THE SENATE, GREETING',
echoing the syntactical formulation used by Roman letter-writers
(and deliberately employed by Erasmus). Its opening sentence is
printed in inscriptional capitals, the words separated with periods,
and the lines right justified, in the style of a Roman epigraph. The
sentence reads 'IF.YOV.CONSCRIPT.FATHERS.VVITH YOVR. CHIL-
DREN.BE. | IN.HEALTH.IT.IS.ABUNDANTLY.VVELL.VVE. VVITH.
OVR. | FRIENDS.HERE.ARE.SO'. A printed marginal note claims that
this formulation is 'according to the *exordium* used in letters by the
Romans [*Solenne exordium Epistolar. apud Romanos*]' and refers the
reader to the eighth and final book of French historian Bernabé
Brisson's *De formvlis et sollemnibvs populi romani verbis* ['cons. Briss.
de formul. lib. 8'.][23] in which Brisson provides a series of variations
on the standard formula for greeting used in Roman letters, 'si vales
bene est, ego valeo'. The standard address he gives from emperors
to the Senate was the one englished by Jonson: 'SI VOS LIBERIQVE
VESTRI VALETIS, BENE EST, EGO EXERCITVSQVE VALEMVS'.[24]

While Jonson's Romanization borders on the pedantic, by contrast, as we shall see, Shakespeare's attempts to incorporate the real-
ities of Roman letters are fleeting and messy. Only his earliest foray
into Roman life, *Titus Andronicus*, insists on the Latin-ness of its culture, and then only partially. Lavinia and Young Lucius together read
'Tully's *Orator*' and Ovid's *Metamorphoses* (*Tit* 4.1.14, 42); Demetrius
finds a Latin quotation, which is recognized by Chiron as 'a verse in
Horace' (4.2.22); and of course Lavinia, finding in the *Metamorphoses*
the story of Philomel to figure what has happened to her, finally
spells out the details in Latin: '*Stuprum—Chiron—Demetrius*' (4.1.78).
But elsewhere the play can be wilfully anachronistic: Lavinia 'turns
the leaves', 'quotes the leaves' (4.1.45, 50) of her Ovid, indicating that
it is, improbably enough, a book-like codex, while Chiron read the
'verse in Horace' 'in the grammar long ago' (4.2.22–3)—a reference
to William Lily's sixteenth-century school textbook, the *Brevissima
institutio*.[25] Similarly confused are the play's multiple letters. When

Titus hands out arrows with letters on them, half seem to be in Latin ('*Ad Jovem*', '*ad Apollinem*', '*Ad Martem*'), half in English ('to Pallas', 'to Mercury', 'To Saturn') (4.3.54–8). Demetrius finds the Horace quotation on 'a scroll . . . written round about' (4.2.18); Aaron gives Tamora 'this fatal-plotted scroll' (2.2.47); the letters that are shot by arrow are 'Sweet scrolls' (4.4.16)—the scroll being the format that might suggest letters from antiquity to early modern audiences, although, as Lipsius points out, in reality Romans tended to write short letters to each other on 'wax-covered tablets made out of beech, fir, boxwood, lime or linden bark, maple, citron, or ivory'.[26]

In Shakespeare's later Roman plays, this tendency to modernize epistolary practices is taken further. In *Cymbeline*, Leonatus' letter to Imogen recommending Iachimo is laid out like an early modern letter, with the Folio printing the sender's name properly pushed to the right-hand margin, 'Leonatus' (*Cym* 1.7.25); the more formal 'Leonatus Posthumus' ends the brusque letter to Imogen (3.2.48). Imogen instructs her lady to 'Fold down the leaf where I have left' reading (2.2.4, see also 2.2.44–6), evidently another codex book with leaves. Pisanio notes the modern writing materials that construct the letter ordering him to kill Imogen: 'Oh damn'd paper! | Black as the ink that's on thee!' (3.2.19–20), and Imogen remarks on the 'Good wax' that seals the letter to her (3.2.35). The letters in *Coriolanus* are not described, although Aufidius orders 'this paper' to be delivered to the lords of Corioles (*Cor* 5.6.1–2). In *Antony and Cleopatra*, it is true that Caesar gives Taurus military instructions on a scroll, 'Do not exceed | The prescript of this scroll' (*AC* 3.8.4–5), and speaks of 'th' roll of conquest' (5.2.180). But these are different kinds of documents; letters in the play remain stubbornly of Shakespeare's day. Cleopatra twice calls specifically for 'Ink and paper, Charmian!' to write her love letters to Antony (1.5.68, 79), and Caesar admonishes Antony that, when he 'wrote to you | When rioting in Alexandria', Antony 'Did pocket up my letters' (2.2.76–7), an act that requires the smallness and flexibility of letter familiar to Shakespeare's audience,

not the folded wax tablets that the historical Caesar would have sent
to Antony.

It would seem from this that Shakespeare had only limited
interest in classical writing practices, or the contemporary scholarship on the subject. Certainly, in writing *Julius Caesar*, he makes
no attempt to depict historically correct Roman textual practices.
When Brutus asks for his book, he remarks 'is not the leaf turned
down | Where I left reading?' (4.3.271–2) betraying the fact that
the book is a codex and not a roll. Here, as elsewhere, Shakespeare adapts his source materials to render them dramatically
compelling to his audience. In Plutarch's account of their lives,
both Caesar and Brutus were noted for their letter-writing. Caesar,
he claimed, had 'alwayes a secretarie with him in his coche, who
did still wryte as he went by the way'. During the Gallic wars,
'he did further exercise him selfe to indite letters as he rode by
the way, and did occupie two secretaries at once with as much
as they could wryte: and as Oppius wryteth, more then two at a
time', and allegedly invented 'wryting ciphers in letters'.[27] For his
part, Brutus, writes Plutarch, was particularly noted for the singu-
larity of his letters: 'But for the Græke tongue, they do note in
some of his Epistells, that he counterfeated that briefe compendious
maner of speach of the LACEDÆMONIANS', quoting examples of
Brutus' laconic 'manner of letters which were honored for their
briefenes'.[28] Shakespeare notably ignores Plutarch's insistence on
the importance of letters to the two men, focusing instead on their
oratory. But elsewhere he allows letters to have huge dramatic
importance.

Brutus is encouraged to move against Caesar by a series of anonymous missives. In Plutarch's life of Caesar, men desiring change and
wanting Brutus to be their prince and governor, 'in the night did
cast sundrie papers into the Praetors seate where he gaue audience,
and the most of them to this effect. Thou sleepest *Brutus*, and art
not *Brutus* in deede.' Brutus' ambition was 'sturred vp the more by

these seditious billes', leaving him vulnerable to Cassius' urging.[29] Plutarch expands in his life of Brutus:

But of *Brutus*, his frendes and contrie men, both by diuers procurementes, and sundrie rumors of the citie, and by many bills also, did openlie call and procure him to doe that he did. For, vnder the image of his auncester *Iunius Brutus*, that draue the kinges out of ROME, they wrote: O, that it pleased the goddes thou wert nowe aliue, *Brutus:* and againe, that thou wert here amonge vs nowe. His tribunall (or chaire) where he gaue audience duringe the time he was Praetor, was full of suche billes: *Brutus*, thou art a sleepe, and art not *Brutus* in deede . . .[30]

Cassius seizes the opportunity, urging Brutus: 'Thinkest thou that they be cobblers, tapsters, or suche like base mechanicall people, that wryte these billes and scrowles which are founde dayly in thy Praetors chaire, and not the noblest men and best citizens that doe it?'[31]

The most striking innovation in Shakespeare's adaptation of these events is in the role of Cassius. Plutarch's Cassius, albeit opportunistically and for his own purposes, seizes on thoughts already inculcated in Brutus by missives written by other Roman citizens. But in Shakespeare's play, it is Cassius who writes those letters and causes them to be distributed, making them the deliberate propaganda campaign of one ambitious man. Allied to this recasting of the origin of the bills and papers is a subtle but vital change to the manner of their dissemination. In Plutarch, those opposed to Caesar urge Brutus to make a stand by affixing 'sundrie papers' and 'billes' in two public places: under the image of his ancestor Junius Brutus, and in his 'Praetors chaire', the 'tribunall' or *sella curulis* where Brutus sits when settling disputes as praetor. In Shakespeare's play, Cassius similarly orders Cinna to leave to leave one 'paper' 'in the praetor's chair | Where Brutus may but find it', and 'set' another 'up with wax | Upon old Brutus' statue'. But Cassius gives him a third letter, to 'throw . . . | In at his window' (1.3.142–6), an option that Plutarch doesn't advance. This instruction is fleshed out in Cassius' earlier description of how he

> will this night
> In several hands in at his windows throw,
> As if they came from several citizens,
> Writings all tending to the great opinion
> That Rome holds of his name—wherein obscurely
> Caesar's ambition shall be glanced at.

> (1.2.314–19)

It is presumably this letter, thrown by Cinna, that Brutus' servant Lucius finds: 'The taper burneth in your closet, sir. | Searching the window for a flint' to light a taper, he explains to his master 'I found | This paper, thus sealed up, and I am sure | It did not lie there when I went to bed' (2.1.35–8).

This third letter places us back in the letters culture of Shakespeare's own times. Like a private letter of the sixteenth century, it is 'sealed up', not an open bill. Unlike the standard letter, however, this paper is not delivered by a bearer or messenger, but is instead thrown in at a window of a private house. In this sense, the third letter shares much with a sub-genre of the early modern libel. As Andrew Gordon has shown, while early modern London had several public sites associated with the publishing of libels—Newgate Market, the Poultry, the Royal Exchange, the Tower gate—the city also witnessed a fair number of libels thrown into private residences.[32] In 1586, there was reported a 'sedytyous lybell lately throwen under my Lorde Mayors gate';[33] in 1595, a libel was 'founde under Sir Richard Martyn [the Lord Mayor] his dore'.[34] Transposed to the early modern stage, a letter thrown in at Brutus' window performs a different function from the letters posted on the sites of his public, state life. Not simply in his household, the letter lands in his 'closet', the most private, inward room of the early modern house, where a man would keep his valuable paperwork, amongst other things. Later, Mark Antony will reveal 'a parchment, with the seal of Caesar', claiming, 'I found it in his closet' (3.2.129–30); the provenance (along with the seal) validates the will. Similarly, it is this letter, found in his closet, to which Brutus is seen to pay especial attention. By the light of the 'exhalations [meteors] whizzing in the air', Brutus *'Opens the letter'*—reiterating that it is a folded, sealed letter and not a bill to be posted—*'and reads'* (2.1.44 and SD):

> 'Brutus thou sleep'st; awake, and see thyself.
> Shall Rome, et cetera. Speak, strike, redress'.
> 'Brutus, thou sleep'st: awake'.
> Such instigations have been often dropped
> Where I have took them up.
> 'Shall Rome, et cetera'. Thus must I piece it out:
> Shall Rome stand under one man's awe? What Rome?
> My ancestors did from the streets of Rome
> The Tarquin drive, when he was called a king.
> 'Speak, strike, redress'. Am I entreated
> To speak, and strike? O Rome, I make thee promise,
> If the redress will follow, thou receivest
> Thy full petition at the hand of Brutus.
>
> (2.1.46–58)

In these lines, we learn that Brutus has previously taken up similar 'instigations' dropped elsewhere, but clearly there is a different impact for one thrown into his own house. He engages with the letter in a new way, attempting to 'piece it out', where the letter only hints: 'Shall Rome, et cetera' urges Brutus to complete the sentence, and provokes a verbal expression of how he inwardly feels: 'Shall Rome stand under one man's awe?' By the end of his reading, he feels he is being addressed directly by Rome, and vows to fulfil the terms of this letter, 'Thy full petition'—although of course, the petition only becomes 'full' 'at the hand of Brutus' as he supplies the words that he, perhaps subconsciously, wants to hear.

A modern audience knows that Brutus is being manipulated by Cassius; to an early modern audience, it would also be evident that Brutus is foolish to pay attention to a letter that comes without a messenger. The recipient a lacks part of the essential transaction of receiving a letter—learning how it reached him. The letter therefore bears important resemblances to the letter to Caesar we will hear, and see received but unread, in Act 3. In Plutarch's account,

> one *Artemidorus* also borne in the Ile of GNIDOS, a Doctor of Rethoricke in the Greeke tongue, who by meanes of his profession was verie familliar with certaine of *Brutus* confederates, and therefore knew the most parte of all their practises against *Cæsar*: came & brought him a litle bill wrytten with his owne hand, of all that he ment to tell him. He marking howe *Cæsar* receiued all the supplications that were offered him, and that he gave them straight to his men that were about him, pressed neerer to him, and sayed: *Cæsar*, reade this memorial to your selfe, and that quickely, for they be matters of great waight and touche you neerely. *Cæsar* tooke it of him, but coulde neuer reade it, though he many times attempted it, for the number of people that did salute him: but holding it still in his hande, keeping it to him selfe, went on withal into the Senate house.[35]

This, then, is a letter that importantly remains unread, its historical function unrealized, and yet its narrative function is heightened. Like the papers posted for Brutus, this letter is transformed subtly in Shakespeare's drama, as some of the signs it carried for a classical audience had been lost. In Suetonius' account of the letter, englished by Philemon Holland, Caesar 'shuffled the same among other skroes and writings which he held in his left hand as if he would haue red it anone',[36] a detail that is picked up in John Higgins' *The Mirror for Magistrates* (1587) where Caesar reports how he was presented by 'a *Romayne* good' with 'a scrole of every name':

> But I supposde that for some suit hee came,
> I heedelesse bare this scrole in my left hand,
> And others more, till leasure, left unscand,
> Which in my pocket afterwards they fand.[37]

The detail of the 'left hand', not in Plutarch, is significant. In the Roman era, books, and indeed texts of any great length, including substantial letters and (here) petitions, were written on rolls, which were unrolled with the right hand.[38] Vives cites Seneca on the proper

brevity of the letter: 'And Seneca says in the sixth book of his letters: "In order not to exceed the limits of a letter, which should
not fill the reader's left hand, I shall put off this dispute with the
dialecticians".'[39] This remark only makes sense when the letter is a
scroll, unrolled with the right hand while the left hand gathers up
the part that has been read. Seneca, Vives noted, ignored his own
advice: 'And yet his own letters sometimes fill the right hand twice
over. . . .'[40] For the famously left-handed Caesar to carry letters in
his left hand makes clear that he has not read them, but that he
intends to momentarily. But this physical sign of whether or not a
letter was being read, so perfectly evident to the Romans, would be
lost on a sixteenth-century audience (as indeed it was muddled by
a knowledgeable scholar: Justus Lipsius read Seneca's line, quoted
above, as referring not to a scroll, but to a letter in the form of
tablets: 'This remark surely refers to the spareness and compact size
of the little book').[41]

In Shakespeare's *Julius Caesar*, Artemidorus' letter is not a scroll
held in Caesar's left hand. It is emphatically an early modern letter.
Despite being unread by Caesar, it is read out onstage by its author,
and thus given theatrical life:

> *Caesar, beware of Brutus. Take heed of Cassius. Come not near Caska. Have an eye*
> *to Cinna. Trust not Trebonius. Marke well Metellus Cimber. Decius Brutus loves*
> *thee not. Thou hast wronged Caius Ligarius. There is but one mind in all these*
> *men, and it is bent against Caesar. If thou beest not immortal, look about you.*
> *Security gives way to conspiracy. The mighty gods defend thee.*
>
> Thy lover, Artemidorus. (2.3.1–9)

Artemidorus here eschews the Roman form of greeting that we saw
in Tiberius Caesar's letter in *Seianvs*: instead of opening 'Artemidorus to Caesar, greeting' (a form that was required by the scroll
format—we need to know who writes the letter as soon as we
unroll it, not at the end), we have the formulations of sixteenth-
century courtesy, with the addressee at the head of the letter, and
the valediction of '*Thy lover, Artemidorus*'. Indeed, the letter is printed

in the First Folio so as to represent typographically the required, deferential layout of a letter to a social superior, with the valediction at the bottom right-hand corner.

With Cassius' libels and Artemidorus' petition, as with the striking clock, Shakespeare is happy to tamper with historical accuracy to present practices that will make sense to his audience. But in the most letter-filled of his Roman plays, *Antony and Cleopatra*, he goes much further, using the play's pitting of Rome against Egypt to explore the theatrical performance of letters, and providing a sustained critique of the value of Roman letters.

'All my Writings': Augustan Historiography

When Octavius Caesar receives the news of Antony's suicide, at the end of Act 5, Scene 1 of *Antony and Cleopatra*, he invites his Council of War to

> Go with me to my tent, where you shall see
> How hardly I was drawn into this war,
> How calm and gentle I proceeded still
> In all my writings. Go with me and see
> What I can show in this.
>
> (5.1.73–7)

Octavius is anxious to furnish textual evidence that will support his account of his 'calm and gentle' actions towards Antony and his reluctant entry into war against him. He is not alone in valuing how he will be viewed by posterity. Antony predicts that 'I and my sword will earn my chronicle' (3.13.180), and applauds the 'nobleness in record' (4.14.100) that suicide brings, while Cleopatra famously frets lest Rome's 'quick comedians | Extemporally will stage us', and, while still alive, she will be forced to witness 'Some squeaking Cleopatra boy my greatness | I'th' posture of a whore' (5.2.215–16, 219–20). W. B. Worthen notes that '*Antony and Cleopatra* is, of course, centrally concerned with how events are written into narrative, transformed into history, literature, and myth';[42] C. C. Barfoot has suggested that 'the chief protagonists in *Antony and Cleopatra* are above all committed to fulfilling the destiny of their names', acutely aware 'of how the future will regard them when they are entirely in the past';[43] indeed, as Garrett Sullivan sums up, *Antony and Cleopatra* is 'a play dominated by the retrospective characterization of people and events'.[44]

Probing this phenomenon more deeply, Linda Charnes has demonstrated how, despite their shared concern for posterity, the characters' approaches to posthumous reputation—and their success in achieving it—vary widely. While noting that 'all the "actors" in this play are obsessed with playing to reviewers near and far', she argues that 'they are not equally in control of the effects of their performances' since Rome is 'the play's "original" center of the narrative imperative, of the incitement to discourse that drives imperialist historiography'. In this reading the play 'represents the ultimate triumph of Octavius, who will later sculpt himself into the Augustus of Virgil, Horace, and Ovid', writers whose influence on Renaissance readers such as Shakespeare was immense. Not only did he have 'a monumental machinery of language at his disposal', but '[a]s Augustus Caesar, Octavius was to become chief executive of a massive discursive empire, the productions of which would be referred to again and again, from Dante to Pope, as models of literary, moral, and historical "authority" '.[45]

The historical Augustus certainly provided for posterity,[46] not only through his patronage of great authors, but also by leaving to the safekeeping of the Vestal Virgins 'a catalogue of his achievements which he wished to be inscribed on bronze tablets and set up in front of his mausoleum', a text that was rediscovered in the sixteenth century in the temple of Rome and Augustus in Ancyra (modern Ankara).[47] This emphasis on documentary culture chimes with the portrait of Octavius given in one of Shakespeare's sources, Sir Thomas North's englishing of 'The Live of Octavius Cæsar Augustus' by the French Calvinist Simon Goulart (included in the

1603 edition of Plutarch's *Lives*). Goulart depicts Octavius as 'learned in the liberall sciences, very eloquent, and desirous to learne', a bookworm for whom reading is a favourite and enthralling pursuit. Delighting in the great authors, he would plunder their works for 'sentences teaching good maners', and 'hauing written them out word by word, he gaue out a copy of them to his familiars: and sent them about to the gouernours of prouinces, and to the magistrates of ROME and of other cities'. Lacking in vanity, he would be 'reading in his booke, or writing, euen whilest the Barber was trimming of him'. Even 'in the middest of all his infinite affairs' during the war of Mutine, 'he did reade, he wrote, and made orations amongst his familiars'. This was no *sprezzatura* performance, but a painstakingly careful and prepared campaign. Although he 'had speech at commaundement, to propound or aunswer to any thing in the field', Octavius 'neuer spake vnto the Senate nor people, nor to his souldiers, but he had first written and premeditated that he would say vnto them'. In order not to 'deceiue his memory, or lose time in superfluous speech' the emperor 'determined euer to write all that he would say' (Goulart claims he was 'the first inuenter' of this habit). No matter to whom he was talking, even his wife, 'he would put that downe in his writing tables, because he would speake neither more nor lesse'.[48]

For Shakespeare's Octavius similarly, the image he will present to posterity lies in 'all my writings'. Charnes' account assumes a triumphalist narrative not only of Octavius' imperialism, but of the Renaissance humanist claims for the continuing dominance of Roman textual achievements. But, as I shall argue, the play's attitude to such a narrative is by no means secure:[49] while Charnes' argument may be a valid claim for the lasting success of Octavius' version of historiography into the Renaissance, it does not address the complexities of the characters' multifarious bids for posterity in *Antony and Cleopatra*. To return to the specific incident of inviting his officers into his tent to view his writings: this moment, surely a crucial point in Octavius' propaganda campaign,[50] is taken directly from Plutarch's life of Antony:

Cæsar [i.e. Octavius] hearing these newes [of Antony's death], straight withdrewe himselfe into a secret place of his tent, and there burst out with teares, lamenting his hard and miserable fortune, that had bene his friend and brother in law, his equall in the Empire, and companion with him in sundry great exploits and battels. Then he called for all his friends, and shewed them the letters *Antonius* had written to him, and his answers also sent him againe, during their quarrell and strife: and how fiercely and proudly the other answered him, to all iust and reasonable matters he wrote vnto him.[51]

But the play's adaptation of this passage seriously weakens the force of Octavius' appeal to his writings. Plutarch depicts an ongoing, responsible epistolary exchange between Octavius and Antony, but in the play, we are promised only 'all my writings', at best only one side of a correspondence, and perhaps not even letters. Moreover, on hearing the news, Shakespeare's Octavius does not retire to his tent to weep, as in Plutarch, but instead launches into his eulogy for Antony, only to interrupt himself:

> Hear me, good friends—
> But I will tell you at some meeter season.
> The business of this man looks out of him;
> We'll hear him what he says.
>
> (5.1.48–51)

The interruption, 'this man', turns out to be an 'Egyptian', his 'business' a message from Cleopatra. Octavius sends the man back with assurances that he will not be 'ungentle' to his prisoner (5.1.60), but is struck with the idea that Cleopatra might kill herself and sends Proculeius, Gallus and Dolabella to prevent it; only after doing this does he issue his invitation to view his 'writings'. The effect of this interruption is twofold: first, it hints at the likelihood of Cleopatra's suicide in the following scene; and second, it ensures, as Octavius dispatches his men on various missions, that the writings are presented to a sadly depleted Council, probably only numbering two, Agrippa and Maecenas. It betrays the fact that Octavius' letters are going to mean little to posterity compared with the iconic act of Cleopatra's suicide.

As I shall argue, this incident is just one of a series of moments when Octavius' textual bid for history is pitted against a non-textual bid by Cleopatra. Far from leading to Octavius' posthumous dominance, *Antony and Cleopatra* consistently challenges the grounds on which Roman historiography is to be built—Octavius' 'writings', perhaps his letters—and, in so doing, offers a different, and determinedly theatrical, challenge to the sway of Roman epistolary historiography.

Rome's Letters, Egypt's Words

It is of course a commonplace to read *Antony and Cleopatra* as a confrontation between two civilizations, west and east, Rome and Egypt, Caesar and Cleopatra.[52] In the words of John F. Danby, Shakespeare is writing 'the vast containing opposites of Rome and Egypt, the World and the Flesh',[53] or as Maurice Charney puts it, 'Rome and Egypt represent crucial moral choices, and they function as symbolic locales in a manner not unlike Henry James' Europe and America.'[54] The play's imagery pits Rome against Egypt relentlessly: cold versus hot, rigour versus luxury, scarcity versus bounty, masculine versus feminine, political versus domestic, rational versus irrational, Attic versus Asiatic, *virtus* versus *voluptas*.[55] Rome takes a passive role in this battle of binaries, often suggested as the negative of Egypt, rather than being fully portrayed in its own right: Rome is not, simply because Egypt is, a place of pleasure, sensuality, sex, appetite, shifting moods, sudden violence, infinite and destabilizing variety. In these readings, Antony is torn between the two: though Roman-born, he is easily swayed by Egyptian pleasures: Danby memorably summarizes his choice as between 'soldiering for a cynical Rome or whoring on furlough in reckless Egypt'.[56] Recent criticism has successfully complicated this binary model, while still preserving its basic terms: we now see the Rome in Egypt and the Egypt in Rome, their complementarity, the specularity of the two cultures, the complex ways in which we are led to see one through the eyes of the other.[57] But an examination of the modes of communication used by the two cultures—letters, messages, messengers, the kinds of communication that by their very nature have to work *across* those cultures—provides us with a way of understanding not only the differences between Egypt and Rome, but also their points of contact, practical and ideological.[58] *Antony and Cleopatra* is a play overrun with messages and messengers,[59] and necessarily so. With its action spread across two continents, events need to be reported, verbally or by letter, in order to provoke a response; its characters spend much of the play recounting, hearing of, and commenting on what has happened elsewhere.[60] While scholars have commented on this abundance of messengers and the effect of reportage they produce,[61] the play's various letters—the letters that Plutarch's Octavius evokes to prove his historiographic case—have yet to be scrutinized in detail.

Rome's power is built on its use of letters, its geographically vast empire controlled by an epistolary network.[62] Messages from Rome arrive in letter form. In Alexandria, Antony receives letters containing the details of Fulvia's death in Sicyon (1.2.123–8); he is petitioned by 'the letters too | Of many our contriving friends in Rome' (1.2.188–9). Silius asks Ventidius, 'Thou wilt write to Antony?' (3.1.30). Rather than mere verbal agreements, Rome insists on written, sealed contracts: we see Pompey asking that 'our composition may be written | And sealed between us' (2.6.58–9), and Enobarbus reports of Pompey's collaborators that 'The other three are sealing' (3.2.3). This Roman empire is epitomized by Octavius, significantly first encountered by the audience in the act of *'reading a letter'* from Alexandria (1.4.0 SD),[63] an entrance motif that is repeated later (4.1.0 SD). He sees letters as documentary evidence, orally paraphrasing to Lepidus 'the news . . . From Alexandria' (1.4.3–4) but then offering the letter containing the news in support of what he says: 'You shall find there | A man who is the abstract of all faults, | That all men follow' (1.4.8–10). He uses letters to control: in planning the sea battle, he commands Taurus with written instructions: 'Do not exceed | The prescript of this scroll' (3.8.4–5). He has respect for petitions submitted in letter form: in temporarily holding back an assault against Antony, he tells his sister Octavia that it was 'Your letters did withhold our breaking forth' (3.6.81). And, as befits a man with such investment in letters, he shows himself to be hyper-efficient in matters epistolary. When he recites to Agrippa Antony's charges against him, Agrippa urges 'Sir, this should be answered', but Octavius is a step ahead: ''Tis done already, and the messenger gone' (3.6.31–2). He sees letters as evidence: when he turns on Lepidus, after their joint victory against Pompey, he 'accuses him of letters he had formerly wrote to Pompey' (3.5.9–10).[64] Material gains from war can be 'Put . . . i'th' roll of conquest' (5.2.180); even physical injuries take on a textual form, as he reassures his prisoner Cleopatra that 'The record of what injuries you did us, | Though written in our flesh, we shall remember | As things but done by chance' (5.2.117–19).

Against Rome's literate culture, Egypt is presented as predominantly oral, a choice that seems to be the playwright's, rather than an effect of dominant opinion. Indeed, discourses about Egypt circulating in the early modern period, surveyed by John Michael Archer, point to the respect paid to Egypt as an early, if not originary, civilization in the development of writing.[65] Philemon Holland, writing in 1603, provides a typical summation: 'The wisdome and learning of the Aegyptians hath bene much recommended unto us by ancient writers, and not without good cause: considering that *Aegypt* hath bene the source and fountaine from whence have flowed into the world arts and liberall sciences, as a man may gather by the testimony of the first Poets and philosophers that ever were.'[66] Shakespeare's Cleopatra, however, is seen to prefer spoken messages to letters. For the queen, news arrives in bodily form, moving violently from the throat to the ear: 'Ram thou thy fruitful tidings in mine ears' (2.5.24); 'Pour out the pack of matter to mine ear' (2.5.54). She refuses to *hear* that Antony is dead: 'If thou say so, villain, | Thou kill'st thy mistress' (2.5.26–7), 'The gold I give thee will I melt and pour | Down thy ill-uttering throat' (2.5.34–5).

Cleopatra's understanding of news in bodily terms renders her incapable of distinguishing the message from its physical vessel, the messenger. When news arrives of Antony's marriage to Octavia, she lectures the messenger:

> Though it be honest, it is never good
> To bring bad news. Give to a gracious message
> An host of tongues, but let ill tidings tell
> Themselves when they be felt.

> (2.5.85–8)

Her analysis is borne out by her behaviour, as the messenger bears the brunt of her anger at the message he bears. Even before he makes the announcement, Cleopatra has said that his reward will depend on the news he brings:

> I have a mind to strike thee ere thou speak'st.
> Yet if thou say Antony lives, is well,
> Or friends with Caesar, or not captive to him,
> I'll set thee in a shower of gold and hail
> Rich pearls upon thee.

> (2.5.42–6)

Ultimately, she opts for the former, in a vicious beating: she '*Strikes him down*' (2.5.61 SD) calling down 'The most infectious pestilence upon thee' (2.5.61); she '*Strikes him*' (2.5.62 SD) again, and '*hales him up and down*' (2.5.64 SD), claiming she'll 'spurn thine eyes | Like balls before me! I'll unhair thy head! | Thou shalt be whipped with wire and stewed in brine, | Smarting in lingering pickle!' (2.5.63–6). Finally she '*Draw[s] a knife*' (2.5.73 SD) and the messenger flees. 'Gracious madam', he claims, 'I that do bring the news, made not the match. | ...What mean you, madam? I have made no fault'

(2.5.66–7, 74). But for Cleopatra, there is no distinction: he is not merely the carrier of written news, but the embodiment of the news itself.

Although this binary of literate, letter-bound Rome versus oral, physical Egypt is attractive, strictly dichotomous models of message-bearing are, perforce, impossible to sustain, since the carrying of messages is by its nature transactive, moving not only within a single culture, but *across* the play's two cultures. So Cleopatra is shown as literate: when Antony leaves her, she proves her love by twice calling for her writing implements: 'Ink and paper, Charmian! . . . Get me ink and paper! | He shall have every day a several greeting, or I'll unpeople Egypt' (1.5.68, 79–81). Once separated geographically, Egypt seems to engage in 'Roman' letter-writing. But, despite her intentions, there is nothing in the text to suggest that Cleopatra ever does write a letter. She certainly sends an army of messengers to her beloved, asking Alexas 'Met'st thou my posts?' 'Ay, madam', he answers 'twenty several messengers. | Why do you send so thick?' (1.5.64–6). The queen replies portentously 'Who's born that day | When I forget to send to Antony | Shall die a beggar' (1.5.66–8): but the verb is 'send', not 'write'. Later, having beaten Antony's messenger, Cleopatra again appears to resort to letter-writing. Plying the hapless messenger with gold, she orders him, 'Go, make thee ready. | Our letters are prepared' (3.3.36–7). But it turns out that the letters are not prepared—or at least, that Cleopatra is not finished with them. Within ten lines, she announces that she has

> One thing more to ask him yet, good Charmian.
> But 'tis no matter; thou shalt bring him to me
> Where I will write. All may be well enough.
>
> (3.3.44–6)

Even in her final moments, when she produces for Caesar 'the brief of money, plate and jewels | I am possessed of', assuring him ''Tis exactly valued, | Not petty things admitted' (5.2.137–9), it turns out to be incomplete, and even her treasurer will not endorse it. These incidents show Cleopatra equipped with the skills to enter into the Roman epistolary world, but temperamentally unsuited to it, refusing to respect its rules.

Antony, as one might expect, is depicted as torn between these two cultures. In Plutarch's account, Antony, in common with every other major political player of his day, is involved in extensive epistolary correspondence, and his affair with Cleopatra is kept afloat during lengthy periods of separation through letters, sometimes to his detriment: Antony is specifically charged 'That diuerse times sitting in his tribunall and chaire of state, giuing audience to all Kings and Princes: he had receiued loue letters from *Cleopatra*, written in tables of Onyx or Christall, & that he had red them, sitting in his Imperiall seat.'[67] In other early modern accounts, too, Antony makes good use of letters. Samuel Brandon's dramatization of Antony's relationship with Octavia hinges on the fact that Antony halts Octavia's journey to him at Athens by sending her letters; Brandon even composed a fictional pair of letters between husband and wife on this emotionally fraught occasion, while Samuel Daniel similarly confected 'A Letter sent from Octauia to her husband Marcus Antonius into Egypt.'[68]

Shakespeare's Antony, by contrast, does not read love letters from Cleopatra, and when he's with her he opts out of his native Roman letter-writing culture. Octavius complains to Antony that 'I wrote to you | When rioting in Alexandria. You | Did pocket up my letters, and with taunts | Did gibe my missive out of audience' (2.2.76–9). Although Antony weakly objects that Octavius's messenger had violated protocol by entering without being properly admitted (2.2.79–84), Octavius' anger is warranted: Antony publicly humiliated his messenger (and therefore Octavius himself), and was seen to put away the letters instead of affording them his attention. Antony's decline from Roman etiquette is measured by his performance in diplomatic relations with Caesar. He decides to send 'our schoolmaster' (3.11.72) as an ambassador, a choice which Dolabella correctly interprets as 'An argument that he is plucked, when hither | He sends so poor a pinion of his wing, | Which had superfluous kings for messengers | Not many moons gone by' (3.12.3–6). The schoolmaster-ambassador himself expresses amazement and shame at his appointment: 'Such as I am, I come from Antony. | I was of late as petty to his ends | As is the morn-dew on the myrtle leaf | To his grand sea' (3.12.7–10). As an ambassador, the schoolmaster is shockingly incompetent, presenting a verbal petition and then immediately, in the same sentence, assuming it will not be granted: Antony '[r]equires to live in Egypt; which not granted | He lessens his requests' (3.12.12–13). It is only when the schoolmaster has returned with Caesar's denials that Antony returns to writing letters, as he challenges Caesar (for the second time) to single combat:

> I dare him therefore
> To lay his gay caparisons apart
> And answer me declined, sword against sword,
> Ourselves alone. I'll write it.
>
> (3.13.25–8)

Presumably this is the letter that Caesar is shown reading at the beginning of act four ('*Enter Caesar, Agrippa and Mecenas with his army, Caesar reading a letter*' (4.1.0 SD)), as he complains

> He calls me boy, and chides as he had power
> To beat me out of Egypt. My messenger
> He hath whipped with rods; dares me to personal combat,
> Caesar to Antony.
>
> (4.1.1–4)

Antony has by this point fallen away from epistolary protocols, allowing his prejudice against Octavius' youth to find its way into a letter (which Octavius characteristically regards as evidence), as well as physically abusing his letter-bearer.

This anti-Roman attitude, however, is by no means consistent. Although enthralled by Cleopatra, Antony necessarily remains part of the Roman epistolary world. As we have seen, he receives news of his wife Fulvia's death by letter, and petitions from his friends in Rome to return home. After his defeat at sea, Antony dismisses his attendants, but uses letters to recommend them to posts elsewhere:

'Friends, be gone. You shall | Have letters from me to some friends that will | Sweep your way for you' (3.11.15–17). It is revealed in passing that Antony is in correspondence with Octavius: when challenged that he was complicit with attacks against Octavius by his brother and wife, Antony points out that 'Of this my letters | Before did satisfy you' (2.2.56–7).

Rome and Egypt, then, can be seen to have different attitudes to the bearing of messages, Rome fixating on written epistolary documentation, Egypt preferring the personally conveyed oral message, although both civilizations are capable—perhaps through necessity—of drawing on the other's techniques. In terms of the posterity of historiography, Rome might seem to have the upper hand here, its messages preservable in written form while Egypt's are by their nature transient. But this notion is not allowed to pass unchallenged. In the figure of Antony—the Roman in Egypt, ostensibly rejecting but often complicit in the culture of Roman letters—we are presented with an uncertain resistance to Roman historiography, focused on his claim to be a Roman, at the moment of his death.

The Self Hand: Antony or Eros?

Antony's final words paint a portrait of how he should be remembered:

> The miserable change now at my end,
> Lament nor sorrow at, but please your thoughts
> In feeding them with those my former fortunes
> Wherein I lived the greatest prince o'th' world,
> The noblest; and do now not basely die,
> Not cowardly put off my helmet to
> My countryman; a Roman by a Roman
> Valiantly vanquished. Now my spirit is going;
> I can no more.

> (4.15.53–61)

According to Antony, he did not submit to a fellow 'countryman', but was 'Valiantly vanquished', in the only way a Roman should be, by an equal, a Roman. The 'countryman' must be Octavius Caesar, whose control he has escaped, since the two Romans are both Antony, vanquisher and vanquished: he has already claimed that 'Not Caesar's valour hath o'erthrown Antony, | But Antony's hath triumphed on itself', and Cleopatra has confirmed approvingly that 'none but Antony | Should conquer Antony' (4.15.15–18). Self-killing is, of course, understood by the Renaissance as the classic Roman gesture of courage,[69] and as he contemplates the act in a rare soliloquy, Antony is drawn, uncharacteristically, to a Roman image of contract: 'Seal then, and all is done' (4.14.50). Yet this confident assertion is belied by what the audience has seen: Antony first asking his servant to kill him, then witnessing that servant bravely kill himself rather than execute his master, then botching his own suicide, before vainly pleading with his guards to finish the job, and then being hauled up to his deathbed by (foreign) women. And there is something very wrong with this sentence: who is Antony's 'countryman' if not a Roman? If the countryman is not a Roman, then what is Antony?

The first official report of Antony's demise, given by Decretas to Octavius explains that he died,

> Not by a public minister of justice,
> Nor by a hired knife, but that self hand
> Which writ his honour in the acts it did
> Hath, with the courage which the heart did lend it,
> Splitted the heart.

> (5.1.20–4)

The awkward reference to Antony's 'self hand' (hyphenated as 'selfe-hand' in F) might alert us to a problem. Hands are prominently portrayed throughout the play, shaken, kissed, read by a soothsayer. But the lovers show a surprising lack of control over their own hands. When Antony exclaims, '[Cleopatra] hath betrayed me and shall die the death' (4.14.26), Mardian replies, 'Death of one person can be paid but once, | And that she has discharged. What thou wouldst do | Is done unto thy hand' (4.14.27–9). The phrasing here is odd, but telling: Mardian means that the action Antony would do (raise his hand to kill Cleopatra) has already been done; but in so doing, the act has been done 'unto thy hand', almost as if an attack on *his* hand. When Cleopatra goes to stab herself, she exclaims, 'Quick, quick, good hands' (5.2.38), but Caesar's man Proculeius is too fast, and disarms her. And, in this case too, the hand is not under Antony's control: although Decretas talks of 'that self hand | Which writ his honour', the audience already knows that Antony's first impulse is to use someone else's hand to do the deed: the hand of Eros.

Antony's confident assertion that he is 'a Roman by a Roman | Valiantly vanquished', and Decretas' report that he was killed by 'that self hand | Which writ his honour in the acts it did', need to be tempered by the knowledge of this call on Eros: to what extent is Antony really vanquished by a Roman, or by his self-hand? Significantly, even before his suicide, Antony's sense of a discrete self is already shaken: indeed, his suicide scene opens with him asking his servant Eros the bewildering question 'Eros, thou yet behold'st me?' (4.14.1). Although Eros answers in the affirmative, Antony objects that, as when we see clouds that bear a certain shape, 'now thy captain is | Even such a body. Here I am Antony, | Yet cannot hold this visible shape, my knave' (4.14.12–14), as a result of Cleopatra's betrayal. In his mind, Antony cannot be seen; yet Eros assures him that *he* can see Antony: Eros' sight is required in order for Antony to be visible. Antony has some comfort for his servant: 'Nay, weep not, gentle Eros. There is left us | Ourselves to end ourselves' (4.14.21–2). Antony's meaning, as will soon become explicit, is that he will end his own life. But his use of the plural form 'ourselves' suggests something else: that it will take both of them to kill themselves. Antony's death then is not at the hand of Antony, but at the combined hand of Antony and Eros; his 'self hand' is not his own, but theirs jointly.

This is made crucial by Shakespeare's depiction of Eros. As Leeds Barroll has demonstrated convincingly,[70] in creating the man whom Antony asks to kill him, Shakespeare goes beyond Plutarch's account. Plutarch tells that Eros was a loved servant, 'whom he had long before caused to sweare vnto him, that he should kill him when he did command him: and then he willed him to keepe his promise'.[71] By contrast to this unexplained long-before swearing, Shakespeare has Antony recalling a specific moment—'When I did make thee free, swor'st thou not then | To do this when I bade thee?' (4.14.82–3)—that makes Eros a freedman, an enfranchised servant. This appears to be a Shakespearean innovation: Thomas North's translation describes Eros merely as 'a man of his', while Jacques Amyot's French makes him 'vn sien seruiteur';[72] Mary, countess of Pembroke follows North in referring to '*Eros* his man' in her closet verse drama *Tragedie of Anthonie* (1592);[73] while the original of her translation, Robert Garnier's *M. Antoine, Tragedie* (1578), follows Amyot in using 'Eros son seruiteur'.[74] These epithets—'his man' and 'his servant' (serviteur)—seem to be standard for Eros: we might add contemporary allusions by Sir Richard Barckley in his 1598 *A Discovrse of the Felicitie of Man* to 'his man *Eros*';[75] and Robert Allott, in his 1599 *Wits Theater of the little World*, where Eros is described as 'the seruant of Antonius'.[76] (Another variant from the Herbert circle, Samuel Brandon's 1598 *The Tragicomoedi of the vertuous Octauia* omits Eros.)[77] Neither does Plutarch's Greek, have Eros as a freedman: he is described as 'οικετης αυτον πιστος'—a trusted household slave of his, emphatically not an απελευτηερον, one of his 'infranchised bondmen'. Shakespeare's Eros is thus notably different from other versions of the story,[78] but why? What does it mean that Eros should be an enfranchised slave?

A Roman freedman was never fully free, but bound to the conditions of his oath (*iusirandum liberti*) by which the freedman might perform certain *operae* or services, perhaps a weekly ration of domestic or skilled labour, or working as a generalized *procurator*, managing the master's affairs.[79] Beyond these, the *operae* might include certain specific tasks, and it is this arrangement to which Antony refers. In rendering Eros a freedman, Shakespeare draws (as Barroll suggests) not only on Plutarch's Eros but also on other characters in Plutarch's *Lives*. The first is Rhamnus, another servant to whom Antony turned in a low moment during the Parthian campaign: '*Antonius* called for one *Rhamnus*, one of his slaues infranchised that was of his guard, and made him giue him his faith that he would thrust his sword through him when he would bid him, and cut off his head, because he might not be taken aliue of his enemies, nor knowne when he were dead'.[80] This identification between Rhamnus and Eros is strengthened by the fact that Antony urges Eros to 'Draw that thy honest sword which thou hast worn | Most useful for thy country' (4.14.80–1), implying that Eros has been a soldier, and Eros himself alludes to the Parthian campaign in this final scene: 'Shall I do that which all the Parthian darts, | Though enemy, lost aim and could not?' (4.14.71–2).[81] In Barroll's argument, Shakespeare's Eros 'has in effect taken on the characteristics of Plutarch's suicide helper B —Rhamnus from the Plutarchan Parthian expedition ... And the manumission (from Plutarch's Rhamnus) has become so significant in Shakespeare that it is part of the structure of Antony's effort to persuade Eros—a persuasion, indeed, telling enough to force Eros either to honor Antony's plea or to kill himself to avoid the debt.'[82]

Second, Eros recalls the man who slays Cassius 'at his earnest request ... a faithfull seruant of his owne called *Pindarus*, whom he had infranchised'.[83] Elsewhere, Plutarch elaborates that Pindarus was one of Cassius' 'freed bondmen, whom he reserued euer for such a pinch, since the cursed battell of the PARTHIANS'; Pindarus decapitates Cassius as ordered, 'but after that time *Pindarus* was neuer seene more. Whereupon, some tooke occasion to say that he had slaine his maister without his commaundement.'[84] In dramatizing this incident in *Julius Caesar*, as Barroll notes, Shakespeare altered the sequence of events,[85] making the enfranchisement a delayed reward contingent on the killing:

> In Parthia did I take thee prisoner,
> And then I swore thee, saving of thy life,
> That whatsoever I did bid thee do,
> Thou shouldst attempt it. Come now, keep thine oath.
> Now be a free man, and with this good sword
> That ran through Caesar's bowels, search this bosom.
>
> (*JC* 5.3.37–42)

Having performed the act, Pindarus meditates on his fate: 'So, I am free; yet would not so have been | Durst I have done my will', and decides to go into exile 'Where never Roman shall take note of him' (5.3.47–50). The Cassius–Pindarus narrative, with its coercive promises and its shameful outcome, makes clear the dangerous bargain that is involved in this claim on the freedman, a bargain repeated in the Antony–Eros encounter. As Antony notes,

> When I did make thee free, sworst thou not then
> To do this when I bade thee? Do it at once,
> Or thy precedent services are all
> But accidents unpurposed.
>
> (*AC* 4.14.82–5)

Antony claims that unless Eros obeys, his previous services are rendered redundant, the terms of his freedom violated.

In both cases, the bargaining of Cassius and Antony belies the supposed freedom of their erstwhile slaves as, despite their enfranchisement, Pindarus and Rhamnus—and, it follows, therefore Eros—are shown to be still committed to certain formidable duties for their masters. Antony has previously invoked another freedman over whom he exerts a control. After beating him, he tells Caesar's messenger Thidias to return to Caesar and tell him how he was treated:

> If he mislike,
> My speech and what is done, tell him he has
> Hipparchus, my enfranched bondman, whom
> He may at pleasure whip or hang or torture,
> As he shall like to quit me.
>
> (3.13. 152–6)[86]

This Hipparchus is introduced by Plutarch as 'the first of all his [Antony's] infranchised bondmen that reuolted from him, and yeelded vnto *Cæsar*, and afterwards went and dwelt at CORINTH'.[87] It is clear from Antony's speech that he still recognizes Hipparchus as his own to punish, despite his doubly removed status, freed from bondage, and then revolted from Antony's mastery. This notion, insistently made, that manumission does not fully free an ex-slave is betrayed in Samuel Daniel's 1607 revision of his *Cleopatra*, which critics have seen as drawing on Shakespeare's play. Following Eros' suicide, Daniel's Antony exclaims, 'Shall I not haue the vpper hand to fall | In death? must both a woman, and a slaue | The start before me of this glory haue?' (G8ᵛ). Antony objects to the fact that two lesser beings, two non-Roman citizens in the form of a woman (Cleopatra) and a slave (Eros), have beaten him to the virtuous Roman act of self-killing. As Eros has just been introduced by Daniel as 'his late infranchis'd seruant' (G8ʳ), this seems inconsistent, but the implication here must be that Daniel's Antony is registering the notion that a slave is never fully manumitted, and equally that a freedman is never considered fully a Roman citizen. So if Shakespeare's Antony had been killed by the hand of a freedman, he would not have been killed by a Roman.[88]

But there is another aspect to Antony's use of Eros, and it takes us back to Antony's relationship to Roman letters. Whereas Plutarch introduces us to Eros only at the moment of Antony's attempted suicide, in *Antony and Cleopatra*, he has made a series of important entries.[89] Eros first appears in 3.5 in a brief encounter with Enobarbus, where, although his social function is not clear, he is seen to be in possession of 'strange news come', knowledge of Antony's whereabouts and action, and the detail that Octavius has accused Lepidus 'of letters he had formerly wrote to *Pompey*' (3.5.9–10). His second appearance is in 3.11, immediately following Antony's ignominious defeat at sea. In Plutarch's account, it is '*Cleopatraes* women', sometime afterwards, who 'first brought *Antonius* and *Cleopatra* to speake together, and afterwards to sup and lie together'.[90] In the play, the scene occurs immediately after Antony has dismissed his attendants, and it is not solely Cleopatra's women who bring about the reconciliation. Eros enters alongside Charmian and Iras, leading Cleopatra; it is here his role to bring the two together, encouraging first the queen ('Nay, gentle madam, to him! Comfort him' (3.11.25)) then the despondent general ('See you here, sir?...Sir, sir!...The Queen, my lord! The Queen!...Most noble sir, arise. The Queen approaches...Sir, the Queen!' (3.11.30–50)). It is still not specified who Eros is, but unlike Cleopatra's women, he seems to be able to talk to both parties. His next appearance is in 4.4, as Antony calls for his servant to prepare him for battle: 'Eros! Mine armour, Eros!...Eros! Come, mine armour, Eros!...Come, good fellow, put thine iron on' (4.4.1, 2, 3). This scene places Eros in competition with Cleopatra: Antony's calls for Eros are at first interrupted by Cleopatra's pleas for him to 'Sleep a little' (4.4.1) and then by her offers to help him arm. Although at first her attempts seem misplaced, soon Antony is impressed: 'Thou fumblest, Eros, and my queen's a squire | More tight at this than thou. Dispatch' (4.4.14–15). Eros is here portrayed as the devoted servant, intent on arming his master before thinking of himself: when Antony orders him to 'Go put on thy defences', Eros puts him off with a 'Briefly, sir' (4.4.10).

The servant's name of course is serendipitous, and it is not left unexploited throughout these scenes. Antony constantly *names* Eros, often calling for him urgently, five times as Eros arms him (4.4), no fewer than fifteen times in the suicide scene (4.14). If Eros equals Love, however, there is no single way of reading that love. In bringing together Antony and Cleopatra following the sea disaster, Eros may be seen as pandering their affair, assuring heterosexual love; but it could equally be argued that Eros is in competition with Cleopatra for Antony's love, as they squabble over who should arm him. Both readings are possible in Antony's distracted speech, as his thoughts of the dead Cleopatra are interrupted by his calls for Eros:

Eros!—I come, my queen.—Eros!—Stay for me.
Where souls do couch on flowers we'll hand in hand
And with our sprightly port make the ghosts gaze.
Dido and her Aeneas shall want troops,
And all the haunt be ours. Come Eros! Eros!

(4.14.51–5)

But perhaps the most telling scene of their relationship arrives when
Antony realizes that Enobarbus has gone, and he orders Eros to
'send his treasure after' him:

Write to him—
I will subscribe—gentle adieus and greetings.
Say that I wish he never find more cause
To change a master.

(4.5.13–16)

Antony expects Eros to draft the letter, according to his general
instructions, and he will provide the subscription and superscription.
Eros is here functioning as Antony's secretary, a position in which
many freedmen continued to serve their erstwhile masters: the
most famous is Cicero's Tiro, who dealt with his master's finances,
appeased his creditors, revised his accounts, supervised his gardens
and building operations, and acted as his confidant and literary
collaborator.[91] To early modern readers, the secretary suggested a
role of unparalleled intimacy based not only on physical proximity
(although Eros's duties in arming and disarming Antony testify to
such a relationship) but on the sharing of intellectual knowledge
and secrets. In his discourse 'Of the Partes, Place and Office of a
Secretorie', Angel Day insists that the secretary is not made merely
by 'the praisable endeuour or abilitie of well writing or ordering
the pen', but rather by his relationship with his master: his position
thus 'containeth the chiefest title of credite, and place of greatest
assurance that may be reposed, in respect of the neerenesse and
affinitie they haue both of trust and fidelitie, each with the other,
by great conceyte and discretion'.[92] Beyond this, and worryingly,

the secretary writes both for and—in this case—*as* his master, as he composes his words. As Richard Rambuss has shown, 'Secretary-ship . . . does not simply mean transcribing, copying down the words of the master; rather it entails becoming the simulacrum of the master himself.'[93] We see this phenomenon at work in Timon of Athens' steward Flavius, who pre-empts an order by Timon to go to the Senate and drum up cash by asserting, 'I have been bold, | For that I knew it the most general way, | To them to use your signet and your name' (2.2.203–5). Flavius is comfortable and probably accustomed to speaking, writing and sealing as his master.

The letter-writing scene is unique to Shakespeare's play, without parallel in any of the possible sources. So why does Shakespeare make Eros a letter-writing secretary? I suggest that the scene is a deliberate foreshadowing of the moment when Antony will demand Eros's hand to perform another task on his behalf: his suicide. The link between these two manual functions (letter-writing and self-killing) is made explicit in Decretas' report: Antony is killed, he claims, by 'that self hand | Which writ his honour in the acts it did' (5.1.21–2). By troping honour as a series of handwritten acts, Decretas unconsciously draws attention to the fact that Antony's hand is not his own: Antony does not do his own writing, so perhaps he did not write his own honour. Here, the contrast with Caesar is vivid: Octavius' focus on writing is entirely individual—he reads, he gathers 'sentences' from the great authors, he writes on tables to prepare his speeches, he writes his own letters. Antony's writing, his very hand, conversely, is the joint work of himself and Eros; and therefore his self-killing cannot be the work of his hand alone. He knows this, and so he calls on his secretary to kill him; but ultimately, the true secretary—the man whose hand is his master's— cannot be his master's hand in this task. Eros thus refuses to do the ultimate secretarial act: to use his (self-)hand against his master's body.

In portraying Eros as both a freedman and a secretary, the play complicates Antony's actions to the point that they no longer mean what he claims they do. The impossible dual place of the secretary—the servant who is also 'the simulacrum of the master'—is imposed on the impossible dual place of the freedman—slave and Roman. Antony's 'self hand' is no longer his, and his position as a Roman, so much a part of his self-vision, is ultimately not assured.

Eternal in her Triumph: Letters and Posterity

If Octavius' Roman historiography fails to find an audience, and even Antony's very status within Roman historiography is compromised, then how does Cleopatra fare? At the climax of *Antony and Cleopatra*, there is a missing letter. Plutarch relates how after a countryman had delivered a basket and figs, and Cleopatra had dined,

> she sent a certaine table written and sealed vnto *Cæsar*, and commaunded them all to go out of the tombes where she was, but the two women, then she shut the doores to her. *Cæsar* when he receiued this table, and began to read her lamentation and petition, requesting him that he would let her be buried with *Antonius*, found straight what she meant, and thought to haue gone thither himselfe: howbeit, he sent one before in all hast that might be, to see what it was.

However, by that time, it was too late: despite running 'in all hast possible', Caesar's messengers 'found *Cleopatra* starke dead'.[94] The play dispenses with Cleopatra's sealed letter to Caesar. Instead, 'an Egyptian' (5.1.49 SD) is sent with a verbal message from Cleopatra asking for Caesar's 'instruction, | That she preparedly may frame herself | To th' way she's forced to' (5.2.54–6). The omission of this letter runs true to form with the play's depiction of Cleopatra as preferring verbal to epistolary communication, and, in that way, it might be said to support the notion that oral Egypt is presented in opposition to literate Rome. But, its omission—or more precisely, the introduction of the Egyptian messenger—can be seen to challenge the efficacy of Rome's documentary culture.

In Shakespeare's treatment, it is this Egyptian's oral message that serves to interrupt Octavius' invitation to his men to view his writings. As noted earlier, the message alerts Octavius that Cleopatra may harm herself, and he gives orders for his men to prevent her doing so, not out of humane compassion, but, once again, with an eye to posterity:

> Give her what comforts
> The quality of her passion shall require,
> Lest, in her greatness, by some mortal stroke
> She do defeat us. For her life in Rome
> Would be eternal in our triumph.
>
> (5.1.62–6)

If a living, captured Cleopatra in Rome would be eternal in Caesar's triumph (as Cleopatra also imagines), then it follows that her death in Egypt could be eternal in Caesar's defeat. This defeat is enacted when Dolabella reaches Cleopatra's monument, and a guard enters, noisily *'rustling in'* (5.2.319, SD) to announce that 'Caesar hath sent—'. The sentence is unfinished, and in the First Folio unpunctuated (modern editors tend to add a dash), and Charmian finishes the sentence with the sardonic 'Too slow a messenger'. Here, the limitations of Octavius' network of messengers are revealed. While Octavius hoped to clinch the narrative by showing his letter-book to his Council of War, instead the Romans march into the monument to examine the corpses, hoping to understand the cause of death, while Caesar pays tribute to the future longevity of this couple's memory:

> No grave upon the earth shall clip in it
> A pair so famous. High events as these
> Strike those that make them, and their story is
> No less in pity than his glory which
> Brought them to be lamented.
>
> (5.2.358–62)

Linda Charnes reads this as the crowning glory of the Roman success in historiography: 'Octavius understands immediately the political uses to which he can put a mythologized "Antony and Cleopatra"...He swiftly translates them from rebellious figures who
escaped his control and punishment into legendary lovers...Antony
and Cleopatra can become epic lovers in the world's report only
once Octavius has full control of the machinery of reproduction.
Only then can they be put to historiographic use.'[95] But to what
extent is this notion of Antony and Cleopatra as eternally embrac-
ing 'legendary lovers' truly Octavius' impulse? The notion that the
queen 'shall be buried by her Antony' (5.2.357) is the request contained in her sealed letter; it is Antony who himself determined to
'be | A bridegroom in my death and run into't | As to a lover's bed'
(4.14.100–2). The historical Octavius ignored Antony and Cleopatra
in his autobiography: the queen disappears altogether, and Antony
is evoked only obliquely as 'the tyranny of a faction' that Octavius
suppressed in his youth.[96] But Shakespeare's Octavius, far from having 'full control of the machinery of reproduction' as he hoped to
have with the writings in his tent, is forced to take Cleopatra and
Antony's version of events; his only power is to enshrine it in Roman
historiography.

   In the play's final two scenes, then, we see competing memo-
rializing impulses played out, in ways that insist again on oppos-
ing values of Rome and Egypt, as Shakespeare depicts them. For
Octavius Caesar, the history of Antony and Cleopatra will be written
from the evidence of his correspondence with Mark Antony. For
Cleopatra, the history will be inspired by the physical tableau of
the almost perfect female corpses, and the oral testimonies of the
man who last saw alive, her guard. And, as Rosalie Colie observes,
Cleopatra gets the last laugh: while Rome may seem to dominate the play, a play that 'begins and ends with expressions of the
Roman point of view', nevertheless, 'seen from another angle, Egypt
commands the play, where the action begins and ends and where
all the major episodes take place'.[97] Colie's formulation implicitly

contrasts Roman 'expressions' versus Egyptian 'action', Octavius' words versus Cleopatra's gestures. In this, Colie subscribes tacitly to the oft-asserted association between Cleopatra and the theatre, in which commonplace anti-theatrical prejudice is deployed against the exotic, foreign, stagy queen.[98] Here however, that same Egyptian theatricality becomes an effective challenge to Roman historiography, and within the terms of the play, may be said to defeat it.[99] For the showing of these 'writings' is superseded by the call to see the queen: the play ends not in Octavius' tent, with the viewing of his letters, but—through heeding the oral message of her Egyptian servant—inside Cleopatra's monument. In allowing that image to occupy the final moments of the play, Shakespeare, or perhaps theatre itself, comes down on the side of Egyptian spectacle, and against Roman letters.

3

Shakespeare and the Carriers

If any solid apology can be offered for the unnatural Tragi-comic mode of writing, the richness of humour in many scenes of this play, must stand for justification; but this of the Carriers is so exceedingly low, and we may add indecent, that it should be cast aside; nay, and might be, without any injury to the plot; indeed it is an injury to let it stand, being the lowest degree of farce.[1]

~

Francis Gentleman's notes to Bell's 1774 acting edition of *Henry IV Part One* Act 2, Scene 1, leave no doubt as to his opinion of 'this [scene] of the Carriers'. The scene is admittedly something of an oddity, comprising two conversations between five lowly characters that barely feature elsewhere in the play: two carriers, an inn's ostler and chamberlain, and the criminal Gadshill. Gadshill is involved in the highway robbery in the following scene, and one of the carriers appears with the sheriff as they pursue Falstaff to the tavern in Eastcheap, but otherwise the characters disappear. Cutting the scene therefore allows for some helpful cast pruning: as early as the 1620s, when Sir Edward Dering drafted his abridgement of *Henry IV Part One* (adding about one quarter of *Henry IV Part Two*), the carriers' scene was among the casualties; together with a reworking of the robbery scene (2.2), the cut allowed him to drop all five characters.[2] And yet there is evidence that some early readers regarded the scene as important, even quotable. In a commonplace book that includes extracts of the play, lines from the exchange between Gadshill and the chamberlain were selected for inclusion, much to the annoyance of its recent editor Hilton Kelliher, who complains that 'Falstaff, the presiding comic genius of Shakespeare's play, surprisingly provided not one sentiment worthy of record. Why Falstaff's ribald wit should have served his turn any less than the rather contrived humour of Gadshill and the Chamberlain is not immediately apparent, unless it was simply too subversive for his purposes'.[3] When in 1700 Thomas Betterton 'Revived, with Alterations' the play, he cut the king's opening speech to ten lines, eliminated Lady Percy and Glendower's daughter from 3.1, cut all of 4.4 and much of 5.4 and 5.5, but included the carriers' scene intact.[4] Moreover, as we shall see, in the riposte to Shakespeare's portrayal of Falstaff, the Admiral's Men's 1599 *Sir John Old-castle*, written by Michael Drayton, Richard Hathway, Antony Munday, and Robert Wilson, the inn scenes involving carriers and ostlers are greatly extended.[5]

The consensus of twentieth-century critics was that these comic scenes have an important but subordinate relationship to the main plot. Fredson Bowers, for instance, believed that the inn and robbery scenes in *Henry IV Part One* constituted 'the mimic world of the underplot', part of 'the larger unity as a form of parody of the main plot', but was keen to assert that 'This action has no independent ideological significance in itself.'[6] More recently, Arden 3 editor David Scott Kastan objects that this 'desire to assert the play's formal coherence' effectively 'subordinat[es] subplot to main plot, commoners to aristocrats, comedy to history', and argues that the play is 'less willing to organize its disparate voices into hierarchies than such demonstrations of the terms of its putative unity would allow'.[7] Here, I build on Kastan's thesis to provide a specific reading of the carriers' contribution to the play, which, as I shall propose, is by no means expendable, and which calls into question the possibility of such hierarchical distinction. Explicitly and articulately, the Gadshill robbery shows how an unholy alliance between career criminals and their high-ranking protectors preyed on a crucial infrastructure of early modern England that has been largely lost to modern view: the network of carriers and carriers' inns on which so much communication depended. The carrier not only provided the primary means of contact in Elizabethan England between London and provincial towns, but also constituted a way of understanding the capital for the provincial men and woman, the 'foreigners' who made it their home either temporarily or permanently. In *Henry IV Part One*, Shakespeare presents the system of carriers and the inns that sheltered them as under threat from precisely those London-dwellers whose lives and livelihoods it makes possible. I here attempt to restore the carriers to their rightful place in the play—and in the life of the playwright, since Shakespeare's own relationship with the carrier system is revealed in the single piece of his surviving correspondence.

'ffrom the Bell in Carter Lane': A Letter to Shakespeare

In the autumn of 1793, Edmond Malone visited Stratford-upon-Avon, performing what he dubbed 'a complete rummage' through a pile of 'not less than three thousand' papers in the archives of the Stratford Corporation. Writing to his friend James Boswell on 1 September, he complained that he had 'been up to my elbows every day this week past in old papers and parchments', working 'every day from ten till it was nearly dark'. He had news, however: 'I met with one letter to Shakespeare, but after the most diligent search, I could not find his answer, which would have been an *eureka* indeed; nor with a single scrap of his handwriting.'[8] In letters to other correspondents, Malone claimed the letter was 'a very fine relic, in excellent preservation, about two inches long by one broad',[9] or alternately, 'about three inches long by two broad'.[10]

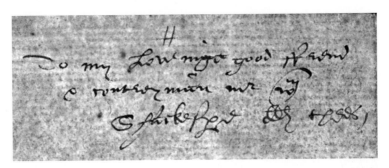

4. Superscription of a letter from Richard Quiney to William Shakespeare, 25 October 1598.

In fact the letter, when folded, is $2\frac{7}{8}$ inches by 2 inches, bearing the superscription 'To my Loveinge good ffrend & contreymann Mr Wm. Shackespere deliver thees'[11] (illustration 4). When opened, it measures $6\frac{1}{2}$ by $5\frac{1}{4}$ inches, and its in-side reads as follows (Illustration 5):

Loveinge Contreyman I am bolde of yow as of a ffrende, craveinge yowre helpe with xxx^{ll} [thirty pounds] vppon Mr Bushells & my securytee or Mr Myttons with me. Mr Rosswell is nott come to London as yeate & I have especiall cawse. Yow shall ffrende me muche in helpeinge me out of all the debettes I owe in London I thancke god & muche quiet my mynde which wolde nott be indebeted. I am nowe towardes the Cowrte in hope of answer for the dispatche of my Buysenes. Yow shall nether loase creddytt nor monney by me the Lorde wyllinge & nowe butt perswade yowr selfe soe as I hope & yow shall nott need to feare butt with all hartie thanckefullenes I wyll holde my tyme & content yowr ffrende & yf we Bargaine farther yow shalbe the paiemaster yowre selfe. My tyme biddes me hasten to an ende & soe I committ thys [to?] yowr care & hope of yowr helpe. I feare I shall nott be backe thys night ffrom the Cowrte. Haste. The Lorde be with yow & with vs all amen. ffrom the Bell in Carter Lane the 25 October 1598.

Yowres in all kyndenes
Ryc. Quyney.

Quiney was in London on behalf of Stratford's Corporation to present a plea to Sir John Fortescue, Chancellor of the Exchequer,

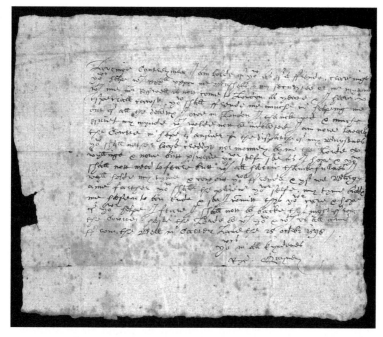

5. Inside of a letter from Quiney to Shakespeare, 25 October 1598.

that the town should be exempted from some harsh taxation measures, citing two recent fires that had caused considerable financial harm; he had now incurred debts in the capital, which he needed to clear. It seems that, as of 25 October, Quiney had not been able to make his case to Fortescue but was now headed for the court; Privy Council minutes confirm that the Council met three times upriver at Richmond that day, and that Fortescue was among their number.[12] Since the letter was first printed in 1821, scholars have argued over the precise financial transactions that this letter aimed to bring about, an issue to which I'll return in Chapter 4.[13] What has been largely ignored is the place where the letter is written: 'ffrom the Bell in Carter Lane'. These six words, I shall argue, tell us a good deal about the way in which a man like Shakespeare might have conducted his own correspondence.

The Quiney and Shakespeare families were long associated, if not necessarily intimate.[14] Richard Quiney's grandfather, his namesake, was acquainted with Shakespeare's grandfather Richard Shakespeare of Snitterfield. Quiney's father Adrian was a colleague of Shakespeare's father John in Stratford's Corporation. And the family connections were made one flesh on 10 February 1616 when Quiney's third son Thomas married Shakespeare's younger daughter Judith; their first child, as if embodying the families' long acquaintance, would be baptized Shakespeare Quiney nine months later, in November 1616.[15] Richard Quiney and William Shakespeare were most likely both educated at the King's Free School, Quiney a few years ahead. Thereafter their lives seem to take different paths: Shakespeare moving to London and entering the theatre, Quiney remaining in Stratford, a successful mercer, town alderman in 1588, and twice bailiff.[16] But those paths are less divergent than might at first be apparent. Shakespeare kept his primary residence in Stratford; his wife and children lived in Stratford; he increasingly invested in property in Stratford, and ultimately he would die in Stratford. Quiney, ostensibly the quintessential Stratford man, spent extensive amounts of time in London, suing on behalf of the Stratford Corporation in various causes. In addition to this winter 1598–9 trip, he also travelled to London in 1593, 1595, and every year between 1597 and 1601,[17] so this was pretty much annual business for him. Ultimately Quiney's offspring would leave Stratford: his second son Richard moved to the capital, finding success as a grocer at the Red Lion in Bucklersbury,[18] and his third son Thomas departed for London in 1652 after a disastrous stint as a vintner, leaving behind his wife and family.[19]

It might be fairly said, then, that in their different ways William Shakespeare and Richard Quiney both led lives spanning Stratford and London. They shared this experience with many provincial men of the time, especially those with mercantile, property and legal interests since, despite the strength of local affiliations, many of the decisions regarding life in the country were made in London and its environs, home to Parliament, the law courts, and the royal court. The letter to Shakespeare is one in a substantial cache of letters, mainly written to Quiney, which survive in Stratford's archives because Quiney died intestate while in office in May 1602.[20] They contain his contact with family and friends, financial and mercantile dealings in London and Stratford, news and gossip about mutual acquaintances—what today would fill telephone conversations, e-mails and instant messages, all then the stuff of letters. Once away from Stratford, Quiney's dealings with his hometown were completely circumscribed by what could be facilitated in the letter form. Shakespeare too would have relied on letters to negotiate his dual lives in the capital and Stratford, and therefore this batch of Quiney's letters gives us some idea what Shakespeare's own correspondence might have looked like. More pertinently to this inquiry, it suggests how that correspondence might have been transacted.

Quiney was an educated man, more showily so than Shakespeare: his letters are peppered with Latin tags, and his schoolboy son Richard and brother-in-law Abraham Sturley both wrote entire letters to him in the language—in one letter, Sturley advises Quiney to 'provide for vr [your] benefit. Read Tullies epistles'.[21] But Quiney's correspondence reveals how the culture of letters extended far beyond grammar-school boys, and indeed, beyond those who could read or write. At home, letters from Quiney were picked up by his family for delivery to others: in October 1598, his father Adrian Quiney passed on letters 'to master bayliffe [John Smith] & master alderman [Sturley]';[22] Quiney's letters of 20 October were delivered 'by candel light' to Sturley; on 27 October. Sturley read his own, and then 'went & deliuered urs [yours] to mi Sister', Quiney's wife Elizabeth.[23] Letters ostensibly from one individual to another were sometimes read by a wider circle: when Sturley delivered that letter to his sister, he was 'made partake[r] of the contentes theareof allso'; Quiney's first official newsletter was addressed to 'ma*ster* B[ailiff]', but the Bailiff 'pr*op*ounded it to a company of purpose gathered'.[24] All this shows that early modern culture participated more fully in a culture of letters than our own, in which illiteracy is condemned and stigmatized. Letters were read aloud to—and thus, in an important sense, received by—those who could not read, and letters were even composed and sent by those who could not write: Abraham Sturley visited Elizabeth Quiney's house to write letters to her husband at her dictation, though with considerable input on his part, once signing off with the striking valediction, 'att vr [your] owne table in vr owne house time for me to go home. late and verj late'.[25]

Most of the letters contain comments that reveal how they were conveyed between Stratford and London. Without a regularized postal system—the royal post was not opened to private letters until 1635—early modern correspondents relied on several different means for transporting letters. If they could, Quiney and his correspondents used one of the unregulated but established 'carriers' who moved between London and various provincial towns.[26] Although slower than a post or foot messenger, the carrier was much cheaper. In the early seventeenth century, it cost only a penny to send a letter from London to Oxford or Ipswich; a letter sent to Quiney on 4 November 1598 by Sturley had its carriage prepaid at a rate of twopence.[27] The carrier was therefore celebrated for consolidating ties between individuals across distances: as John Earle puts it in his 1628 *Micro-Cosmographie*, 'Hee is the ordinarie Embassadour betweene Friend and Friend.' Although superficially 'Churlish blunt', the carrier was 'no vnletter'd man, though in shew simple' with privileged access to knowledge: 'hee has much in his Budget, which hee can vtter too in fit time and place; Hee is the Vault in Gloster Church, that conueyes Whispers at a distance; for hee takes the sound out of your mouth at Yorke, and makes it bee heard as farre as London.'[28] The possible risk that the carrier might read letters and broadcast information is suggested in Claude Holibrand's multilingual phrasebook *Campo di Fior* (1583) which tells of a son who 'hath sent a letter to his father all full of mourning, ...Which, bycause it was not sealed, was read by the carier'.[29] Despite these concerns, however, the carrier seems to have been a trusted means of transport.

Carriers conveyed much more than letters, as Earle suggests: 'Hee is the young Students ioy a[n]d expectation, and the most accepted guest, to whom they lend a willing hand to discharge him of his burthen. His first greeting is, Your Friends are well; then a piece of Gold deliuers their Blessing.'[30] Letters often served as little more than a covering note describing what else was being sent by the carrier. Quiney's wife sent him via the carrier Carlisle spoons and silver bound up with tobacco, cheeses, and collars of brawn; he sent her back from London 'garnets' (gurnards?), oranges and 'stampes' (oil vessels); and she asked for raisins, currants, pepper, sugar, '& some other grocerye yff the prices be reasonable & that you may have caryage resonable'.[31] On other occasion, she reminded him to buy 'a sute of hattes for v [your] boies the yongst lined & trimmed with silke',[32] while his eleven-year-old son Richard wrote from Stratford's school to ask him to buy two paper copybooks ('duos chartaceos libellos') for himself and brother Thomas.[33] His nephew Daniel Baker asks, 'Yff therbee any cloth for mee to bee sent downe: send it by Edward bromly', Stratford's 'long carrier'.[34]

Besides letters and goods, the carrier was accompanied by men and women, who for company and safety either walked alongside the carrier, or hired a horse from him, or even were taken as part of his load. There were occasional dangers with the last of these: Saffron Walden's parish register has a sad entry on 12 May, 1611, telling how 'Martha Warde, a young mayd coming from Chelmsford on a carte, was overwhelmed and smothered with certayn clothes which were in the carte, and was buried here.'[35] From the

1560s onwards, some passengers rode in covered wagons,[36] although Fynes Moryson, accustomed to more refined modes of transport, dismissed the carrier possibility out of hand: 'Carryers haue long couered Waggons, in which they carry passengers from City to City: but this kind of iournying is so tedious, by reason they must take waggon very earely, and come very late to their Innes, as none but women and people of inferiour condition, or strangers (as Flemmings with their wiues and seruants) vse to trauell in this sort.'[37]

Catering primarily to these 'people of inferiour condition', carriers acquired a reputation that was on occasion less than salubrious. Allusions in plays and ballads suggest that girls 'coming up' with the carrier to London rendered themselves vulnerable to solicitation from bawds. In Thomas Dekker's *The Second Part of the Honest Whore* (1630), Bots reports that 'wee heare of two or three new Wenches are come vp with a Carrier, and your old Goshawke here [the bawd Mistress Horsleach] is flying at them'. Later, demolishing Horsleach's claim to be 'a motherly honest woman, and no Bawd', Catyryna Bountinall demands of her 'how many Carriers hast thou bribed for Country Wenches?'[38] In *Robin Good-Fellow, His Mad Prankes, and merry Iest* (1628), Robin sings of the inexorable decline of country Virtue to alcohol, smoking and marriage to 'a Tobacco-man, | A Stranger', all via her journey with the carrier: 'She came vp with a Carriers Iade, | And lay at racke and manger.'[39] It seems that the country girls outdid the locals: 'One your Carrier brings to Towne, | Will put downe your City bred: | Put her on a Brokers Gowne, | That will sell her mayden-head ...'[40]

Perhaps the most popular carrier-related story introduced the legendary 'Long Meg of Westminster', a Lancashire lass in Henry VIII's reign with the height, stature, and physical strength of a man.[41] Wanting to live in London 'to serue, and to learne City fashions', she and three girlfriends opt to 'come vp with a Carrier a neighbour of hers called Father *Willis*'.[42] Unfortunately Willis turns out to be 'a hard man' who 'asketh more than wee haue in our purses, for letting vs ride a little on his pack-saddles', demanding ten shillings per girl as they reached Islington, then a village just north of London. Meg appeals to his sympathy, offering him 'a gallon of Wine, and if euer we come to keepe houses of our owne here in London, looke for amends; in the meane time to make vp the bargaine; you shall haue of euery one of vs a kisse for a fauour'. When Willis angrily resists the wine, future hospitality, and kisses, Long Meg beats him into submission, and makes him promise to give them an angel each, and to place each one with a mistress; Meg herself is placed, as many immigrants to the city were, at an alehouse, the Eagle in Westminster.[43] In making her case, Meg appeals to their shared Lancashire roots: 'no Father *Willis*, you are our Countrey-man and our neighbour, and we are poore wenches, and farre from our friends'.[44] It is an appeal that is later played out when Willis and his man, flush with one hundred marks from another trip to London, are ambushed at St James's Corner, on their way to see Long Meg at the Eagle; they call on Meg, and she rescues them without question.[45] Their shared Lancashire provenance is reinforced by their experience travelling together to London; and these new friendships are continued through meetings in taverns.

Each carrier would regularly stay at, and was therefore associated with, a particular London inn. A survey of extant correspondence would no doubt clarify which carriers used which inn, but records for the 1590s are scanty. The Caroline period is better served by John Taylor's 1637 *The Carriers Cosmographie* which noted the specific 'Innes, Ordinaries, Hosteries and other lodgings' in which carriers from certain towns lodged, and 'what daies of the weeke they doe come to London, and on what daies they returne', so that 'all sorts of people may finde direction how to receiue, or send, goods or letters, unto such places as their occasions may require'.[46] 'The Carriers of *Buckingham*,' for example, 'doe lodge at the saracens head in carter lane, they come and goe fridaies and saturdaies.'[47] As this suggests, carriers where feasible worked on a weekly schedule, arriving in

London on one assigned day, and leaving to return to the provinces on the next. This model would fit with the Stratford-upon-Avon to London journey, a route of some 94 miles via Chipping Norton, Oxford, Tetsworth, and High Wycombe, which seems to have taken three days one-way in decent weather.[48]

The carrier's London inn had an extended social function, as can be seen in the journal left by the seventeenth-century seaman Edward Barlow. Born and raised in Prestwich, four miles outside Manchester, Barlow follows his brother and sister in making the 140-mile journey to London with a carrier. He leaves home abruptly in March 1657, '[k]nowing it was the day that the carriers were passing for London', and chooses one 'Thomas Haye, who had carried a sister of mine up to London, as I thought he might show me more favour than one whom I had never seen. And finding him making ready I stayed till his yokes were ready.' He gives Haye six shillings, from which the carrier pays for his 'charges' (expenses) *en route*; this does not include any place on a horse or cart, however, as Barlow travels on foot. The carrier and his entourage progress slowly to London, through Cheshire, Derbyshire, Leicestershire, Northamptonshire, Buckinghamshire, and Hertfordshire, making eight overnight stops. By the time they reach St Albans, Barlow 'began to tire and my legs began to fail me by reason of my long journey and going afoot all the way', and his condition worsens to 'faint and exceeding weary' the following day at Barnet, but he finally makes it to London, where they 'took up our lodging at the "Sign of the Axe" in Aldermanbury, for there the carriers lay'.[49]

Barlow thus spends his first night in the capital at the inn habitually used by the Manchester carrier, and it is from there that his London life starts. While he is out the following day attempting to find his sister, 'my uncle that lived in Southwark came to the inn to look for me, for my father had sent him word by the post that I was coming up to London against their wills, and desired of him that he would go to the inn and take me to his house till such time as he could put me out to some place'.[50] It is assumed by his father and uncle that the 'Sign of the Axe' in Aldermanbury is where a recent Manchester immigrant is likely to be—and they are right.[51] Fact or fiction, the logic behind all these stories is that the experience of the provincial man or woman travelling by carrier to London, is in large measure defined by, and dependent on, that carrier, and the inn he patronizes in London. These associations are not shaken off the minute that the travellers reach town: rather, they remain a material point of contact between the newly minted Londoners and their hometown—or at least a handy excuse for a drink, as when the second prentice in Thomas Heywood's *The Second Part of, If you know not me, you know no bodie* (1605) claims to his fellows, 'I must needes step to the Dagger in Cheape to send a Letter into the Countrie vnto my father.'[52]

News from home arrives via the carrier at a particular inn on a particular day. The power of this geographical and temporal schedule to affect the lives of individuals can be seen in the case of John Donne, as witnessed by his letters to Sir Henry Goodere, a friend who lived at Polesworth Hall in Warwickshire, four miles from Tamworth in Staffordshire.[53] Donne wrote regularly to Goodere on a Tuesday, a fact he remarks on in the letters themselves: 'Every tuesday I make account that I turn a great hour-glass, and consider that a weeks life is run out since I writ'; once, writing irregularly on a Saturday, he apologizes that 'by taking me before my day (which I accounted Tuesday) I make short payment of this duty of Letters'. Closing one letter, Donne writes that if 'there intervene new subject of writing, I shall relieve my selfe upon Tuesday, if *Tamworth* carrier be in town'. On another occasion, he includes a postscript explaining that 'Lest your *Polesworth* carrier should cousin [cozen] me, I send my man with this letter early to *London*.'[54] Living south of London in Mitcham, Donne had to ensure that he or at least his letters made it to town on Tuesday each week. In August 1607, he wrote to Goodere that his 'course of writing' was 'a sacrifice', and that 'we must sepose some certain times for the outward service thereof, though it be but formall and testimoniall: that time to me towards you is Tuesday, and my Temple, the Rose in Smith-field'.[55] The Rose in Smithfield was evidently the base for the carrier who went to Tamworth and Polesworth—a decade later Taylor noted that one set of 'carriers from *Coventry* . . . doe on Thursdaies and Fridaies come to the Rose in *Smithfield*'[56]—and for Donne his adherence to their schedule is nothing short of a ritual.

Like Donne, Shakespeare had a personal relationship to the carrier system. At least three men—William Greenway (or Greenaway), his son Richard, and Edward Bromley—served Stratford-upon-Avon as carriers in the late Elizabethan period. William Greenway was himself a Stratford man, a mercer who lived on Henley Street, near the Shakespeares, and leased a couple of small shops in Middle Row.[57] The carriers' schedule dictated the rhythms of letter-writing in Stratford as well as London. Abraham Sturley had wanted to report to Quiney that the Bailiff came home on 11 November, 'but the Carrier hath with his haste prevented me'.[58] On 20 November, Sturley wrote to tell Quiney that he had written to him 'a long letter for our Longe Carrier E: B: [Edward Bromley] to have brought v [you] but bj his haste he prevented me'.[59] As this suggests, it would be wrong to assume that the carriers' routines were always constant. Even the *Carriers Cosmographie* was forced to admit that the carriers 'doe often change and shift from one Inne or lodging to another'.[60] Carriers could be delayed on the road for any number of reasons, interrupting their schedules; letter-writers might need to send letters while their regular carrier was out of town or left early. On the occasion when the 'long carrier' Bromley had already gone, Sturley was forced to resort to a stranger who just happened to be travelling to London: an acquaintance named John Tubb had heard of 'one that laj that night att *Master* Lanes' (the house of Richard Lane in Bridge Town), and undertook to send it by him.[61] When a message had to be sent immediately, one might need to resort to another town's carrier: when Quiney's nephew Daniel Baker urged him to correspond he wrote, 'I pray you let mee heare from you by the Carrier of shipston vppon saterdaie com sennet [sevennight] yff you cannot beefore',[62] Shipston-upon-Stour being a south Warwickshire town near Stratford-upon-Avon where Baker might reasonably be able to pick up a letter.

But these are exceptions, and are always highlighted as such by the writer. We know from the directions on letters to him that Richard Quiney's usual *modus operandi* while in London was to lodge at, and receive letters at, the Bell Inn in Carter Lane.[63] Carter Lane, running parallel to the Thames just south of St Paul's, was then one of the city's main thoroughfares; the Bell Inn lay (from at least 1404 to 1708) at the east end of the street in what is now Bell Yard.[64] Over time, Carter Lane's inns became popular with carriers: the Saracen's Head, the Paul's Head and the Mermaid were listed by Taylor as operative there in 1637, serving as the bases for carriers from various locations in Oxfordshire, Gloucestershire, and Monmouthshire. Although comparable information is not available for the 1590s, Carter Lane's Saracen's Head certainly had an established history as a carriers' inn: in John Eliot's multilingual phrase book of 1593, *Ortho-Epia Gallica*, we are given the useful phrase, 'To the Sarasens head to deliuer a letter'.[65] Richard Quiney stayed at the Bell Inn precisely because the Bell was the Stratford carriers' London base: the carrier businesses thus effectively defined the parameters of Quiney's existence in London. It may well be that this routine led to some form of ex-provincial communities being formed in London. Although social historians have determined that ethnic immigrants such as the Welsh and Irish and overseas 'strangers' such as the French, Dutch, and later, Jewish arrivals, clustered together in their lodgings,[66] the patterns are not reproduced in the case of other provincial 'foreigners'; as Peter Clark argues, 'There is nothing to show that distinct geographical concentrations of Kentishmen or Yorkshiremen existed in the capital.'[67] It seems probable, however, that each carriers' inn provided a ready-made and convivial venue, at least every time the carrier was due in town, for meetings between countrymen in London, and those coming to or leaving the capital via the carrier. Indeed, Quiney's correspondents not only wrote to him at the Bell, but made arrangements for financial transactions with him there: William Parsons wrote to tell 'Mr. Quene' that 'I have taken order withe William Wenlocke to pay unto you or to Misterise Greffine at the Bell in Carter Lane tenne poundes',[68] Mistress Griffin being, presumably, the landlady at the Bell, who had a long-standing arrangement with Quiney.[69] For all that we do not know about William Shakespeare's daily routine, we can make a strong case that throughout his years in London he also visited the Bell, or another Stratford-oriented inn, once a week to pick up letters, messages and packages, and to hand over others to be taken by the carrier, on the evening when the carrier stayed overnight.

This arrangement might explain an enduring mystery about Quiney's letter. Although addressed to Shakespeare, it appears not to have reached him, since it remained in Quiney's cache of letters. His-torians have suggested that Shakespeare received the letter and then handed it back to Quiney, or (anachronistically) that he passed it to his solicitor to be dealt with.[70] I would suggest instead that Quiney did not send the letter to his countryman. Rather, he left it at the Bell to be picked up by Shakespeare, whom he knew would visit that day (a Wednesday) to meet the carrier. Perhaps he was used to meeting Shakespeare at the Bell on Wednesday, hence his explanation that he did not expect to be there that evening, because he would be held up at the court upriver at Richmond. But we know that Quiney *did* return to the Bell that evening, because he wrote to Abraham Stur-ley the same day, and included news that Shakespeare was going to co-operate. (Although Quiney's letter is lost, Sturley acknowledges the news on 4 November with a notable lack of enthusiasm: 'that our countryman Master William Shakespeare would procure us monej, I will like of as I shall heare when & wheare & howe'.)[71] My sug-gestion, then, is that having made arrangements for the possibility that he and Shakespeare would not coincide at the Bell, Quiney did meet Shakespeare that evening, not by accident, but by following the natural rhythms of lives that were transacted, to a large extent, by letters taken by carriers between London and the provinces.

Richard Tarlton's Poor Carrier

Despite, or perhaps because of, their ubiquity in Londoners' lives, carriers are not frequently portrayed in the canonical works of early modern drama. But one stage carrier did leave his mark: Dericke, created by Richard Tarlton in the popular 1580s Queen's Men play *The Famous Victories of Henry the Fifth.*[72] Tarlton's persona was that of a 'clown', a new-fangled term that denoted both rustic and stage comedian, or rather, a novel blend of the two. As Peter Thomson has noted, Tarlton himself 'arrived in London as a provincial immigrant. It was as a rustic clown, dressed in a russet suit and buttoned cap, that he stamped his enduring image on the city.'[73] John Davies' epigram on Tarlton claims,

> all *Clownes* since haue bene his Apes:
> Earst he of Clownes to learne still sought;
> But now they learne of him they taught
> By Art far past the Principall;
> The *Counterfet* is, so, worth all.[74]

In other words, Tarlton based his act on the countrymen he knew, but his influence was such that, after his death, they seemed to model themselves on him: in Richard Helgerson's words, 'Rustics came to be seen as Tarlton portrayed them.'[75] As David Wiles has argued, 'The rustic clown was a response to London...Tarlton tapped spectators' anxieties about the rustic boor latent within themselves.'[76] Or, as Thomson claims, 'The role enabled him to speak to and for the uprooted countrymen struggling to come to terms with urban living, and the effectiveness of his comic improvisations owed much to his natural ability to observe the customs of the city from the outside.'[77]

The theatrical appeal of 'uprooted countrymen' should not be underestimated. It has been calculated that early modern London absorbed immigrants at a rate of six to ten thousand *per annum*. The lower estimate comes from analysing the discrepancy between baptism and burial statistics in London parish registers, but such a calculation ignores all those who came to London and then left again before dying.[78] William Shakespeare was one of these missing statistics: parish registers will tell us he was baptized, married, and buried in Stratford-upon-Avon, and that his children were baptized and buried there; but the records fail to tell us he spent twenty years of his adult life in London. In short, there was a vast adult market that could recognize and sympathize with the plight of the provincial woman or man turned Londoner. Theatre audiences may have included carriers themselves: one Italian witness stereotyped the audience at the Curtain in 1613 as a 'gang of porters and carters' ('la canaglia di facchini e carrettieri'; John Florio pungently rendered 'canáglia' as 'raskaly people only fit for dogs company').[79] And in *The Famous Victories*, in the figure of Dericke the carrier, *alias* 'Goodman Hoblings man of Kent', one of the 'gentlemen Clownes in Kent' (B3ʳ, A4ʳ), the man who still straddles the rural and urban worlds by virtue of his occupation, the man who may have set many immigrants on their London lives, Tarlton found the perfect encapsulation of that section of London society.

It is clear even from the flawed printed playtext that this role gave Tarlton ample opportunities to improvise his trademark comic business. The audience is drawn to the carrier's side from the beginning, as he enters 'rouing' through the audience, displaying the signs of a beating, crying pitifully 'Who [whoa], who there, who there?' to his missing horse, lamenting he has been robbed, calling for 'maister Constable', and insisting 'ile haue the law at his hands' (A4ʳ). He immediately finds sympathetic support in the watch of three civic-minded Londoners—John Cobler, Robin Pewterer, and Lawrence Costermonger—who patrol the city streets at midnight. When Dericke identifies the man that assaulted him, they throw him into 'the country prison' (B^v), Newgate, to await the sessions, although he is the prince's servant. The thief, who is revealed to be one Cuthbert Cutter (B2^v) ('cutter' being slang for highway robber),[80] is formally indicted by a clerk in terms that emphasizes the carrier's poverty and vulnerability: 'I indite thee by the name of *Cutbert Cutter*, for robbing a poore carrier the 20 day of May last past, in the fourteen yeare of the raigne of our soueraigne Lord King *Henry* the fourth, for setting vpon a poore Carrier vpon Gads hill in *Kent*, and hauing beaten and wounded the said Carrier, and taken his goods from him' (B2^v). In a typical comic moment of rustic ignorance, Dericke points out 'he hath not beaten and wounded me also, but hee hath beaten and wounded my packe, and hath taken the great rase of Ginger, that bouncing Besse with the iolly buttocks should haue had; that greeues me most' (B2^v).

Deciding he has had enough of his dangerous trade—'Faith ile be no more a Carrier'—Dericke informs one of the watch, John Cobler, that 'Ile dwell with thee and be a Cobler' (B4^v), and spends some time in a knockabout *ménage à trois* with the poor cobbler and his wife. Learning of Cutter's imprisonment, Prince Harry intervenes to free his man, but the Lord Chief Justice refuses to waive the law and threatens to hang Cutter, leading the prince to punch him in the face and get himself thrown into the King's Bench prison.[81] Once Henry IV is dead, however, the Lord Chief Justice frees Cutter, fearing reprisals from the new king. Tom, Ned, and Jockey Oldcastle advise the freed thief that the new king will not want a 'Scab'd knaue as thou art' in his service (D^r), and the thief disappears once Ned gives him two angels, emphasizing his mercenary nature. Cutter turns up only once more, pressed into military service alongside Cobler and Dericke, who immediately worries about his shirt: 'I am sure heele steale it from me, | He is such a filching fellow' (E^r). This is the final word on Cutter: as the play moves to France, he disappears entirely. Dericke, meanwhile, survives the war—'once kild, why it is nothing, | I was foure or fiue times slaine' (F4^v)—and makes his last appearance 'with his girdle full of shooes' (F4^v) stolen from dead

French soldiers, planning to sneak back into England with the duke of York's funeral entourage.

Beyond giving Tarlton a great part, the play also served as a source for Shakespeare's Henriad; as such, it provides a useful starting point for an analysis of Shakespeare's treatment of the Elizabethan carrier. In recasting these events in his own play, I suggest, Shakespeare exploited some crucial ambiguities in his source materials. The raw stuff of episodes in *Henry IV Part One* is evident in *The Famous Victories*, notably the highway robbery, the carrier, the Kent location of Gads Hill, and the character known as Gadshill. We might add to this list the 'old Tauerne in Eastcheape' (A3^v) where Cutter is due to meet with the prince, and small details such as Dericke's favourite curse 'A bots on you' (C^r) echoed in the 'bots' (1 H 4 2.1.9) that afflict the carrier's jade, and his load of a 'great rase of Ginger' (B2^v) that becomes 'two races of ginger' (2.1.24–5) in *Henry IV Part One*. In more significant ways, however, the treatment of carrier robbery in the two plays differs radically. In *The Famous Victories*, the attack on the two richly laden receivers is separate from the attack on the carrier; in Shakespeare's play, Gadshill lays the groundwork for the raid by Falstaff and his friends on two rich gentlemen travelling with a carrier. And this distinction, I would argue, has profound implications for our understanding of the relationship between London and its carriers.

'The most villainous house in all London road': The Carrier and the Inn

The *Famous Victories* centres its action on London. We first meet Harry and his associates in the aftermath of their assault on the receivers near Deptford, only 'about a mile off' London (A2^v). Although the carrier Dericke is attacked on Gads Hill, over twenty miles south-east of the capital, we do not see him until he reaches London and seeks help from the watch. In *Henry IV Part One*, however, the action is more widely dispersed: while the unnamed tavern in London's Eastcheap is seen as a base of operations (1.2, 2.4, 3.3), we are also taken to an inn at Rochester (2.1), and on to Gad's Hill, slightly west of Rochester (2.2), both of them on the road to London.[82] Shakespeare's introduction of the Rochester inn focuses the play's examination of the interdependence of the provincial system of carriers, the inns that sustained them, the inn's employees, their customers and the criminals who preyed on them.

It is in the Rochester inn that we meet Mugs and an unidentified carrier, preparing for the next day's journey (2.1). Although their occupation is not immediately named (until Gadshill greets them at 2.1.31), carriers were apparently familiar enough figures to be clearly identifiable by their dress: in George Chapman's play *The Conspiracie, and Tragedie of Charles Duke of Byron Marshall of France,* Byron enters '*solus disguizd like a Carrier of letters*'.[83] Tarlton's Dericke may also have served as the model for the stage carrier. Although the scene is broadly comic, these carriers are a long way from the lovable Dericke. Here, the carriers' dialogue is coarse, both in tone and content, and (in the 1598 Q1 edition at least) filled with oaths and curses: 'by the Masse', 'Gods bodie', 'I faith', and 'Marry'.[84] Their main concern is for the commodities they carry—'I have a gammon of bacon, and two races of ginger to be delivered as far as Charing Cross' (2.1.24–5), the other side of London, says the second carrier, while Mugs complains that 'the turkeys in my pannier are quite starved!' (2.1.26–7), suggesting that the poultry he carries is just about alive, to be delivered fresh for slaughter at one of London's markets.[85]

Rochester, as every member of Shakespeare's audience would know, was a key town on the road from London to Kent, one of the busiest roads in England, which ran through Dartmouth, Gravesend, Rochester, Sittingbourne, and Canterbury to Dover—a route important enough to be included in the continental road-book *The Post for Diuers Partes of the World* (1579).[86] The road's heavy traffic traditionally came from two groups: merchants and travellers

coming from Dover, and pilgrims travelling to and from Canterbury: Poins talks up the robbers' potential booty as coming from
'pilgrims going to Canterbury with rich offerings and traders riding
to London with fat purses' (1.2.119–21). From the fourteenth century on, the road was organized enough to have split into established 'stages' to facilitate faster journeys by the use of relays. The
route even left its marks on equine vocabulary, giving us the term
'Rochester hackney' and even the verb 'to canter', a contraction of
'Canterbury'.[87]

Significantly, the men are introduced not on the road but at an
inn, and it is the inn that is the cause of their complaints. The
two men deplore the substandard quality of their bed and board
and the treatment of their horses. The Rochester inn is 'the most
villainous house in all London road for fleas. I am stung like a tench'
(2.1.14–15), claims the second carrier; Mugs concurs that 'there is
ne're a king christen could be better bit than I have been since the
first cock' (2.1.16–18). The second carrier diagnoses the problem's
source in the inn's toilet arrangements: 'you will allow us ne'er a
jordan [chamberpot], and then we leak in your chimney, and your
chamber lye breeds fleas like a loach' (2.1.19–21). Their conversation
also reveals their longstanding association with the Rochester inn
and its staff. The ostler is important because he cares for their horses,
crucial to their livelihood: Mugs wants him to 'beat Cut's saddle, put
a few flocks in the point' (2.1.5–6), that is, to soften the horse's saddle
leather and stuff some padding wool under the pommel.[88] They
recall with nostalgic regret the passing of the previous ostler: 'This
house is turned upside down since Robin Ostler died' (2.1.10–11).
In the rose-coloured vision of William Harrison's 'Description of
England', the horses of a guest at an English inn 'are walked, dressed
and looked vnto by certeine hostelers or hired seruants, appointed
at the charges of the goodman of the house, who in hope of extra-
ordinarie reward will deale verie diligentlie ... in this their function
and calling'.[89] Harrison's caring ostler appears in *Sir John Oldcastle*
in the form of Old Jack, welcoming the carrier to the Bell Inn in

St Albans, on the Lancashire to London route, with a friendly 'What gaffer Club, welcome to saint Albons, | How does all our friends in Lancashire?' '[H]ow does old Dick Dunne?' asks the ostler, of the carrier's own horse: when the carrier replies that due to 'abhomination weather', 'old Dunne has bin moyerd in a slough in Brickhillane' [near Fenny Stratford, also on the London-Lancashire route], the ostler makes it up to the horse with 'one half pecke of pease and oates more for that, as I am Iohn Ostler, hee has been euer as good a iade as euer trauel'd'. Caring for both carrier and his horse, Old Jack urges him, 'Come Gaffer Club, vnlode, vnlode, and get to supper, and Ile rub dunne the while'.[90]

Even Harrison has to admit that in their job, 'neuerthelesse are manie of them [ostlers] blame worthie, in that they doo not onelie deceiue the beast oftentimes of his allowance by sundrie meanes, except their owners looke well to them'.[91] That reputation is verified (albeit negatively) by the dwarf in *The Knight of the Burning Pestle*, who claims that the ostler 'will our Palfries slicke with wisps of straw, | And in the Maunger put them Oates enough, | And neuer grease their teeth with candle snuffe',[92] implying that a lack of slicking, inadequate feeding and teeth-greasing were considered commonplace. In Robert Wilson's *Three Ladies of London*, the 'goodly gentleman ostler' is Fraud himself;[93] Marlowe's Ithamore boasts that 'One time I was an Hostler in an Inne, | And in the night time secretly would I steale | To trauellers Chambers, and there cut their throats.'[94] In *Henry IV Part One*, the good ostler is lamented, while a bad ostler, Tom, is hinted at offstage. Robin saw his life cut short by the rising price of oats—'Poor fellow never joyed since the price of oats rose; it was the death of him' (2.1.12–13)—possibly, as Kastan suggests, a reference to actual contemporary economic conditions.[95] The current ostler, despite repeated and increasingly angry calls from the carriers, seems to have no interest in serving them, and Robin's oats have been replaced by cheaper, substandard fare: 'Peas and beans are as dank here as a dog, and this is the next way to give poor jades the bots' (2.1.8–9), the second carrier claims.

The two carriers are not working together, but they see themselves as 'neighbours', or 'countrymen', travelling the same road, in the same direction, and, it seems, on the same schedule. Taylor's *Carriers Cosmographie* suggests that carriers from particular regions tended (though not necessarily) to travel in packs,[96] timing their journeys to and from London so that they would coincide as they neared the capital, perhaps because they were hoping for safety in numbers. The progression of the scene in *Henry IV Part One* would support the interpretation that carriers had something to fear. The carriers' easy banter is instantly banished by the arrival of Gadshill. 'Good morrow, carriers. What's o'clock?', he asks, and Mugs replies 'I think it be two o'clock' (2.1.31–2), even though he has earlier remarked that it must already be 'four by the day' (2.1.1): he is attempting to obscure from Gadshill the precise time of their departure. As Gadshill then tries to persuade each of the carriers in turn to lend him a lantern, this suspicion becomes more evident. 'Nay, by God, soft. I know a trick worth two of that' (2.1.35–6), Mugs says. 'Ay, when, canst tell?' retorts the other, ' "Lend me thy lantern", quoth he. Marry, I'll see thee hanged first' (2.1.38–9). When Gadshill pushes them to tell him at what time they intend to reach London, the response is evasive and rude: 'Time enough to go to bed with a candle, I warrant thee' (2.1.42–3).

For all their kneejerk suspicion, however, the two are foolish enough to let Gadshill hear the information he wants: namely, that there are 'gentlemen' in the inn, who 'will along with [want to travel with] company' because 'they have great charge' (2.1.43–5), valuables to be transported. Later, during the ambush, we see something of the relationship between carrier and these gentlemen travellers. Two of the travellers dismount as they descend the hill: 'Come, neighbour', says one, 'the boy shall lead our horses down the hill. We'll walk afoot awhile, and ease our legs' (2.2.76–8). Presumably the boy works for the carrier, helping to lead the horses that the gentlemen have hired. It is at this moment, as the travellers move into 'the narrow lane' (2.2.58), that Falstaff, Peto, Bardolph, and

Gadshill make their ambush.[97] By the time we first meet the carriers, we already know, from Poins, of the plan:

[T]omorrow morning, by four o'clock early, at Gad's Hill, there are pilgrims going to Canterbury with rich offerings, and traders riding to London with fat purses. I have vizards for you all; you have horses for yourselves. Gadshill lies tonight in Rochester. I have bespoke supper tomorrow in Eastcheap. We may do it as secure as sleep.

(1.2.118–24).

The ambush will take place on Gad's Hill, a high-lying forested area on the London road between Rochester and Gravesend, already a by-word for danger to travellers. In *Sir John Old-castle*, the robber priest Sir John of Wrotham provides a checklist of such spots on Kent's London road: 'theres nere a hill, heath, nor downe in all Kent, but tis in my parish, Barrham downe, Chobham downe, Gads hill, Wrootham hill, Blacke heath, Cockes heath, Birchen wood, all pay me tythe'.[98] Of these, Gad's Hill was the most infamous. In his 1592 sermon *The Poore Mans Teares*, Henry Smith decried 'some beggers that boldly on Gads hill, Shooters hill, and suche places take mens horses by the heads, and bids them deliuer their purses'.[99] Black Will, in *Arden of Faversham*, boasts of how he 'robbed [a Constable] and his Man once at Gades hill'.[100] In Jonson's *Every Man Out of his Humour*, Sogliardo sings the praises of '*Caualier Shift*', 'the only *Bidstand* that euer was', who robs on 'all the high places of any Request', such as '*New-Market, Salisburie* Plaine, *Hockley* i'the hole, *Gads-Hill*', carrying out 'fiue hundred Robberies in his time, more or lesse'.[101] In Dekker and Webster's *West-ward Hoe*, Mistress Birdlime laments 'how the poor gentlewoman lies . . . as the way lies ouer *Gads-hill*, very dangerous'.[102]

At this point in 1.2, Poins and the gang are in Eastcheap and have booked supper there for the following evening as an alibi: no-one would suspect that they had galloped out of London in the middle of the night, carried out a highway robbery twenty miles away around dawn, and then ridden back. The only gang member placed at the scene is Gadshill, who is spending the night at the inn at Rochester, on a reconnaissance mission. But in Poins' speech we encounter what seems to be an awkward confusion: Gad's Hill is the place where the robbery will take place, but is also the name of one of the gang. Obviously, 'Gadshill' is an appropriate nickname for a man in his line of business—in *The Famous Victories*, Dericke recognizes Cutter not by his given name, but as the place of his criminal activity: 'Whoope hollo, now Gads Hill, knowest thou me? ... I know thee for a taking fellow, | Upon Gads hill in *Kent*' (A4ᵛ). Here, however, I want to propose another reading. In adapting this episode in *Henry IV Part One*, Shakespeare alters the thief's character by depriving him of his crime-related identity as Cuthbert Cutter, and instead names him exclusively as a product of the *place* of his crime, Gad's Hill, personifying the carrier's perception of the threat posed by that place. The doubling of place and person means that the statement 'Gadshill lies tonight in Rochester' sits awkwardly, as if one geographical place were spending the night in another. The effect is deliberate: to collapse the site of the robbery with the inn (the place where he 'lies') and to highlight the collusion of some of the inn's workers in the ambush. The Gadshill character is then developed in a combative scene with the carriers and a conspiratorial scene with the inn's chamberlain to make clear the causal links between the crime of highway robbery and the inns on which the carriers rely.

Poins celebrates Gadshill as the evil mastermind: 'Now shall we know if Gadshill have set a match. O, if men were to be saved by merit, what hole in hell were hot enough for him? This is the most omnipotent villain that ever cried "Stand!" to a true man' (1.2.102–5). It is Gadshill who elaborates the detailed information that there are 'Some eight or ten' in the company (2.2.62). But Gadshill's intelligence source, the enabler of his villainy, is made clear: he has this information because 'Gadshill lies tonight in Rochester', or more precisely, because he has an informant at the inn where he lies.

This collusion between inn-servant and criminal is a common-place, but, as I shall suggest, the play provides an unusual analysis of the situation. In the midst of his description of England's beautiful inns, William Harrison embarks on a lengthy digression on the nefarious tricks of inn staff. Ostlers, he begins, not only mistreat the horses but also 'make such packs with slipper merchants which hunt after preie . . . that manie an honest man is spoiled of his goods as he trauelleth to and fro'. In this enterprise, he alleges, 'the counsell of the tapsters or drawers of drinke, and chamberleins is not seldome behind or wanting', to the extent that 'Certes I beleeue not that chapman or traueller in England is robbed by the waie without the knowledge of some of them.' The tricks are multiple. When a guest comes into the inn and dismounts from his horse, the ostler 'forthwith is verie busie to take downe his budget or capcase in the yard from his sadle bow, which he peiseth [weigheth] slilie in his hand to féele the weight thereof'. When the guest goes to his chamber, the chamberlain will 'be sure to remooue it from the place where the owner hath set it as if it were to set it more conuenientlie some where else, whereby he getteth an inkling whether it be monie or other short wares'. The tapster for his part observes 'what plenty of monie he draweth' when a customer 'paieth the shot'. In short, 'it shall be an hard matter to escape all their subtile practises'. Armed with this information, the ostler, chamberlain, or tapster 'giueth warning to such od ghests as hant the house and are of his confederacie, to the vtter vndoing of manie an honest yeoman as he iournieth by the waie'.[103] Even those thinking it 'a gay matter' to 'commit their budgets at their comming to the goodman of the house', can cause their own undoing, since 'there cannot be a surer token vnto such as prie and watch for those booties, than to sée anie ghest deliuer his capcase in such maner'.[104] The dangers are dramatized in the so-called 'Tapster Manuscript', a single leaf of dramatic text that came to light in 1988, in which an inn's tapster tips off two thieves about a 'man that lodged in our house last night that hath 3 hundred markes in [gold.] he carries yt vnto the kings exchequer for certaine lands was latelye forfeited & that same man must needes go ore the [hill] where you may very well goe meete with <h>[im]', since 'there is not anye beares him companye'. He is certain of his information, 'for I did see the gold last night when as he gaue my master yt to lay vp tyll he calld for yt today'. In this brief scene, the tables are turned when the thieves depart promising the tapster a share in their profits, but failing to pay their beer bill.[105]

In Shakespeare, tapsters and ostlers are usually by-words for lowly, borderline-criminal characters: Coriolanus mocks the ostler as one 'that for th'poorest piece | Will bear the knave by th' volume', that is, for the smallest remuneration will bear being called knave a multitude of times (*Cor* 3.3.32–3). Falstaff asserts that 'A tapster is a good trade: an old cloak makes a new jerkin; a withered serving-man a fresh tapster' (*MW* 1.3.15–17). Celia opines that 'the oath of a lover is no stronger than the word of a tapster. They are both the confirmer of false reckonings' (*AL* 3.4.27–9) while the fact that Pompey is 'a tapster' is taken as evidence that he's also 'parcel-bawd', part pimp (*MM* 2.1.62). But in *Henry IV Part One* ostlers and tapsters are not the guilty party at the Rochester inn. Instead, by contrast, there is a marked distinction between corrupt inn servants and good, exploited inn servants. And in making this distinction, the play lines up carriers, innkeepers, tapsters, and ostlers against the chamberlain and his cronies.

The Custom of the Realm

In the final scene of Act 2, the play-acting of Falstaff, Hal and their comrades is interrupted by the entrance of a flustered Bardolph, who announces, 'O my lord, my lord, the sheriff with a most mon-strous watch is at the door' (2.4.469–70). Seconds later, the Hostess enters with the same news: 'The sheriff and all the watch are at the door. They are come to search the house.' (2.4.470–1). According to the printed stage direction, however, the 'most monstrous watch' turns out to be only 'Sheriff and the Carrier' (2.4.491 SD). The Sheriff explains that 'two gentlemen | Have in this robbery lost three hundred marks' (2.4.506–7), and that a 'hue and cry | Hath followed certain men unto this house' (2.4.493–4). A 'hue and cry', the 'outcry calling for the pursuit of a felon . . . by a constable, etc.' was usually 'raised by the party aggrieved',[106] but the men we might expect to be 'the party aggrieved', the two gentlemen, are not present. Why is the carrier in this scene? He barely speaks: when the Sheriff reports that 'A gross, fat man' is among the suspected thieves, the carrier elaborates only that he is 'As fat as butter' (2.4.497–8). Evidently, his presence is required for more than these four words.[107] In what follows, I shall suggest that the carrier needs to enter alongside the sheriff, because he, rather than the gentlemen, is indeed legally the 'party aggrieved'.

Shakespeare is at pains to exonerate the ostler and tapster from the suspicion of foul play. Gadshill's informant is specifically the chamberlain, the servant who, as *The Knight of the Burning Pestle* reminds us, has responsibility for the inn's chambers: he 'will see | Our beds prepar'd, and bring vs snowy sheetes, | Where neuer foote-man stretch'd his butter'd Hams'.[108] But the luxury provided by the chamberlain carried its own danger. When John Milton writes his elegy on the death of Hobson, the Cambridge University carrier, in 1631, he imagines Hobson being welcomed by 'the kind office of a Chamberlin', but that Chamberlain is Death:

> [Death,] lately finding him [the carrier] so long at home,
> And thinking now his journeys end was come,
> And that he had tane up his latest Inn,
> In the kind office of a Chamberlin
> Shew'd him his room where he must lodge that night,
> Pull'd off his Boots, and took away the light:
> If any ask for him, it shall be sed,
> *Hobson* has supt, and's newly gon to bed.[109]

The chamberlain's inherent threat, tacitly registered in Milton's elegy, derives from his intimate access to guests. The chamberlain is in a prime position to learn what they are carrying: 'It holds current that I told you yesternight. There's a franklin in the Weald of Kent hath brought three hundred marks with him in gold' (2.1.52–5). He has this knowledge from overhearing the guests' conversation: 'I heard him tell it to one of his company last night at supper—a kind of auditor, one that hath abundance of charge too, God knows what' (2.1.55–7). With responsibility for their board, he can give Gadshill precise information on their schedule: 'They are up already, and call for eggs and butter. They will away presently' (2.1.58–9).

Despite their collusion, the chamberlain and Gadshill have very different notions about what that collusion means. Gadshill is at pains to stress their mutual involvement in the crime, the direct connection between the chamberlain's information and the planned robbery. When the chamberlain answers Gadshill's call with a cheery ' "At hand", quoth Pickpurse', Gadshill observes sardonically, 'That's even as fair as "At hand", quoth the chamberlain', he claims, 'for thou variest no more from picking of purses than giving direction doth from labouring: thou layest the plot how' (2.1.47–5 1). The tension registered in this exchange is recapitulated when the two men shake hands on their deal. '[T]hou shalt have a share in our purchase' (2.1.90–1), Gadshill confirms, but the preceding conversation has established that, in practice, there is an important difference between the thief's actions and the chamberlain's intelligence, and a hint of it surfaces when the subject of hanging is broached. 'Sirrah, if they [the guests] meet not with Saint Nicholas's clerks [highwaymen]', insists Gadshill, 'I'll give thee this neck' (2.1.60–1). The chamberlain wants none of this talk of hanging: 'I pray thee keep that for the hangman, for I know thou worshippest Saint Nicholas as truly as a man of falsehood may' (2.1.62–4). Perhaps this insult is why the scene ends with Gadshill calling the chamberlain 'you muddy knave' (2.1.96).

Underlying this cooperation between the thief and the chamberlain is an important legal reality: as early as the 1360s, the king's council had issued a writ stating that any loss of goods brought into the inn by guests was answerable by the innkeeper.[110] This was the first use of what became known as 'custom of the realm' in which such liability did not have to be proved because 'the custom of this realm is common law'.[111] As William Harrison notes, 'If [a guest] loose oughts whilest he abideth in the inne, the host is bound by a generall custome to restore the damage, so that there is no greater securitie anie where for trauellers than in the gretest ins of England.'[112] This means that when a guest is robbed, his thoughts turn not to the thief, but to the innkeeper. In *Sir John Old-castle*, the carrier Club, whose clothes have gone missing, demands, 'Zwookes, do you robbe your ghests? doe you lodge rogues and slaues, and scoundrels, ha? they ha stolne our cloths here?'[113] Note here the strange progression of his thought: first, does the innkeeper rob his guests? second, does the innkeeper allow criminals to lodge in his inn? and only finally, a poor third, does he assert that *they* (other people) have stolen his clothes. Club determines to 'forzweare your house', since 'you lodgde a fellow and his wife by vs that ha runne away with our parrel'.[114] The threat here is more severe than it appears, since the carrier brought with him considerable custom: the inn trade and the carrier trade were inextricably linked. The bullish carrier here is echoed in Earle's sketch, where 'No man domineers more in his Inne, nor cals his Host vnreuerently with more presumption, and this arrogance proceeds out of the strength of his Horses.'[115] By contrast with these stereotyped portrayals, Shakespeare's carriers are churlish, but notably less arrogant.

The liability of the innkeeper is not raised in the carrier scenes, but it is clearly echoed when Falstaff is robbed of the papers in his pocket whilst in a drunken stupor. He demands of the Hostess that she discover who stole his property: 'How now, Dame Partlet the hen, have you enquired yet who picked my pocket?' (*1H4* 3.3.51–2). The hostess is properly enraged: 'Why, Sir John, what do you think, Sir John? Do you think I keep thieves in my house? I have searched, I have enquired, so has my husband, man by man, boy by boy, servant by servant. The tithe of a hair was never lost in my house before' (3.3.53–7). She is keen to deny that she keeps thieves in her house because, as innkeeper, she is vulnerable to claims for property stolen from her premises. Falstaff's insistence on the innkeeper's responsibility comes to nothing when the Hostess points out that he is in debt to her: for 'your diet, and by-drinkings', twenty-four pounds lent to him in cash, and twelve shirts she has bought him made of 'holland of eight shillings an ell' (3.3.70–2). She accuses him of fabricating the robbery story to evade his debts: 'you owe me money, Sir John, and now you pick a quarrel to beguile me of it' (3.3.65–6).

In *Henry IV Part One*, of course, the plot is not to relieve the guests of their goods at the inn, but to rob them once those guests are back on the road—and this is where the carrier comes in. For, as Harrison writes, 'you shall not heare that a man is robbed in his inne, yet after their departure the host can make no warrantise of the same, sith his protection extendeth no further than the gate of his owne house'.[116] Once the guests have left the inn, the innkeeper is not responsible for their stolen goods. But if they leave with a carrier, the carrier takes responsibility. The carrier's legal status was like the innkeeper's: through the custom of the realm he too was a bailee, that is, 'a man who in taking charge of another man's goods assumes an absolute liability for them to the owner', and is thus responsible for all loss and damage to the goods.[117] The principle is made clear in Christopher St German's *Doctor and Student*, a dialogue discussing legal issues first published in 1528 and frequently reprinted throughout the following century:

as it is commonly holden in the lawes of Englande if a common carier goe by the wayes that bee daungerous for robbing, or driue by night, or in other inconuenient time, & be robbed, or if he ouer charge a horse, whereby he falleth into the water or otherwise, so that the stuffe is hurt or impeyred, that he shal stande charged for his misdemeanour, & if hee would percase refuse to cary it, vnles promise were made vnto him that he shall not bee charged for no misdemeanor that should be in him, that promise were void. For it were against reason & against good maners and so it is in al other cases like.[118]

Despite legal challenges, in the last years of Elizabeth's reign verdicts in Woodlife's Case (1596–7) and Southcote's Case (King's Bench, 1601) restated the carrier's liability. Edward Coke advised that the only way out for the carrier was to establish beforehand a sense of limited liability:

Note reader, it is good policy for him who takes any goods to keep, to take them in a special manner, *sci[licet]*, 'to keep them as he keeps his own goods', or 'to keep them the best that he can at the peril of the party', or 'if they happen to be stolen or purloined, that he shall not answer for them'; for he that accepteth them ought to take them in such or the like manner, or otherwise he may be charged by his general acceptance.[119]

In practice, then, carriers had little recourse to legal remedy: they could be ruined by large claims on their liability. This is what Long Meg of Westminster means when she teaches a lesson to the assailants of the carrier Father Willis. She makes them swear (by the hem of her skirt) never to 'rob no Pack-men nor Carriers: for their goods nor mony is none of their owne':[120] carriers stand to lose even more by the fact that their goods and money are not their own. Dericke makes his entrance in *The Famous Victories*, it will be remembered, calling for a constable; he is trying to raise a hue and cry. Even John Earle's unsympathetic sketch of the carrier testifies to his vulnerability to robbery and the consequences, although in Earle's eyes, this is only just deserts for the carrier's assault on the roads: 'He is a great afflicter of the High-way, and beares them out of mesure, which iniury is somtimes reuengd by the Purse taker; & then the Voyage miscaries.'[121]

This is why, then, it is the carrier who appears in the Eastcheap tavern alongside the sheriff: if the goods are not found, or the highwaymen are not prosecuted, he is liable for the theft. The play emphasizes that the robbery affects not only rich individuals, but also the poor carrier who transports them, a familiar real-life figure and popular stage character notable for his rustic lack of urban sophistication. Carriers were naturally vulnerable on many fronts. In 1600, Stratford's 'long carrier' Edward Bromley was forced to resort to legal action to secure payment from one of his clients, Nicholas Jevens: Jevens, he claimed, owed him sixteen-pence, 'the price agreed for carrying for the said Nicholas from London to

Stratford' a 'certain fish called a thorn-back', as well as 'threepence for [to carry] a hamper called a dorsor' and two gallons of ale.[122] Bromley was charged, by Quiney's nephew Daniel Baker, with 'a case of negligent loss by a common carrier between London and Stratford', for losing 'a box containing a starr ryall, &c., valued altogether at £3'.[123] But in *Henry IV Part One*, the carrier's vulnerability is presented as the result of deliberate, cold-blooded victimization, and here, Shakespeare's play departs significantly from its inspirations and sources.

The ultimate source for the Gadshill episode is probably John Stow's *Chronicles of England* (1580), which tell how the prince, 'accompanyed with some of his yong Lords & gentlemen...wold waite in disguised araye for his owne receyuers, and distresse them of theyr money'.[124] This scenario is rehearsed in *The Famous Victories* when Harry with his friends Ned, Tom, and Jockey Oldcastle are said to have ambushed receivers and taken a thousand pounds—raising the odds from Stow's account, as Harry and his friends here 'rob my fathers Receiuers' (A2ʳ), attacking the king's men rather than his own. As we have seen, *The Famous Victories* contrasts this with the other and more prominent robbery by Cuthbert Cutter upon 'a poore Carrier' (A2ᵛ), Dericke—and makes it clear that Dericke should be seen as the play's comic hero, and Cutter as its villain. The play is in no doubt that these two crimes are ethically different, the attack on the receivers a piece of fun, whereas the carrier attack is blameworthy and worthy of vengeance. This distinction is borne out in the prince's dreams of the time when he will be king, appointing Ned as his Lord Chief Justice:

thou shalt hang none but picke purses and horse stealers, and such base minded villaines, but that fellow that will stand by the high way side couragiously with his sword and buckler and take a purse, that fellow giue him commendations; beside that, send him to me and I will giue him an anuall pension out of my Exchequer, to maintaine him all the dayes of his life.

(Cᵛ)

The dashing highway pursetaker, standing with his sword and buckler, is to be admired; but sneaky pickpurses and horse-stealers are beyond the pale: the prince berates Cutter as a 'base minded rascal to rob a poore carrier' (A2ᵛ). Despite this distinction, the two robberies cannot be kept entirely separate: the thief who attacks the carrier is, after all, the prince's man who had 'parted from vs the last night' (A2ᵛ) and the prince does intervene to save Cutter from jail. Harry and his cronies use Cutter 'to spie | Out our booties' (A2ᵛ), to facilitate Harry's attack on the receivers. So if the play condemns Cutter outright, how can it simultaneously permit a grudging admiration for Harry's highway ambush?

In *Henry IV Part One*, Shakespeare builds on this ambiguity, merging the two offences to produce an attack that could ultimately wreck the lives of not only the two gentlemen (here downgraded to a franklin and an auditor), but also the carrier who transports them. The play does present, albeit fleetingly, a different version of the robbery, when it is reported that 'there's money of the King's coming down the hill, 'tis going to the King's exchequer' (2.2.52–3).[125] This is at odds with what Gadshill has gathered from the chamberlain— perhaps because this is a ghost of an earlier version, or perhaps because the robbers are deliberately obscuring and misrepresenting the lowly nature of their victims.

Whatever the case, Shakespeare's play refuses an easy separation between evil lowly villains and the reckless, dashing elite characters. To reinforce this identification, the carriers' scene echoes and resonates strangely with the first scene between Hal and Falstaff at the tavern in Eastcheap (1.2). At Rochester, it is still dark: the first carrier enters '*with a lantern in his hand*', and claims 'Hey-ho! An it be not four by the day, I'll be hanged. Charles's Wain [ursa major, the plough] is over the new chimney, and yet our horse not packed' (2.1.0 SD and 1–3). Here we see something of the schedule and labour of the carrier: travel must be accomplished during daylight hours, so the horses have to be ready to leave at dawn. But asking the time also echoes Falstaff, on his first entrance in the play: 'Now, Hal, what time of day is it, lad?' to which the prince objects that 'What a devil hast thou to do with the time of the day?' (1.2.1, 5–6). Given Falstaff's unscheduled, hedonistic lifestyle, Hal can 'see no reason, why thou shouldst bee so superfluous to demand the time of the day' (1.2.10–11). Falstaff admits that the prince has a point: 'Indeed you come near me now, Hal, for we that take purses go by the moon and seven stars, and not by Phoebus, he, that "wand'ring knight so fair" '(1.2.12–14). As one who takes purses, Falstaff aligns himself with Gadshill, but as one who goes by the moon, he associates himself with carriers who rely on nocturnal astronomy to time the pre-dawn beginning of their working day. The image is developed through the play. While the carriers rely on their lanterns for their work, and Gadshill attempts to borrow them to aid his, Bardolph's nose becomes a lantern for Falstaff: 'thou bearest the lantern in the poop, but 'tis in the nose of thee. Thou art the Knight of the Burning Lamp' (3.3.25–7). Falstaff details the uses he makes of it: Bardolph's nose is the 'sun of utter darkness' (3.3.37) because it only serves to light the nightworld of criminals: as he 'ran...up Gad's Hill in the night to catch my horse' (3.3.37–8), saving Falstaff 'a thousand marks in links and torches walking with thee in the night betwixt tavern and tavern' (3.3.41–3).

Falstaff's poetic conceits are not allowed to go unchallenged. In 1.2, Falstaff develops his self-description as a nocturnal pursetaker, claiming such as he are 'Diana's foresters, gentlemen of the shade, minions of the moon...being governed, as the sea is, by our noble and chaste mistress the moon, under whose countenance we steal' (1.2.24–8). In response, Hal perversely picks up on the ebbing that is destined for 'us that are the moon's men': 'a purse of gold most resolutely snatched on Monday night and most dissolutely spent on Tuesday morning, got with swearing "Lay by!", and spent with crying "Bring in!", now in as low an ebb as the foot of the ladder, and by and by in as high a flow as the ridge of the gallows' (1.2.30–7). The tone shifts as Hal reminds Falstaff of the consequences of 'swearing "Lay by!" '—death by hanging. Falstaff begs Hal not to 'hang a

thief' 'when thou art king' (1.2.59); and Hal equivocates by saying
that instead Falstaff will, 'and so become a rare hangman' (1.2.64–5).
The conversation resonates with the curse-laden speech of the two
carriers, highlighted by an inventive variety of hanging oaths: 'I'll
be hanged', 'Come away, and be hanged!' 'Come and be hanged!'
'Marry, I'll see thee hanged first' (1.2.1–2, 22, 30, 39). (Here again, we
might find an echo of *The Famous Victories*: 'Dericke' was at that time
synonymous for the hangman or the gallows, and was even used as
an active verb meaning 'to hang'.)[126]

This 'hanging' figure reveals Falstaff's identification with the
world of Gadshill—and forces us to take seriously Gadshill's insistence, in a speech to the chamberlain, that thanks to high-level
protection, he is safe from prosecution and punishment:

What talkest thou to me of the hangman? If I hang, I'll make a fat pair of
gallows; for, if I hang, old Sir John hangs with me, and thou knowest he
is no starveling. Tut, there are other Trojans that thou dreamest not of,
the which for sport sake are content to do the profession some grace, that
would, if matters should be looked into, for their own credit sake make all
whole. I am joined with no foot-landrakers, no long-staff sixpenny strikers,
none of these mad mustachio purple-hued maltworms, but with nobility
and tranquility, burgomasters and great oneyers, such as can hold in, such
as will strike sooner then speak, and speak sooner then drink, and drink
sooner then pray—and yet, zounds, I lie, for they pray continually unto
their saint the commonwealth, or, rather, not to pray to her but prey on
her, for they ride up and down on her, and make her their boots.

(2.1.65–81)

In Gadshill's boastful account, his safety is vouched for by his collab-
orators, the undreamed-of 'other Trojans', 'nobility and tranquility,
burgomasters, and great oneyers', with whose support, he and his
fellows 'steal as in a castle, cocksure', and 'walk invisible' (2.1.85–6).
But Gadhill's speech reveals the cost: these supporters not only 'pray
to' the Commonwealth but 'prey on her'—and his image is one of
their trampling the land: 'they ride up and down on her, and make
her their boots' [plunder] (2.1.81). These are the terms with which

King Henry opens the play, with his premature speech of joy at the end of civil war:

> No more the thirsty entrance of this soil
> Shall daub her lips with her own children's blood;
> No more shall trenching war channel her fields,
> Nor bruise her flowerets with the armed hoofs
> Of hostile paces.
>
> (1.1.5–9)

As the play progresses, Falstaff, Gadshill's most prominent supporter, proves himself to be a second Gadshill: as he moves towards Warwickshire, pressing soldiers (and pocketing the collateral profits), exploiting the innkeepers: 'There's not a shirt and a half in all my company, and the half-shirt is two napkins tacked together and thrown over the shoulders like a herald's coat without sleeves; and the shirt, to say the truth, stolen from my host of Saint Albans, or the red-nose innkeeper of Daventry' (4.2.41–6). In a macabre parody of the carrier's journey, Falstaff's itinerary is mapped and remembered by the inns and innkeepers that punctuate it, at St Albans and Daventry, both on the carriers' London road to Coventry.[127] And once again we find the inns as scenes of crime: he has stolen a shirt (and probably napkins) from an innkeeper. More gravely, among his declared choice of categories of impressed men, Falstaff again victimizes those lower-ranked men who serve the realm's highways: 'Such as indeed were never soldiers, but discarded unjust servingmen, younger sons to younger brothers, revolted tapsters and ostlers trade-fallen—the cankers of a calm world and a long peace, ten times more dishonorable-ragged than an old-feazed ensign' (4.2.26–3 1). Here among England's disaffected are 'revolted tapsters and ostlers trade-fallen', recalling the tapster Francis, the hapless victim of Falstaff and Hal's merriment in the Eastcheap tavern, and the Rochester inn's Robin Ostler, whose death was attributed to the rise in the price of oats. When Hal rebukes him for pressing 'such pitiful rascals' (4.2.63), Falstaff callously dismisses his objections: 'Tut, tut, good enough to toss; food for powder, food for powder. They'll fill a pit as well as better. Tush, man, mortal men, mortal men' (4.2.64–6). In due course, inevitably, his words come true: 'I have led my ragamuffins where they are peppered; there's not three of my hundred and fifty left alive, and they are for the town's end to beg during life' (5.3.35–8). While Gadshill and Falstaff are glibly happy to exploit the 'custom of the realm' by abusing carriers and innkeepers, Falstaff ultimately proves himself capable of a fatal exploitation of the subordinates in the same system, the ostlers, and tapsters, supposedly in the service of the realm.

If Falstaff is deeply implicated in such abuse, then where does this leave Hal? When the robbery is first mooted by Poins, the prince notably refuses Falstaff's invitation to 'make one' of the crew: 'Who? I rob? I a thief? Not I, by my faith... Well, come what will, I'll tarry at home' (1.2.131, 137). He is persuaded specifically not to take part in the robbery of the pilgrims and traders ('yourself and I will not be there', Poins insists), but to 'rob the thieves' (2.2.91); having recovered the money, and shamed the robbers, Hal swears that 'The money shall be paid back again with advantage' (2.4.533–4). He attacks Falstaff when Sir John accuses the Hostess of theft: 'Charge an honest woman with picking thy pocket? Why thou whoreson, impudent, embossed rascal' (3.3.154–6). Against the false lanterns of Falstaff and Bardolph, Shakespeare weaves the dominant imagery of Hal as the sun/son yet to come, 'Who doth permit the base contagious clouds | To smother up his beauty from the world' (1.2.188–9), the clouds and mist to be dispelled by his change, 'My reformation, glittering o'er my fault' (1.2.203).

But is Hal as guiltless as he insists? He wants to separate himself from this world of corrupt chamberlains who betray their customers, lazy ostlers who maltreat their horses, highway robbers who collude with inn-workers, duplicitous and thieving guests who make false claims against innkeepers and steal their property. He angrily resists the language of the inns: when Falstaff asks him to help him get back on his horse, the prince retorts, 'Out, ye rogue;

shall I be your ostler?' (2.2.41). Yet he gleefully takes part in the 'playing holidays' and 'loose behaviour' of the tavern (1.2.194, 198), the taunting of the tapster Francis, and the picking of Falstaff's pocket. More damagingly, he does nothing to stop the Gadshill robbery, which not only leads to the theft of money (which he can put right) but also to the vicious assault on the bodies of the travellers (which he cannot). Indeed, the robbery has to take place for him to have his 'sport'. And even at the end of the play, he declares himself happy to 'grace' Falstaff's 'lie' (5.5.157–8). Far from separating out a comic 'underplot' that mimics and absolves the main plot, the play refuses to allow an easy absolution to Hal's continued indulgence in the world of Falstaff and Gadshill.

To excise the carriers' scene is not simply to lose a few actors, costumes or stage time. It also comes at the price of unpinning the play's finely plotted connections between the worlds of the Eastcheap tavern and the Rochester inn, and the mutual support system between the high-placed 'Trojans' and the low, vicious criminals whom they protect. By drawing on the figure of the carrier, familiar both from his audience's own lives, and from the comic creation of Richard Tarlton, Shakespeare is able to point out everyone's vulnerability to the corruption of men like Falstaff—and, by extension, the unreformed Hal. The carrier is not a faceless, hapless victim: he is, for most London audiences, the face of home—it is he, along with the inn's retinue of honest innkeepers, tapsters, and ostlers, who provides the conduit from and back to the provinces that allows their new London lives to flourish. Gadshill and his protectors, personified in Falstaff, 'prey' on the commonwealth, attacking precisely those who, by the 'custom of the realm', cannot protect themselves, and have no legal redress. Far from providing a comic 'underplot', the carriers' scene begins to suggest an analysis of how 'nobility and tranquility' might be responsible for the fate of 'revolted tapsters and ostlers trade-fallen', as their paths cross on London road.

4

Shakespeare is Shylock: Letters of Credit in *The Merchant of Venice*

Given Edmond Malone's commitment to tracking down every piece of archival evidence related to Shakespeare, *An Inquiry into the Authenticity of certain Miscellaneous Papers and Legal Instruments*, his monumental and pitiless demolition of Samuel Ireland's Shakespeare letters, is perhaps most remarkable for what it omits— the letter from Richard Quiney to William Shakespeare that Malone had himself discovered and which was, in 1795, in his possession.[1] For all the excitement he expressed in private correspondence to friends, Malone maintained an uncharacteristic public silence about this discovery, and even more significantly, failed to mention the Quiney letter in his letters to Stratford-upon-Avon correspondents.[2] Malone took thousands of documents with him when he returned to London, and kept hold of them for over twelve years until in December 1805 the Stratford authorities threatened to take him to the Court of King's Bench to recover them,[3] so we can only assume that this relic was among those papers. Nevertheless, Malone died in 1812 without either publishing the letter or advertising its existence, and ultimately the letter did not make it to the printed page until James Boswell junior edited Malone's *Life of William Shakespeare* in 1821, almost thirty years after its discovery.[4] What was there in this letter that made Malone so reluctant to trumpet his discovery to the world?

As Mark Eccles has detailed, the letter refers to the way in which Quiney would usually receive financial help: via Peter Roswell, servant to Sir Edward Greville, local lord of the manor. In Roswell's absence, however, Plan B involves asking Shakespeare, as a 'Loveinge Countreyman' (that is, fellow Warwickshire native) and 'ffrende' to help him with raising £30 to pay 'all the debettes I owe in London'; Quiney offers as security against the loan his own credit-worthiness in combination with that of either Thomas Bushell or Richard Mytton, both kinsmen and associates of Greville.[5] When he printed the letter in 1821, Boswell attempted (using Malone's notes) to explain the letter as evidence of Shakespeare's financial success. Since thirty pounds was 'no inconsiderable sum in those days', he argues that 'Such a request could not have been made to a person who was not possessed of means which enabled him readily to comply with it'; and that the writer 'was addressing one from whom he had no apprehension of receiving a churlish denial'. He reads the Quiney letter as another proof that Shakespeare 'appears at an early period to have placed himself in circumstances of ease and comfort', a sensible man cognizant of his 'duties as a husband and a father'.[6] But in truth, this was not the kind of letter Malone himself advertised that he wanted to find. Victorian scholars detected a less palatable truth, that might explain Malone's reluctance to publish, and Boswell's extravagant apologia—that Shakespeare was approached because he was a known money-lender.

This awkward possibility was first mooted by James Orchard Halliwell in 1848: 'I am scarcely willing,' he wrote, 'to hazard the conjecture that after Shakespeare had obtained a capital in ready money, he increased it by supplying loans at interest; but there really seems to be fair grounds for such an opinion.'[7] More recently, this interpretation has been pursued by Ernst Honigmann, who suggests that 'Like his father, John, who had lent large sums (£80, £100) at the illegal rate of 20 per cent, William seems to have had a sideline as a money-lender, while at the same time Shylock thrilled audiences in London.'[8] Honigmann's ironic coupling of Shakespeare and

Shylock is not the empathetic bonding of Christian playwright and persecuted Jew that Stephen Greenblatt and Kenneth Gross have recently celebrated[9]—Honigmann intends to shock us by posing Shakespeare as usurer. I should say at the outset that the identification of Shakespeare as a moneylender is, in strict terms, misleading. In the letter, Quiney quite clearly claims that he will 'hold my time and content yowr frende', that is pay back 'yowr frende' fully on the due date, implying not that Shakespeare would directly fund him, but instead that he would act as an intermediary to Quiney's hoped-for source of funds.[10] Nonetheless, Honigmann is right to suggest that Shakespeare in London and Shylock in Venice have something in common. But to define what this is we need to develop a different understanding of the place of moneylending in early modern England, an understanding that moves us away from the charged and censorious rhetorics against usury that have dominated critical discussion of Shylock's role in *The Merchant of Venice*. And to demonstrate how this works, I turn again to the play's letters, which we can appreciate better through an examination of Richard Quiney's correspondence.

Stratford's Man in London

The letters he sent home and received from Stratford-upon-Avon did more than keep Richard Quiney in contact with his townsfolk: they made things happen. During his 1598–9 stay in London, for example, Quiney was called on by numerous family members and neighbours as Stratford's man in London to perform tasks for them. At Roger Smith's request, William Walford wrote twice concerning a matter at King's Bench, requesting that Quiney speak to Smith's attorney Horbone.[11] Brother-in-law Abraham Sturley asked Quiney to intervene in an Exchequer case brought by one Briscow against Quiney, Sturley, and three other Stratford men, 'seinge vr opportunitj is theare to staj att some leasure'.[12] Sturley conveyed to Quiney that

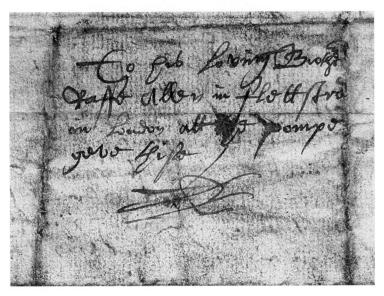

6. Superscription of a letter from Robert Allen to Raffe Allen, 8 October 1598.

John Tubb 'praith u to certifie his atturnej master Thomas Hunte that ffor Thomas Grenes band of Marson he is satisfied'.[13] George Bardell's widow Isabell wrote to ask her 'Good Cozen' and 'lovinge kinsman' Quiney to find a situation for her eldest son Adrian, then twenty, who had lost his place with 'my cozen Parker'. Since 'I haue gott noe place for hym in the contrey', she pleaded, 'I would therefore entreat yow to stand soe much my good ffrend as to helpe me now and I shall be bound to praie for yow the longest daie of my lieffe.' In a postscript she added, 'if yow can procure me a place if yt please yow to send me word I will send him vp vnto yow'.[14]

Many of the tasks Quiney undertook were financial in nature, had implications in both London and Stratford, and were not only recorded but facilitated and accredited by letters. A letter remaining in the Stratford archives gives some sense of how such transactions might take place (illustrations 6 and 7). Written by Robert Allen in 'starttforde of haven' on 8 October, 1598, to his brother Raffe (Ralph), staying 'att the pompe' in London's Fleet Street, it asks Raffe to

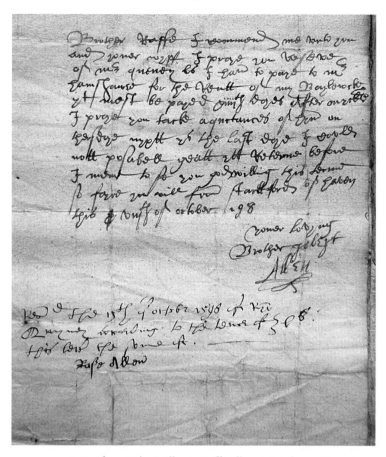

7. Letter from Robert Allen to Raffe Allen, 8 October 1598.

'reseve of [i.e. from] ma*ster* queney ls [50 shillings] I haue to paye to ma*ster* hamshawre for the Rentt of my Bayleweke [bailiwick] *that* mest be payed'. Raffe was to take the money from Quiney, and then use it to pay Hamshaw. Below the letter-text, the paper then bears, in Quiney's hand, the sentence 'Rec*eaue*d the 13th of octob[e]r 1598 of Richard Quyney according to the tenor of this letter the sv*mme* of ls' (50 shillings), and the signature of 'Rafe Allen'. Quiney obviously took the letter with Raffe's signature as proof that he had indeed handed over the fifty shillings, hence its survival in the Stratford papers.[15]

Whereas Allen's negotiations proceeded smoothly, a series of letters from Quiney's wife's nephew Daniel Baker amply testifies to the problems that could be encountered in such long-distance transactions.[16] Baker owed money to a number of London drapers— 'To master Randulfe woollie at the signe of the starr & pheasant in watlinge street 30[ll] To master ffrauncis Evington draper at the signe of the Checker in watlinge street 14[ll] To master John weston draper at the signe of the kinges head in watlinge street 26[ll],[17]—and made arrangements by letter to have the debts cleared, only to find that the sums were paid either in part, or not at all. When cash did come available in London for him, as when Sir Edward Greville allegedly paid him some £40 in November 1598, the hapless Baker could not trace to whom the monies had been paid. His letters quickly deteriorate into an increasingly complex mesh of transactions, the tenor of which can be gauged in this, of 13 November, where the seven uses of 'if' betray the uncertainty with which he writes:

Sir I vnderstand by your Letter derected to master Alderman that Sir Edward Grevile hath paid mee but 40[ll] but to whom it is paide I know not but only 10[ll] to master John west at the signe of the kinges head in watlinge street: the other 30[ll] I willed should bee payd 20[li] to master wolly and 10[li] to master ffrauncis Evington draper at the signe of the Checker in watling street. but whether master Evington haue that 10[lll] I know not and therfore dessier to bee certefyeth {sic} therof from you. neyther doe I know whether by your meanes or Leonard Bennetes the 3[ll] 7[s] bee yet payd to master kympton at the black boie in watling strete. and therfore for most Assuerance I haue taken order with master Barber to pay 3[ll] for mee to master kympton this weeke I pray yow certefy master kympton therof. and yff you can paie hi, the od vij[s]. Yf master kympton haue Receaue his monie beefore then I haue appointed master Barber to pay the sayd 3[ll] to master woolly. And yff Sir Edward haue payd master woolly but 20[ll] then I pray you entreat Sir Edward yff it maybe to paye hym 10[ll] more or yff you can heare of any Spare monie to bee taken vp theer yff Sir Edward canot doo it I pray you yet 10[ll] more payd for mee to master woolly. or 13[ll] Rather yff it may bee & I will Repaie it heere and so in great haste I end...[18]

The experience of Daniel Baker acts as a salutary reminder that this system of financial transaction-via-letter was hardly foolproof, but it also underscores the fact that Baker has no alternative but to continue to send more letters and set up more letter-transacted deals. As Baker's letter suggests, also, the money moved about in London could lead directly to money being moved about in Stratford-upon-Avon. Quiney's wife Elizabeth borrowed £7 from William Smith the younger in Stratford, to be repaid at a price of £10 to him by her husband in London.[19] On 20 October, Quiney's father Adrian urged him to 'wryght earnestly' to one Master Parsons to persuade Parsons to give Adrian the £3 13s 4d he needed.[20] In return, Parsons in Stratford arranged via one William Wenlock for Quiney to receive ten pounds on All Saints' Eve or the following day, to be held by him until passed on to Master Richard Woodward.[21]

I would suggest that it is in this context of lives and financial dealings conducted between Stratford-upon-Avon and London that we need to read Richard Quiney's letter written to William Shakespeare on 25 October, 1598. The Quiney–Shakespeare deal clearly has ramifications in both locations. Most immediately, the promise of the Shakespeare-procured money in London helped Quiney's wife in Stratford: her nephew Daniel Baker wrote to Quiney that 'my Aunt Quyne telleth mee that you are to Receaue 20 or 30ll In London & that you will pay som monie for mee yff neede bee: & in that respect I haue lent her som monie allredy to serue her occasions'.[22] But other letters show that the money requested by Quiney's letter had a purpose beyond its immediate alleged use. Adrian Quiney had already advised his son 'to bye some such warys as yow may selle presently with profet. Yff yow bargen with William sha {sic} or R[ec]eave money ther or brynge your money home yf yow maye. I see howe kn[i]te stockynges be sold ther ys gret byinge of them at Aysham. Edward Wheat & Harrye your brother man were both at evysham thys daye senet & as I harde bestow 20ll ther in knyt hosse, wherefore I thynke yow maye doo good yff yow can have money.'[23] Were Quiney to get hold of some money, he should not use it directly to pay off debts in London (as he claims to Shakespeare) but to invest in commodities that might yield a good profit on his return to Stratford. Replying on 4 November to Quiney's news 'that our countryman Master William Shakespeare would procure us monej', Abraham Sturley seemed underwhelmed: 'I will like of [it] as I shall heare when & wheare & howe' he writes tersely. But he was keen to invest the money in a lease: 'I pray let nat go that occasion if it may sorte to anj indifferent condicions. Allso that yf monej might be had for 30 or 40^{ll} a lease &c. might be procured: Oh howe can u make dowbt of monej who will not beare xxx^{ll} or xl^{s} towards sutch a match?'[24] As Stratford archivist Robert Bearman has argued, Quiney is not acting alone: 'the approach to Shakespeare was indeed made on Sturley's and Quiney's joint behalf ("would procure *us* money")... The final two sentences... clearly hint at the terms at which a loan might be secured.'[25] So Quiney, and his fellows in Stratford, are looking for Shakespeare, a Stratford man in London, to use his credit to raise money in London for Quiney's use. Quiney claims it is to pay off debts, but in reality, he might well use that money to purchase commodities in London, or elsewhere on the route home, in order to sell those commodities for profit in Stratford. What the Quiney letter represents, in other words, is not a single isolated instance of 'moneylending', but an entire series, even a network of financial transactions that are forged across two distant places.

We should not think of this as suspicious or even as odd or anomalous. As the work of the economic historian Craig Muldrew is showing us, a complicated mesh of credit arrangements (rather than cash payments) accounted for the majority of financial trans-actions in early modern England, partly because of a lack of coin, but also because these credit relationships constituted social relationships.[26] As Deborah Valenze summarizes Muldrew's argu-ment, '[t]he social import of contractual obligation was so great that all social life was practically indistinguishable from the enforced relationality of trust generated by credit'.[27] But how are these credit relationships brought about? In most cases, they are transacted through personal contact: I buy something from the butcher, I owe the butcher money, the butcher becomes my creditor, I become his debtor. But in dealings such as Quiney's with Shakespeare, we are dealing with long-distance arrangements, and the medium of their transaction is the letter. We know of these arrangements because Quiney's correspondence happens to have survived. But what I want to stress is that his letters do not simply describe those transactions—rather, they *are* those transactions. It is the letters moving between Quiney and his fellow Stratfordians that transact these business initiatives, instructing what monies should be moved where, acting as guarantors for those moves. In other words, the letters themselves become carriers of credit, and often, as we shall see, a legal record of the credit arrangements they transact.

This chapter explores how such an understanding of credit might be brought to bear on one of Shakespeare's most misunderstood plays, *The Merchant of Venice*. The 'pound of flesh' bond story, although structurally subservient to Bassanio's wooing of Portia, has come, through its compelling portrayal of the Jew Shylock, to dominate the play. Shylock is the star part, and the play's treatment of Jews, anti-Jewish prejudice and toleration is usually held up as its most significant feature, focusing critical attention on Shylock-related topics: usury and the law. Inspired by the onstage court scene, the play's longest, critics have interpreted Shylock's battle with Balthasar/Portia as relating to different legal systems, Shylock's contractual literalism versus Portia's merciful equity (or the English common-law courts versus the courts of equity), a legal battle that is then mapped onto the play's pitting of (Jewish) usury versus (Christian) charity. In truth, the play presents a far more complex understanding of the interactions between finance and the law, and between various different monetary dealings of the early modern world. For, as I shall demonstrate, the disparate elements of *The Merchant of Venice* harp on a single theme, of *credit*, in the fullest early modern senses of the word, ranging from financial trustworthiness to forensic believability. And the treatment of credit in *The Merchant of Venice*, I shall argue, is inextricably linked to its depiction of letters.

As in many of his plays, Shakespeare uses letters to convey news and to make arrangements: Bassanio tells his man to 'see these letters delivered', presumably invitations to 'My best-esteem'd acquaintances' to 'feast to-night' (2.2.110–11, 163–4); Jessica charges her father's erstwhile servant Lancelot Gobbo to 'Give . . . this letter,— do it secretly' to her suitor Lorenzo directing him in her plan to escape (2.3.5–8, delivered in 2.4). But here, perhaps more than in any other play, he is fascinated by the ways in which letters transact commercial business and legal business, the ways in which letters carry credit. Critics have been unhappy with the two letters produced by Portia at the play's conclusion:

> Here is a letter, read it at your leisure,—
> It comes from Padua from Bellario,—
> There you shall find that Portia was the doctor,
> Nerrissa there her clerk. . . .
>   Antonio you are welcome,
> And I have better news in store for you
> Than you expect: unseal this letter soon,
> There you shall find three of your argosies
> Are richly come to harbour suddenly.
> You shall not know by what strange accident
> I chanced on this letter.
>
>   (5.1.267–79)

In 1926, Arthur Quiller-Couch and J. Dover Wilson admired 'This beautiful example of Shakespeare's dramatic impudence' while noting that it had 'been severely criticized by some pundits'.[28] They presumably had in mind the type of complaint forwarded by Isaac-Ambrose Eccles in his 1805 edition of the play: 'There is not, perhaps, to be found in the dramatic writings of any poet a more lame, awkward, and inartificial expedient for suddenly bringing on a general satisfaction in the catastrophe, than that which is here had recourse to.'[29] This chapter will contend that this final move is anything but lame, awkward and inartificial. Instead, it is structurally the lynchpin of the play where letters act both as instruments of financial credit, and as forensic proofs of credibility.

The Place Where Merchants shall Write

The iconic image of the merchant on England's early modern stage was of a man discovered counting his money—'*Enter Barabas in his Counting-house, with heapes of gold before him*'.[30] But this is a powerful theatrical shorthand that obscures more about social practice than it reveals. In reality, the counting house was, according to advice tracts, the 'place wher they [the merchants] shall write'. As a consequence, it 'ought to be quiat or still, and furnisshid with al thingis necessarie, belonging unto the same, as bokis paper, yncke, standishe pennes, penkniff, wex, seallinge threde, seale &c',[31] the raw materials of letter-writing.

That heavy-duty writing was a merchant's lot can be seen in two of the most familiar images of sixteenth-century merchants, Hans Holbein the Younger's portrait of George Gisze (1532) (illustration 8) and Jan Gossaert's *c.* 1530 portrait of an Antwerp merchant (illustration 9).[32] Each merchant is painted not with gold, spices or other valuable commodities, but with the paraphernalia of his account-keeping: quills and ink, sealing wax, scales, a pile of coins, paper in book form, a sandbox, and (in Gossaert's painting, in the bottom right corner) a set of tables.[33] Holbein's merchant is surrounded by letters on a filing mechanism; another is displayed centrally on the wall; he eyes the painter without warmth, visibly keen to open another, sealed letter in his hands. Gossaert places the merchant centrally between two sets of letters, each on 'file', that is, hung upside down and backwards, and threaded (through holes punched into the bottom of the sheet) onto a wire. The set on his right (our left) is labelled 'Alrehande Missiven' (miscellaneous letters), the other 'Alrehande Minuten' (miscellaneous

8. Hans Holbein the Younger, *Portrait of the Merchant George Gisze* (1532).

drafts, originals, copies). I would suggest we are to see the letters in some way analogous to the double-entry accounting depicted in the merchant's hands.

Critics have recently insisted on the importance of the rise of double-entry book-keeping in the early modern period.[34] But to date no one has focused attention on the role of letters in that book-keeping. After Luca Pacioli included a section on book-keeping in a 1494 Venetian book on arithmetic, tracts on accountancy were

9. Jan Gossaert, *Portrait of a Merchant* (*c.* 1530).

published in Europe's vernacular languages, first in Italian, then in French, Dutch, and German and from 1543, in English.[35] Without exception, these manuals, usually drawing tacitly on Pacioli, devote a chapter to advising merchants how to deal with their letters. They prescribe periodically arranging the letters into bundles, relating to the cities where the correspondents are based; some propose keeping copies of letters sent; some suggest keeping a register of correspondence. Letters should, like the various ledger books, be kept in a secret, locked location—and presumably, for the same reasons: that these constitute a record, and ultimately, legal evidence of the financial transactions.

The accounts in the English sixteenth-century manuals, by Hugh Oldcastle, James Peele, and John Mellis, are largely similar. Each theorist advises that in addition to the memorial, the journal, and the ledger in which business transactions are detailed, some subsidiary books must be kept. In 1553, James Peele advises that the record-keeper should 'be circumspect aboute all thinges committed to his charge, as billes, Obligacions or Statutes' (various types of bonds or recognizances), sorting, endorsing, and dating them and periodically surveying what action needs to be taken on them. But he also deals with letters. Letters from overseas should also be ordered: 'in all letters receiued from any partes beyonde the seas, to be at eche voiages retourne, bounde vp and written on them, of what Marte or voiage thei were of: and in what yere: and so orderly piled vp in your Comptyng house'. In addition, a book should be kept for taking 'copies of letters sent to any parties beyonde the seas: to whom, and by whom thei be sent, and what numbre and date thei were of'.[36]

The 1588 edition by mathematics teacher John Mellis of Hugh Oldcastle's 1543 tract on account-keeping[37] extends these directions, including an entire chapter in which Mellis exhorts the merchant to pay attention to 'the sure keeping and ordering of your letters which are sent to you from your friends and factors: and also your especialties, as are billes of hande, formall obligations and acquittances, concerning any part of your occupying' (F6^{r-v}). He advises him to have

a little booke of paper called a register, wherein yee shal register euery letter and especialty that yee receiue, after that you haue written the day of the moneth that you receiued it vppon the backe of your letter, and in this manner yee shall write in your said register, in the beginning of the date of our Lorde, and then the day of the present moneth directly vnder: and then begin to write at the margent in this manner. *M*. receiued at Maister Anthony Rose *de Mysina* a letter concerning so much Ginger sent to me from him the 24 day of February. And then begin againe, and say: Item receiued a letter from him concerning so much suger that I had of him the 12. day of March: also recieued a letter the 4 day of July, from my factor such a man, being at *Cyuill*, concerning diuers wares that hee sent mee, as appeareth in my Journal: also to bee remembred that I receiued sent to mee an obligation canceled of *40* li. that I paid him the eight day of May: and so continue your booke or register till the ende...

(F7^v)

In addition to this registering of the traffic in letters, one should have 'a chest in your counting house for your letters, wherein you shall put them as soone as you haue read them, and written the day of receite on the backe side'. At the end of each month, the month's letters should be gathered: 'fold them somewat large, and binde them in a bushel'. Letters from a single place—he gives as examples Venice, Genoa, Florence, London, Seville, and Antwerp—'should be bound in a bundell by themselues, and write vppon the vpper letter Uenice, or Iene, or any other place that they come from'. The remaining 'desperate [disparate] letters that you receiue from sundry places, may happen one or two in a yeare', should be given their own bundle. At the end of the year, 'put all the bundels of letters of that yeare together in a bagge or large boxe meete for that purpose, & write the date of our Lord vppon the said bagge or boxe' (F8^r). The imperative to register and archive letters effectively even impacts on the layout of merchants' letters. Mellis notes that in normal correspondence the 'name is accustomed to bee written vnder the letters in the corner of the right hande'. In the case of trade-related correspondence, however, the format is different: 'But among marchantes it is vsed to write the date of our Lorde, and the name of the place aboue the letters at the beginning', presumably to facilitate the kind of ordering described above.

A more developed example of this letter-based transaction can be seen in *The marchants avizo*, attributed on its titlepage to '*I B* [John Browne] *merchant*', which was first printed in 1589, and went through at least four subsequent editions before 1640, making it one of the most popular of all such manuals.[38] As its titlepage suggests, it was designed for merchants trading with the Iberian peninsula, or rather for those working for them there: it was '*Very necessarie for their sonnes and seruants, when they first send them beyond the seas, as to Spaine and Portingale or other countreyes*'. Browne's instructions are specific to the markets to which the factor is dispatched: he provides 'A briefe instrvction for the Better Knowledge of certaine wares of Portingale, Spaine, and France' (D.iiij.^{r}), notably pepper, cloves, maze, cinnamon, nutmeg, ginger, sugar, calico, salt, cochineal, oils, soap, woad, iron, train oil and wines (D.iiij.^{r}–E.ij.^{r}), the 'weights, measures and values of monies' in Portugal, Spain and France (D^v–D.iij.^{r}), and the models of contract document particular to the Spanish are given (a bill of lading, a letter of remembrance, a bill of exchange, an acquittance, a letter of attorney, a bill of debt, a bond or obligation, and a policy or writing of assurance) (H^r–I.ij.^{r}).

The master explains to the factor how he should proceed when he reaches Spain:

presently vpon your ariuall . . . make diligent inquirie, whether anie ships be bound either to this Port of Bristowe, or to any part of England. And then haue especiall care, that the neerest that commeth to this Port, you write letters by them vnto me, and to them that you haue to deale for, of the arriuall of your ship: according to this plaine and briefe forme of inditing, as I will hereafter shew you. And so write likewise by your first letters, of the state of your businesse, and of the newes of the country, according as that time passeth. And when you haue learned of anie ship that commeth for England, doe not yourselfe make it knowne to anie bodie at all: but write and deliuer your letters secretlie, for it shall sound much to your especiall credit and good liking, when your diligence shall be so seene, that your letters shall shew the first arriuall of your Ship: because it is the thing that euerie Marchant doth especially long after to vnderstand.

(B^{r-v})

As with the London–Stratford correspondence of Richard Quiney, the letters here function *as* the transactions they both arrange and record. Browne's manual includes 'a briefe forme of all such letters as you shall neede to write throughout your whole voyage', models from which he advises his servant not to depart: 'The which forme is effectual & sufficient inough, and may still be obserued, vntill by experience you may learne to indite better you selfe' (B.iiij.^{v}). The types of letters give a sense of the eventualities that the factor might expect: 'A Letter written to your Master, if your ship be forced by weather into any place, before you come to your Port of discharge' (B.iiij.^{v}); 'A Letter to be written to your Master presently upon arriuall at your Port' (C^r); 'A Letter to be written to your Maister, or some other man that is of worship, next after your first letter' (C^v); 'A Letter to be written upon your arriuall from Lisbon vnto your second Port' (C.ij.^{v}); 'A Letter to be sent in that ship where you haue laden goods for any Marchant (C.iij.^{r}); 'A Letter to be writen to one that hath left some busines to doe for him under your handes, there in the Country' (C.iij.^{v}); and so on.

Some of the model letters make clear how the traffic in letters might interact with the exchange of monies and commodities. 'A Letter to be written to a friend, giuing him thanks for some pleasure he hath done for you, and requesting againe some farther good turne of him' (C.iiij.^{r}), for example:

Desiring you hartily yet once more, to let me craue so much your good wil, as to do me againe this one plesure: which is, to deliuer this letter hereinclosed to master P.R. Draper, that dwelleth in Lisbon in *Roa noua*: and that you would receaue for me of him 100. Duckets which I haue written to him to pay you. And when you haue receaued it, that you would be so good as to imploie it all in good pepper, & to set my Masters mark on it, which is as in the margent. Praying you to agree for freyte, and to procure to haue it laden in the *Pleasure*, & to write a letter vnto my Master about it.

(C.iiij.$^{r-v}$)

The enclosed letter will raise one hundred ducats in cash from master P. R., which the friend is to spend on a commodity of pepper, to be shipped on *Pleasure* to the factor's master in England. Note how many letters are involved here: one letter from the factor to his friend; a second from the factor to master P. R.; a third from the friend to the factor's master to confirm this arrangement. The second letter, of course, is a bill of exchange that guarantees the payment of one hundred ducats, but the first and third letters act in a related manner, although not in the text: they contain in the margin the merchant's mark that is to be, and later has been, placed on the casks containing the pepper (illustration 10).[39] So the letters here become the guarantor of the shipment. This interaction is made visually compelling in Holbein's portrait of George Gisze. Attached to his office walls are letters bearing a merchant's mark that have been identified as Gisze's own on contemporary documents—but which can also be seen, in reverse, within a shield on Gisze's seal, which lies on his table (illustration 8).[40]

Now What News on the Rialto?

Antonio is said to be trading with Tripolis, the Indies, Mexico, England, Lisbon, Barbary, and India.[41] As a sitting merchant who does not travel himself, he must transact his trade via factors in these places, through the medium of letters. From the first scene, Antonio is shown waiting for news-bearing letters that do not arrive, and his financial health is ultimately confirmed only by the receipt of a letter (via Portia) in the final scene. But the usual *modus operandi* of the long-haul trade merchant is vividly depicted in a memorable scene set in London's Royal Exchange, the equivalent of Venice's Rialto, in William Haughton's 1598 *English-Men for My Money*,[42] a play that, as Jean Howard has recently argued, reworks many of *The Merchant of Venice*'s motifs to different and comic effect, in an English setting.[43]

The Exchange was the meeting place for London's merchants, and, not coincidentally, the place where posts (letter-bearers) headed for overseas locations could be found. In John Eliot's 1593 French

16   *The Marchants*

good as to imploy it all in good Pepper, and to
set *my masters marke on it, which is as in the
margent. Praying you to agree for freyte, and
to procure to haue it laden in the *Pleasure*, & to
write a letter vnto my Master about it.   I am
sorie that I am driuen to make still so bold vpon you: wishing that you had the like or greater occasion to trie also my good will towards
you.   Little newes I heare worth the writing,
&c. Thus taking my leaue, I commit you to
Almightie God. From Ciuel 25.day of Ianua-
rie 1589.

Your assured to my
power. R.A.

*A Letter to be written to a friend when you
would haue him to pleasure you in
any matter.*

Emanuel.

A Eter my very hartie commendations vnto
you : I pray for your good health and pro-
speritie, &c. These are most hartelie to desire
so much your friendship and good will, to doo
me this pleasure: as to receiue for me out of the
Gabriel when she cometh to S.Lucar, 6.tunnes
of Lead conteining 150.peeces, being marked
as in the * margent: & to doo so much as make
present sale of it , the best you can as the time
serueth. And when you haue made sale and receiued

10. Page from John Browne, *The marchants avizo* (London: William Norton, 1589), C4ᵛ showing the use of merchant's marks in the margin of letters.

conversation manual, *Ortho-Epia Gallica*, the post is highlighted in a chapter on the Exchange:

> Where dwelleth the ordinarie post to Calis, to Bruges, to Antuerpe?
> He dwelleth in the Iewrie.
> At what signe?
> At the white Lyon, at the grenning Iackanapes . . .
> How shall I doe to deliuer him a packet of letters?
> You shall find him vpon the Exchange about halfe an hower after
>   eleuen a clocke.
> But when will he depart, can you tell?
> He will embarke peraduenture with the first tide?
> Where is the wind? It is in the South. It is against him then, it was this
>   morning North North-east.[44]

Each ordinary post had a specific city to which he travelled. Although his dwelling place was known, it was customary to hand over packets of letters on the Exchange itself, at a specified time. But beyond that, the arrangements were out of the post's control, since he left London by ship, and ships were dependent on the tides and the winds. In Haughton's play, the post is portrayed as a young man who bears the physical traces of his travel: one character taunts him by saying 'thou seemes to haue bin in the hot countries, thy face looks so like a peece of rusty Bacon' (C2^r). Letters have been handed to him in Spain; when the ships made their initial English docking at Plymouth, on the south coast, the post disembarked and made his way by land to London's Exchange; the ships themselves will follow (the post estimates that 'the Ships will be come about from *Plimmouth* . . . Next weeke'). When the post arrives, he is immediately mobbed, much to the concern of those characters unaccustomed to Exchange business: 'Sure, yonder fellow will be torne in peeces . . . Whats hee, sweete youths; that so they flocke about.' As the post hands out letters, the tumult suddenly subsides: 'Looke, looke, how busely they fall to reading' (C^r).

The play is at pains to emphasize the unreliability of the Exchange-news brought by the post under these conditions. The

Portuguese-born London usurer Pisaro, trading with Iberian territories, meets a merchant named Towerson who informs him verbally that a south-west wind has 'driuen home our long expected Shippes, | All laden with the wealth of ample *Spaine*', and just yesterday they arrived 'Safely at *Plimmouth*, where they yet abide' (B4ʳ). But this oral news is then altered by letters delivered by Towerson:

> But heare you sir, my businesse is not done;
> From these same Shippes I did receiue these lines,
> And there inclosde this same Bill of exchange,
> To pay at sight; if so you please accept it.
>
> (B4ʳ).

Towerson's polite addendum 'if so you please accept it' is well-chosen, for Pisaro immediately doubts the validity of the letter and of the bill of exchange that he is expected to reimburse, since he has not himself yet received any letters by the post, suspicious that letters may be forged:

> Accept it, why? What sir should I accept,
> Haue you receiued Letters, and not I?
> Where is this lazie villaine, this slow Poast:
> What, brings he euery man his Letters home,
> And makes mee no bodie; does hee, does hee?
> I would not haue you bring me counterfeit;
> And if you doe, assure you I shall smel it:
> I know my Factors writing well enough.
>
> (B4ʳ)

When the post finally hands over his letters, Pisaro, still complaining ('I am the last, you should haue kept it still: | Well, we shall see what newes you bring with you') reads out his factor's letter:

Our duty premised, and we haue sent vnto your worship Sacke, siuill Oyles, Pepper, Barbery sugar, and such other commodities as we thought most requisite, we wanted mony therefore we are fayne to take vp 200 l. of Maister *Towersons* man, which by a bill of Exchange sent to him, we would request your worship pay accordingly. . . . The newes here is, that the English shipes, the Fortune, your shipe, the aduenture and good lucke of

London coasting along by *Italy* Towards *Turky*, were set vpon by to *Spanish-galleis*, what became of them we know not, but doubt much by reason of the weathers calmnesse.

(C^r)

Here, just as in *The marchants avizo*, the merchant's factor writes back to England with information of what has been bought and dispatched on the ship leaving Spain. Just as the letter bears the merchant's marks that will identify the commodities shipped for Pisaro, so it acts as proof of the validity of the bill of exchange issued to Towerson's factor in Spain, which he has forwarded to his master in London.

While *The marchants avizo* presents smooth textbook examples, Haughton's play dramatizes the confusions that epistolary trade can carry. The factor's letter also provides the unwelcome news that three English ships, Pisaro's *Fortune* amongst them, were ambushed by Spanish galleys off the Italian coast on their way to Turkey: 'what became of them we know not, but doubt much by reason of the weathers calmnesse' (C^r). But that news is suddenly pre-empted by information conveyed via Italy, provided in a letter to the Italian merchant Alvaro from his factor, that reports a northerly wind caused such storms on the sea that the Spanish galleys 'run away for feare be almost drownde'(C3^r). Pisaro is unconvinced, and Alvaro has to show him the letter: 'Wil you no beleeue me? see dare dan, see de lettre'(C3^v). News on the Exchange is shown to be unreliable, but the play does not present written information as necessarily superior: instead, it is locally sourced intelligence that takes precedence. So while Pisaro's factor's letter, sent from Spain, is proper evidence for the validity of Towerson's bill of exchange, its knowledge of the incident off the Italian coast is necessarily second-hand ('The newes here is . . .') and proved to be mistaken.

Shakespeare places this desire for epistolary news centrally in *The Merchant of Venice*. The immediate explanation for Salerio and Solanio of Antonio's self-proclaimed sadness is the uncertain status of his argosies, an uncertainty that stems from a lack of letter-news.

Filling the void is rumour, circulating energetically on the Rialto. Salerio recounts how he 'reason'd with a Frenchman yesterday', who told him that in the English Channel 'a vessel of our country richly fraught' had 'miscarried' (2.8.27–32), but his description of this rumour as 'reason'd' soon comes under attack. When Solanio later asks 'Now what news on the Rialto?' (3.1.1), Salerio offers the following, less positive version: 'Why yet it lives there uncheck'd, that Antonio hath a ship of rich lading wrack'd on the narrow seas . . . if my gossip Report be an honest woman of her word' (3.1.2–7). Solanio retorts: 'I would she were as lying a gossip in that, as ever knapp'd ginger, or made her neighbours believe she wept for the death of a third husband: but it is true' (3.1.8–10). The news 'lives there uncheck'd', has a life on the Rialto that has not been restrained, contradicted or stopped (rather than unverified) but the men's characterization is significant. She is 'my gossip Report', merging the traditional sense of 'gossip', a godparent, and by extension an old woman, with a newer notion of an unreliable tattle-tale: here Report is an old woman who munches ginger, and who is given by temperament to lying, faking grief for a third dead husband.

Whereas Solanio and Salerio rely on Rialto gossip they know to be uncertain, Shylock by contrast asks not 'Now what news on the Rialto', but 'How now Tubal! what news from Genoa?' (3.1.72), relying for his intelligence on personally conveyed information from a man with whom he is familiar, who has been to Genoa himself. As it happens, Tubal is forced to relate news that is still on the level of oral gossip, 'heard in Genoa!' as Shylock puts it (3.1.97): 'I often came where I did hear of her, but cannot find her' (3.1.74–5); 'Antonio (as I heard in Genoa) . . . hath an argosy cast away coming from Tripolis' (3.1.89–92); 'Your daughter spent in Genoa, as I heard, one night, fourscore ducats' (3.1.98–9). But Tubal's news items 'heard in Genoa' are then confirmed by personally accredited sources: of Antonio's bad luck, he has confirmation, because 'I spoke with some of the sailors that escaped the wrack' (3.1.94–5) and 'There came divers of Antonio's creditors in my company to Venice, that swear, he cannot choose but break' (3.1.103–05). Above and beyond the creditors' sworn testimony, Tubal has ocular proof: 'One of them showed me a ring that he had of your daughter for a monkey' (3.1.108–9).

The play constantly toys with these different levels of news: written and oral, gossip and personally witnessed. 'What's the news from Venice? | How doth that royal merchant good Antonio?' (3.2.237–8) demands Gratiano in Belmont, of the newcomer from Venice, Salerio. At precisely the same moment, Antonio in Venice informs Bassanio in Belmont by letter: '*My ships have all miscarried*' (3.2.314). Having read the letter silently, Bassanio immediately asks for verification from the man who has come from Venice with the letter: 'But is it true Salerio? | Hath all his ventures fail'd? what not one hit?' (3.2.265–6). Even here, reading a letter in Antonio's hand ('The paper as the body of my friend' (3.2.263)), carried by a man known to both writer and recipient, Bassanio's instinct is to ask for oral confirmation beyond the letter. It is this tension, between written and spoken word, that carries over dramatically into the play's most celebrated confrontation, between Antonio and Shylock.

The Sealed Bond

It is standard critical practice to pit Shylock's bond with Antonio against the openness of the arrangement between Antonio and Bassanio—and then to call the former an instance of usury, the second an instance of charity. This reading, I shall argue, merely reproduces a logic that the play itself is careful to avoid: instead, Shylock and Antonio are depicted as operating in similar ways, for all their rhetoric. For Shylock too is seen to have unsecured financial understandings with his friends: he tells Bassanio and Antonio that he cannot 'instantly raise up the gross | Of full three thousand ducats' but that 'Tubal (a wealthy Hebrew of my tribe) | Will furnish me' (1.3.50–2). Some editors have assumed that this is a rhetorical ploy on Shylock's part: John Russell Brown, for example, quotes the claim of Thomas Bell's 1596 *Speculation of Usury* that the usurer customarily 'protesteth that hee hath no money at all, but that himselfe seeketh where to finde an vsurer'.[45] M. M. Mahood more charitably points out that by involving Tubal in the deal, Shakespeare 'shows that the Jews in Venice follow the injunction of Deut. 23.20 in lending freely to each other and taking interest only of non-Jews'.[46] Following Mahood, it can be argued that both Antonio and Shylock have non-interest-bearing financial dealings within a certain circle.

We might also want to reconsider that understanding between Antonio and Bassanio. 'My purse, my person, my extremest means | Lie all unlock'd to your occasions' (1.1.138–9), Antonio offers initially. It soon becomes clear that this offer *is* rhetorical: Antonio's purse is empty, because 'all my fortunes are at sea', both in terms of 'money' and 'commodity'. It is at this point, and for this reason, that he has to turn to his 'credit' to finance his friend:

> therefore go forth
> Try what my credit can in Venice do,—
> That shall be rack'd even to the uttermost
> To furnish thee to Belmont to fair Portia.
> Go presently inquire (and so will I)
> Where money is, and I no question make
> To have it of my trust, or of my sake.
>
> (1.1.179–85)

That final line, lost in the scene's concluding couplet, is significant: Antonio still holds out hope that he can raise credit 'of my sake', for himself, simply because people love him. But as becomes evident two scenes later, neither his 'sake' (for himself) nor his 'trust' (his credit) is enough, and he has to turn to a money-lender.

The deal that Bassanio strikes with Shylock is specific in terms of the monies involved, the duration of the loan, and the nature of contract—'Three thousand ducats for three months, and Antonio bound' (1.3.8–9), which means that Shylock 'may take his bond' (1.3.24). Later, Shylock reiterates the nature and terms of the bond:

> Go with me to a notary, seal me there
> Your single bond, and (in a merry sport)
> If you repay me not on such a day
> In such a place, such sum or sums as are
> Express'd in the condition, let the forfeit
> Be nominated for an equal pound
> Of your fair flesh, to be cut off and taken
> In what part of your body pleaseth me.
>
> (1.3.140–7)

Initially, Shylock offers a 'single bond', one without a condition; but then, 'in a merry sport' he proposes a ludicrous penalty. Since Shylock is known to be a usurer, critical commentary on this bond has often deemed it to be usurious. But Shylock does not stand here to make any financial profit by interest, and the forfeit seems to be a 'merry sport'. This is why Antonio remarks 'The Hebrew will turn Christian: he grows kind', and even Bassanio admits that these are 'fair terms', even if preferred by 'a villain's mind' (1.3.174–5).

The sport loses its merriment, however, when Shylock loses his daughter, and he determines that Antonio's flesh 'will feed my revenge' (3.1.48). In court, he shows absolute allegiance to the wording of the obligation: 'Ay, his breast, | So says the bond, doth it not noble judge? | "Nearest his heart", those are the very words' (4.1.248–50); when Balthasar suggests that a surgeon should be on hand to staunch Antonio's bleeding, Shylock objects, 'Is it so nominated in the bond? . . . I cannot find it, 'tis not in the bond' (4.1.255, 258). Some have seen the battle between Shylock and Portia/Balthasar as predicting the forthcoming struggle between the common-law courts and the courts of equity;[47] others have detected a dramatization of changes in understanding of the law of obligation that culminated in the fin-de-siècle *Slade's Case*.[48] But in fact, both Shylock *and* Balthasar insist on the wording of the bond, and it is that adherence that Balthasar ultimately uses to stymie Shylock's plans: 'This bond doth give thee here no jot of blood, | The words expressly are "a pound of flesh" ' (4.1.302–03).

Although we may find the sealed bond an alien concept, it would have been all too familiar to Shakespeare's audience. As Craig Muldrew has shown, 'By far the most important form of indebtedness after sales and service credit—certainly much more important than moneylending—was lending on sealed bonds.'[49] C.W. Brooks agrees: the bond 'was the most significant single legal ligament in early modern society, a fact which is no less true because it has received so little attention from scholars'.[50] The reason for the bond's popularity were clear, according to Muldrew: 'Bonds were a much more secure form of lending, and took the form of either writings, or bills, obligatory, which had to be written in proper legal form. They were often drawn up by a lawyer or scrivener, and then signed and sealed by two witnesses, and many had penal clauses.'[51] Shylock is insistent that the bond should be drawn up by a notary and sealed ('Go with me to a notary, seal me there | Your single bond', 'meet me forthwith at the notary's' (1.3.140–1, 168)). In its form, his bond is quite particular. 'Most bonds did not state a specific date of payment, nor was there any penalty listed for non-payment', Muldrew continues: indeed, most bonds 'still left a great deal of room for discretion by leaving the date of repayment negotiable if the debtor could not pay on time'. So in its particularity, Shylock's bond corresponds to the English 'bill obligatory', often known as an 'obligation'. Shakespeare uses the term in this sense only once when it is satirically claimed that Justice Shallow 'writes himself *Armigero*, in any bill, warrant, quittance, or obligation' (*MW* 1.1.8–9), but as I shall argue, imagery associated with the obligation permeates *The Merchant of Venice*. In what was known as the 'condition', the bill obligatory 'set a date on which payment was required (and often the place where the payment was to be made), and a specified penalty of about 100 per cent if the debtor failed to pay by the specified date'.[52] Clearly Shylock's suggested 'forfeiture' (1.3.160) is a bizarre twist on the usual penalty of 100 per cent, but that more common forfeiture is precisely what Portia automatically suggests ('Pay him six thousand, and deface the bond', 3.2.298) and what Bassanio, acting for Antonio, first offers in the courtroom ('For thy three thousand ducats here is six'; 'twice the sum', 4.1.84, 206).

This understanding of the obligation also helps to explain the movement of the court scene. As S. F. C. Milsom notes, in debt on an obligation, 'when the plaintiff had a sealed deed, questions of proof were effectively excluded'.[53] The defendant's only real defence was to prove that the document was not his deed (*non est factum suum*)— either that it was not a deed, that it was forged, that he was illiterate and the contents had been misread to him, that the bond had been tampered with, or that it had been made at a time of incapacity or under particular duress. But if those objections could not be made— and when Balthazar asks 'Do you confess the bond?' Antonio replies, 'I do' (4.1.179–80)—then there was no further debate to be had. So when Balthazar says 'Then must the Jew be merciful', his meaning is not necessarily one of 'compulsion', as Shylock takes it (4.1.178–9), but simply the legal fact of the matter: since there is a sealed bond that the defendant confesses, then its terms stand, and the only way out of this situation is for the Jew not to take what is legally his.

Indeed, the sealed bond's power was such in English law that it continued to operate even after the debt had been repaid unless the bond were destroyed, if for example, the obligee stole back the bond and sued on it. The onus was on the obligor to obtain an acquittance, similarly sealed, stating that the money was repaid, or, more simply, have the bond destroyed, hence the insistence of Balthazar that they 'deface the bond', 'bid me tear the bond' (3.2.298, 4.1.230). In this instance, as legal historian J. H. Baker notes, 'there was no way in the world that a valid deed could be contradicted by oral evidence'.[54] Baker quotes the landmark 1542 case of *Waberley v. Cockerel*, where the ruling went with the bond against what had actually occurred: it was declared that it was 'better to suffer a mischief to one man than an inconvenience to many, which would subvert the law. For if matter in writing could be so easily defeated and avoided by such a surmise, by naked breath, a matter in writing would be of no greater authority than a matter of fact.'[55] *Waberley v. Cockerel* here rehearses an argument in Christopher St German's much published dialogue, *Doctor and Student*, in which a doctor attempts to push a law student on questions relating to English law. Significantly, the very first point on which the Doctor challenges the English law on grounds of conscience and reason is precisely this point about sealed conditional bonds:

I haue heard say, that if a man that is bound in an Obligation pay the money, but he taketh no acquitaunce, or if he take one and it happeneth him to leese it, that in that case he shall bee compelled by the lawes of Englande to pay the money againe, And howe may it be said then, that that Lawe standeth with reason and conscience? For as it is grounded vpon the Lawe of reason, that debtes ought of right to be payed, so it is grounded vpon the Lawe of reason (as mee seemeth) that when [t]hey be paid that he that payed them shoulde be discharged.

(C.vi.^{r})

The Student replies, that it is not the case that, in such a case, 'the law determineth *that* he ought of ryght to pay the money eftsoones [a second time]'. Indeed, such a law 'were both against reason and conscience', but

there is a generall Maxime in *the* law of England, that in an action of debt sued vpon an Obligation, the defendant shall not pled that he oweth not the mony, ne can in no wise discharge himself in that action, but he haue acquitance or some other writing sufficient in the law, or some other thing like, witnessing that he hath paied the mony, and that it is ordained by the lawe to auoide a great inconuenience that els might happen to come to many people, that it so say, that euery man by a *Nude paroll* and by a bare *Auerrement* should auoide an Obligation. Wherefore to auoid that inconuenience the law hath ordained that as the defendant is charged by a sufficient writing, that so he must be discharged by sufficient writing, or by some other thing of as high aucthoritie as the obligation is.

(C.vi.$^{\text{r-v}}$)

So Shylock's insistence on the primacy of the sealed bond, and Balthazar's assent to that primacy, is entirely in line with English law: indeed, it is the first lesson that has to be learned by fledgling lawyers, precisely because it appears to go against conscience and reason.[56] The Student points out that 'a *Nude paroll* and ... a bare *Auerrement*' cannot be allowed to 'auoide' [make void] a sealed bond. And as Shylock says, as if ventriloquizing the bond, 'There is no power in the tongue of man | To alter me,—I stay here on my bond' (4.1.237–8). This is not the first time that Shylock pits his bond against another man's speech: 'I'll have my bond, speak not against my bond', he tells Antonio four times within a dozen lines: 'I'll have my bond. I will not hear thee speak, | I'll have my bond, and therefore speak no more. | ... I'll have no speaking, I will have my bond' (3.3.4–5, 12–13, 16). The English law's pitting of bond versus *paroll* is manipulated dramatically, as is the law's fear that the acceptance of *paroll* against a bond would lead to 'a great inconuenience that els might happen to come to many people', in the words of the Student. It is no accident that Shylock's formulation 'There is no power in the tongue of man | To alter me' (4.1.237–8) directly echoes Balthazar's dictum that 'there is no power in Venice | Can alter a decree established: | 'Twill be recorded for a President, | And many an error by the same example, | Will rush into the state' (4.1.214–18)'.

It would be wrong to read from this that Antonio stands for *paroll*, and Shylock for the bond. For there is a sly pun here that takes us somewhere else: Shylock refuses the strength of *paroll* as speech, 'the tongue of man', while uttering these words precisely as a *paroll*, an oath of honour: 'by my soul I swear' (4.1.236–7). Indeed, while Shylock stands on his bond, he does it through an insistent oath-swearing: 'by our holy Sabbath have I sworn | To have the due and forfeit of my bond', he declares to the Duke (4.1.36–7), and later to Balthazar he says, aghast, 'An oath, an oath, I have an oath in heaven,—| Shall I lay perjury upon my soul? | No not for Venice' (4.1.224–6). This oath is first mentioned when Shylock entrusts Antonio to the gaoler: 'I'll have my bond, speak not against my bond, | I have sworn an oath, that I will have my bond' (3.3.4–5), perhaps an oath sworn in the synagogue where he earlier purposed to meet Tubal (3.1.118–20): despite his constant standing on his bond against the *nude paroll* of Antonio, Shylock's stance is preceded by the swearing of a solemn, holy oath. And in this apparent contradiction, we get to the heart of the sealed obligation. What the bond contains, ultimately, is an oath under seal. The standard English bond would contain, in Latin, the form: 'Know all men etc. that I, *AB*, am firmly bound to *CD* in £*n* to be paid at Michaelmas next following.'[57] As George Norbury puts it in his widely circulated analysis of 'The Abuses and Remedies of Chancery' (1621), 'a man's bond under hand and seale is his oathe, whereby he testifieth before all men'.[58] The bond captures the moment when the oath is sworn in front of witnesses—that moment captured by the sealing of the bond witnessed by a notary.

This complex association of, and opposition of, bond and oath is ironically recapitulated in the final scene, as Bassanio and Gratiano try to rehabilitate themselves in the favour of their wives, after giving away their rings. '[I]n the hearing of these many friends', insists Bassanio, 'I swear to thee, even by thine own fair eyes | Wherein I see myself—' (5.1.240–3). Portia's response is devastating, as she literalizes his metaphor of seeing himself in her eyes: 'In both my eyes he doubly sees himself: | In each eye one,—swear by your double self, | And there's an oath of credit' (5.1.244–6). As she mocks his 'oath of credit', Bassanio makes one final attempt, and in so doing unconsciously repeats Shylock's self-defeating oath-swearing of the trial scene: 'Pardon this fault, and by my soul I swear | I never more will break an oath with thee' (5.1.247–8). As he has earlier told Balthasar, Portia 'made me vow' that he would not sell, give or lose it (4.1.438–9). Now, having broken that oath, he swears, probably by the same oath, never to 'break an oath' with her. The redundancy of this latest oath is self-evident: Portia does not even have to repudiate it. It is at this point that Antonio intervenes, tacitly bettering Bassanio's swearing and oaths with the offer of a new bond:

> I once did lend my body for his wealth,
> ...   I dare be bound again,
> My soul upon the forfeit, that your lord
> Will never more break faith advisedly.
>
> (5.1.249–53)

Portia takes him up on the offer, handing him a ring and telling Antonio to 'bid [Bassanio] keep it better than the other', and that, in doing this, 'you shall be his surety' (5.1.254–5). The term is, of course, loaded: in this new arrangement, Antonio will stand liable for Bassanio's debt to Portia. Antonio turns to Bassanio and hands over the ring: 'Here, Lord Bassanio, swear to keep this ring' (5.1.256). But Bassanio never swears: instead, he is sidetracked by the revelation that the ring is the same ring he gave to the doctor. Even at the end of the play, it seems, *paroll* and bond exist in an uneasy relationship to each other.

Obliged Faith: Sealing Love's Bonds

The sealed bond, the bill obligatory, is thus at the centre of *The Merchant of Venice*'s transactions. But, as I shall suggest, its terms creep into several other relationships in the play. The English 'bill obligatory' was also known as a 'letter obligatory'[59] and, although the bond did not necessarily resemble an epistle, it possesses characteristics in common with letters. First, it is a written transaction between two people. Second, in mercantile terms, letters, and bonds have a similar function: merchants' manuals suggest they should be filed and archived in the same manner. Third, and most importantly to this discussion, both bonds and letters are sealed. Indeed, some obligations remaining in Richard Quiney's papers at Stratford-upon-Avon, are written on the same paper, and with a similar layout to his letters.[60] As I shall show, Shakespeare is at pains to point up the parallels between this sealed bond and the other letters of the play.

The language of sealing is extended, for example, to comment on the relationship of Lorenzo and Jessica. As they wait for Lorenzo to arrive on the night of Jessica's escape, Salerio comments, 'O ten times faster Venus' pigeons fly | To seal love's bonds new-made, than they are wont | To keep obliged faith unforfeited!' (2.6.5–7).[61] The words 'seal', 'bonds', 'obliged', and 'unforfeited' conjure up the image of a sealed bond obligatory carrying a forfeit: they claim that lovers are keener to 'seal love's bonds' (the moment when cash is paid out), than to hold to the terms of the bond ('keep[ing] obliged faith') and avoid the penalty ('unforfeited'). The image is particularly telling here, because the speakers are remarking on Lorenzo's tardiness: 'it is marvel he out-dwells his hour, | For lovers ever run before the clock' (2.6.3–4). Lorenzo is late like an uneager, long-term lover, constrained by contract, might be late; Lorenzo himself acknowledges his tardiness, claiming 'Not I but my affairs have made you wait' (2.6.22). Here we have the first inkling here that all is not well with the Lorenzo-Jessica match. Is their relationship, like the enforced relationship of Antonio and Shylock, now a conditional bond carrying a forfeit?

Other letters may be profitably considered through the prism of the sealed bond. The terms of the forfeit push Antonio into issuing his own letter to Bassanio.

Sweet Bassanio, my ships haue all miscarried, my creditors grow cruel, my estate is very low, my bond to the Jew is forfeit, and (since in paying it, it is impossible I should live). all debts are clear'd between you and I, if I might see you at my death: notwithstanding, use your pleasure,—if your loue do not persuade you to come, let not my letter.

(3.2.314–20)

The specific charge of this letter can be seen by comparing it to the corresponding moment in Shakespeare's source story. In Ser Giovanni Fiorentino's *Il Pecorone* (1558), day 4, story 1, this one demand by the older man Ansaldo of his young godson Giannetto is made verbally before Giannetto sets out: 'My son, you are going and you see the bond under which I stand. I ask of you one promise, that should any misfortune occur, you will please come back to me, so that I may see you before I die, and with that die content.' Giannetto replies, 'Messer Ansaldo, I will do anything to please you.'[62] When the due date (the feast of St John) arrives, Ansaldo pleads with the Jew for a few days' respite 'so that, if his dear Giannetto arrived, he might at least see him once more', which gives Giannetto time to return.[63] But in Shakespeare's play, this promise is in a letter—and one, I would argue, that demands to be understood as a variant on the letter obligatory to which Antonio set his seal with Shylock. It couches his relationship with Bassanio in the language of debt, and the clearance of debt. The letter draws attention to itself, as it speaks: '*if your love do not persuade you to come, let not my letter*'. But this is disingenuous: it is precisely the letter that persuades Bassanio, since it carries its own penalty clause—'*all debts are clear'd between you and I, if I might see you at my death*'. And if not, what happens? Does Bassanio owe Antonio's executors three thousand ducats? This letter, I argue, raises the spectre that Antonio's provision of monies to Bassanio was not without its own forfeit, at least in Antonio's mind.

This might give us pause in accepting the initial dealings between Antonio and Bassanio as open-hearted charity. Bassanio's voyage to Bellemont is a venture that is couched in terms of amorous pursuit, but is of course also a hard-headed financial speculation, since Portia is a very valuable portion or dowry. Bassanio is asking Antonio to invest in a venture with high profit-margins; his agreement comes with its own demands. Bassanio's ensuing explanation to Portia of the situation makes plain the analogy between his dealings with Antonio, and Antonio's dealings with Shylock: 'I have engag'd myself to a dear friend, | Engag'd my friend to his mere enemy | To feed my means' (3.2.260–2). The repetition of 'engag'd' not only renders the Bassanio-Antonio arrangement analogous to the Antonio-Shylock arrangement, but also recalls Bassanio's earlier description to Antonio of their relationship: he talks of

> the great debts
> Wherein my time (something too prodigal)
> Hath left me gag'd: to you Antonio
> I owe the most in money and in love,
> And from your love I have a warranty
> To unburthen all my plots and purposes
> How to get clear of all the debts I owe.
>
> (1.1.128–34)

The torturous logic of this speech lays bare the contradictions of Bassanio's resorting to Antonio to get free of his debts. He is 'gag'd' to his debts, as he will be 'engag'd ... to a dear friend' Antonio, and Antonio 'Engag'd' (by Bassanio) to Shylock. But his chief creditor—the one to whom he 'owe[s] the most in money and in love'—is Antonio. Both Antonio and his debts are creditors, but Antonio's love provides him with 'a warranty' that will allow him to rid himself of 'all the debts I owe'.

My point here, then, is that instead of portraying neatly opposed systems—usury versus charity, Judaism versus Christianity, contractual literalism versus merciful equity—all the relationships of the play are better understood on a sliding scale of credit relationships. While the Shylock-Antonio transaction clearly requires a sealed bond to assure it, Shakespeare shows how the supposedly openhearted relationships between Antonio and Bassanio and between Lorenzo and Jessica are also implicated in such forfeitful credit transactions, with their language of sealed bonds and acquittances. And in each case, these analogies and parallels are pointed up in performance through a particular piece of stage business, the physical delivery of a sealed letter.

When Lancelot Gobbo reaches Lorenzo and his friends with a letter from Jessica, Lorenzo asks, 'friend Launcelot what's the news' (2.4.9). Lancelot's response is significant. As he hands over the letter, he draws attention to the fact that it is sealed: 'And it shall please you to break up this, shall it seem to signify' (2.4.10–11); the letter's message will become clear, when the seal is broken. Similarly, when Salerio hands over Antonio's letter to Bassanio, the breaking open of the letter is dramatically delayed. 'Ere I ope his letter,' says Bassanio, 'I pray you tell me how my good friend doth.' Salerio evades the question by focusing attention again on the unopened letter: 'Not sick my lord, unless it be in mind, | Nor well, unless in mind: his letter there | Will show you his estate' (3.2.233–5). In both the Quarto and Folio editions of the play, there follows the instruction, *'Opens the Letter'*. This is a rare stage direction: there are plenty of *'Reads the Letter'* cues in early printed play-texts, but very few placing emphasis instead simply on the *opening* of a letter; furthermore, we do not hear the letter's content until about eighty lines later. The reason Shakespeare draws attention to the breaking open of the seal, I suggest, is to make clear the analogy between the sealed letter from Jessica to Lorenzo, the sealed letter from Antonio to Bassanio, and the sealed bond between Shylock and Antonio.

Three Final Letters

The play ends, as we've seen, with the breaking open of further sealed letters: one containing an explanation of the plot, another providing assurance of Antonio's continued financial sufficiency, and a final sealed letter, 'a special deed of gift' that assures the financial stability of Jessica and Lorenzo (5.1.293). The critical opprobrium levelled at the letter Portia hands over to Antonio has taken the heat off another suspicious epistle: Bellario's letter from Padua. This is supposed to provide evidence of Portia's impersonation as Balthazar, and Nerissa's as her clerk, which is, of course, the truth. But this Doctor Bellario, Portia's legal expert cousin, has already provided a letter in which he 'doth commend | A young and learned doctor in our court' (4.1.143–4). The letter is read aloud in full by the duke:

Your grace shall understand, that at the receipt of your letter I am very sick, but in the instant that your messenger came, in loving visitation was with me a young doctor of Rome, his name is Balthazar: I acquainted him with the cause in controversy between the Jew and Antonio the merchant, we turn'd o'er many books together, he is furnished with my opinion, which (bettered with his own learning, the greatness whereof I cannot enough commend), comes with him at my importunity, to fill up your grace's request in my stead. I beseech you let his lack of years be no impediment to let him lack a reverend estimation, for I never knew so young a body with so old a head: I leave him to your gracious acceptance, whose trial shall better publish his commendation.

(4.1.150–62)

Most of this is untrue. The young lawyer is not Balthazar, not a man, not a doctor of Rome, not of great learning. He and Bellario have not even 'turn'd o'er many books together', since, as Portia advises her messenger Balthazar, Bellario is required only to send 'notes and garments' (3.4.51) back with Balthazar, not to meet with Portia.

There is some indication that this episode was not fully conceptualized: in all early editions of the play, Portia instructs her messenger to give the letter to her cousin Doctor Bellario in Mantua (3.4.49n.) but all other references to Bellario place him in Padua which was well known to early modern England as a centre for civil law training.[64] Similarly, Portia's messenger is named Balthazar, the name she will take for her male lawyer *alter ego*. Nonetheless, Shakespeare deliberately moves beyond Giovanni's notion of having the Portia-figure merely claim to be 'a young lawyer who had finished his studies at Bologna'. In making the case for one of literature's most eloquent pleas for mercy, *The Merchant of Venice* has its voice, Balthazar/Portia, be a cross-dressed imposter, bolstered by a recommendation from a lying family member, and this lie is transacted by a letter of recommendation. The sealed bond is then undone by a lawyer with fake letter-credentials. And that same writer, and the same medium, is the source for the evidence of the play's plot. In other words, perhaps critics are right to see something awry with Portia's neat production of letters bringing the play to its conclusion. But if we are to undo the ending in this way, we have to consider what it means to the rest of the play. If we are suspicious of the letter that guarantees Antonio his continued solvency, then we must also be suspicious of the letter that will tell the plot, sourced as it is from the phantom Bellario who provides the false credentials for Balthazar as a judge. Or perhaps we should treat Antonio's final speech with more attention: 'Sweet lady, you have given me life and living' (5.1.286). In a play where giving never happens without the incurring of debt, what does Antonio now owe to Portia?

The letters that Portia gives to Bassanio and Antonio are thematically the logical climax of a play that has dealt extensively not only in letters, but in the ways in which letters are used. Letters are essential to the long-distance trade dealings of a merchant such as Antonio; a specific sort of letter, the sealed bill of obligation, constitutes the crux of Antonio's deal with Shylock, and of Shylock's encounter with Venetian law; a letter enforces Bassanio's return to Venice; letters allow Portia in Belmont to correspond with Bellario in Padua, and allow Bellario in Padua to accredit Portia-as-Balthazar in Venice; and letters provide the proofs—narrative, mercantile, and of a transfer of property—that will bring the play to its ostensibly happy end. In deploying letters in this multitude of ways, however, Shakespeare does not provide a happy ending: instead he brings vividly into relief the relations between mercantile trade, moneylending, and legal evidence—and forces a meditation on the discrepancy between the written word and what Shylock derides as 'the power of the tongue'.

5

The Matter of Messengers in *King Lear*

EDMUND   How now, what's the matter?.....
GLOUCESTER ...What's the matter here?
CORNWALL ...What is the matter?
REGAN   The messengers from our sister and the King. (*KL*, 2.2.43–9)

∼

At Gloucester's house, Kent, in disguise, and Goneril's steward Oswald enter '*severally*', (2.2.0 SD) and soon fall into a slanging match that ends with Kent striking Oswald with his sword, and Oswald calling out 'Help, ho! Murder, murder!' (2.2.42). Edmund, Cornwall, Regan, and Gloucester rush in, and in turn the three men ask, in almost identical words, 'what is the matter?' Regan's response, 'The messengers from our sister and the King', a statement in the quarto editions, and a question in the Folio, appears at first glance to be less of an explanation of the 'matter', and more a simple identification of the parties involved. But, as this chapter will suggest, 'messengers' *are* the matter here.

As Stanley Wells puts it in a nice understatement, *King Lear* calls for the props department to supply 'rather a lot of letters'.[1] In fact, more letters appear on stage in *King Lear* than in any other Shakespearean play, while yet more letters, unseen on stage, are mentioned, discussed, and take on dramatic importance. The first is held by Edmund, quickly hidden, and then demanded by Gloucester in 1.2: a letter penned by Edmund, but signed as Edgar, and supposedly thrown in at his closet window. Oswald writes a letter in Goneril's name which he then takes to Regan (1.4). Lear writes a letter to Regan, which is taken by Kent, disguised as Caius (1.5). Kent receives and reads a letter from Cordelia (2.2), and perhaps sends a letter to her with his ring (3.1). Gloucester speaks of receiving a dangerous letter that he is hiding in his closet (3.3); Edmund steals it and gives it to Cornwall (3.5), who gives it to Goneril (3.7), to be shown to Albany. A messenger delivers a letter from Regan to Goneril (4.2) demanding an answer. A gentleman reports to Kent on Cordelia's response to his letter (4.3). Oswald, en route with a letter to Edmund from Goneril, is intercepted by Regan (4.5), but refuses her demand to show her the letter. Lear may show the blind Gloucester a penned 'challenge', to which Gloucester replies, 'Were all thy letters suns, I could not see one' (4.6.136). As Edgar kills Oswald, the steward asks him to deliver letters to Edmund (4.6.241–95): Edgar reads out a letter from Goneril. Edgar hands over the letter to Albany, asking him to read it later; Edmund gives Albany a 'note' of the enemy's forces (5.1). Edmund gives another 'note' to a captain to be delivered to the gaol, while a herald reads out a challenge from Edmund, and Albany confronts Goneril with the letter she wrote to Edmund (5.3). Even ignoring the notes and challenges, there are eight letters in the play that appear in twelve scenes of the play, two of which are read aloud on stage.

King Lear is thus a play riddled with letters—letters written, letters delivered, letters read, letters forged, letters recalled, letters denied. Since the time of A.C. Bradley at the turn of the twentieth century, critics have drawn attention to the play's letter communications, and

especially to how perverse they are.[2] Rather than present straightforward missives, the play dwells on letters that are forged, intercepted,
undelivered, and misdelivered, and the epistolary transactions are
obscured, confusing, and even preposterous. But far from being
an inconsistent mess, as some critics have alleged, the epistolary
transactions are more firmly and particularly plotted in this play
than in any other Shakespeare drama. By tracing the play through
its letters—a process that the playwright has, I admit, deliberately
made as difficult as possible—we can find a consistent attempt to
reconceptualize the relationships between individuals, and the letters and messengers that facilitate and maintain them. For, as I
shall argue, above all, the letters of *King Lear* are letters that are
delivered, letters that turn men of all social stations—Edmund, Kent,
Oswald, Edgar, Albany, and one or two nameless gentlemen—into
messengers. The quarrel between the two messengers brings to
centre-stage the question of how characters communicate with each
other, the inter-relatedness of message and messenger, of letter and
letter-bearer. This chapter will suggest that it is in conflicting ways
of being messengers that we find the central opposition of the play,
oft invoked in criticism of the last century. Or, as Cornwall asks
explicitly as he confronts Oswald and Kent, these two 'messengers'
on parallel missions 'from our sister and the King', 'What is your
difference?' (2.2.50).

'Messenger and familiar speeche'

For Erasmus of Rotterdam, letters are famously 'a kind of mutual
exchange of speech between absent friends'.[3] Throughout the sixteenth century, this notion, repeated in every letter-writing manual
and textbook, became hardened into a truism. 'A letter of epistle,
is the thyng alone *that* maketh men present which are absent',
writes Myles Coverdale.[4] 'An Epistle or letter is a kinde of conference or communication, of one that is absent, with another that is

not present', says the scholar in Abraham Fleming's *A Panoplie of Epistles*.[5] At first glance, Angel Day's opening gambit in his popular *The English Secretarie* (1586) does no more than provide another echo of Erasmus' dictum: *'Touching an Epistle*, which usually we terme a letter, no other definition needeth therof, that wherein is expresslye conueied in writing, the intent and meaning of one man, imme- diately to passe and be directed to an other, and for the certaine respects thereof, is termed the messenger and familiar speeche of the absent.'[6] But by the end of his first sentence, almost impercep- tibly, Day has departed from his Erasmian model, when he glosses the letter in that combination image: 'the messenger and familiar speeche of the absent'.[7] The bifurcation of the letter into messenger and familiar speech is important; for while the letter may contain the standard conceit of the absent friend's speech, the messenger is not purely metaphoric: it betrays the fact that the letter cannot exist without 'the messenger', that the messenger is part of the letter.

Every early modern letter required a messenger, and who the messenger was mattered. Much of the correspondence of early modern England was not carried by the employees of impersonal, organized postal systems, but by identifiable and often personally known individuals. These might be the carriers or the royal post making journeys up and down England's thoroughfares, a feed rider or runner, or a household servant whose sole mission was to deliver a single letter to a particular person. These letters *rely* for their meaning on a specific messenger whose employment as bearer impinges on, or indeed creates, the conditions of the relationship between writer and recipient. He is the third party, without whom these letters would not come into being. In Angel Day's exemplary letters, the messenger is a constant presence. One writer writes to his friend, 'attending by the returne of this messenger the newes of your good health' (D4[r–v]), while another uses the bearer to carry ten pounds in money 'which I pray you of all loues see disbursed to his vses' (H[v]). The crucial component of some messages is not contained in the letter, but is conveyed by the messenger orally:

'Sir I am so bolde in my great necessitie . . . to entreate your especiall ayde and furtheraunce in two thinges, the one whereof this bearer shall instruct you in' (M5^v); 'This bearer shall informe you of some especiall causes, concerning my affaires in the country, whom I do pray you to conferre with . . .'. (N2^v). Sometimes a messenger's duties might extend further—'I haue sent this bearer to attend you to those places' (M8^r)—or sometimes he merely needed to be paid off 'depending vpon your courteous dismission of this bearer' (Q8^r). A messenger could be used to further the correspondence, allowing the writer to set the terms of later transactions: 'Meane while I woulde gladlye be informed by the returne of this messenger, at what time I maye expect to see you, according to which I will appoint horses, and send some vp to accompanye you' (L4^v); 'The messenger I haue appointed to morrow morning to retourne againe to my lodging, at which time I will not fayle to finishe, what in the best sort I can conceaue to be vnto your occasions most fur-thering' (M6^r). Sometimes the bearer could serve as the means for establishing a new relationship, as when the writer claims, 'This bearer and my seruant whom I greatly credite, hath signified vnto me manye matters tending to your great commendation' (L4^r). But occasionally the bearer was not to be trusted, because he was not familiar with the letter's content: 'I praye you sir acquaint not this bearer with the cause, who thereunto is as yet a straunger' (M8^{r-v}). The messenger also provided a direct and effective means of pro-moting the cause of a particular person. *The English Secretorie* has several examples of letters carried by the very men those letters are discussing. A bearer might carry a letter that contained his own complaint or petition or suit, with the support of the writer;[8] or a letter of personal recommendation from the writer.[9] The genre was so established that Day was able to provide a parody, 'A Letter Commendatorie pleasantly conceited in preferring an vnprofitable seruaunt', in which the bearer is accused, at length, of being a hope-less drunk, glutton and general slattern—and a bad messenger: '*if you haue occasion to credite him with a small parcell of money in dispatche*

*of a iourny, doe but say the word, that it shal once lie in his charge, and
you may stand assured, that it shalbe laid vp so safe, as any liquor in the
worlde can safe conduct it from his bellie'* (N7ᵛ–N8ᵛ).

For a first-hand glimpse into the mechanics of personal letter-
carrying and message delivery in élite circles, we can turn briefly
to a letter written by the young Francis Bacon during his time in
the household of Sir Amias Paulet, Elizabeth's ambassador to the
French king, from 1576 to 1579. At some point, probably in 1577,
Paulet sent Bacon with a packet of letters to the English court.[10]
Leaving Paris on Friday, Bacon arrives at court the following Tuesday afternoon; he writes back to Paulet on the Wednesday with a
report of his progress. The letter tells how he went first to Secretary
of State Sir Francis Walsingham, whom he found 'scant well at ease;
and delyue*r*ed vnto him my chardge of L*ett*res beinge laide vppon
his bedd'. Walsingham 'opened them and rendred vnto me twoo
L*ett*res directed to my Lo*r*d of Leicester to deliu*er* wi th mine owe
hand*es*', saying that he could see the others 'deliu*er*ed him self'.
The Secretary dismissed Bacon, and he 'repayred to my Lo*r*d of
Leice*s*te*r*s Chamber whome I found there wi th the Queene'. Astutely
realizing this was not the most opportune moment to interrupt,
Bacon 'thought good to wayte vppon my Lo*r*d Tresaurer', his uncle
William Cecil, Lord Burghley, to deliver Paulet's letter to him. Luckily, their paths crossed: 'Yt was my chaunce to meete him between
the Courte and his howse, and there he receyved of me the saide
L*ett*re and toulde me that he woulde speake wi th me farther some
oth*er* time'. An hour later, as instructed, Bacon 'attended on him
at his Chamber', but Burghley was not there; instead, Bacon 'went
thence into the pa*r*ke where I spake wi th him, and receyved of
him many good word*es*', as Burghley told him that 'her ma*i*esties
meaninge was I should com me to her p*r*esence that eveninge'. Bacon
raised the question of a verbal message he had from Paulet for
Burghley, but his uncle said 'he woulde heare it at his firste leasure'. Shortly afterwards, Bacon 'founde her ma*i*estie in the gardenie
(*sic*) where it pleased her ma*i*estie to vse vnto me so manye and

so gratious woord*es* as coulde not be vttered in most ample and effectuall sorte'. There he was also greeted by Leicester, to whom he delivered the relevant letters. Later, returning to Burghley, he was once again 'put ou*er*' (put off) 'towchinge my messuage vntill some oth*er* tyme'. At the time of writing, Bacon reports, he still had not been able to deliver his message to Burghley.[11]

This letter is instructive on several counts. First, it testifies to the absolutely peronalized nature of letter delivery at this exalted level of society: Bacon has to encounter Walsingham, Burghley, the queen and Leicester in person to hand over their letters (although Walsingham takes responsibility for conveying other, less important letters). Second, it makes explicit the way in which envoys had to memorize messages to be given orally to particular recipients. Third, it reveals the importance of reporting back how letters are received: to a modern reader, Bacon may seem to be boasting of the 'good word*es*' he won from Burghley, Leicester, or the queen, but they are in fact a signal to Paulet as to how his letters have been received. It would not be enough for Bacon to write that he had delivered all the letters, and was still waiting an opportunity to pass the verbal message to Burghley. Instead, he has to detail when and where each letter was handed over, and what the response was.

It is this still crucial field of personally conveyed letter, with its particular dynamics of delivery, reception, report and response, with which *King Lear* is centrally concerned. The Shakespearean messenger is often seen as a bit-player, to be ignored alongside the proverbial spear-carrier. Usually unidentified, his function simply to bring news from another location to propel the action forward. But Shakespeare toyed with this necessary convention to great effect in many of his plays. Often news is received staggered between several messengers; sometimes those messengers bring conflicting intelligence to be weighed. But Shakespeare also shows an interest in assessing the nature not only of the news or intelligence, but also of the messenger.

In the opening scene of *Henry IV Part Two*, for example, Bardolph claims to have 'certain news from Shrewsbury' that the king is wounded, and Prince Harry killed (1.1.12, 14–20). Northumberland needs to know his source: 'How is this deriv'd? | Saw you the field? Came you from Shrewsbury?' (1.1.23–4). It transpires that Bardolph has not seen the battlefield, but he 'spake with one...that came from thence', a well-bred gentleman '[t]hat freely render'd me these news for true' (1.1.25–6). Northumberland's servant Travers, who had been dispatched 'On Tuesday last to listen after news' (1.1.29), then appears. Bardolph insists that Travers can tell nothing new: 'I over-rode him on the way, | And he is furnished with no certainties | More than he haply may retail from me' (1.1.30–2). But he is mistaken. Travers reports that Sir John Umfrevile gave him the 'joyful tidings' from the battlefield, and 'turned me back', soon outriding him 'being better hors'd' (1.1.34–6) (most editors alter Umfrevile to Bardolph here, to make the two accounts tally). But since he was slower, Travers was then caught by 'A gentleman almost forspent with speed...spurring hard' with a 'bloodied horse', looking for Chester (1.1.36–9). He reported, contrary to Bardolph or Umfrevile, that the 'rebellion had ill luck, | And that young Harry Percy's spur was cold', taking off before Travers could question him further (1.1.39–48). 'Look, here comes more news' (1.1.59): a third version of events then comes in, in the form of Morton, who 'ran' from the battlefield to bring an eyewitness account of the tragic news (1.1.65–7). Shakespeare uses the confusion to probe notions of rank—Bardolph trusts the word of a well-bred gentleman and derides Travers' source as 'some hilding fellow that had stol'n | The horse he rode on, and, upon my life, | Spoke at a venture' (1.1.56–9) swearing 'my barony' that Hotspur won the day (1.1.51–4). Speed is emphasized: Bardolph is 'better hors'd' than Travers, and Travers' source is 'almost forspent with speed...spurring hard' with a 'bloodied horse'; ultimately, Morton 'ran'. Although all three are oral messengers, only one, Morton, is an eyewitness, and he is interestingly figured as a book:

'this man's brow, like to a title leaf, | Foretells the nature of a tragic volume' (1.1.60–1).

There is no strict hierarchy of news operating across Shakespeare's plays. Letter-evidence is not always to be trusted over oral evidence; gentlemen are not always to be trusted over hilding fellows; speed is important, but needs not to be hasty. But the increasing interest in the identity of the messenger in *Henry IV Part Two* to some extent hints at what is to come in *King Lear*. As we've already seen, the choice of messenger to convey a particular letter has ramifications. When Burgundy sends his curt letter to Henry VI, his loaded choice of the cowardly Sir John Fastolfe as bearer prefigures and reinforces the insult of the letter's breach of protocol. For a theatre audience, I would argue, the physical presence of this ludicrous messenger counts for far more than the 'churlish superscription' that Gloucester reads out (1*H*6 4.1.53). Antony's use of his old schoolmaster as letter-bearer to Caesar is seen by the Romans as a sign of his weakness (*AC* 3.12.3–6). When Lucetta first presents a letter to Julia in *The Two Gentlemen of Verona*, Julia immediately wants to know who the letter-bearer was: 'Say, say, who gave it thee?' Lucetta's answer—'Sir Valentine's page; and sent, I think, from Proteus' (*TGV* 1.2.38)—should alert us from the start to a problem with Proteus's courtship: the letter is coming through the wrong channels. But in *King Lear*, Shakespeare's concern is not with the news they carry, nor even necessarily in the identity of the bearer, but the way they carry it.

What is your Difference? Kent and Oswald as Messengers

For at least the past century, criticism of *King Lear* has seen the play as a struggle between two groups of individuals, a reading noted by G. Wilson Knight: 'all the persons of *King Lear* are either very good or very bad'.[12] A.C. Bradley observed that the 'two distinct groups' represented 'unselfish and devoted love' (Cordelia, Kent, Edgar, the Fool) and 'hard self-seeking' (Goneril, Regan, Edmund, Cornwall, Oswald),[13] and that division has subsequently been mapped onto various politicized readings, with the unselfish, devoted love becoming a traditional, aristocratic, feudal, medieval vision of society based on loyalty and honour, and the hard self-seeking representing a materialist, nascent capitalism based on unfettered dog-eat-dog competition. In these readings, the latter was for decades personified by Edmund, as John Danby writes: 'Edmund belongs to the new age of scientific inquiry and industrial develop-ment, of bureaucratic organization and social regimentation, the age of mining and merchant-venturing, of monopoly and Empire-making, the age of the sixteenth century and after: an age of com-petition, suspicion, glory.'[14] As Margreta de Grazia has concluded, 'In all these readings, the influence of periodization is at work, predisposing criticism to see the play's issues in terms of the great historical shift from the Medieval to the Modern', and specifically, to identify 'that momentous transition from one social formation to another (feudal to capitalist) and from one type of individual to another (loyal to self-interested)'.[15]

Recently, however, Edmund has been pre-empted as the locus for the new order. As John Turner points out, Goneril, Regan, and Edmund are odd representatives for an anti-feudal capitalism: 'it is surely unlikely that two king's daughters and one illegitimate nobleman's son, all of whom are killed, should have been chosen by Shakespeare to express an emergent bourgeois ideology'.[16] Richard Halpern has proposed instead a new pair of antagonists: 'If Edmund evokes the Renaissance new man,' he argues, 'he does so only for the purpose of driving it back to a culturally anterior form. He cannot simply be opposed to Kent, for he is the efficient cause that realizes Kent's nostalgia. There *is* a new man in *King Lear*, however, and his name is Oswald.' The steward 'is clearly wheeled in solely as a foil to Kent, and his very existence is conjured up only to complete the play's set of social "types" ... the finical, flattering courtier'.[17] Much earlier, Jonas Barish and Marshall Waingrow recognized that Kent serves as 'the quintessence of the good servant and the touchstone for service throughout the play', while 'Oswald is Kent turned inside out, the bad servant anatomized', and as a result, 'their altercation in the courtyard of Gloucester's court presents in almost schematic form the confrontation of true service with false'—the humble, humbly dressed true servant versus the fastidious, liveried steward.[18]

But I would resist this reading of Oswald as a 'finical, flattering courtier', which is drawn from Kent's outburst against him. As Richard Strier has argued in relation to Oswald,[19] the early modern steward was no ordinary servant but a valued official, literate and experienced, and typically not of low birth: some 190 Members of Parliament in Elizabeth's reign served as stewards at some point in their lives, indicating (as D.R. Hainsworth argues) 'not simply that in the sixteenth century stewardship was a respectable calling, but that it could be a means of climbing the ladder of degree'.[20] The steward's power is clear from a 1595 book of household orders established by Anthony Viscount Montague, in which 'My Stewarde of Householde' has the 'carriage and porte of my chiefe officer'; he is responsible for purchasing provisions, making repairs to his property, paying the servants' wages and providing other monies, riding through the estates to check on them, and keeping accounts.[21] The steward should 'holde a superioritye over all my domesticall officers, servantts and attendantts' and must 'be by them obeyed in all things whatsoever and how inconvenient soever they deeme ytt to be ... Yea and albeitt he exceede the boundes of office. For if he soe doe, ytt shall lye in noe servantts or childes power to controwle him.'[22] But most important, he is also charged to 'assiste me with sounde advice in matters of most ymportance and greatest deliberaci on, and therein faythfully keepe all my secretes'. The steward increasingly served in an ambassadorial function, representing his master or mistress outside the household, and on occasion taking on 'what would seem to twentieth-century eyes a most extraordinary surrogate role'.[23] Since the status of a steward was in large part dependent on the status of the master or mistress, audiences would have expected Goneril, a king's daughter married to a duke, to have a steward of appropriate rank. Although he is still responsible for entertainment at Goneril's house—she orders him to 'prepare for dinner' (1.3.27)—Oswald is also the figure whom Goneril naturally employs as her personal ambassador to her sister.

The fight at Gloucester's house should be seen, therefore, not as between base servant and disguised master but as between two different conceptions of ambassador or 'messenger', as Regan identifies them. While Goneril sends a personal ambassador, Lear turns to an apparent stranger, Caius. Back-to-back scenes in which the two sets of ambassadorial instructions are given speak to rival technologies of communication. Goneril tells Albany that 'I have writ my sister' to tell her 'What he [Lear] hath uttered' (1.4.325). In reality, as we learn lines later, she has instructed her steward Oswald to write the letter: 'How now Oswald? | What, have you writ that letter to my sister?' (1.4.329–30). When he replies in the affirmative—'Ay, madam' (1.4.331)—Goneril then clearly tells him that he may add to the letter, presumably in a verbal message: 'Inform her full of my particular fear, | And thereto add such reasons of your own, | As may compact it more' (1.4.333–5). Her use of 'compact' inevitably if reluctantly carries a negative charge of conspiracy: Oswald himself will later describe Kent negatively as 'compact and flattering [Lear's] displeasure' (2.2.116, F only).

Lear, by contrast, explicitly forbids Kent to add anything to a letter that he himself has written: 'Go you before to Gloucester with these letters. Acquaint my daughter no further with anything you know than comes from her demand out of the letter. If your diligence be not speedy, I shall be there afore you' (1.5.1–5). This is of a piece with Kent's depiction of his own abilities: he has told Lear that 'I can keep honest counsel, ride, run, mar a curious tale in telling it and deliver a plain message bluntly' (1.4.32–3). Although message delivery is among the 'services' Kent offers to Lear, it is offered alongside various forms of silence and verbal ineptitude: this is a man who will not tell a story well—the line plays on the proverb 'A good tale ill told is marred in the telling'[24]—and whose delivery will be 'blunt', unceremonious. 'That which ordinary men are fit for, I am qualified in, and the best of me, is diligence' (1.4.34–5), Kent concludes. Now Lear calls him on his vaunted 'diligence'; he answers, 'I will not sleep, my lord, till I have delivered your letter' (1.5.6–7), and sets out.

We might expect Kent's outstanding quality of 'diligence' to denote simply the earnest and assiduous application of a sincere servant: in his 1578 *A Short discourse of the life of Seruingmen,* Walter Darell advised that the 'foure especiall pointes...whereby to knowe a Seruingman' are 'Godlinesse, Clenlinesse, Audacitie, and Diligence'.[25] But the term is more specific, as Lear makes clear when he picks up Kent's promise later. 'If your diligence be not speedy', he remarks, 'I shall be there afore you' (1.5.4–). Alongside its primary meaning of assiduousness, diligence had come to carry a sense of speed—when Joan LaPucelle conjures her fiends she exclaims that 'This speedy and quick appearance argues proof | Of your accustomed diligence to me' (*1H6* 5.2.29–30); 'Tarquin's foul offence' is 'publish[ed]' 'with speedy diligence' (*Luc* 1852–3); Prospero bids Ariel 'Go! Hence with diligence' (*Tem* 1.2.305) and later even fondly dubs the spirit 'my diligence' (5.1.241). Diligence thus becomes the particular quality of a trusted and *speedy* messenger. In the fourteenth century, Dame Juliana Berners had even thought the best collective noun for a group of messengers was 'a Diligens of Messangeris' as distinct from the more general 'an Obeisians of seruauntis'.[26]

Kent does indeed show diligence in speed, arriving at the Cornwalls' home before Oswald. But once there, the two messengers carry out their duties in radically different ways. In his own account, after entering into the presence of Cornwall and Regan, Kent falls to his knees, 'the place that showed | My duty kneeling'. By contrast, Oswald enters, 'a reeking post, | Stewed in his haste, half breathless, panting forth | From Goneril his mistress, salutations; | Delivered letters, spite of intermission' (2.2.219–23). Without waiting, Oswald moves directly from salutation to delivery of the letters, ignoring the fact that he is, against protocol, pushing in front of someone else. Kent's poised and reverential dignity is thus positively contrasted to Oswald's sweaty, rude bursting in—but Kent loses. It is Oswald's letters that Regan and Cornwall read and act upon, immediately giving orders to leave, and commanding Kent 'to follow, and attend | The leisure of their answer' (2.2.226–7). This failure to answer the king's messenger is doubly a breach of decorum: as Lear notes, ''Tis strange that they should so depart from home | And not send back my messenger' (2.2.193–4).

How then are we to judge these two? For all Kent's diligence, it is the letter carried by Oswald that gets read first. Moreover, Kent isn't the 'blunt' man he appears. We first see him alongside Gloucester, discussing matters of state, a seasoned politician. His first intervention with the king reveals an adept courtier, whose verbose preamble prompts an impatient Lear to remark, 'The bow is bent and drawn, make from the shaft' (1.1.144). His attack on Oswald, couched as a parody of a formal introduction with its 'addition', its litany of titles, is an articulate *tour de force* of alliteration and word-minting. When Cornwall remarks that Kent's bluntness is a guise that can 'Harbour more craft and more corrupter ends | Than twenty silly-ducking observants | That stretch their duties nicely' (2.2.100–2), Kent shows he has more than one 'dialect' by reverting to a pastiche of the courtier's tongue, a parody of the great Marlovian line:

> Sir, in good faith, or in sincere verity,
> Under th'allowance of your great aspect,
> Whose influence, like the wreath of radiant fire
> On flicking Phoebus' front—
>
> (2.2.103–6)

Ironically, in this move, Kent gives substance to Cornwall's argument—that Kent hides 'craft' that could be used for 'corrupter ends'. Some critics have recently argued that audience sympathy is tested by this character: as Kent Cartwright has noted, 'Kent is Lear's and *Lear's* principal respondent, registering the progress of the "hero" and the play', standing for 'self-sacrificing, persistent, and deeply felt' service. Yet ultimately, 'He does not achieve what he seeks; his service 'verges on the futile and sentimental. . . . Kent can become downright annoying himself. He represents both the rectitude of the *Lear*-world and its unmalleability, its violent stasis.'[27] To make sense of this impasse, I shall argue, we are required to pass judgement on the *type* of service Oswald performs so well—and which leads directly to his death.

'Post unsanctified': The Limits of Service

Much to critics' bemusement, Oswald seems to be a good and faithful servant who does his job exceedingly well, reprehensible but utterly loyal. 'I know not well why *Shakespeare* gives to the steward, who is a mere factor of wickedness, so much fidelity', wrote Dr Johnson, giving as instances of his fidelity his refusal to hand over Goneril's letter to Regan, and the fact that 'afterwards, when he is dying, [he] thinks only how it may be safely delivered'.[28] Similarly, A.C. Bradley, while believing Oswald to be 'far the most contemptible' of the 'evil beings' of the play, found him sympathetic on the same two occasions: in 4.5, 'Regan cannot tempt him to let him open Goneril's letter to Edmund; and his last thought as he dies is given to the fulfilment of his trust. It is to a monster that he is faithful, and he is faithful to her in a monstrous design. Still faithfulness is faithfulness, and he is not wholly worthless.'[29] As both Johnson and Bradley suggest, Oswald's conduct in his role as messenger seems to contradict our perhaps instinctive contempt for him.

Oswald takes on the role of letter-deliverer in a particular manner, when Goneril tells him to 'add such reasons of your own, | As may compact it more' (1.4.334–5). This licence to amplify is developed more fully as Oswald (who has been sent ahead) welcomes Goneril

and Edmund to Regan's palace. Asked by Goneril where his master
is, Oswald replies,

> Madam, within; but never man so changed.
> I told him of the army that was landed;
> He smiled at it. I told him you were coming;
> His answer was 'The worse'. Of Gloucester's treachery
> And of the loyal service of his son,
> When I informed him, then he called me sot,
> And told me I had turned the wrong side out.
> What most he should dislike seems pleasant to him,
> What like, offensive.
>
> (4.2.3–11)

What is remarkable here is the scope of Oswald's answer. Solicited
only to give the location of his master, he offers instead a heavily
opinionated account of Albany's behaviour that includes a none too
oblique comment on the state of Albany and Goneril's marriage.
We are surely meant at this point to wonder about the nature of
Oswald's relationship with Goneril. Certainly, Regan has her doubts.
She later says to the steward,

> I know your lady does not love her husband,
> I am sure of that; and at her late being here,
> She gave strange oeillades and most speaking looks
> To noble Edmund. I know you are of her bosom.
>
> (4.5.25–8)

Oswald seems shocked by the insinuation. 'I, madam?' he asks,
to which Regan replies, 'I speak in understanding; y'are: I know't'
(4.5.29–30). Regan's response here implies, even as she denies it, that
there are ways of Oswald being 'of [Goneril's] bosom' that would
not be about 'understanding', but closer to the 'most speaking looks'
that Goneril shares with Edmund. So Oswald's stewardly closeness
to Goneril here tips into sexual innuendo, and he comes dangerously
close to embodying the stock character that Edgar, in disguise as
Tom, claims to have been: 'A serving-man, proud in heart and mind,
that curled my hair, wore gloves in my cap, served the lust of my

mistress' heart, and did the act of darkness with her; swore as many oaths as I spake words and broke them in the sweet face of heaven' (3.4.83–7). Even Bradley was tempted to see this as a reference to Oswald: 'I will not go on to hint that Edgar had Oswald in his mind when he described the serving-man', he claims, in the process hinting precisely that.[30] Oswald may be seen as playing into a particular dramatic stereotype of the socially ambitious steward, often portrayed as avaricious and sexually profligate,[31] tragedy's version of comedy's Malvolio.

Shakespeare puts pressure on this relationship in a scene that is clearly inspired by his source play, *The True Chronicle Historie of King Leir, and his three daughters, Gonorill, Ragan, and Cordella.*[32] After Gonorill has mistreated Leir, and, unbeknownst to Cornwall, the king has departed to visit Ragan, Cornwall decides to 'send a Poste immediately to know | Whether he be arriued there or no' (D2^v). In a soliloquy, Gonorill explains her plan to foil her husband's manoeuvre:

> But I will intercept the Messenger,
> And temper him before he doth depart,
> With sweet perswasions, and with sound rewards,
> That his report shall ratify my speech,
> And make my Lord cease further to inquire . . .
> Well, after him Ile send such thunderclaps
> Of slaunder, scandall, and inuented tales,
> That all the blame shall be remou'd from me,
> And vnperceiu'd rebound vpon himselfe.
> And thus with one nayle another Ile expell,
> And make the world iudge, that I vsde him well.
>
> (D2^v–D3^r)

The Messenger (who remains unnamed, despite the extent of his role in the play) enters 'with letters from the king' (Cornwall) bound 'To Cambria . . . Vnto your father, if he be there' (D3^r). Gonorill demands 'Let me see them', and *'opens them'*, causing the messenger quite understandable concern: although she is his queen, he is required not to let the king's letters be opened except by Leir himself, on pain of death:

> Madam, I hope your Grace will stand
> Betweene me and my neck-verse, if I be
> Calld in question, for opening the Kings letters.

$$(D3^r)$$

When Gonorill objects, ''Twas I that opened them, it was not thou', the messenger points out that she 'need not care' about consequences, but he, 'A hansome man', will 'be quickly trust vp, | And when a man's hang'd, all the world cannot save him' ($D3^r$) Gonorill insists that no one will harm him, since 'we make great account of thee': he responds with verbose praise, claiming he would give ninety-nine out of a hundred lives to his 'Kind Queene', and the remaining life 'is not too deare for my good Queene'.

When Gonorill *'Flings him a purse'*—'A strong Bond, a firme Obligation' ($D3^r$), as he deems it—their pact is sealed. Gonorill gives him a mission that will make 'a hye way of preferment to thee | And all thy friends' ($D3^v$):

Instead of carrying the Kings letters to my father, carry thou these letters to my sister, which contayne matter quite contrary to the other: there shal she be giuen to vnderstand, that my father hath detracted her, giuen out slaundrous speaches against her; and that hee hath most intollerably abused me, set my Lord and me at variance, and made mutinyes amongst the commons.

$$(D3^v)$$

He must affirm these things to be true, even though they are not, larding his speech '[w]ith othes and protestations' to turn Ragan against their father. She broaches 'a further matter', asking 'If my sister thinketh conuenient, as my letters importeth, to make him away, hast thou the heart to effect it?' The messenger swears 'By this booke I will', *'kisse[s] the paper'*, presumably the letter containing the plan, and departs ($D3^v$).

This scene is readily recognizable in *King Lear*, even when reworked in a different context. In 4.5 Oswald carries a letter from Goneril to Edmund. Not finding Edmund at Gloucester's house, he is encountered by Regan, who questions him about Albany's military manoeuvres—here again Oswald offers too much opinion, answering that Albany is in person with his troops, only 'with much ado; your sister is the better soldier' (4.5.5–6). But when Regan starts to question why Goneril might want to write to Edmund, Oswald refuses to speak. 'I know not, lady...I must needs after him, madam, with my letter' (4.5.9, 17). Regan offers him a place to stay overnight but he refuses: 'I may not, madam: | My lady charged my duty in this business' (4.5.19–20) and of course he objects when, against all letter etiquette, Regan asks him to 'Let me unseal the letter' (4.5.24) addressed to another. But then Regan gets to the point, saying she knows that Goneril does not love her husband and is involved with Edmund, and that Oswald is 'of her bosom' (4.5.28). 'Therefore', she continues,

> I do advise you take this note.
> My lord is dead; Edmund and I have talked,
> And more convenient is he for my hand
> Then for your lady's. You may gather more.
> If you do find him, pray you give him this;
> And when your mistress hears thus much from you,
> I pray desire her call her wisdom to her.

> (4.5.31–7)

While the detail is vague, the gist of her argument is clear: the widowed Regan is a better match for Edmund than the still-married Goneril. 'You may gather more' allows Oswald to make what he will of her suggestion. She also exhorts him to kill Gloucester: 'If you do chance to hear of that blind traitor, | Preferment falls on him, that cuts him off' (4.5.39–40). Oswald departs declaring, 'Would I could meet him, madam, I should show | What party I do follow' (4.5.41–2).[33] This line seems to have been mangled in its printing. Whereas F reads 'Would I could meet madam' editors usually restore the first phrase to read (as it does in the quarto): 'Would I could meet him Madam . . . ' In Q, however, there is a second change: 'party' is emended to 'Lady'. With this clarification, Oswald seems here to be saying that if he met with Gloucester (or possibly Edmund), his actions would show which lady he was serving—a strangely ambiguous response that signally fails to reiterate his allegiance to Goneril.

Far from showing unswerving faithfulness to Goneril, as Bradley alleges, Oswald, following the model of the *True Chronicle Historie*'s Messenger, seems to display the capacity to be bribed when needed. Regan apparently gives him a letter (or possibly token) to pass to Edmund, so that Oswald is now carrying two letters to the man. In his final moments he begs Edgar to 'give the letters which thou find'st about me, | To Edmund, Earl of Gloucester' (4.6.244–5)— does that mean plural letters from both Goneril *and* Regan, or a single letter from Goneril (often conventionally referred to in the plural)? Ultimately, as we shall see, the only letter Edgar finds is from Goneril, but does that mean that Oswald has remained 'A serviceable villain, | As duteous to the vices of thy mistress | As badness would desire' (4.6.247–9), destroying Regan's letter, or simply that Edgar fails to find the letter that would prove Oswald less than 'duteous'?

'What I haue heard, what passions I haue seene': How to Read the Reading of Letters

Diligence, speed in delivery, is only half the job. Both Oswald and Kent are expected to report back to the letter-sender: 'hasten your return', says Goneril to her steward (1.4.336); ''Tis strange that they should so depart from home | And not send back my messenger' (2.2.193–4), muses Lear, when Regan, Cornwall, and Kent are not to be found at Cornwall's house. Even Regan admits that she needs to send back Oswald and Kent, whom she has dragged to Goneril's house: 'The several messengers | From hence attend dispatch' (2.1.126–7). The returning messenger was vital for two things. Second, to bring back any verbal or written answer. But first and foremost, his role was to report on the reception of the letter. Here again, we're made aware of the public, almost theatrical nature of letter-receiving and reading: what we regard as a silent, textual act clearly made for compelling performance to its early modern audience. Many plays have letters being read on stage, with the reader's reactions being indicated either in stage directions, or in others' responses. This reaction was precisely what gave the letter-giving its drama: theatre audiences were trained to read the body language of the reader, just as messengers were trained to capture this moment to be reported back to the letter's sender.

In Robert Greene's play *Friar Bacon and Friar Bungay* (c.1589), for example, a post arrives carrying letters from the earl of Lincoln for Margaret, and a pot of gold.[34] He asks her, 'Sweete bonny wench read them and make reply' (F4^v), Margaret opens the letters, making conversation as she does—'Tell me whilest I doe vnrip the seales'— and then reads aloud Lincoln's admission that he is to marry another woman. Despite the awkwardness of the situation, the post is compelled to repeat his request that she 'make reply': 'What answere shall I returne to my Lord?' Margaret gives a long, poised response, returning the dowry money and saying she will never marry another man but enter a convent. Finally, she gives the post money, 'not for the newes, | For these be hatefull vnto Margret, | But for that thart [thou art] Lacies man once Margrets loue'. As he leaves, the post says, 'What I haue heard what passions I haue seene | Ile make report of them vnto the Earle' (G^v). The scene neatly encapsulates the multifaceted role of the letter-bearer. First, of course, he must deliver the letter in person to the recipient; finally, he must report back to the sender the response of the recipient. But crucially, he serves as an observer of the moment of delivery. And in this case, the post's success in conveying both what he has heard and the passions he has seen leads Lacy to the conviction that he must indeed marry Margaret.

In *Frier Bacon* we hear the letter that produces the emotion that the post needs to report. In other contemporary plays, however, the letter-text is not as important as the emotional response. In Beaumont and Fletcher's *The Custome of the Countrey* (1631), the letter-bearer Duarte watches the reaction of the letter-recipient Guiomart—although on this occasion, he has not told her from whom the letter is sent, and her reaction is an increasingly angry response to both the letter *and* the messenger:

> What a frown was ther? She looks me through, & through,
> Now reades again, now pauses, and now smiles;
> And yet there's more of anger in't then mirth,
> These are strange changes; oh I understand it,
> She's full of serious thoughts.[35]

In its treatment of this reporting, *King Lear*'s debt to the *True Chronicle Historie* is once again clear. In the earlier play, the reporting is made part of the action. Arriving at the Cambrian king's palace, the messenger from Cornwall's wife formally greets Ragan, explains his message ('Kind greetings from the Cornwall Queene: | The residue these letters will declare'), and reports on his queen's good health. Ragan *'opens the letters'*, *'reads the letter, frownes and stamps'* (E[r]), while the messenger comments on her response:

> See how her colour comes and goes agayne,
> Now red as scarlet, now as pale as ash:
> See how she knits her brow, and bytes her lips,
> And stamps, and makes a dumbe shew of disdayne,
> Mixt with reuenge, and violent extreames.
> Here will be more worke and more crownes for me.
>   (E[v])

It may well be this passage that suggested to Shakespeare the scene in the 1608 quarto version of *King Lear* where a gentleman recounts to Kent how he brought letters to Cordelia. Cordelia's face, as reported by the Gentleman, expresses the emotion caused by the letter. Since the letter that produces that affect is notably absent,[36] the scene offers a textbook example of the messenger's crucial role in carrying back and reproducing to the letter-sender the emotion provoked by the letters. Kent needs the messenger, not merely to hand over the letters and impart any verbal message, but also to make observations about their reception and to report these back to the sender. First the recipient must accept the letters physically, entailing the admission of the messenger to her presence: 'She took them, read them in my presence', the Gentleman assures Kent (4.3.11). Then she must read them, and her reactions should be observed: 'Did your letters pierce the queen to any demonstration of grief?...O, then, it moved her?' asks Kent (4.3.9–10, 15). The Gentleman describes how Cordelia's 'patience and sorrow' 'smiles and tears' strove to win control (4.3.16–24). Then we move to any response in words: 'Made she no verbal question?' (4.3.25) Here the Gentleman reports not a direct answer made to him, but her private response, which he overheard: 'once or twice she heaved the name of father | Pantingly forth, as if it pressed her heart; | Cried "Sisters, sisters, shame of ladies, sisters! | Kent, father, sisters! What i'th' storm, i'th' night? | Let pity not be believed!"' (4.3.26–30). Usually, the messenger would then expect to take back a verbal message, or at the very least, thanks for the letters, and possibly to wait for a written letter in response. But here the transaction is broken off halfway through, as Cordelia, failing to control the physical and verbal expression of her deep emotions ('clamour mastered her' (4.3.32)), rushes off '[t]o deal with grief alone' (4.3.33). Kent hopes for a further meeting—'You spoke not with her since?' (4.3.36)—but the Gentleman confirms that he did not. Here, then, *Lear* gives us a letter whose complete transaction might be said to be stymied, since Cordelia does not send a written or even verbal answer. But at least here the messenger is able to do most of his job; elsewhere in the play, by contrast, letters appear but the messenger is nowhere in sight.

Closet Letters: Letters without Messengers

— When came you to this? Who brought it?
— It was not brought me, my lord, there's the cunning of it.

(1.2.57–60)

The play's most explosive letter is supposedly written by Edgar and sent to Edmund to suggest that they murder their father. This letter vexed A.C. Bradley. 'No sort of reason is given,' he complained, 'why Edgar, who lives in the same house with Edmund, should write a letter to him instead of speaking; and this is a letter absolutely damning to his character. Gloster (*sic*) was very foolish, but surely not so foolish as to pass unnoticed this improbability; or, if so foolish, what need for Edmund to forge a letter rather than a conversation, especially as Gloster appears to be unacquainted with his son's handwriting?'[37]

To answer this complaint, we need to turn to Gloucester's reaction. After reading the letter, and learning that his son and heir is planning to ensure that he 'would sleep till I waked him' (1.2.52–3), Gloucester in fact has four questions: 'My son Edgar, had he a hand to write this? A heart and brain to breed it in? When came you to this? Who brought it?' (1.2.56–8). The first two questions raise the presence of Edgar's physical writing of the letter ('hand'), and the relationship of that hand to his emotion and reason ('heart and brain'). This relationship is then elaborated as Gloucester asks Edmund whether 'You know the character to be your brother's?' (1.2.62), prompting the usual Shakespearean play on 'character' as handwriting and personal qualities.[38] Edmund feigns an attempt to unpick the connection: 'If the matter were good, my lord, I durst swear it were his; but in respect of that, I would fain think it were not' (1.2.63–5). Under continued questioning from his father, however—'It is his?'—Edmund admits 'It is his hand, my lord': his added 'hope' that 'his heart is not in the contents' (1.2.66–8) has already been rendered vain by the 'character', simultaneously hand/writing and 'heart and brain'. Later, as Edgar flees his father's house, Edmund invents a speech where Edgar claims that no one would believe a bastard's words against him, 'ay, though thou didst produce | My very character' (2.1.71–2). But now his 'very character' is no more than the letter: 'O strange and fastened villain', laments Gloucester, on hearing this: 'Would he deny his letter, said he?' (2.1.77–8).

But it is Gloucester's last two questions which are the most revealing: 'When came this to you? Who brought it?' He wants to know the nature of the letter's delivery—when it was brought, and who brought it. Note that he doesn't have to ask 'where' it was delivered, because he assumes that the letter was handed over to Edmund in person, as most letters were. But on this occasion, that assumption is mistaken. 'It was not brought me, my lord', replies Edmund, 'there's the cunning of it. I found it thrown in at the casement of my closet' (1.2.59–61). The closet, often the only lockable room in the early modern house, represents the individual's most private space.[39] The 'thrown' letter then is not delivered to the recipient's hands, but made to appear in the room most intimately associated with him, where the recipient can be depended on to find it, while the messenger remains hidden.

The play has another closet letter, one that seals Gloucester's fate, but this second letter does not raise the same questions. When Gloucester reveals to Edmund that 'There is division between the dukes, and a worse matter than that' (3.3.8–9), he backs up his verdict by invoking epistolary evidence:

I have received a letter this night—'tis dangerous to be spoken, I have locked the letter in my closet. These injuries the King now bears, will be revenged home. There is part of a power already footed; we must incline to the King. I will look him, and privily relieve him.

(3.3.9–14)

Once Gloucester has left, Edmund reveals his plan: 'This courtesy, forbid thee, shall the Duke | Instantly know and of that letter too' (3.3.20–1). Beyond telling Cornwall of the letter, Edmund evidently breaks into his father's closet and steals it, revealing Gloucester's plans to Cornwall by producing the paper: 'This is the letter which he spoke of, which approves him an intelligent party to the advantages of France. O heavens! That this treason were not, or not I the detector ... If the matter of this paper be certain, you have mighty business in hand' (3.5.10–16). Cornwall is convinced, and produces the letter as evidence to his sister-in-law: 'Post speedily to my lord your husband, show him this letter: the army of France is landed. Seek out the traitor, Gloucester' (3.7.1–3).

Once Gloucester is seized, it is this letter that is invoked against him: 'Come, sir, what letters had you late from France? ... And what confederacy have you with the traitors, | Late footed in the kingdom?' (3.7.42, 44–5) to which Gloucester responds, 'I have a letter guessingly set down | Which came from one that's of a neutral heart, | And not from one opposed', an answer that Cornwall admits is 'Cunning' (3.7.47–9). 'Cunning' because it aims to evade any implication of partial involvement: the content of the letter is merely 'guessingly set down', a speculation, its author 'a neutral heart' rather than 'one opposed'. But without a messenger to be identified, Gloucester's claim will not stick. The letter is, as he has already admitted, 'dangerous to be spoken'. With the transaction of delivery obscured, what Gloucester perceives as a 'neutral heart' can equally be one of Cornwall's 'traitors'. Its danger lies, therefore, not simply in its content, but in the fact that it comes without an identifiable messenger that can vouchsafe its provenance.

These two letters, housed in the closets of Gloucester's castle, speak to each other intriguingly. Their very presence in the closets confirms their dangerousness: Gloucester realizes the danger of the letter to him, while Edmund creates the danger of the letter he writes by claiming it came to him in his closet. The letter to Edmund is in fact a letter from Edmund; without a known author, responsibility for the letter to Gloucester is ultimately pinned on Gloucester himself. In each case, these identifications and misidentifications are made possible precisely through their lack of a messenger.

Undirected Letters: Critical Confusion in King Lear

The letters in *King Lear* have infuriated critics. Exhausted with coping with the play's idiosyncratic time schemes and wilful geographical vagueness, scholars from A.C. Bradley to Jonathan Goldberg have admitted defeat when faced with the vagaries of the play's letters. Letters circulate at high speed, miraculously reaching characters who are hiding in disguise; characters appear to be in receipt of information that cannot possibly have reached them. Rosalie Colie's response is representative: she sums up the epistolary exchanges in the play as 'odd...Letters pass at an amazing rate from hand to hand—but there is no hint of how they do so...All we know is that letters and people pass from here and there to Dover.'[40] Many of the critical complaints about inconsistency centre on questions of place: in a world where characters depart from one space to another on the spur of the moment, how do letters reach them? Bradley's objection is typical: 'Lear and Goneril, intending to hurry to Regan, both send off messengers to her, and both tell the messengers to bring back an answer. But it does not appear either how the messengers *could* return or what answer could be required, as their superiors are following them with the greatest speed.'[41] But these qualms disappear once we accept that early modern messengers are not sent from place to place but from person to person; their address, as we've seen, is to a person not a place; the messenger must report back, or carry a letter back, to the original sender, who might well be mobile, and so locating that sender is part of the messenger's duties.

The letter problem is compounded by a geography problem. The geography of *King Lear* is notoriously inadequate. As Stanley Wells has noted, Shakespeare 'opens up the play's action', by replacing specificity with 'multiplicity of suggestiveness'—or, in other words, 'delocalization'. Although some scenes are situated—Gloucester's castle, Albany's seat, Cornwall's palace—we don't know where any of these are geographically located. Reason would assert that Albany would have his seat in Scotland, and Cornwall in the extreme south-west of England, but the distances between these places would make the play's action implausible—so even characters deliberately known by geographical signifiers are then detached from those places. The result, I shall suggest, is a play of purely interpersonal relations between individuals, in which letters brought by personal bearers are crucial.

The most egregious example is the peculiarly healthy correspondence transacted between Cordelia in France, and Kent, flitting between the court, Albany's house, Cornwall's house, Gloucester's house and the so-called heath. In 2.2, Kent, in the stocks at Gloucester's house very early in the morning, produces a letter and calls on the 'warm sun' to '[a]pproach' so that 'by thy comfortable beams I may | Peruse this letter' (2.2.160–2)

> I know 'tis from Cordelia,
> Who hath most fortunately been informed
> Of my obscured course, [*reading the letter*] 'and shall find time
> From this enormous state, seeking to give
> Losses their remedies'. All weary and o'erwatched,
> Take vantage, heavy eyes, not to behold
> This shameful lodging.
> Fortune, good night: smile once more; turn thy wheel.
>
> (2.2.164–71)

This passage has caused editors considerable grief. How does Kent have a letter from Cordelia in his possession? How did it reach him? Does he open it and read it at this point? Are some of these words then Cordelia's—as R. A. Foakes's edition, cited here, suggests—or all of them Kent's?[42]

Richard Knowles argues that Kent 'himself must somehow have informed Cordelia of his disguise', pointing out that 'no one else knows of it until the end of the play', so Cordelia 'hath most fortunately' ('*happily*, not *accidentally*') 'been informed' of his state. Cordelia, meanwhile, 'must have had available to her some unmiraculous means of corresponding from France to her friends in England, perhaps through a network hurriedly arranged . . . when she left England for France'. Building on this supposition, Knowles speculates that 'Kent most probably has just gotten the letter from someone in Gloucester's household, where he has recently arrived'—since he has not read it, he is unlikely to have received it previously at Goneril's house. 'If a realistic explanation can be imagined', he concludes, 'the letter must have been sent first to Goneril's house, where Cordelia expected Lear and Kent to be, and it (or a duplicate) must have followed him to Regan's or Gloucester's house. How, we do not know, nor are we invited to ask.'[43]

Knowles' analysis here is astute, but it importantly misunderstands what it would mean for Cordelia to send a letter to Kent. Once again, it follows our modern assumption that the letter would be sent to the *place* where Kent is thought to be, and then forwarded to the place where Kent actually is (say, from Goneril's to Regan's or Gloucester's house), and finally handed over by 'someone in Gloucester's household'. But this is not how early modern letters operated, and especially not the kind of letter Cordelia would be sending to Kent, from the king's disowned daughter to a banished nobleman. By simply existing, such a letter would be dangerous, its messenger liable to extreme punishment if found. Cordelia would instruct a personal servant to deliver it *to Kent*: not to the house where he was expected to stay, not to the house where he was staying, not to someone else in that house, but to Kent in person. But this then begs the question: how would a bearer know of Kent's disguise, or his whereabouts?—and his disguise and whereabouts are inexorably linked, since in using the phrase 'obscured course' (2.2.166) Kent himself conflates his physical disguise and his erratic journey. The play does not provide an answer: it simply demands that we accept that the mechanics of letter delivery are such that a good bearer will find his man, even when that quarry is on the run, in disguise, and moving swiftly between multiple locales.

Details of the Cordelia to Kent message are later revealed in Kent's reply. In 3.1, Kent encounters a Gentleman whom he recognizes ('I know you' (3.1.3)), perhaps the Knight remaining in

Lear's retinue.[44] After enquiring about the state of the king, Kent reiterates, 'Sir, I do know you | And dare upon the warrant of my note [Q: Arte] | Commend a dear thing to you' (3.1.17–19). He tells of the hidden 'division' between Albany and Cornwall, who both have servants working as intelligencers for France. The Gentleman offers to 'talk further with you' (3.1.39) but Kent has a different plan.

> For confirmation that I am much more
> Then my out-wall, open this purse, and take
> What it contains. If you shall see Cordelia,
> As fear not but you shall, show her this ring,
> And she will tell you who that fellow is
> That yet you do not know.
>
> (3.1.40–5)

Kent here gives the Gentleman ample money and a ring, probably his personal signet ring bearing his family arms or personal identification. (In Q, he also specifies that the Gentleman should 'make your speed to Dover' and asserts that 'I am a Gentleman of blood and breeding' (3.1.32, 36)). The dialogue does not mention a letter, but in 4.3, as we have seen, a Gentleman reports Cordelia's reception of a letter. So does Kent silently hand over a letter here? Does 'this office', a function that is not specified, refer to a letter? Does the purse contain not only money but a folded, sealed letter?

The attempt to pin down a realistic explanation is misplaced. Here, even the letter disappears: all we're left with is an unnamed gentleman being commissioned to go from a man whose identity he does not know to a place where he may / will meet Cordelia. Whereas all other letter transactions are between individuals, Kent sends the gentleman to a *place*, Dover. However, Dover is a place where the letter transaction can only be consummated by the presence of Cordelia, which is simultaneously only possible and yet undoubted—hence the strange formulation: 'If you shall see Cordelia, | As fear not but you shall' (3.1.42–3). It has been noted by several critics that in a play of only the vaguest geographical specificity, Dover is the only location imbued with any reality. Gloucester advises Kent to 'drive toward Dover', with Lear, 'where thou shalt meet | Both welcome and protection' (3.6.88–9). It is this that propels the interrogation of Gloucester by Regan and Cornwall ('Wherefore to Dover?' they repeat three times, 3.7.50–4). Blinded, Gloucester begs Edgar to help him to the cliff at Dover (4.1.45, 58, 74). As Jodi Mikalachki notes, 'the word "Dover" stands for the saving, redemptive possibility that Shakespeare excised from his tragic revision of the Lear story. In Gloucester's belief that it will provide his deliverance, as well as Kent's intelligence of Cordelia's projected landing there, Dover assumes something like the saving function of Jerusalem on a *mappamundi*.'[45] Edgar pretends to help but, as the audience is well aware, they never reach Dover.[46] In Jonathan Goldberg's words: 'The refusal to allow the word "Dover" to arrive at the place it (apparently) names, the failure, in other words, of the signifier to reach the signified—the failure of the sign—establishes the place that "Dover" occupies in the text. It is the place of illusion: the illusion of the desire voiced by Kent or Gloucester, the illusion of recovery, *and* the illusion of respite and end.'[47]

It might be argued, *pace* Mikalachki and Goldberg, that Dover *is* reached in the play—by this Gentleman. And it is at the moment that he reaches Dover, and therefore Cordelia, that the letter from Kent materializes, and he witnesses her emotional response. After letters without messengers, Shakespeare here gives us a messenger apparently without a letter—but a letter appears as soon as *Lear*'s Jerusalem, Dover, is reached.

Preposterous Letters: Critical Confusion in King Lear

Place is not the only form of measurement that letters confuse in *King Lear*. Even more so, time slips out of our control, as actions appear to be reported before they happen, with letters again identified as the main culprits. Jonathan Goldberg pins down a particular problem:

In the second act of *King Lear* . . . Regan claims to have received a letter from Goneril a scene before the letter carrier arrives, and the delivery of the letter as later recounted by Kent describes a scene that cannot have taken place. In the letter as Regan reads it, Goneril tells her that she is about to arrive, something she could not possibly have written in act 1 when she dispatched the letter, since her decision depends on events subsequent to the posting of the letter. These dizzying refusals remind us of the 'post' in 'posting'. They make plotting and retrospection coincident. If letters can arrive before they were sent, or vice versa, then before and after are—literally—preposterous.[48]

Goldberg's sense of the *effect* of the play's use of letters is spot-on: *King Lear* does indeed perform 'dizzying' tricks with time and letters, that 'make plotting and retrospection coincident', and render the action 'literally preposterous'. But his account of the letter's transaction is mistaken. In fact, the play's temporal plotting of the writing, sending, and receiving of these letters is absolutely precise. But, as Bradley states, 'it needs the closest attention to follow these movements',[49] and it is by no means clear that an audience *can* follow them. It is the play's *presentation* of those processes to the audience that threatens our sense of linear chronology.

To take Goldberg's complaints: 'Regan claims to have received a letter from Goneril a scene before the letter carrier arrives, and the delivery of the letter as later recounted by Kent describes a scene that cannot have taken place.' In 2.1, Regan claims that 'I have this present evening from my sister | Been well informed of them, and with such cautions | That if they come to sojourn at my house, | I'll not be there' (2.1.101–4).[50] It is true that the messenger who brings this letter, Oswald, is not seen until 2.2, when he asks Kent where he might 'set our horses' (2.2.4) but this does not mean that he does not arrive until that moment, merely that his first duty on arrival with an urgent message was to deliver it to its recipient, before stabling his horses—as we'll hear later, Oswald runs in 'reeking . . . | Stewed in his haste, half breathless, panting forth | From Goneril, his mistress, salutations' (2.2.220–2). We might compare Thomas Heywood's play

Edward IV Part One, in which '*a Messenger [enters] booted with letters, and kneeling giues them to the King*': here, the 'booted' shows that he has not changed from his riding costume, because the delivery of letters takes precedence.[51] When Kent encounters Oswald in 2.2, he knows already who Oswald is, because he's previously met him at Goneril's house, and seen him 'come with letters against the King' to Regan (2.2.34–5); Oswald, by contrast, intent on his delivery, does not recognize Kent, and so asks him 'Art of this house?' (2.2.1–2). But the audience does not hear of their second (offstage) meeting at Regan's house until two hundred lines later in the scene, when it is related by Kent to Lear.

So the sequence of events is:

Goneril asks Oswald to write letter to Regan (unseen; referred to 1.4.329–30)

Oswald writes letter to Regan (unseen; confirmed 1.4.331)

Goneril confirms that Oswald has written letter to Regan and dispatches him, telling him to add more details when he informs Regan (1.4.329–36)

Lear dispatches Kent to Regan with letters (1.5.1–7)

At Cornwall's house, Kent kneels to present letters to Regan and Cornwall (unseen; implied 2.1.124; reported 2.2.217–20)

At Cornwall's house, Oswald enters with letters, which they read (unseen; implied 2.1.124; reported 2.220–4)

At Cornwall's house, Regan and Cornwall command Kent to follow them (to Gloucester's castle) to receive their answer (unseen; reported 2.1.125–7; 2.2.226)

They all ride from Cornwall's house to Gloucester's castle (unseen; reported 2.1.125–7; 2.2.225)

At Gloucester's house, Curan informs Edgar that he has told Gloucester that Cornwall and Regan will be with him that night (2.1.2–5)

Cornwall and Regan arrive at Gloucester's house (2.1.86)

At Gloucester's house, Kent encounters Oswald and they fight (2.2.1–42)

Kent tells Lear of the reception of his and Oswald's letters (2.2.217–27)

Kent tells Lear of his fight with Oswald (2.2.228–35)

The sequence of events is, in fact, quite sound, but as Goldberg rightly points out, the audience does not experience it in order.

Why would a playwright go out of his way to plot such an intricate series of delivery transactions and then effectively sabotage it when dramatizing that plot? The answer must be that by not staging certain moments—notably the reception of Oswald's and Kent's letters by Regan and Cornwall—Shakespeare throws our attention onto the messengers rather than the letters they carry. The play, once again, is a matter of messengers.

(There is, I must admit, one moment that still eludes a rational explanation. Lear dispatches Kent with letters to *Gloucester*—'Go you before to Gloucester with these letters. Acquaint my daughter...' (1.5.1–2)—but Kent heads off first to Regan, and only subsequently to Gloucester, accompanying Regan as she travels to Gloucester's castle. Critics and editors have suggested that 'Gloucester' might be a place;[52] or that 'letters' refers to two sets of letters, one to Gloucester, one to Regan. But it may simply be an error: Lear should say 'Cornwall'.)

Ask Me Not what I Know: Messengers Interrupted

In the final moments of the play, Albany waves at Goneril a letter that, he claims, proves her to be bigamously 'sub-contracted' to Edmund. As she objects, he responds violently, threatening to use the letter to choke her, and claiming 'Lady, I perceiue you know't':

GON.   Say if I do, the lawes are mine not thine, who shal arraine me
　　　for't.
ALB.   Most monstrous know'st thou this paper?
GON.   Aske me not what I know.
                    Exit Gonorill.
ALB.   Go after her, shee's desperate, gouerne her.

                                        (Q, L2^r)

So runs the scene in the Quarto. In the Folio version, the question 'know'st thou this paper?' is answered not by Goneril, who has already exited, but by Edmund, who continues: 'That you haue charg'd me with, | That haue I done, | And more, much more, the time will bring it out' (F, ss2ᵛ). The discrepancy in these two readings points, I suggest, to an interesting lapse in the play's logic. We as audience already know the letter's provenance and contents. As Oswald dies, he says to his killer Edgar:

> Slave, thou hast slain me. Villain, take my purse.
> If ever thou wilt thrive, bury my body,
> And give the letters which thou find'st about me
> To Edmund, Earl of Gloucester. Seek him out
> Upon the English party. O untimely death, death!
>
> (4.6.242–6)

Edgar goes through the corpse's clothes ('Let's see these pockets: the letters that he speaks of | May be my friends' (4.6.251–2)), apologetically breaks open the letter's seal ('Leave, gentle wax; and manners, blame us not' (4.6.253–4)), and reads it aloud:[53]

'Let our reciprocal vows be remembered. You have many opportunities to cut him off. If your will want not, time and place will be fruitfully offered. There is nothing done if he return the conqueror; then am I the prisoner, and his bed my gaol, from the loathed warmth whereof, deliver me and supply the place for your labour. Your (wife, so I would say) affectionate servant and for you her own for venture. Goneril'.

(4.6.257–65)

On this paper much of the action of the fifth act depends. The disguised Edgar importunes Albany for his attention, and begs him, 'Before you fight the battle, ope this letter' (5.1.41). Albany agrees to 'o'erlook thy paper' (5.1.51), but does not mention it again for quite some time. Instead, he challenges Edmund's assumption of power, which provokes Goneril and Regan, who is increasingly ill, to a squabble over which of them will have Edmund. Finally, Albany arrests Edmund on charges of capital treason, asserting that he bears the claim 'in the interest of my wife, | 'Tis she is sub-contracted to this lord' (5.3.86–7), presumably extrapolating this fact from the 'reciprocal vows' recalled in the letter by Goneril. The herald blows the trumpet three times, the signal for Edgar to appear, and he challenges Edmund.

Goneril recognizes the paper, and tries in vain to destroy it, as we can tell from her husband's comments: 'Nay, no tearing, lady; I perceive you know it' (5.3.154–5)—he does not want his evidence torn, blown to the winds. Edmund will not answer whether or not he knows the letter. But, in truth, he does *not* know it: despite being intended for him, and carried by Goneril's personal messenger to him, the letter has failed to reach its recipient. Moreover, there may be nothing in its material form that links it to him, since, in all probability, it lacks a superscription. While signed by Goneril, and suggesting that a man with whom she has exchanged 'reciprocal vows' should ensure that her husband does not return, so that she can become 'Your wife', the letter does not name its intended recipient. That information is vouched for only by Edgar who assumes that the letter was bound for Edmund, because with his dying breath Oswald tells him to deliver the letter to 'Edmund, Earl of Gloucester' who is with 'the English party'. Presumably Albany had his suspicions about Goneril and Edmund. But Edmund cannot know that the evidence identifying him is so flimsy, and that there is no need for him to admit guilt at this moment.

The play's final letter, like its first, is written by Edmund. After ordering Lear and Cordelia to be taken away (5.3.19), Edmund calls over a captain, commanding him 'Take thou this note' (5.3.26), 'follow them to prison', and obey the instructions 'As I have set it down' (5.3.38)—if he undertakes this 'great employment' (5.3.33) he will 'make thy way | To noble fortunes' (5.3.30–1), a line that recalls Ragan's to the messenger in the *True Chronicle Historie*: 'This do, thou winst my favour for ever, | And makest a hye way of preferment to thee | And all thy friends' (D3ᵛ). In the captain's response, too, we hear a final echo of the avaricious messenger: he agrees, realizing 'I cannot draw a cart, nor eat dried oats' (i.e. I cannot be a horse), but 'If it be man's work, I'll do't' (5.3.39–40). This letter also produces the final struggle between postal and stage action. As Edmund struggles

to stay alive after his duel with Edgar, he makes a last-ditch attempt
at practical redemption:

> I pant for life. Some good I mean to do,
> Despite of mine own nature. Quickly send—
> Be brief in it—to the castle, for my writ
> Is on the life of Lear and on Cordelia;
> Nay, send in time.
>
> (5.3.241–5)

While Albany calls for men to 'Run, run, O run', (5.3.245), Edgar is
more practical: 'To who, my Lord? Who has the office?' (5.3.246).
He also knows that Edmund's orders must be countermanded by
something more compelling than the writ or note he has written.
'Send | Thy token of reprieve', (5.3.246–7) he suggests; 'Well thought
on', responds Edmund, 'take my sword; the captain, | Give it the
captain' (5.3.248–9).

'Haste thee for thy life', Edgar commands a gentleman—and
here he turns that gentleman into a letter. By 1606 'haste for thy
life' had become a cliché of messenger rhetoric. Important missives
were superscribed with a series of instructions denoting mounting
urgency: 'Haste', 'Post-haste', 'Post-haste for life' (plus any number
of reiterated 'for life's)—Mary Tudor sent a letter to the City of
London asking for men to relieve Calais, which was superscribed.
'Hast, Hast Post, Hast, For lief, For lief, For lief, For lief.'[54] The
instruction was topped by a crude portrait of the gallows, giving the
messenger no doubt whose 'life' might be at stake if the letter were
not delivered. In Edgar's mouth, however, the phrase has another
truth: it is not the messenger's life at stake here but Cordelia's. For
once again, the full explanation is the last to be revealed, in what
turn out to be Edmund's final lines:

> He hath commission from thy wife and me
> To hang Cordelia in the prison and
> To lay the blame upon her own despair,
> That she fordid herself.
>
> (5.3.250–3)

Then, telescoping time, we see the letter's results: as Edmund is borne out through one door, Lear enters at another with Cordelia, dead, in his arms.

And here lies a final irony. As he instructs the captain, Edmund notes, 'Know thou this, that men | Are as the time is; to be tender-minded | Does not become a sword' (5.3.31–3). He opposes tender-mindedness to the sword, and yet is unable to speak his commission, leaving that instead to the pen: even his instruction to 'carry it so | As I have set it down' and 'write "happy", when thou'st done' (5.3.36–8) projects the act of murder as a simple textual transaction. He does not carry out the task himself—and even if he did, the hanging of an imprisoned woman to look like a suicide is not an act of the sword, and surely not high on the list of honourable war crimes. When he does finally use his sword, it is only as a token to supersede the authority of his written letter—and the letter wins.

It's a hollow victory for epistolary culture. With its letters forged, intercepted, delivered by men in disguise, delivered by no apparent means, thrown in at casements, and undelivered, *King Lear* can be seen as the most advanced exploration in Shakespeare's *oeuvre* of the myriad problems and challenges facing communication via letters in the early modern world. So when Angel Day writes that of a letter, 'no other definition [is] needeth thereof, that wherein is expresslye conceiued in writing, the intent and meaning of one man, immediately to passe and be directed to an other, for the certeine respects thereof, is termed the messenger and familiar speeche of the absent',[55] one need only turn to *King Lear* to dismantle every phrase of his confident dictum.

6

Lovers' Lines: Letters to Ophelia

As Simon Palfrey has recently noted, of all the 'puzzled questions' to which *Hamlet* gives rise, 'perhaps the most irresistible of all involves curiosity about the true status of Hamlet's relationship with Ophelia. Does he really love her? Did they have sex?' Palfrey promptly rejects his own question, saying it has a 'basic absurdity. If you are going to answer, you are not going to find your rationale for doing so in the text. It has to be answered at some extra-textual level, in the space where a play gathers a life of its own, for instance in the private mind of a reader or the practice of a company.'[1] In this chapter, I shall argue instead that the play does carry answers to these questions, but through signals that we have lost the skills to read, not all of which are clearly 'in the text'. Instead, the nature of the relationship between Hamlet and Ophelia is conveyed through a complex interplay of spatial and transactional markers, represented through architecture and gift-giving, that would have been vividly evident to the play's early audiences. These markers are drawn from powerful contemporary ideologies, and bear some relation to legal evidence, but they find their full power only on stage. And those signals coalesce on Hamlet's letter to Ophelia.

Ophelia believes that Hamlet's attentions are evidence of his honourable intentions towards her, claiming to her father that Hamlet 'hath…of late made many tenders | Of his affection to me' (1.3.98–9). Polonius however contemptuously mocks her use of

'tenders', re-casting Hamlet's tender affections as counterfeit coins
and suggesting that she needs to force a harder bargain:

> Marry, I will teach you; think yourself a baby
> That you have ta'en these tenders for true pay
> Which are not sterling. Tender yourself more dearly;
> Or—not to crack the wind of the poor phrase,
> Wronging it thus—you'll tender me a fool.
>
> (1.3.104–8)

Ophelia remonstrates more passionately that Hamlet has 'impor-
tuned me with love, | In honourable fashion', making his speech
'with almost all the holy vows of heaven' (1.3.109–10, 113) but again
her father turns the prince's 'vows' into a bad bargain:

> ... In few, Ophelia,
> Do not believe his vows, for they are brokers
> Not of that dye which their investments show
> But mere implorators of unholy suits,
> Breathing like sanctified and pious bonds
> The better to beguile.
>
> (1.3.125–30)

Despite Polonius' dismissive attitude, however, Ophelia is not alone
in believing that Hamlet will marry her. As Claudius and Polonius
are priming Ophelia for her ambush of Hamlet, Gertrude says:

> for your part, Ophelia, I do wish
> That your good beauties be the happy cause
> Of Hamlet's wildness. So shall I hope your virtues
> Will bring him to his wonted way again
> To both your honours.
>
> (3.1.37–41)

'Honours' here hints at marriage, the 'honourable fashion' that
Ophelia insists Hamlet used in his courting of her; it also carries
the implication that if Hamlet does not return to 'his wonted way'
then both of them will be dishonoured. The marriage hint is made

explicit only after Ophelia's death when Gertrude bids farewell at
her funeral:

> I hoped thou shouldst have been my Hamlet's wife:
> I thought thy bride-bed to have decked, sweet maid,
> And not have strewed thy grave.

(5.1.233–5)

So why does Gertrude believe that Hamlet would have married
Ophelia? This chapter will suggest that, in important ways, Hamlet and Ophelia were already contracted to be married. As many
historians have shown, the question of what constituted a valid
and binding marriage in early modern England was legally vexed,
although it does not seem to have unduly worried men and women
in their everyday lives.[2] Although there were clear definitions of
marriage, it was possible for a so-called 'clandestine marriage'—
one which involved an official, but might lack the reading of banns
or a licence, have taken place outside church, outside the home
diocese of the husband and wife, and outside the proper hours and
season—to be binding under canon law. In fact, as Richard Adair has
written, 'any agreement between a couple in words of the present
tense (*de praesenti*) to marry by mutual unforced consent, no matter
how irregular—perhaps in a field, with no witnesses or priest—
constituted a valid and binding marriage in itself'. An agreement
de futuro, where the couple used words of the future tense to pledge
themselves, could be dissolved by mutual consent 'unless followed
by intercourse which transformed its status into the equivalent of a
de praesenti case'.[3]

Marriage is a pervasive theme in Shakespeare's plays, especially
in the comedies:[4] as Anne Barton notes, 'In play after play, Shakespeare evokes the specifics of marriage contracts and solemniza-
tions among familiar contemporary lines, regardless of whether
the setting is Catholic, Protestant, or pre-Christian'.[5] Shakespeare
seems particularly interested in the theme of clandestine marriage,
to which he returns in a number of his plays, across all genres.[6]

Juliet reminds the friar that 'God join'd my heart and Romeo's, thou our hands' (*RJ* 4.1.55); Othello and Desdemona elope into such a marriage. In *The Merry Wives of Windsor*, Fenton arranges for a tavern-keeper to 'procure the vicar | To stay for me at church,' twixt twelve and one' to perform his clandestine marriage with Anne Page: this, he is aware, will 'give our hearts united ceremony … in the lawful name of marrying' (*MW* 4.6.46–50). Olivia and Sebastian 'plight' their 'faith' in a chantry in front of a clergyman; a bigger, social wedding will take place in time to come (*TN* 4.3.22–31). When Nell Quickly marries Pistol, Bardolph tells Nim 'certainly she did you wrong, for you were troth-plight to her' (*H5* 2.1.19–20): they were precontracted by virtue of pledging their troths but she broke her promise. Lucentio and Bianca are married at the unlikely hour of supper time by 'the old priest at Saint Luke's church' who fortuitously 'is at your command at all hours' (*TS* 4.4.84–5), he is advised to 'take the priest, clerk, and some sufficient honest witnesses' (4.4.90–1) in order for the marriage to be legal. Biondello supportively assures Lucentio that such a spontaneous, ill-timed marriage is quite proper: 'I knew a wench married in an afternoon as she went to the garden for parsley to stuff a rabbit. And so may you, sir' (4.4.95–7).

The more serious aspects of such marriages are explored in *Measure for Measure* with multiple variations on the theme.[7] Claudio tells Lucio that 'upon a true contract | I got possession of Julietta's bed' (1.2.134–5), where their 'most mutual entertainment' (1.2.143) ended in her pregnancy. Julietta is, Claudio insists, 'fast my wife, | Save that we do the denunciation lack | Of outward order' (1.2.136–8), since they are waiting for the dowry in the possession of Julietta's 'friends' (1.2.140–2). There is no question here that both parties consented to the sex: this is 'most mutual entertainment'. When Claudio claims she is 'fast my wife', he is alluding to 'handfasting', another term, alongside contracting or troth-plighting, for a binding engagement (Iago similarly asks Othello, 'Are you fast married?' (*Oth* 1.2.11)). The situation of Claudio and Julietta is contrasted with the sad case of Angelo and Mariana. Mariana 'was affianced to her oath, and the nuptial appointed' (*MM* 3.1.213–14), but between the 'time of the contract, and limit of the solemnity', her brother died in a shipwreck, 'having in that perished vessel, the dowry of his sister' (3.1.215–18). Suddenly, the newly 'poor gentlewoman' loses not only her brother and 'the portion and sinew of her fortune, her marriage dowry' (3.1.222–3), but 'with both, her combinate husband, this well-seeming Angelo' (3.1.222–3). Here Angelo and Mariana have entered into a spousal *de futuro*, an arrangement with an expiration clause ('contract, and limit'); again, what is lacking is the dowry, and when that dowry is lost at sea, Angelo allows the spousal to lapse. But he covers himself by 'pretending in her discoveries of dishonour' (3.1.226–7), claiming that she was hiding dishonourable conduct grave enough for him not to follow through on the betrothal. And there is a third marriage of this sort in *Measure for Measure* that often gets lost. When Mistress Overdone, 'a bawd of eleven years' continuance' is brought before the authorities, she claims that the information against her derives from Lucio who has a grudge against her: 'Mistress Kate Keep-down was with child by him in the Duke's time, he promised her marriage. His child is a year and a quarter old come Philip and Jacob. I have kept it myself and see how he goes about to abuse me' (3.2.192–7). Here the same situation: promise of marriage, sex, pregnancy: so far, so much like Claudio and Julietta. But in this case, the man walks out on the woman: so much like Angelo and Mariana. Of course, no comparable clandestine marriage between Hamlet and Ophelia is referred to in the text of the play: it is significant that a monograph devoted to 'broken nuptials in Shakespeare's plays' does not identify this relationship among them.[8] Ann Jennalie Cook states categorically—and correctly—that 'the text shows no promise of marriage'.[9] But as long ago as 1954 William G. Meader saw evidence of a broken engagement in *Hamlet*,[10] and my work here builds on that suggestion. We need to look beyond the words that survive on the page, I shall argue, and examine instead what else is transacted between the two characters.

According to early modern English marriage laws, in cases where marriages were contested, priority was given to the wording of the vows and the testimony of witnesses. But attention might also be given to other evidence: '[t]he giving and receiving of gifts, especially a ring, between courting couples was also taken to ratify a relationship in some circumstances'.[11] As Ralph Houlbrooke's researches show, 'Some reference to gifts is to be found in the records of over a quarter of the cases in the sample, whether in depositions, personal answers, or acts of court', primarily rings of gold and silver (often linked with oral pledges), but also coins, personal ornaments and trinkets.[12] Depositions suggest parental anxiety as to the meaning of gifts bestowed on women by men. At Christmas 1521, the mother of Agnes Farman of Norwich said to Thomas Coddenham: 'ye resorte ofte tymes hether to my dawghter and she to yow and yow gaue her many giftes. I pray yow shew me in what entent ye do soo whether it be in the way of matrimony or noo and be content to haue her to your wiff; and if it be so I am very gladde.'[13] If it were not so, we infer, Mistress Farman would not be very glad; the visits between households and the gifts from Coddenham would then mean something very different. Laura Gowing has concluded that 'Women and men both gave and received the gifts of courtship, but it was women who found themselves most obligated by them, and who made efforts to avoid accepting gifts with implications. A man's gifts held, as a woman's did not, the implication of an emotional and, potentially, a marital bond, and a woman's receipt of gifts implied consent to that bond.'[14] This is the fear that Egeus expresses in *A Midsummer Night's Dream*, when he claims that Lysander has 'interchang'd love-tokens with my child' including 'bracelets of thy hair, rings, gauds, conceits, | Knacks, trifles, nosegays, sweetmeats', all of them 'messengers | Of strong prevailment in unharden'd youth' (1.1.28–35): in other words, the love tokens would prevail, influence or persuade a young, and not yet fully formed, woman. If no marriage transpires, then the woman is compromised by the actions of the male sender.

In what follows, I propose that Ophelia understands that she and Hamlet are to be married: and that the letter that he sends her constitutes both the most compelling piece of evidence of this, and the most disastrous proof of Ophelia's acquiescence to his sexual attentions. While the clandestine marriages of *Measure for Measure* present three unhappy outcomes of contracts that are not honoured for whatever reason—sex, pregnancy, and abandonment (Kate Keepdown); abandonment, enforced lifelong virginity, and moated dejection (Mariana); sex, dowry-less poverty, pregnancy, and prosecution (Claudio and Julietta)—*Hamlet* suggests a fourth, even more extreme possibility: madness leading to suicide.

The Ambassadors of Love

The relationship between Hamlet and Ophelia is sketched in only a few scenes. Ophelia may appear along with the rest of the court in 1.2 (she is named in F but not in Q2), but she does not speak. In 1.3 we learn, from conversations with her brother and father, that Hamlet has shown her 'favour' (1.3.5, 'favours' in F) and 'made tenders | Of his affections' (1.3.98–9) towards Ophelia. In 2.1 Ophelia enters 'affrighted' (2.1.72), and reports to her father that Hamlet has burst into her private room in a state of undress and distraction, which Polonius diagnoses as 'the very ecstasy of love' (2.1.99). The following scene shows Polonius sharing with the king and queen Hamlet's letter to Ophelia. The first onstage meeting of the pair is not until the third act (3.1), when Ophelia attempts to return to the prince his 'remembrances' to her (3.1.92); it is at this moment that Hamlet turns on her. In 3.2, during the performance of *The Mousetrap* Hamlet taunts Ophelia with lewd comments. When we next see Ophelia, twice in 4.5, she is 'distract' (4.5.2). Two scenes later (4.7), Gertrude brings news to Laertes that 'Your sister's drowned' (4.7.162) and she appears in Act 5, if at all, only as a corpse.

This simple sequence of events is telling. We are not shown any
love scene between Hamlet and Ophelia. We are given Ophelia's
word that he has made unspecified 'tenders | Of his affection' to
her; Polonius and Laertes are alarmed that Hamlet has made such
'tenders' to Ophelia, but feel the situation is salvageable if she keeps
away from him. The situation deteriorates when (offstage) Hamlet
bursts into her private room, apparently exhibiting the physical
characteristics provoked by love. As Polonius notes, Hamlet's dress
and demeanour betray all the signs of (theatrical) love: when John
Marston's Jacomo, in his 1607 play *What you Will*, appears 'mad,
starke mad, alasse for loue', the stage direction specifies that he
enters '*vnbraced and careles drest*', and speaks in highflown poetics that prompt another character to comment, 'now I see hee's
madde most palpable, | He speakes like a player, hah! poeticall'.[15]
One might think that Hamlet's invasion of Ophelia's space and
his brutal holding of her might constitute the most egregious element of their relationship—and Ophelia certainly thinks so. But
her father does not. For Polonius, the critical moment comes with
the discovery of the letter that she has received from the prince.
As A. C. Bradley noted a century ago, this letter must have been
written, delivered and received before Ophelia was commanded by
her father to cut off contact with the prince,[16] but it is not revealed
dramatically until after the traumatic invasion of Ophelia's closet.
This, I would suggest, is because it is the letter that constitutes
the most dangerous element of Hamlet's courtship. And it is the
ill-advised return of the letter and other tokens that leads directly
to Hamlet's rejection of Ophelia, her madness and subsequent
suicide.

Before I pursue this argument any further, a caveat is in order.
Love-letters, as I shall argue, could be taken extremely seriously—or
they could be taken extremely lightly. The key factor here is precisely
how they are *taken*. To give a counter example, the comedic possibilities of love-letters sent from men to women are well exploited in
the final scene of *Love's Labour's Lost*. The princess receives from the

king a diamond-encrusted image of lady plus 'as much love in rhyme | As would be crammed up in a sheet of paper | Writ o' both sides the leaf, margin and all, | That he was fain to seal on Cupid's name' (*LLL* 5.2.6–9). Rosaline receives from Biron a 'favour' and 'verses too . . . | O, he hath drawn my picture in his letter!' (5.2.33–8), although she approves of the penmanship rather than the poetry ('Much in the letters, nothing in the praise . . . Fair as a text B in a copy-book' (5.2.40, 42). Katherine receives from Dumaine a glove and 'Some thousand verses of a faithful lover. | A huge translation of hypocrisy, | Vilely compiled, profound simplicity' (5.2.48–52), while Maria is sent from Longueville pearls and a 'letter . . . too long by half a mile' (5.2.53–4). Later, when confronted with the wooers themselves, the princess states,

> We have received your letters full of love,
> Your favours, the ambassadors of love,
> And in our maiden counsel rated them
> At courtship, pleasant jest and courtesy,
> As bombast and as lining to the time.
> But more devout than this in our respects
> Have we not been, and therefore met your loves
> In their own fashion, like a merriment.
>
> (5.2.771–8)

Dumaine is horrified by the cavalier response to their amorous efforts: 'Our letters, madam, showed much more than jest' (5.2.779). But, as Rosaline points out, what the letters showed, what their writers intended, is beside the point, because 'We did not quote them so' (5.2.780). Rosaline's offhand retort gets to the heart of the matter: the 'letters full of love' mean what the recipients let them mean.

What would happen, however, if the female recipient of love-letters did choose to 'quote them so'? Letters could be used as evidence in a case of clandestine marriage. In his *The Practice of the Spiritual or Ecclesiastical Courts* (1685), Henry Consett included 'Private Letters, betwixt one Friend and another, one Tradesman and other', as among the written 'Instruments' that might be invoked as *mortua voce* evidence in disputed cases.[17] As Diana O'Hara writes, 'By law, [letters] were admitted as a form of proof and as a means of contracting spousals if they contained words deemed appropriate for matrimony, were delivered by special messenger and were willingly accepted by the other party.'[18] But it was not merely a question of the text's content: O'Hara notes, citing Henry Swinburne's *Treatise of Spousals* that 'It was necessary for the person, upon receipt of the letter, to express mutual consent to the message imported, and for witnesses to prove that the letter was read and understood.'[19] In everyday life, as I have already suggested, court cases concerning disputed marriages were likely to resort first to witnesses and then to the exchange of gifts or tokens as evidence. However, stage plays are not everyday life: the stage tradition developed its own shorthand for determining whether or not parties had consented to marriage. In this stage tradition, I shall argue, the reception of letters—as of the various 'favours' that the *Love's Labour's Lost* group send with their letters—played an important role.

To explore the theatrical importance of Hamlet's letter to Ophelia, and its relation to his other actions, I turn to a play that predates *Hamlet* by almost half a century, Nicholas Udall's schoolboy comedy *Ralph Roister Doister* (1553).[20] The delicacy of an unmarried woman accepting a letter is vividly portrayed in Udall's play when the virtuous widow Christian Custance is presented with a letter by her old nurse Margery Mumblecrust. She refuses to accept it, instead demanding of her nurse,

> C. Custance. Who tooke thee thys letter Margerie Mumblecrust?
> M. Mumbl. A lustie gay bacheler tooke it me of trust,
> And if ye seeke to him he will lowe [allow] your doing.
> C. Custance. Yea, but where learned he that way of wowing?

To Custance, the sending of a letter from a man to a woman is, perforce, a 'way of wowing'. Seeing the letter, she had assumed 'verily thys had bene some token | From my dere spouse Gawin Goodluck' who is away from home; as she claims, Custance is 'bespoken' (C.ij^v) to Goodluck (it is later confirmed she is 'ensured to an husband'). Madge Mumblecrust, believing Roister Doister to be '[a] ioyly man', urges Custance to 'open the writing and see what it doth speake', but Custance is adamant: 'At thys time nourse I will neither reade ne breake'—neither read the superscription on the outside, nor break the seal open to read the letter's content. It is clear that she finds even the possibility that she would be seen to receive this letter from a strange man compromising to her reputation: 'see thou no more moue me folly to begin, | Nor bring mee no mo letters for no mans pleasure, | But thou know from whom' (C.ij^v).

Ralph follows up the letter with 'a ring, with a token in a cloute' (C.v.[i.e.iij]^v), sent by his servant Dobinet Doughty, who complains of the excessive 'trotting' he has to do to fulfil his master's commands: 'Go beare me this token, carrie me this letter, | ... Trudge, do me thys message, and bring worde quick againe' (C.v.[i.e. C.iij]^r). Doughty tries to deliver the ring and token to Madge but, once bitten, the old nurse is twice shy: 'by the token that God tokened brother | I will deliuer no token one nor other' (C.v. [i.e. C.iij]^v). Scared to return to his master without fulfilling his commission, Doughty decides to hang around the Custance house, reasoning that if he 'tary here his moneth, ... some of the house | Shall take it of me' (C.iiij.^{r}). It takes no more than a brief song and dance before Custance's maid Tibet Talkapace volunteers to deliver the token and ring. With comic promptness, she feels the force of her mistress's displeasure, as she gets blamed for being 'stil ... a runner vp and downe | ... a bringer of tidings and tokens to towne' (D.^{v}). Custance warns her maids:

> Well ye naughty girls, if euer I perceive
> That henceforth you do letters or tokens receiue,
> To bring vnto me from any person or place,
> Except ye first shewe me the party face to face,
> Eyther thou or thou, full truly abye [pay the penalty] thou shalt.
>
> (D.^{v})

A similar sequence arises in *The Two Gentlemen of Verona*, where Lucetta brings a letter to her mistress Julia. Requested to 'Peruse this paper', Julia reads its superscription—'*To Julia*'—but then wants to know, 'Say, from whom?' (1.2.34–5). Lucetta attempts to push her into reading it ('That the contents will show' (1.2.36) but, at Julia's urging, reveals that it came from 'Sir Valentines page; and sent, I think, from Proteus. | He would have given it you, but I, being in the way, | Did in your name receive it. Pardon the fault, I pray' (1.2.38–40). Julia's reaction is similar to Custance's:

> Now, by my modesty, a goodly broker:
> Dare you presume to harbour wanton lines?
> To whisper and conspire against my youth?
> Now trust me, 'tis an office of great worth,
> And you an officer fit for the place.
> There, take the paper. See it be returned,
> Or else return no more into my sight.
>
> (1.2.41–7)

When Julia accuses Lucetta of being a 'broker' she alludes obliquely to the role that servants play vis-à-vis their female employers, a role that is more fully examined in *Ralph Roister Doister*. Throughout this epistolary episode, access to Christian's chastity is figured consistently as access to her house, of which she, as a widow, is head. This association is of course absolutely standard for the day. Edmund Tilney enjoins good wives 'to be resident in hir owne house' in order 'to preserue and maintaine this good fame',[21] a preservation and maintenance required because, as Peter Stallybrass notes, 'woman', and especially her chastity, 'is produced as a *property* category', 'that treasure, which, however locked up, always escapes'. Bodily and architectural images are superimposed in depictions of this dangerous treasure: 'She is the gaping mouth, the open window, the body that "transgresses its own limits" and negates all those boundaries without which property could not be constituted'.[22] Letters, rings, and tokens, moving from the outside world to the inside of the woman's house, transgress these boundaries, proving her house to be open, and calling into question her chastity. And the agents of that transgression are servants, who constantly—and gleefully—move across these boundaries, hence Julia's accusation of Lucetta's brokerage.

This set of concerns focusing on women, letters, servants, and the boundaries of the household can be found in compelling visual form in the familiar Dutch genre paintings of the seventeenth century, by artists including Gabriel Metsu, Jan Steen, and Johannes Vermeer, in which a woman writes, receives, or reads a letter.[23] In some ways, this genre merely complements the male letter-writer genre, whose exponents include Metsu, Gerard ter Borch, and Adriaen van Ostade. But the female letter-writer, I shall suggest, required the development of a new set of motifs. In many of these paintings, the woman is shown reading by the sunlight coming in from a window (sometimes an open window):[24] a practical necessity, of course, but also a sign of the boundary the letter has crossed in coming into the household from outside (by contrast, women are usually shown writing by candlelight). But letters do not fly through casements, except in Shakespearean plays, and the paintings indicate how they might be transmitted. In the paintings of male letter-writers, there is often another man waiting, presumably to take the letter: he is sometimes depicted as the post, with his characteristic horn.[25] In the paintings of female letter-writers, by contrast, letters reach the lady by a personal servant. In Gabriel Metsu's *A Young Woman Receiving a Letter* (c. 1658) (illustration 11), '[a] servant boy dressed in a rusty brown coat and trousers doffs his hat deferentially and delivers a letter to the lady';[26] in his *Woman Reading a Letter* (illustration 12), while the lady reads a letter, a maidservant holds a letter cheekily addressed to Metsu himself.[27] In Johannes Vermeer's *The Love Letter* (c. 1667–70) (illustration 13) the lady looks up enquiringly at the maidservant who has brought the letter—the maidservant, of course, can tell her who gave it to her;[28] in Vermeer's *Lady Writing a Letter with her Maidservant* (illustration 14) a maidservant looks out of the window, waiting while her mistress writes a letter, presumably

11. Gabriel Metsu, *A Young Woman Receiving a Letter* (*c.* 1658).

for her to deliver.[29] Perhaps most tellingly, in Jan Steen's *Bathsheba with King David's Letter* (1659–60), Bathsheba is shown holding a letter which she has taken from an old woman, dressed as a procuress.[30]

The architectural specificity of these paintings cannot be reproduced on stage. Instead, it is evoked by the mention of certain private spaces, or by the comings and goings of servants. Custance's maids' trespass in accepting the ring and token is related, in their mistress's analysis, to their 'delite and ioy | In whiskyng and ramping abroade like a Tom boy': 'Good wenches would not so rampe abrode ydelly', she opines, 'But keepe within doores, and plie their work earnestly' (D.ᵛ–D.ij.ʳ). Christian is proved to be correct in her

12. Gabriel Metsu, *Woman Reading a Letter* (1662–5).

fears: Sim Suresby, the faithful servant of her betrothed, hears talk that she has received letters, rings, and tokens from another man, who hails her as 'wife', and reports back to Goodluck, almost scuppering the planned marriage. These diverse examples, a century apart and from different media and cultures, speak to the resilient

13. Johannes Vermeer, *De lieftesbrief* (*The Love Letter*) (*c.* 1666).

and widespread appeal of the role of the transaction of letters in ideas of women's chastity in the early modern period, especially in relation to the trangressing of household boundaries. The logic of both the plays by Udall and Shakespeare, and the Dutch genre paintings is that the woman's acceptance of a letter already calls into question the boundaries of her household, chamber, and body.

14. Johannes Vermeer, *Lady Writing a Letter with her Maid* (*c.* 1670).

We don't have to look far in Shakespeare's plays to find women's chastity figured by and vouchsafed by the household walls. We have Portia in Belmont, Mariana in her grange, Olivia who will see no visitors. There is no shortage of fathers keen to contain daughters within the family home, and keep suitors outside—but they are often foiled by the doors and windows of their houses.

Shylock memorably admonishes Jessica to 'Lock up my doors', 'shut doors after you: | Fast bind, fast find' (2.5.29, 51–3). Windows are anthropomorphized: when Jessica hears the drum and fife, Shylock warns, 'Clamber not you up to the casements then, | Nor thrust your head into the public street . . . | But stop my house's ears, I mean my casements: | Let not the sound of shallow foppery enter | My sober house' (2.5.31–6). He is, of course, correct in his fears: within a few lines, Lancelot has exhorted Jessica to 'look out at window, for all this, | There will come a Christian boy, will be worth a Jewess' eye', and presumably Jessica escapes through a window (2.5.40–2). In *The Two Gentlemen of Verona*, the Duke provides for his daughter Silvia's chastity: 'Knowing that tender youth is soon suggested', he proudly tells Proteus, 'I nightly lodge her in an upper tower, | The key whereof myself have ever kept; | And thence she cannot be convey'd away' (*TGV*, 3.1.34–7). Proteus has to disabuse him, revealing how Valentine and Silvia have 'devised a mean | How he her chamber-window will ascend | And with a corded ladder fetch her down' (3.1.38–40). Hero's chastity is compromised when her woman 'leans me out at her mistress' chamber window' (*MA* 3.3.139–41). And when Juliet appears to Romeo, he exclaims, 'what light through yonder window breaks?' (*RJ* 2.2.2). Consistently, the window is the weak link in the containment of the young women's sexuality. In other plays, men are welcomed into the home, only to be made unwelcome when they become suitors to the immured daughters, as when Brabantio invites Othello, and Desdemona falls in love (*Oth* 1.3.79–95); or when Prospero houses Caliban, only to have him attempt to violate Miranda (*Tem* 1.2.346–9); or when Lucentio disguises himself as a schoolmaster to get to Bianca, whose father has 'closely mew'd her up' (*TS* 1.1.183). All these instances speak to a theatrical shorthand that links a daughter's chastity to the apertures of her father's house—and letters often play a role in this weakness of the walls. Jessica uses letters, sent via the servant Lancelot Gobbo to Lorenzo, to plan her escape (and the theft of her father's valuables);

Valentine's plan to free Silvia is foiled when her father finds a letter to her concealed on Valentine's person (*TGV* 3.1.136).

Ophelia's situation is more complicated. In 1.3, Laertes advises Ophelia to

> weigh what loss your honour may sustain
> If with too credent ear you list his songs
> Or lose your heart, or your chaste treasure open
> To his unmastered importunity.
> Fear it, Ophelia, fear it, my dear sister.
>
> (1.3.28–32)

Ophelia's body is figured as a set of vulnerable apertures ('too credent ear', 'your chaste treasure open') that needs to be protected from Hamlet's 'songs' and 'importunity'. To protect it, he advises his sister to 'keep you in the rear of your affection' (1.3.33), that is, not in the frontlines of the army, and thus 'Out of the shot and danger of desire' (1.3.34). By rendering Ophelia's body in spatial terms, Laertes raises the moot question of exactly *where* Ophelia might be able to keep out of Hamlet's range. For Ophelia does not have a house, not even her father's. Instead, they are both part of the court household, of which Hamlet is the heir. Ophelia's chastity is therefore immediately compromised by any access to her person. Polonius reiterates his son's warnings in similar terms, complaining that Ophelia has 'of your audience been most free and bounteous' (1.3.92), and advising her 'From this time | Be something scanter of your maiden presence; | Set your entreatments at a higher rate | Then a command to parle' (1.3.119–22). Polonius forbids Ophelia 'from this time forth' to 'so slander any moment leisure, | As to give words or talk with the Lord Hamlet' (1.3.131–3). Ophelia is not to give Hamlet 'audience', 'presence', 'parle', 'words', or 'talk:' her father, like her brother, insists that she must withdraw herself from any physical or verbal interaction with the prince.

The precise nature of her withdrawal, however, is by no means fixed. As James Knowles has shown,[31] the location of Hamlet's encounters with Ophelia shifts significantly in each early printed version of the play. In Q1, Ophelia admits to her father that Hamlet accosted her when 'Hee found mee walking in the gallery all alone' (D2ᵛ). Clearly, Ophelia has done little to heed her father's warning here: she is discovered in a public space, unaccompanied, and therefore clearly vulnerable. But in Q2 and F, Ophelia does as she's told by her brother and father, and takes up 'sowing in my Chamber' (according to F), or 'sowing in my closset' (according to Q2). The activity of sewing, as Lena Cowen Orlin has shown, signifies as 'a badge of virtue' for a woman, giving her 'an invisibility that in this respect paralleled that of the man of good fame'.[32] By secluding herself in chamber or closet, as Richard Brathwait advises *The English Gentlewoman*, she withdraws from 'the clamours and turbulent insults of the *World*', 'the mutinous motions and innouations of the *flesh*': 'Be you in your Chambers or priuate Closets; be you retired from the eyes of men.'[33] The meaning of Hamlet's assault of Ophelia therefore becomes ever more determined, as it moves from the public gallery to the usually female space of the chamber to the private stage space of the closet.[34]

Initially, neither man mentions letters: they are concerned with Hamlet's physical access to Ophelia, and—typically, in a play obsessed with dangers poured in at the ear—with his speech, his words, his vows. But later, after Hamlet has invaded her closet, Ophelia assures her father she had not 'given him any hard words of late', but instead 'as you did command | I did repel his letters and denied | His access to me' (2.1.104–7). Her reference to 'repel[ling] his letters' 'as you did command' is strange here: we have not heard Polonius say anything about letters. But this is perhaps a residual trace of an earlier version of the play that survives in Q1, where Corambis, the Polonius figure, ends his warning speech to his daughter with a more specific injunction:

Ofelia, receiue none of his letters,
'For louers lines are snares to intrap the heart;
'Refuse his tokens, both of them are keyes
To vnlocke Chastitie vnto Desire;
Come in *Ofelia,* such men often proue,
'Great in their wordes, but little in their loue.

(C2ᵛ)

As Corambis commands her to 'Come in *Ofelia*', he spatially links his advice to Ophelia to refuse Hamlet's letters and tokens with her physical withdrawal within doors. Here, letters and tokens have the power to 'intrap the heart' and 'vnlocke Chastitie', especially when they are combined with 'wordes'—and Corambis' words are graphically marked in the printed text as a gnomic *sententia* worth marking, as several of his / Polonius' lines are.[35]

This particular injunction is lost in Q2 and F. But its force is brought to bear in all versions of the play, when Ophelia does receive a letter from Hamlet, which she dutifully passes to her father, who reads it aloud in its entirety to the king and queen. The superscription reads '*To the celestial and my soul'd idol, the most beautified Ophelia*'—and here, Polonius interrupts himself to comment that 'that's an ill phrase, a vile phrase, "beautified" is a vile phrase, but you shall hear'—before continuing, '*thus in her excellent white bosom, these,* etc'.[36] The bosom was, of course, the preferred location for a love-letter, next to the heart. Imogen keeps letters from her beloved, 'The scriptures of the loyal Leonatus', as 'stomachers to my heart' (*Cym* 3.4.82, 85), comparing them to the ornamental breast covering worn by women under the lacing of their bodices, and to the medicated cloths applied to ease pain of the heart. But while a love-letter might be properly stored by its recipient next to her heart, to *deliver* a letter to a white bosom is another matter entirely. Proteus assures Valentine, 'Thy letters may be here, though thou art hence, | Which, being writ to me, shall be delivered | Even in the milk-white bosom of thy love' (*TGV* 3.1.246–8) but Proteus's promise comes shortly before he attempts to seduce Valentine's beloved, rendering his supposed friendly letter-delivery into something overtly sexual, pre-figured here by the way he sexualizes the recipient. In *Hamlet*, the superscription works together with physical and sexual assault that is implied by Hamlet breaking into Ophelia's closet, 'with his doublet all unbraced, | No hat upon his head, his stockings fouled, | Ungartered and down-gyved to his ankle' (2.1.75–7) holding her 'hard' by the wrist (2.1.84) and staring into her face (2.1.87–8).

The inside of the letter contains a poem and Hamlet's own commentary on it:

> *Doubt thou the stars are fire,*
> *Doubt that the sun doth move,*
> *Doubt truth to be a liar,*
> *But never doubt I love.*
>
> *O dear Ophelia, I am ill at these numbers. I have not art to reckon my groans, but that I love thee best, O most best, believe it. Adieu.*
>
> *Thine evermore, most dear lady, whilst this machine is to him.*
>
> Hamlet. (2.2.114–21)

This letter is, at best, doubtful, but as Harold Jenkins points out, the nature of the doubt seems to shift.[37] In the first two lines, Ophelia is given two apparent truisms—that stars are fire, that the sun moves around the earth—which, it is implied, she should 'doubt' rather than doubt his love. In the third line she should 'doubt' (suspect) truth to be a liar. Whatever doubt the 'numbers' contain, the prose is quite clear: 'I love thee best, O most best', 'Thine evermore ... whilst this machine is to him.' It is not my intention here to claim that this letter is in itself an offer of, or proof of, a clandestine marriage. It is not. At most, it is a declaration of monogamous love present and future, until death. But the text of the letter is its least important element, as Polonius, Claudius, and Gertrude all recognize. The crucial point is what the letter's transaction means.

Gertrude immediately has a question: 'Came this from Hamlet to her?' (2.2.112). Polonius is not willing to be led: 'Good madam, stay awhile: I will be faithful' (2.2.113). He wants the letter, faithfully read out, to serve as its own evidence. He concludes by implying that he has all the corroborating evidence that the queen needs:

> This in obedience hath my daughter shown me;
> And more about hath his solicitings,
> As they fell out, by time, by means, and place,
> All given to my ear.

$$(2.2.122–5)$$

Hamlet's parents are not satisfied, since they have not been given the vital information: 'But how hath she | Received his love?' (2.2.125–6). As Laura Gowing explains, 'women's responses constituted the main point of courtship negotiation'.[38] The correct female response to unwanted male attentions is demonstrated in *All's Well That Ends Well*. The chaste Diana is primed, Polonius-like, by Mariana about the tricks employed by male suitors:

Beware of them, Diana; their promises, enticements, oaths, tokens, and all these engines of lust, are not the things they go under; many a maid hath been seduced by them; and the misery is, example, that so terrible shows in the wrack of maidenhood, cannot for all that dissuade succession, but that they are limed with the twigs that threatens them.

$$(AW\ 3.5.18–25)$$

Forewarned, Diana knows how to repel the (married) Bertram. Although able to speak with Diana, Bertram cannot get her to accept his 'enticements, oaths, tokens', even when proferred by a third party:

> I spoke with her but once,
> And found her wondrous cold, but I sent to her [by Parolles] . . .
> Tokens and letters, which she did re-send.

$$(3.6.106–9)$$

Diana's failure to respond to his advances is epitomized by her re-sending of his 'tokens and letters'.

For those less determined than Diana, matters could get more complicated. Gowing explains how 'Women who accepted tokens and regretted it tried, when they came to court, to explain how they were received unwittingly.'³⁹ They had received the gifts unknowingly, they alleged, handed over in the dark, or left in rooms. There are records of cases where gifts were allegedly given by force, with occasions where the form of the giving 'served as a sexual affront, with gifts stuffed into a girl's bosom'; Houlbrooke finds two accounts of coins 'thrust into their bosoms'.⁴⁰ In one case, *Longley* v. *Marchant*, Joanne Marchant testified that one Longley 'forced [her] to take of him a token against her will, which she refused, and said she wold not take it, but he nevertheless did put it into [her] bosom being in a paper, which whan [she] went to bed fell from her, and she toke it up, not loking into the paper what it was'.⁴¹

Ophelia must make it appear that Hamlet forced the letter on her—or, at the very least, Polonius must make it clear that he did not encourage his daughter to solicit Hamlet's attentions. The real issue is not explicitly spoken, but it haunts the conversation between Polonius and the king and queen nevertheless. When Polonius introduces the letter, saying, 'I have a daughter . . . | Hath given me this', he characteristically interrupts himself with a digression: 'I have a daughter—have while she is mine— | Who in her duty and obedience, mark, | Hath given me this' (2.2.105–7). Polonius tries to assure his listeners that Ophelia gave him the letter in 'duty and obedience' (which he exhorts his audience to 'mark'), but simultaneously raises the possibility that Ophelia (soon?) will not be his daughter, but another man's wife. While adamantly denying that he knew anything of the letter from Hamlet to Ophelia, Polonius admits the severity of the situation if he *had* known: 'What do you think of me? . . . what might you think?' he repeats four times (2.2.126, 128, 131–2, 136), rhetorically conjuring the situation if either the king or queen thought that he had known.

> But what might you think
> When I had seen this hot love on the wing—
> As I perceived it (I must tell you that)
> Before my daughter told me—what might you,
> Or my dear majesty your Queen here, think

If I had played the desk or table-book,
Or given my heart a working mute and dumb,
Or looked upon this love with idle sight,
What might you think? No, I went round to work.

(2.2.128–36)

While some of the images convey merely a closing of the eye, a failure to speak or hear or see, one is more active: 'If I had played the desk or table-book', if I had been the materials on which letters are physically written (the desk) or in which the raw materials of a letter are composed (the table-book, or note-book, of which more later). Polonius is anxious to assure his master and mistress that he did not collude in the courtship between Hamlet and Ophelia, a courtship that, if successful, might one day see his grandchild on the Danish throne.[42]

Polonius once again closes down the conversation by implying that they are impugning his integrity, telling them that 'Before my daughter told me' he had no knowledge of the exchange; and immediately upon knowing, 'I went round to work', and told Ophelia that Hamlet was 'a prince out of thy star. | This must not be' (2.2.136–9). Characteristically, he gave her 'Precepts': 'That she should lock herself from his resort, | Admit no messengers, receive no tokens' (2.2.140–1). Letters are not mentioned explicitly, but they are clearly implied by 'messengers', as *Ralph Roister Doister* and the Dutch paintings demonstrate. Ophelia, he claims, 'took the fruits of my advice' and 'repelled' Hamlet, as a result of which he fell '[i]nto the madness wherein now he raves' (2.2.142–7). He deftly refocuses the conversation on the prince, and Ophelia is forgotten, except as a bait to trap Hamlet so that they can observe their 'encounter' and see for themselves that he loves her.

It is in that encounter—midway through the play, and perhaps the drama's most painful scene—that the true impact of Hamlet's letters can be felt most keenly. But of course the scene is not of Ophelia's making: it is instead staged by the king and her father. Claudius asks his queen to leave,

> For we have closely sent for Hamlet hither
> That he, as 'twere by accident, may here
> Affront Ophelia. Her father and myself—
> We'll so bestow ourselves that, being unseen,
> We may of their encounter frankly judge.
>
> (3.1.29–33)

Although their ostensible goal is to assess whether or not Hamlet's love for Ophelia is causing his current 'affliction', I propose that the deliberateness of the staging suggests something more specific. In the Folio version of these lines, Claudius says, 'Her Father, and my selfe (lawful espials) | Will so bestow our selues, that seeing vnseene | We may of their encounter frankely iudge' (F, 005^r). The hypometric addition of 'lawful espials', according to John Jones, 'add an appealing touch in the area of intellectual yet farcical yet dangerous comedy which is absolutely of this play, they further the spying, the groping, the hide-and-seek cause of the whole'.[43] But rather than simply meaning 'legally justified onlookers', 'lawful espials' may mean 'those who spy for legal reasons', an interpretation that is bolstered by Claudius' assertion that the two men will 'frankely iudge' the meeting. For an encounter between two lovers with two men as witnesses is the classic form for a clandestine but valid marriage: the witnesses are the 'lawful' element to verify the match. This scene, therefore, is in effect an anti-marriage, an undoing of marriage: whereas in a real, clandestine marriage, Ophelia would accept Hamlet's ring in the presence of two witnesses, here Ophelia returns Hamlet's letters in the unacknowledged but 'lawful' presence of two witnesses.[44]

Ophelia attempts to return the letters not only physically, but also verbally, in clear and unambiguous terms:

> My lord, I have remembrances of yours
> That I have longed long to redeliver.
> I pray you now receive them.
>
> (3.1.92–4)

Her placing of the letters into a narrative of their previous relationship tacitly encourages Hamlet to admit that he sent them. But Hamlet, almost as if he knows he is being overheard, staunchly objects that 'No, not I. I never gave you aught' (3.1.95). This moment, like many of the most emotionally fraught moments in the play, is one where the early versions differ. F has 'No, no, I never gaue you ought' to which Ophelia replies 'My honor'd Lord, I know right well you did' (F, 005^r). In Q2 Hamlet almost seems to imply that *he* is not the writer, 'No, not I, I neuer gaue you ought', and Ophelia persists 'My Lord, you know right well you did' (Q2, E^r), stressing his knowledge rather than her own.[45] In both she continues, 'And with them words of so sweet breath composed | As made the things more rich' (3.1.97–8). With the withdrawal of his sweet breath, 'perfume lost' (3.1.98), she no longer wants the letters: 'Rich gifts wax poor when givers prove unkind' (3.1.100). And it is at the very moment that she gives them back—'There, my lord' (3.1.101)—that Hamlet begins his relentless assault on her reputation: 'Ha! Ha! Are you honest?... Are you fair?' (3.1.102, 104). If she were indeed honest and fair, he argues, 'your honesty would admit no discourse to your beauty' (3.1.106–7): her very admitting of discourse, the evidence of which is the 'remembrances' she attempts to return, has compromised her honesty. Now, even 'If thou dost marry, I'll give thee this plague for thy dowry: be thou as chaste as ice, as pure as snow, thou shalt not escape calumny... Or, if thou wilt needs marry, marry a fool, for wise men know well enough what monsters you make of them' (3.1.137–9)—that is, cuckolds.

As Lisa Jardine has argued, what is at stake in Ophelia's decline is a broken betrothal, and more specifically that Ophelia's return to Hamlet of his gifts is 'a sign of a betrothal broken off'. Jardine comments that, 'Ophelia is honest (chaste) or a bawd (a whore) depending on how Hamlet now chooses to describe his own behaviour towards her. If he loved her, declared that love to her, and she accepted his gifts and embraces, then she is chaste. If he never loved her, but attempted to seduce her only, then *she* is lewd and lascivious, because *Hamlet* trifled with her.'[46] I would argue further that this situation only arises because she attempts to return the 'remembrances', a result of the dynamics of gift-giving within clandestine marriage.

From that moment on, both Hamlet and Ophelia evince an obsession with sex. In their conversation at the performance of *The Mousetrap*, Hamlet makes lewd references to lying in Ophelia's lap, 'country matters', and lying 'between maids' legs' (3.2.110, 112). The next time we see Ophelia, she is '*distracted*', according to the Folio's stage directions, singing catches of songs that are, as Maurice Charney writes, 'markedly bawdy. After monumental repression, she seems finally to be expressing herself.'[47] But what exactly do these ballads express? They tell of dead or departed lovers, and of maids who lose their virginity to lovers who then disappear:

> Then up he rose and donned his clothes
> And dupped [opened] the chamber door—
> Let in the maid that out a maid
> Never departed more . . .
> Quoth she, 'Before you tumbled me
> You promised me to wed'. . . .
> 'So would I ha' done by yonder sun
> An thou hadst not come to my bed'.
>
> (4.5.52–66)

The man's reply suggests that precisely her willingness to sleep with him is what makes him unwilling to marry her afterwards.

In the German touring version of *Hamlet, Tragœdia der Bestrafte Brudermond oder: Prinz Hamlet aus Dænnemark*,[48] which might serve as a contemporary interpretation of *Hamlet*, Ophelia is quite definitely portrayed as a betrothed and jilted woman. Wearing a spoiled wedding dress (II.ix; 134), Ophelia takes Phantasmo (the Osric character) to be Hamlet, and is quite sexually forward with him: 'What sayest thou, my love? We will go to bed together. I will wash thee quite clean' (II.ix; 134). It is clear that the goal here is marriage: 'Listen, my love: I have been at the priest's, and he will join us this very day. I have made all ready for the wedding, and bought chickens, hares, meat, butter, and cheese. There is nothing else wanting but the musicians to play us to bed' (III.xi; 135).

But when Phantasmo decides that he might as well play along, in order to get Ophelia into bed, she suddenly refuses, now quite properly insisting that they must marry before consummating their love: 'No, no, my poppet, we must first go to church together, and then we'll eat and drink, and then we'll dance. Ah, how merry she shall be!' (III.xi; 136). Ophelia's inconsistency here again plays out the double bind of sex and marriage: sexual consummation can provide evidence of a marriage, as long as both parties consent, but if the man refuses this interpretation, sex makes the woman a whore. Finally, she rejects Phantasmo's advances and, seeing her beloved in another man, runs towards him; ultimately, in her delusion, she falls off a high hill (IV.vi; 141).

If, as Palfrey suggests, *Hamlet* does indeed provoke 'curiosity about the true status of Hamlet's relationship with Ophelia', it is for good reason: because the play deliberately invites it. But the questions we are invited to ask are perhaps not 'Does he really love her? Did they have sex?' because the answers to these questions can never be represented on stage. The real question is: are Hamlet's intentions towards Ophelia honourable, as she claims they are? Does he initially intend to marry her? And the answer must be, through the play's consistent coding of the place of letters in relation to the courtship of women: yes, he does. The tragedy of Ophelia is that she is forced by her father not only to break off the relationship (in modern terms) but to attempt the impossible, to undo what has gone before by returning his letters. As Hamlet brutally tells her, there is only one place for a woman who returns the letters by which she has been courted, who denies herself the marriage that would have legitimized the breach of her chastity: 'Get thee to a nunnery!' (3.1.120).

In proposing this understanding of what happens to Ophelia, I am implicitly demonstrating the limits of a historicist criticism that would seek to find the representation of real social processes in Shakespeare's plays. In 'real life', Ophelia would not have been sexually compromised by accepting Hamlet's letters, unless she had wanted to call off the marriage and he wanted to pursue it. But in a parallel form of 'stage life', the return of love-letters under disputed terms ('I never gave you aught'—'you know right well you did') has real consequences. Ophelia's fate speaks to the successful development of a new grammar of stage letters, where letter-giving and letter-receiving, processes borrowed from the real world, have been encoded with specific meanings and heightened with particular emotions. Shakespeare's letter-writers and readers all subscribe to this grammar—and it is to the most prolific of his writers that I turn in my final chapter: Hamlet.

7

Rewriting Hamlet

Hamlet is the most prolific letter-writer in Shakespeare's drama. He writes a love letter to Ophelia. He writes to his uncle and stepfather king Claudius, advising him that he has returned to Denmark. He writes to his mother. He writes to his friend Horatio, with news and instructions on how to deliver other letters. He writes to the king of England, although not under his own name. Three of his letters are read out on stage in their entirety. Four, if not all, of these letters make a physical appearance on stage. In addition to Hamlet's letters, the play witnesses a letter sent from Claudius to the king of England, carried by Rosencrantz and Guildenstern, and 'notes' written by Polonius for his son Laertes ('these letters' in the equivalent exchange in Q1, D2$^\mathrm{v}$),[1] carried to Paris by Reynaldo. *Hamlet* is thus filled with letters, its plot often dependent on them, and its hero its leading writer. Unlike the king, who employs secretaries, Hamlet routinely writes his own letters: Claudius can identify Hamlet's handwriting and as we shall see, Hamlet's letter-writing skills are second to none. And yet critics have not made much of this letter-writing.[2] If they note it at all, they diagnose it as one symptom of Hamlet's general intellectualism, another manifestation of the metaphorical 'inky cloak' (1.2.77) he wears as a perennial graduate student, alongside his inclination to solitude, book-reading, melancholy, and madness. As I shall suggest in this chapter, however, it is through the writing—or rather the rewriting—of one of Hamlet's letters that Shakespeare provides a different perspective on one of the play's central themes: how and what to remember.

Rewriting Bellerophon's Letters

The letter to which the play devotes most time is written by Hamlet to the king of England. It serves a crucial plot function: Hamlet has been sent, with his university friends Rosencrantz and Guilderstern, on an embassy to England ostensibly to demand the unpaid tribute that England owes to Denmark. In reality, the letters of introduction that Rosencrantz and Guilderstern are carrying from Claudius to England contain instructions that Hamlet should be executed. Already suspicious of his companions, Hamlet sneaks into their shipboard chamber at night, and finds, opens, and reads the letter. Discovering what Claudius has planned for him, Hamlet substitutes a letter requesting that the king of England execute its bearers. Soon after, the ship carrying the embassy is pursued by pirates, and Hamlet ends up in their hands, while Rosencrantz and Guilderstern continue to their fate; the play ends as English ambassadors reach Denmark, with joyful news for Claudius that they have carried out his instructions to kill the two Danish envoys.

It's the oldest letter story in the book, quite literally. The earliest possible reference to literate culture in western art comes in book six of *The Iliad* (6:167–70), when King Proteus' queen, Anteia, falls in love with her husband's guest, a younger man named Bellerophon. Enraged when her passion is not reciprocated, the queen tells her husband that Bellerophon has made advances towards her. Rather than break the rules of hospitality by murdering his guest, Proteus dispatches Bellerophon to Anteia's father, the king of Lycia, sending him with a deadly messsage contained in folded tablets [γράψας ἐν πίνακι], namely an instruction to kill him.[3] In English Renaissance translations, these written tablets become 'letters': George Chapman has Proteus 'sending him with letters seald (that, opened, touch his life)',[4] while another contemporary englishing, by Arthur Hall from a French translation, describes how 'Malicious, false, and ful of guile he letters doth compose.'[5] The story was familiar enough to become one of Erasmus's *Adagia* (II.vi.82), and indeed

Chapman's translation of Homer refers the reader to Erasmus in a printed marginal note.[6] The point for Erasmus was the treachery involved in giving the letter to Bellerophon: 'Thus', he concludes, 'of anyone who from imprudence either tells or does something that betrays him, one can rightly use the phrase A Bellerophon letter, or of anyone who suffers an injury under pretext of doing him a kindness'.[7] But ultimately, Bellerophon does not die. The Lycian king proves equally unwilling to kill his new guest in his own house, and instead sends the young man on a series of seemingly deadly missions against the Chimaera, the Solymi, and the Amazons, and sets an ambush by Lycian men, all of which Bellerophon survives. Convinced that the gods must be on Bellerophon's side for a reason, the king offers him his own daughter and a half-share in his kingdom and the Lycians give him the best lands in the country.[8] Bellerophon's divine protection overcomes the treachery of the letter he carries.

Hamlet has it both ways. The Bellerophon letter given to Hamlet clinches Claudius' evil for anyone who still doubts it. Echoing Bellerophon, Hamlet speaks of 'heaven' being 'ordinant' (5.2.48) in his discovery of the scheme, detects a providential 'divinity that shapes our ends' (5.2.10), and survives. But he then uses the same trick himself, providing his erstwhile friends Rosencrantz and Guildenstern with a second Bellerophon letter that leads directly to their deaths. This is perhaps the play's most difficult moral issue, since in order for Hamlet's action, nothing more than a repetition of Claudius', to have any ethical validity, we must be certain that Rosencrantz and Guildenstern colluded in the plot to murder the prince. Hamlet is himself sure of this: 'They are not near my conscience', he tells Horatio, 'Their defeat | Does by their own insinuation grow' (5.2.57–8). In the Folio, an extra line makes his sense of their guilt explicit: 'Why man, they did make loue to this imployment' (F, Pp8ʳ). Against this, though, Horatio's worried concern for their lives, 'So Guildenstern and Rosencranz go to't' (5.2.56), suggests that he does not share in Hamlet's certainty.

I draw attention to this letter because the play does, at great length and almost clumsily: this is the passage that Samuel Taylor Coleridge singled out to explore the workings of Hamlet's newly detected 'psychology'.[9] Hamlet leaves Denmark early in Act 4. In the final scene of that act, Horatio is sought out by sailors who bring him a letter from Hamlet, and seek his influence to deliver letters to the king. Hamlet's letter, read aloud by Horatio, explains only that the prince has been seized by pirates, who have ultimately helped him, while Rosencrantz and Guilderstern *'hold their course for England'* (4.6.26–7). It is not until the final scene of the play— after the graveyard scene, and Ophelia's funeral—that Hamlet gets around to telling Horatio about his discovery of Claudius' letter and the substitution of his own, an incident that must have occurred in real time sometime soon after Act 4, Scene 3. The strangeness of this chronological placing demands that we question why we are treated to such a detailed account of the letter incident long after the events have taken place, and when a narrative about them must have lost any immediate plot significance.

Hamlet's story is dramatic and urgent. At sea, he lies in his cabin sleepless. In the dark, he recounts,

> Groped I to find out them, had my desire,
> Fingered their packet, and in fine withdrew
> To mine own room again, making so bold,
> My fears forgetting manners, to unseal
> Their grand commission.
>
> (5.2.14–18)

Hamlet's statement that he needed to 'unseal | Their grand commission' reveals that the commission takes the form of a sealed letter. In breaking the seal of a letter directed to another, that utter breach of epistolary protocol, Hamlet's implied apology for 'forgetting manners' here prefigures Edgar's regret when he opens letters bound for Edmund: 'Leave, gentle wax; and manners, blame us not' (*KL* 4.6.254).

Reading the letter, Hamlet finds 'an exact command' that 'My head should be struck off' (*Ham* 5.2.19, 25). Realizing that he is 'benetted round with villains' (5.2.29), Hamlet 'sat me down' and '[d]evised a new commission' (5.2.31–2), '[a]n earnest conjuration from the King [Claudius]' that the king of England '[w]ithout debatement further more or less' 'should those bearers put to sudden death, | Not shriving time allowed' (5.2.38–47). But this substitution of letters demands more explanation, and Hamlet gives it, unasked. Not only did he devise and pen the commission, he 'wrote it fair' (5.2.32) adding

> I once did hold it as our statists do
> A baseness to write fair and laboured much
> How to forget that learning, but, sir, now
> It did me yeoman's service.
>
> (5.2.33–6)

Hamlet is here rehearsing the social codes that traditionally equated advanced literacy, and especially the ability to write well, with the lower orders of men who had received clerical or university training. It was a cliché of humanist literature that the aristocracy could not write: a speaker in Juan Luis Vives' schoolboy dialogues *Linguae Latinae exercitatio* (1539) claims that the nobility 'think it fine and proper . . . not to know how to shape their letters properly. You would think that it was a lot of chickens scratching about; unless you know beforehand who the writer was, you'd never guess. We see them signing letters composed by their secretaries with totally illegible signatures.'[10] Indeed, those who could write well might be tempted to deny their skill, as Michel de Montaigne claimed: 'I have in my time seene some, who by writing did earnestly get both their titles and living, to disavow their apprentissage, marre their pen, and affect the ignorance of so vulgar a qualitie.'[11] Jonathan Goldberg has rightly noted that in penning the letter Hamlet 'descends to the base matter, the materiality of the letter, a social descent to the yeoman's secretarial skill, manual labor that nonetheless produces the royal word'.[12] But I would argue that Hamlet's descent to the 'materiality of the letter' goes well beyond the ability to pen well that is Goldberg's primary concern.

Hamlet's letter requires considerable skill. This is more than a matter of fine penmanship, although a mastery of the Continental italic hand used in diplomatic documents would be the first step. The scholars who drafted and wrote the kind of commission that Claudius sends to the king of England would also need to be thoroughly schooled in the rhetoric of international diplomacy, and quite possibly the civil law that underpinned that diplomacy, not to mention the elegant Latin in which all such documents were couched.[13] As Hamlet notes, 'our statists', the fashionable politicians of the day, lack these skills, but the prince can put together a passable 'earnest conjuration from the king', couched in the long-winded dependent clauses typical of such documents, which he parodies for Horatio:

> As England was his faithful tributary,
> As love between them like the palm might flourish,
> As peace should still her wheaten garland wear
> And stand a comma 'tween their amities,
> And many such like 'as'-es of great charge.
>
> (5.2.39–43)[14]

But beyond the penmanship, the language, and the style, Hamlet has to understand and reproduce the now lost material protocols of letter-writing operating at the highest administrative levels. While letter-writing manuals advised a wide audience on the proper use of paper, folding, and the layout and wording of subscription and superscription (see Chapter 1), Hamlet is here producing a document of immense diplomatic delicacy. He recounts how he 'Folded the writ up in the form of th'other' (5.2.51), revealing that he knows that the letter must be folded in a particular way, and takes pains to replicate the folding provided by Claudius' secretaries. He also 'Subscribed it' (5.2.52) ending the letter with a valediction and adding Claudius' 'sign manual' (signature), once again an act requiring a knowledge of letter-writing decorum.

Hamlet's account of this process of composition is effectively a monologue, interspersed only with rhetorical invitations to Horatio to request more: 'But wilt thou hear now how I did proceed?' 'wilt thou know | Th'effect of what I wrote?' (5.2.27, 36–7). But Horatio interjects with one eminently practical query about the substitute letter: 'How was this sealed?' (5.2.47).[15] It is this intervention that hits at the heart of Hamlet's story, as is suggested obliquely by the version of events given in Q1. This 1603 printing does not include Hamlet's lengthy account of letter-rewriting—indeed Hamlet's adventures at sea are not revealed by Hamlet at all, but by Horatio, speaking to the Queen. Horatio describes to her the contents of a letter he has received from Hamlet:

> Madame, your sonne is safe arriv'de in *Denmarke*,
> This letter I euen now receiv'd of him,
> Whereas he writes how he escap't the danger,
> And subtle treason that the king had plotted,
> Being crossed by the contention of the windes,
> He found the Packet sent to the king of *England*,
> Wherein he saw himselfe betray'd to death,
> As at his next conuersion [*sc.* conversation?] with your grace,
> He will relate the circumstance at full.
>
> (Q1, H2^v)

Later in the exchange, the Queen asks 'But what become of *Gilderstone* and *Rossencrast*?' and Horatio takes up the story:

> He being set ashore, they went for *England*,
> And in the Packet there writ down that doome
> To be perform'd on them poynted for him:
> And by great chance he had his fathers Seale,
> So all was done without discouerie.
>
> (Q1, H2^v–H3^r)

It's a remarkable variation on the Q2, Folio and all subsequent conflated versions, with its half-digested, half-remembered details pouring forth so disorderedly, muddled syntax reflecting confused chronology. But even amidst the chaos, we hear the last minute recollection that 'by great chance he had his fathers Seale'. Whether Q1 is an inept memorial construction of the play, or a (still inept) record of an adaptation,[16] and while the paper and ink, folding and format specificity of Hamlet's intricate rewriting of the commission are all lost, the question of the seal shines through.[17]

Horatio is not alone in his concern. The play is permeated by a rhetoric of sealing, in which sealing stands for a potent mix of finality and authentification. After King Hamlet kills the elder Fortinbras in single combat, Fortinbras forfeits lands 'by a sealed compact | Well ratified by law and heraldy' (1.1.85–6). After Laertes at length wrings from his father 'my slow leave | By laboursome petition', Polonius '[u]pon his will . . . sealed my hard consent' (1.2.58–60). Hamlet assures a doubting Horatio that 'Since my dear soul was mistress of her choice | And could of men distinguish her election | Sh'ath sealed thee for herself' (3.2.59–61). Trying to woo Laertes and turn him against Hamlet, Claudius begs him, 'Now must your conscience my acquittance seal | And you must put me in your heart for friend' (4.7.1–2). In all these instances, whether sincere or not, the state of being sealed confers finiteness and authenticity, or in the language of the period, 'assurance': in speaking of his father, Hamlet claims the king was 'A combination and a form indeed | Where every god did seem to set his seal | To give the world assurance of a man' (3.4.58–60). Contrarily, without a seal, words have no real power. When debating with himself how to approach Gertrude, Hamlet decides to be 'cruel, not unnatural': 'How in my words somever she be shent | To give them seals never my soul consent' (3.2.385–9). Hamlet deliberately leaves his words to Gertrude unsealed.

By contrast, the letters at the heart of this chapter are very definitely sealed. In organizing Hamlet's departure, Claudius refers to 'everything' being 'sealed and done | That else leans on th'affair' (4.3.54–5), and his use of 'sealed' picking up Hamlet's earlier

observation that there are 'letters sealed' (3.4.200). This must strike
Hamlet, and his audience, as odd. Hamlet is, after all, the son of the
king, acting here as part of an embassy from Denmark to England,
and the usual means of dispatching an ambassador were lengthy and
ornate. Bernard du Rosier, in his short 1436 treatise on ambassadors,
advised envoys to demand that their instructions be given to them
privately and orally, so that questions could be raised and ambiguity
avoided.[18] Jean Hotman writes in his 1603 treatise *The Ambassador*
that 'an Ambassador ought to desire that his commission be giuen
him in writing, where the affaire he goeth about to treat, is of
great consequence, or that the effect thereof is odious'.[19] In striking
contrast, Hamlet is given no formal public audience, no private
instruction, no written commission to which he is privy, but only
'letters sealed' that he cannot read. It is not then surprising that
he immediately suspects a plot between the king and his erstwhile
friends Rosencrantz and Guildenstern.

In Hamlet's account, it is specifically in the matter of the seal that
Providence intervenes:

> Why even in that was heaven ordinant:
> I had my father's signet in my purse—
> Which was the model of that Danish seal.
>
> (5.2.48–50)

A signet usually took the form of a ring containing a smaller version
of a personal seal. In Shakespeare's plays, the signet ring serves as
a token of identification—in the macabre gloom of *Titus Andronicus*, Martius reports that it is because of the ring that he can
identify Bassanius's corpse '[i]n this detested, dark, blood-drinking
pit': 'Upon his bloody finger he doth wear | A precious ring that
lightens all this hole' (*Tit* 2.3.224–7). Beyond simple identification,
the personal ring serves as a form of proxy verification in extreme
circumstances. The Duke of York, facing military disaster in *Richard
II*, commands a serving-man to go to his sister Gloucester at Plashy
and 'Bid her send me presently a thousand pound'—then pauses,

and adds 'Hold, take my ring', knowing that a servant's word would not be enough by itself to raise such a large sum of money (*R2* 2.2.90–2). When the disguised Kent instructs a gentleman to take news of Lear's travails to Dover, he again hands over this token: 'If you shall see Cordelia . . . show her this ring | And she will tell you who your fellow is, | That yet you do not know' (*KL* 3.1.42–5). The most dramatically striking instance of this personal verification comes in *King Henry VIII*, in a scene ripped from John Foxe's *Acts and Monuments*, when the King saves Cranmer, about to face the Privy Council. 'If entreaties | Will render you no remedy', he says, 'this ring | Deliver them, and your appeal to us | There make before them' (*H* 8 5.1.149–52). When faced with arraignment, Cranmer plays his trump card: 'Stay, good my lords, | I have a little yet to say. Look there, my lords. | By virtue of that ring, I take my cause | Out of the gripes of cruel men and give it | To a most noble judge, the King my master.' The privy councilors all concur that the ring is 'the King's ring', 'no counterfeit', 'the right ring, by heaven', and realize they have gone too far: as Norfolk points out, the ring says it all: 'Do you think, my lords, | The King will suffer but the little finger | Of this man to be vexed' (5.2.131–41). The King's ring is instantly recognizable, its message unequivocal. Within seconds, the powerful councillors are displaced, and Cranmer takes his seat at the head of the Council table.

The signet bestows on its borrower the letter-writing powers of its owner, whether legitimately or illegitimately, a phenomenon often exploited in fictions of the day. In Robert Parry's romance *Moderatus* (1595), Priscus sees a letter fall from his page's bosom, and 'the indorsement thereof, perceiued it to be his friend *Moderatus* hand-writing, and that the direction was to *Florida*'. Under examination, the page confirms the letter's provenance, and Priscus becomes 'great with childe till he might viewe the contentes of his letter', although he cannot open it without the fact being detected. However, there is a way out: 'in the ende after long studie, he bethought him of the print of *Moderatus* signet, which he had in yuorie, and therefore might well open the same without knowledge, whereupon presently vnripping the seale, he perused his friendes lines to *Florida*'. After reading, he 'sealed the letter a-new', and sent it back on its intended journey.[20] Whereas having the signet of his friend permits Priscus merely to open, read and re-seal the letter, Hamlet's allows him to finish a more complex task. As he explains to Horatio, he

> Folded the writ up in the form of th'other,
> Subscribed it, gave't th'impression, placed it safely,
> The changeling never known.
>
> (5.2.51–3)

Here the signet gives 'th'impression' produces an entirely new 'changeling'. Crucially, too, Hamlet's seal-ring is also a family heirloom. When Falstaff has his pocket picked, he complains that he 'lost a seal ring of my grandfather's worth forty mark' (*1H4* 3.3.81–2). Although Hal challenges this valuation, sardonically commenting that the ring is in fact 'copper', 'A trifle, some eightpenny matter' (3.3.84, 104), Falstaff's lament is only partly financial: this is his grandfather's seal-ring, a family inheritance.[21] Shakespeare gives greater dramatic life to such a ring in *All's Well That Ends Well* where Bertram initially refuses to give up to Diana the ring she requests, claiming, 'It is an honour 'longing to our house, | Bequeathed down from many ancestors, | Which were the greatest obloquy i' th' world | In me to lose' (4.2.42–5). In Hamlet's case, of course, the family seal-ring is also the nation's: his possession of it speaks to his claim to the Danish throne.

Hamlet spends forty lines sketching his actions with the letters— and one can see why: it takes a lot of explaining. As early as 1736, Sir Thomas Hanmer pondered that Hamlet's stratagem 'was possible, but not very probable; methinks their [Rosencrantz and Guildenstern's] Commission was kept in a very negligent Manner, to be thus got from them without their knowing it'.[22] Beyond the theft, in producing the letter to England, Hamlet has to lay claim to a host of letter-related skills: locating a suitable piece of paper, folding in the correct manner, writing in a secretary's fair italic hand in the language and rhetorical style of international diplomatic correspondence, subscribing it as if by Claudius. But it is the sealing with the 'Danish seal', a copy of which he just happens to have on him, that is the finishing touch for the letter.

Forged Letters

We should not underestimate the gravity of Hamlet's actions in rewriting the king's letter: he successfully manufactures a high-level forgery that moves the king of England to put to death two Danish envoys.[23] Even leaving to one side the fatal consequences, forgery in the king's name was a capital offence in England. While Hamlet does not contravene the statute passed (25 E. 3, Statute of Purveyors, cap. 2) that made treasonable the crime of 'counterfeit[ing] the kings great or priuie seale' (he merely places the genuine seal to a document without authority, a relatively minor offence of, at worst, 'a very great misprision'), he is clearly guilty of 'the forging ... of the signe manuall' (the autograph signature that certifies a document): he claims categorically that he has 'Subscrib'd' the letter. This 'forging ... of the signe manuall' had been explicitly made a crime of high treason during the reign of Mary I.[24]

The creation of this letter can be seen as tapping into contemporary anxieties about the ability to forge or doctor official documents. In an era where personal documents, and especially letters, were often produced in court as evidence against those accused, there was a heightened understanding that letters could be dangerous. When Robert Devereux, earl of Essex realized that his February 1601 coup was doomed, his first impulse was to burn his papers— a move that implied his guilt.[25] Others were more subtle. When the earl of Somerset was about to be arrested for the murder of Sir Thomas Overbury in 1616, he took the advice of the famed manuscript collector Sir Robert Cotton on what to do with his papers.

Cotton, the prosecution alleged, 'advised you not to burn, but to keep them: And all of them being without dates, Cotton told you there might be such dates given them as would be much to your advantage: So you gave him order for that purpose, to give dates to those letters…he dated some of them with a purpose to cross the Indictment: and some of the letters he razes, some pastes, some pares, as they were advantageous or disadvantageous to him; and all this to obscure the fact.'[26] Cotton believed that simply to *destroy* the papers was not enough to 'obscure the fact' of them; instead, the letters had to exist, but be razed, pasted, and pared to say the right thing.

Unfortunately for Cotton, ink-and-paper letters allow only limited possibilities for rewriting. As Juliet Fleming has noted, erasures from paper 'are neither readily effected nor infinitely repeatable: they are possible, but not practical. The cutting or burning of pages aside, marks left by ink on paper are more easily erased by being crossed or blotted out'—one could use the penknife or a pumice-stone to scrape or cut the paper, or one could blot (use excess ink to cover) or strike through a word or phrase—but 'neither blotting nor crossing can restore a clean writing surface'.[27] The teacher in Vives' schoolboy dialogues points to this dilemma: 'Since you have tried to change these letters into others, having erased parts with the pointed end of your knife, you have disfigured your writing. It would have been better to draw a thin stroke through it', although that solution would leave the paper with the traces of both the mistake and the attempt to delete.[28] Moreover, as the *vulgaria*-like phrases of John Palsgrave's 1530 French–English dictionary make clear, the perception of such amendments come at a moral price. Translating '*Ie efface des motz*' Palsgrave offers 'I Race a writynge I take out a worde with a pomyce or pen knife / so *that* I may write in the same place'. But the effect is that 'All the worlde maye se *that* this writynge hath be raced.' This sort of effacement or erasure betrays itself, is by its nature suspicious, suggesting falsification: 'I Race a worde out of a writing by falshoode / *Ie faulce*… This writing is raced:

Ceste escripture est faulcée. This indenture is raced all the worlde may see it: *Ceste indenture est faulcée tout le monde le peult veoyr.*' Similarly with blotting (the use of excess ink to cover a written word): 'Who hath blotted out this worde / by al symlytude he mente no good faith.'[29]

Beyond the ethical considerations hinted at by Palsgrave, there are legal implications: official documents (including, ideally, diplomatic letters) needed to be 'clean', free of ink blots, and signs of deletion and erasement. In John Weddington's manual *Breffe Instruction* (1567), he advises the merchant that his register 'boke ought to be verri faire writton, without ani blottinge or eror, and with one manner of hande, for to avoide variance, that might come, yf you do occapie in compani &c'.[30] Gerard Malynes in his *Lex Mercatoria* (1622), explains why: the Spaniards, he claims, 'keepe a Borrador or Memorial, wherein all things are first entred, and may vpon occasion be blotted, altered, or (by error) be miscast, or not well entred. But in the Iournall and Leidger Booke, there may not be any alteration of cyphers, blotting (nor places left in blanke in the Iournall) but one parcell without intermission must follow another, otherwise the bookes are of no credit in law, or before any Magistrat.'[31] In other words, the very trace of erasure or amendment—for whatever purpose—compromises the evidential validity of the document.

It is not surprising then that Cotton and Somerset were caught out. Bureaucrats, then as now, had developed highly specific protocols, not evident to the layman, by which they could distinguish an official document from a forgery. Such detective work can be seen in action in a case dating from 1630 when the Privy Council called on manuscript expert William Boswell to verify a letter dated 6 March 1630 signed by the king, recommending one William Poe to the Lord Justices of Ireland.[32] On receiving the letter, however, the Lord Justices suspected it to be 'surreptiously and vnduly gotten', and forwarded it for verification to the man whose office had produced it, Secretary of State Dudley Carleton, Viscount Dorchester. Boswell's

researches revealed that Poe had petitioned the king complaining
about the behaviour of Stephen Allen and others for 'disturbing him
in the operation of a Comm ission' in Ireland, and for indicting him
twice without cause. As a result on 14 July 1629 Dorchester ordered
the Clerk of the Signet that a letter recommending Poe's petition be
written to the Lord Deputy and Council of Ireland and prepared
for Dorchester to present to the King. As Boswell's investigation
soon realized, the story was true up to the point of the Dorchester
authorization: the viscount had the letter drawn up, but 'vpon some
consideration had of the contents, it was reiected by his *Lordsh*ip;
& layed aside for some tyme'. In March 1630, however, Poe 'having
casually gotten this *Lett*re into his hands' contrived to have the king
sign the document at Newmarket. So the question here is not that
the letter was not prepared, nor that it was signed by the king,
but that it was not authorized by Dorchester's office in the proper
manner.

Boswell presented the Privy Council with evidence that the letter
failed on several grounds, in the formulae used, the handwriting, the
'fold and makeing up', and the subscription:

3. In this Letter I observe the vsuall clause of Warranty for doeing the
   contents thereof is (after these words—And these our Letters) cutte off
   with, &c. And the date thereof Giuen att our Palace of Westminster this
   sixth of March in the fourth yeare of our Raigne) is added in another
   hand (whose I cannott finde) much different from the hand wherein the
   whole body of the Letter is written by one [*illeg.*] Read an vnderclerke
   in that office.
4. The fold, and makeing vp of this Letter is much narrower, then the
   ordinarie manner observed with said office; besides it was neuer entred,
   or docquetted there, for ought I can learne.
5. The subscription is not according to the *Lord Viscount* Dorchesters
   direction to the office. Besides the first twoo lynes thereof are in one
   hand (whose I cannott discouer, either by Poe, or any other) And all
   the rest downward to the end, is written in an other hand, by one
   George Hare a Scrivene r dwelling in Westm*inste*r, whoe acknowledgeth
   the same . . .

Some of these points were simply a matter of record-keeping: a document emanating from a particular office should be entered or docketed in the register of that office. Some of these related to personnel: a document emanating from a particular office should be in the identifiable hand of someone working in that office. Other protocols were embedded in the material letter itself, particularly in its use of folding and layout. The key, however, was the seal, which Boswell detected was taken from another document:

6. The Seale is apparently his *Maiesties* Signet, and as I coniecture by some parts of the waxe, somewhat different in colour from other, & by some small raggs of paper in it, hath ben formerly vpon some other Letter, or writing. But when, by whome, or with whose notice it was put vnto this Letter in question, I cannot absolutely determine.

The question naturally arose as to how Poe could have obtained a seal bearing the mark of the king's signet. Under examination by Boswell, Poe claimed that one John Woodison, 'a young man, whoe sometime with permission wrote in the office, & is nowe one of Judge Whitlocks clerkes', had promised at a meeting in Gloucester 'to procure the Kings signet within twoe, or three dayes vnto this Lettre', and had delivered the letter 'sealed vnto him (Poe) walking vnder the Gallery att Whitehall' in exchange for a payment from Poe of 37 shillings.

Although the insistence on the details of handwriting, folding, and sealing are shared with Hamlet's letter, these examples, however, are not substantively the same: Cotton and Poe tamper with existing documents while Hamlet replaces one document with another, forged document. It is precisely the choice of this method of forgery that interests me here, for in making Hamlet create a new document, Shakespeare departs radically from his source materials, and introduces a new level of complexity to the prince's story.

From Erasure to Rewriting: Saxo, Belleforest, and Shakespeare

Shakespeare's immediate source was the fifth volume of François de Belleforest's *Histoires tragiques*, first published in Paris in 1570.[33] In its earlier volumes, the *Histoires tragiques* was primarily a French translation of Matteo Bandello's Italian *novelle*, but by the fifth book, Belleforest had run out of Bandello, and found room for a few additional tales from elsewhere, including the adventures of a Danish prince named Amleth following the remarriage of his mother to the evil Fengon. He took this from a work by a medieval Danish historian known as Saxo Grammaticus;[34] Saxo's *Historiae Danicae* had been made available in a Latin print edition by Jodocus Badius Ascensius in May 1514 in Paris through the labours of the Danish humanist Christiern Pedersen[35] (the text was reprinted in 1576 in Frankfurt by the exiled Huguenot André Wechel).[36]

Belleforest's telling follows Saxo quite closely. In Saxo's version, Feng wants to kill his stepson, but is fearful of the reactions of his wife and of Amleth's grandfather Rorik. So he decides that the King of Britain could be made to do the act. A contemporary English translation of Belleforest, *The Hystorie of Hamblet*, printed in 1608, takes up the story:

Now, to beare him company were assigned two of Fengons faithfull ministers, bearing letters ingraved in wood, that contained Hamblets death, in such sort as he had advertised the king of England. But the subtile Danish prince (beeing at sea) whilst his companions slept, having read the letters, and knowne his uncles great treason, with the wicked and villainous mindes of the two courtyers that led him to the slaughter, raced out the letter that concerned his death, and in stead thereof graved others, with commission to the king of England to hang his two companions; and not content to turne the death they had devised against him upon their owne neckes, wrote further, that king Fengon willed him to give his daughter to Hamlet in marriage. And so arriving in England, the messengers presented themselves to the king, giving him Fengons letter; who having read the contents, sayd nothing as then, but stayed convenient time to effect Fengons desire.[37]

As will be immediately apparent, the technologies of rewriting in the source materials and Shakespeare are radically different. Saxo's Amlethus and Belleforest's Amleth have merely to raze (*abradi, rasa, raced out*) certain characters in the wood, and then cut or engrave (*figurarum apicibus, graua & cisa, graved*) new characters. For Shakespeare's Hamlet, however, working in a different technology, everything has to be replaced—paper, ink, folding, handwriting, subscription (including sign manual), superscription, wax, and seal.

Belleforest's telling of the Amleth story is very close to Saxo's, but there is one fleeting difference: whereas Belleforest's translation introduces the wooden letters without further comment, Saxo (or perhaps his editor Pedersen) takes pains to distance himself from this single feature of his story with a parenthetical comment. Explaining that the messengers carried with them 'litteras ligno insculptas' ('letters engraved in wood'), he qualifies the statement: 'nam id celebre quondam genus chartarum erat' ('for that kind of letter was common at that time'). This comment serves to historicize the wooden letter, and to distance it from more familiar modern media. In the first scholarly edition of the *Historiae Danicae*, published in 1644 by the Danish historiographer Stephan Hansen Stephanius, that seven-word pronouncement is amplified in almost a full folio page of learned commentary about ancient writing technologies.[38] Stephanius draws not only on instances in early sources (Zenodotus, Pliny, Virgil, Juvenal, Livy, St Brovverum, and the sixth century CE poet Venantius Fortunatus) but also on the research of a new generation of antiquarian scholars fascinated by the writing materials of antiquity: among them the Portuguese historian Jerónimo Osório, the Danish physician Ole Worm, the Italian jurist Guido Panciroli, and the Jesuit emblematist Herman Hugo. In different ways, then, the 1514 Pedersen Saxo, Shakespeare, and Stephanius all register the importance and perhaps difficulty of Saxo's wooden letter, but Belleforest chooses to omit Saxo's comment that this practice is now uncommon, presumably in the interests of telling the story without interruption.

In choosing to depart from the Saxo-Belleforest model of a letter carved into wood, Shakespeare once again brings his story into a recognizably sixteenth-century milieu, but then goes out of his way to alert the audience that, for some reason, this is an important moment in the story of Hamlet. Once again, this demands the question: why? My contention is that in his replacement of the razed and re-graved letter with the substitute letter, Shakespeare is working through a debate that he has raised earlier in the play: namely, what it means to rewrite, or more specifically, what it means to be able to erase or not erase that which is written.

Technologies of Remembrance

At the heart of the play, Hamlet vows and fails to remember. The play constantly invokes and questions memory: for how long and how one should remember a dead father; what is the rightful 'king's remembrance' (2.2.26); Fortinbras has 'rights of memory in this kingdom' (5.2.373). Hamlet, we know, has some powers of memory: he does a fair job recalling to the players a version of Aeneas' tale to Dido ('If it live in your memory begin at this line . . .' (2.2.385–6)). But his memory wants to be selective. Even in his first soliloquy, Hamlet tries to avoid remembering: as he recalls 'So excellent a king, that was to this | Hyperion to a satyr', he exclaims, 'Heaven and earth, | Must I remember?' (1.2.139–43). This outburst prefigures the struggle that will ensue when the ghost appears, and tells his son to 'remember me' (1.5.91). Despite his vow to follow this order, Hamlet signally fails to remember his father in the correct way: the Ghost has to return in his mother's closet to berate him: 'Do not forget! This visitation | Is but to whet thy almost blunted purpose' (3.4.106–7).

The failure to remember is introduced simultaneously with the injunction to remember: 'Adieu, adieu, adieu, remember me' (1.5.91). This is the key instruction spoken by the ghost of King

Hamlet to his son. Hamlet's response is at first one of mental, physical, and metaphysical collapse, reiterating his 'Heaven and earth,
Must I remember?':

> O all you host of heaven, O earth—what else?—
> And shall I couple hell? Oh fie! Hold, hold, my heart,
> And you my sinews, grow not instant old
> But bear me swiftly up.
>
> (1.5.92–5)

But then he attends to his father's words:

> Remember thee?
> Ay, thou poor ghost, whiles memory holds a seat
> In this distracted globe. Remember thee?
> Yea, from the table of my memory,
> I'll wipe away all trivial fond records,
> All saws of books, all forms, all pressures past
> That youth and observation copied there
> And thy commandment all alone shall live
> Within the book and volume of my brain,
> Unmixed with baser matter.
>
> Yes, by heaven (1.5.95–104)

The oddness of this speech has long been recognized. In his
Shakespearean Tragedy, A. C. Bradley devoted a note to it, claiming
that it had 'occasioned much difficulty, and to many readers seems
even absurd'.[39] He explains Hamlet's breakdown and reiteration of
the word 'remember':

He is, literally, afraid that he will *forget*—that his mind will lose the message
entrusted to it. Instinctively, then, he feels that, if he *is* to remember, he
must wipe from his memory everything it already contains; and the image
of his past life rises before him, of all its joy in thought and observation
and the stores they have accumulated in his memory. All that is done with
for ever: nothing is to remain for him on the 'table' but the command,
'remember me'.[40]

And yet that doesn't happen. Having made up his mind to remember only to remember his father, Hamlet instantly bursts out,

'O most pernicious woman, | O villain, villain, smiling damned villain' (1.5.105–6), only to be struck by a thought:

> My tables! Meet it is I set it down
> That one may smile and smile and be a villain—
> At least I am sure it may be so in Denmark.
>
> (1.5.107–9)

And so Hamlet reaches for his 'tables', and writes down 'one may smile and smile and be a villain'—a maxim worth remembering—and then announces, pleased with himself, 'So, uncle, there you are. Now to my word. | It is "Adieu, adieu, remember me". | I have sworn't' (1.5.110–12).[41]

This speech refers us to two writing technologies, one metaphorical and one material, that share a basic concept. Over the past half century a series of distinguished studies has detailed the elaborate mnemonic devices, the 'theatres of memory' that were developed in the medieval and early modern periods.[42] But Hamlet's 'table of my memory' does not strive for this complexity: it is perhaps the most basic image of memory, as a waxed surface in which an image is imprinted.[43] In Plato's dialogue *Theaetetus*, Socrates suggests:

Please assume . . . that there is in our souls a block of wax, in one case larger, in another smaller, in one case the wax is purer, in another more impure and harder, in some cases softer, and in some of proper quality . . . Let us, then, say, that this is the gift of Memory, the mother of the Muses, and that whenever we wish to remember anything we see or hear or think of in our own minds, we hold this wax under the perceptions and thoughts and imprint them upon it, just as we make impressions from seal rings; and whatever is imprinted we remember and know as long as its image lasts, but whatever is rubbed out or cannot be imprinted we forget and do not know.[44]

As Mary Carruthers points out, even for Plato's first audience, that reference to 'block of wax' would gesture towards an existing material phenomenon, to the 'pair . . . of wooden slabs fastened together, familiar to every ancient student' that 'served for memoranda of all sorts—ephemeral and occasional writings, like school notes and

exercises, sketches, or compositions, bills and accounts'.[45] Throughout the classical and much of the medieval period, the waxed tablet
was the primary writing surface. As Michael Clanchy has shown,
something similar formed the primary material for composition in
the twelfth century: 'tablets...ordinarily made of wood, overlaid
with coloured wax, and often folded into a diptych which could be
worn on a belt. When something needed noting down, the diptych
was opened, thus exposing the waxed surfaces, which were written
on with a stylus.'[46] Letters were also written on wax tablets: as
Juan Luis Vives writes, 'Men of ancient times used to write letters
on tablets [in tabellis], as the poet Homer teaches us in the tale
of Bellerophon. That custom lasted until Roman times, as Latin
writers like Plautus, Cicero and others make clear. From this custom
those who carried letters were called *tabellarii*, which name remains
even now, although we no longer use tablets, but, as in other matters, through force of custom.'[47] In fact, Vives underestimates the
longevity of the tradition: tablets remained the standard medium
for letters until the time of Abelard and Heloise.

The continuity of the wax tablet to the Elizabethan tables meant
that ancient and scriptural accounts of writing still resonated in the
late sixteenth century. Preachers often recounted the story in the
first chapter of Luke of how John the Baptist's speechless father
Zacharias had signed for 'writing tables to declare that thinge by
dombe letters whiche by liuely voice he could not bring forth', and
by using these tables, confirmed that his son's name was John.[48] In
each successive translation, from the Greek $\pi\iota\nu\alpha\kappa\iota\delta\iota\omega\nu$ to the Latin
pugillarem to the 'writing tables' of the Geneva Bible, the same basic
technology was at stake: Zacharias could as easily have been a father
in Elizabethan England. As the technology persisted, so did the
notion of memory as a waxed tablet through ancient Greek, Roman,
patristic, and Renaissance writers.[49] Even in the late sixteenth century, one can find writers insisting on a literal understanding of the
memory as wax, with medical advice suggesting that heat be applied
to the head to soften up the wax and aid memory.[50] Although it had

its detractors (notably Francis Bacon),[51] the memory as wax tablet analogy was deeply embedded in the culture of Shakespeare and his audience, so when Hamlet speaks of a 'table of my memory' that can hold 'pressures past' and be 'wiped', the image is clear.

The second technology is the one on which Hamlet jots down his thoughts: 'my tables', the early modern variant of the classical hinged writing tablet. Recent research in early modern writing technologies has increased our understanding of the nature of these tables.[52] In situations where writing with ink, pen and paper would be physically cumbersome and messy,[53] these 'writing tables', requiring only a stylus, were a favourite device, especially for notetaking: we find them being used at the theatre, or during sermons.[54] Tables were also the principal writing materials used by students, from schoolboys to university men, and we might see them here as part of the natural paraphernalia of Hamlet the eternal student. Francis Goyet has suggested that, like any other good Wittenberg alumnus, the prince is here following the advice given to students by the university's leading light Philip Melanchthon that they should note down in their tables ('in tabulas referatur') every sentence, adage or apophthegm that they extracted from books, and then recopy these extracts into their commonplace book, judiciously arranging each extract under its 'locus' or commonplace heading.[55] Hamlet's ultimate goal, then, Goyet continues, may be to enter his epigram into a commonplace book, perhaps under the heading 'Villainie'.[56]

But this studious interpretation requires reading Hamlet against the grain of a powerful theatrical tradition. For the prince is by no means alone in pulling out his tables on London's stages before the Civil War, and the depiction of the table-user is surprisingly consistent.[57] Only occasionally are tables used to write down important information, and then during commercial transactions—for example, by a tailor in *Every Man Out of his Humour*,[58] and by a goldsmith in the comedy *The Cuck-Queanes and Cuckolds Errants*.[59] Usually, however, characters use the tables,

in Thomas Nashe's dismissive terms, 'to gather phrases',[60] to jot
down some *bon mot* or piece of arcane vocabulary. They signal not
Melanchthonian common-placing, but fashionable gullery. When
Matzagente exclaims 'I scorne to retort the obtuse ieast of a foole',
in John Marston's *Antonios Reuenge*, Balurdo 'drawes out his writing tables, and writes', 'Retort and obtuse, good words, very good
words'.[61] In Robert Greene's *James the Fourth*, the clown Slipper
instructs his master to 'Draw your tables, and write what wise
I speake', before embarking on a litany of 'what properties of a
woman hath a Horse' ('a merry countenance...a soft pace...a
broad forehead...broad buttockes').[62] In *Everie Woman in her Humor*,
a verbose declamation by Sernulas is interrupted by Scillicet, who
calls for 'Boy my Tables'. The tables are produced, and Sernulas
continues approvingly: 'A gracefull enquirie, and well obseru'd: Sir
my company shal make ye copious of nouelties: let your Tables
befriend your memorie.'[63] Also depicted bearing tables are spies,
women, and pedantic schoolmasters. Jonson's *Euery Man Out of his
Humour* has Cordatus berating 'narrow-ey'd Decipherers...that will
extort straunge and abstruse meanings out of any Subject': 'the
Authour defies them, and their writing-Tables'.[64] In Dekker's *Blurt
Master-Constable*, the courtesan Imperia and her ladies enter 'with
table bookes' to take notes on Lazarino's lecture, although they have
trouble keeping up: 'The what?...Oh againe sweet *Signior*?'[65] And
in *Love's Labour's Lost*, when Holofernes claims that Don Adriano
is 'too picked, too spruce, too affected, too odd, as it were, too
peregrinate, as I may call it', Nathaniel seizes on 'peregrinate' as
'A most singular and choice epithet' and '*Draws out his table-book*'
(5.1.12–15). All these characters are being mocked, either gently or
more vigorously, for their note-taking habits—a consistent stage
tradition which might make us pause to consider the expected effect
of Hamlet suddenly pulling out his tables mid soliloquy.

In fact, Hamlet himself comments on such table-users in a passage
that exists only in Q1. In the midst of his instructions to the players,

the prince exhorts them not to let their clowns speak 'more than is set down', or 'laugh themselves' to cause the spectators to laugh. In QI, the passage continues:

> And then you haue some agen, that keepes one sute
> Of ieasts, as a man is knowne by one sute of
> Apparell, and Gentlemen quotes his ieasts downe
> In their tables, before they come to the play as thus:
> Cannot you stay till I eate my porrige? and, you owe me
> A quarters wages: and, my coate wants a cullison:
> And your beere is sowre: and, blabbering with his lips,
> And thus keeping in his cinkapase of ieasts,
> When, God knows, the warme Clowne cannot make a iest
> Vnlesse by chance, as the blinde man catcheth a hare.
>
> $\qquad$ (QI, F2^{V})

For Hamlet, tables are the repository of the catchphrases of second-rate clowns—and yet he himself pulls out tables to take down his maxim. If not wholly comic, Hamlet's resort to his tables at the very least betrays his superficiality—his reliance on surfaces in a very particular sense. In moving from the 'table of my memory' to his 'tables' (and in QI, the two are identical, the phrase being 'tables | Of my memorie', C4^{V}) as we have seen, Shakespeare literalizes an absolutely commonplace figure.[66] This is in keeping with Margaret Ferguson's argument that Hamlet's language 'produces a curious effect of *materializing* the word, materializing it in a way that forces us to question the distinction between literal and figurative meanings'.[67] But by resorting to the material reality of his 'tables', by materializing the figurative, Hamlet also materializes a *problem* with his memory.

For tables are not a medium of long-term memory. As Henry Woudhuysen points out, 'the essential feature of these writing-tables was that they could be wiped clean and reused'.[68] The blank pages of early modern tables were covered by a coating made of plaster, a sticking agent and varnish,[69] a process that rendered the leaves, in

Francis Bacon's description, 'shining',[70] or in John Florio's, 'a kind of sleeked pasteboord'.[71] This coating meant that words could be written on the page, erased by a wet piece of sponge or linen and the tables written on again.[72] But to push this point further, the essential feature of these writing-tables is not that they *could*, but that they *must* be wiped clean to be used. Erasure is a prerequisite for writing. The Latin term for a 'clean slate' still in use is *tabula rasa*, not a mint, virgin tablet but a used-and-razed tablet.[73] Even the phrase 'clean slate' derives from the phrase 'to wipe the slate clean', so a 'clean slate' is in fact a previously soiled-and-now-cleaned slate.[74] And just as Hamlet's 'tables' were designed to be erased, so is the 'table of my memory'—as Plato puts it 'whatever is imprinted we remember and know as long as its image lasts, but whatever is rubbed out . . . we forget and do not know'.[75] A couplet in an early Jacobean satire addressed to Sir Nicholas Smith makes the analogy clear: 'The mind, you know is like a Table-book, | Which, th'old unwept, new writing never took.'[76]

In other words, the standard model of memory from Plato to these early modern notepads—both the theoretical notion and the practical expression—is one of impermanence, of required erasure. Hamlet fully subscribes to this. He claims he must 'wipe away' everything currently in his memory in order that he might write in it his father's 'commandment all alone'. But the minute he does this mental wiping he writes down 'one may smile, and smile and be a villain'. It is not clear from the text whether Hamlet goes on to write down 'Adieu, adieu, remember me' in his tables, but even if it does, it is too late: his first note, that 'one may smile, and smile and be a villain', remains unwiped, and that is what sustains him, and dictates his action, through much of the play to come.[77]

Hamlet's problems here are usefully illuminated by Sigmund Freud's attempt to schematize the workings of memory through different writing technologies.[78] Freud noted that supplementary aids to memory take two forms, neither of them completely helpful. One, a 'permanent memory-trace' such as 'a sheet of paper which I can write upon in ink', has the advantage of being permanent, and the disadvantage of being finite: at a certain point, the paper will be filled with ink and unable to hold any more (175). The other, such as writing as with 'a piece of chalk upon a slate', has 'unlimited receptive capacity' but, since the marks can be wiped, no permanence. As a result, he notes, 'an unlimited receptive capacity and a retention of permanent traces seem to be mutually exclusive properties in the apparatus which we use as substitutes for our memory: either the receptive surface must be renewed or the note must be destroyed' (176). Freud however found in the children's writing tablet named the *Wunderblock* a model for how the memory actually functions:

The *Wunderblock* is a slab of dark brown resin or wax with a paper edging; over the slab is laid a thin transparent sheet, the top end of which is firmly secured to the slab while its bottom end rests upon it without being fixed to it. This transparent sheet...itself consists of two layers, which can be detached from each other except at their two ends. The upper layer is a transparent piece of celluloid; the lower layer is made of thin translucent waxed paper. When the apparatus is not in use, the lower surface of the waxed paper adheres lightly to the upper surface of the wax slab.

(177)

A pointed stylus presses the waxed paper's lower surface onto the wax slab, producing grooves 'visible as dark writing' on the celluloid; this writing may then be destroyed by raising the double covering sheet away from the wax. However, underneath the celluloid, the traces of the writing remain on the wax slab—not visible, admittedly, but present, in a system that Freud compares to the unconscious (177). Hamlet's memory—both his mental memory and its supplemental form of the tables—can be seen, in Freud's terms, to belong to the category of 'unlimited receptive capacity'. Seeking to supplement a memory he regards as wipable, Hamlet turns to another surface, but this is also wipable: neither of them possesses the capacity to retain permanent traces. Hamlet's reliance on his tables thus metaphorically figures and literally reinforces the failure of the 'table' of his memory.

That this is particular to Hamlet rather than a shared experience can be gauged by a contrasting moment in *Cymbeline*, when
Iachimo inveigles his way into Imogen's chamber. He states his
'design': 'To note the chamber: I will write all down' (*Cym* 2.2.24),
and at this point modern editors often add to a stage direction
to that effect that he takes out his tables. But after jotting down
notes about the contents of her room and distinguishing signs on
her body, Iachimo reconsiders: 'Why should I write this down,
that's riveted, | Screw'd to my memory?' (2.2.43–4). His point is
well taken: if something is really memorable, why would he need
turn to the supplemental technologies of memory?[79] Can Hamlet
really not remember to remember his father, without writing it
on his tables? The workings and failings of Hamlet's memory are
further highlighted by comparison with those of Polonius' family.
Polonius and his children do not turn to supplemental technologies
of memory, but instead see memory as engraved on the heart, subscribing to a hierarchy of memory iterated in many early modern
texts in which Hamlet's writing-tables model is the lowest. In a
1605 sermon, Thomas Playfere argued that it was 'proper to the
child of God, to haue the law of his God in his heart. Not noted
in writing tables, or written in tables of stone, but noted & written
in the fleshie tables of the heart.'[80] A more secular expression of
the same idea comes from the widow in John Gough's *The Academy
of Complements* (1639) who says to a would-be suitor, 'I would not
have you imagine, that my love to my former husband was written on a Table booke, the letters whereof may bee soone wiped
out againe; no, it was engraved upon my heart.'[81] When Polonius
says farewell to his son Laertes, he famously provides him with a
string of precepts (1.3.58–79), far too many to be jotted down in
tables. But unlike Hamlet, Laertes will not use supplemental technologies of memory: Polonius instructs him, 'these few precepts
in thy memory | Look thou character' (1.3.57–8). In turn, when
Laertes bids farewell to his sister, he orders her to 'remember well

| What I have said to you', and she assures him that "'Tis in my memory locked | And you yourself shall keep the key of it' (1.3.83–5). The recall of this family is not perfect: Polonius has a moment of memory lapse, for example.[82] But their heart-engraved, memory-charactered, memory-locked model serves to throw into relief the external textuality of Hamlet's memory. Polonius' family provides us with another model of memory but it is one which is also flawed, since these memories, locked in living bodies, die along with their owners.

It is consistent that Hamlet's other writings, his letters, also are described as memories: when Ophelia attempts to return his letters to him, she calls them 'remembrances of yours | That I have longed long to redeliver' (3.1.92–3), prefiguring her doling out of 'rosemary: that's for remembrance. Pray you, love, remember' (4.5.169–70), which in turn inadvertently parodies the words of the ghost. Given Hamlet's reliance on technologies of 'unlimited receptive capacity' and no permanence, then, it is all the more striking that when he comes to rewrite the letter containing his death letter he does not raze and rewrite his name (the wax tablet model) but writes a new, fair copy (the ink and paper model). Shakespeare's choice to have Hamlet—the great wiper of memory—rewrite the letter is significant, since in Saxo and in Belleforest he was presented with a beautiful example of Amleth using erasure to his advantage, of the positive aspects of being able to wipe out an unwanted text. But instead, Shakespeare chooses to have Hamlet replace one paper letter with another paper letter, written fairly, according to identical protocols, and sealed with the correct seal. This undoubtedly increases its chances of being accepted by the English king (Rosencrantz and Guildenstern will, of course, vouch for its authenticity, since they believe they received it from the king's hands). But the successful replacement also tells us that Hamlet wants this letter survive his memory, that he is making a play for posterity.

Act 5, Scene 3

> let me speak to th' yet unknowing world,
> How these things came about. So shall you hear
> Of carnal, bloody and unnatural acts,
> Of accidental judgements, casual slaughters,
> Of deaths put on by cunning, and for no cause,
> And in this upshot purposes mistook
> Fallen on th'inventors' heads. All this can I
> Truly deliver.

                              (5.2.363–70)

As Hamlet dies, and Fortinbras comes to claim his 'rights of memory' (5.2.373), Horatio promises to explain what has happened, why
Elsinore's court is littered with corpses. Before he can do this,
Fortinbras orders that Hamlet's body be borne 'like a soldier to
the stage', with 'soldiers' music and the rite of war' (5.2.380, 383).
The play therefore ends without explanations, the plot left tangled
as the proper respect is shown to Hamlet, who, Fortinbras claims,
again with no evidence, 'was likely, had he been put on | To have
proved most royal' (5.2.381–2).

   By the end of the play all the main characters who may
know what has happened—Hamlet, Claudius, Gertrude, Laertes,
Polonius, Ophelia, Rosencrantz, and Guilderstern—are dead. The
only characters living are Fortinbras, Horatio, young Osric and the
English ambassadors, and of them only Horatio has any idea of the
whole story. Hamlet implores Horatio three times to tell what he
knows, preventing Horatio's suicide: 'Horatio, I am dead. | Thou
livest: report me and my cause aright | To the unsatisfied' (5.2.322–4);
'If thou didst ever hold me in thy heart | ... in this harsh world draw
thy breath in pain | To tell my story' (5.2.330–3); 'tell him [Fortinbras]
with th'occurrents more and less | Which have solicited' (5.2.341–2).
If Horatio were to launch into his explanation, what would he say?
After explaining the duelling deaths, and the accidental running
through of Polonius, Horatio would spend most of his time dealing
with Claudius' plot to kill Hamlet, and the subsequent deaths of

Rosencrantz and Guildenstern. These are the 'deaths put on by cunning', the 'purposes...| Fallen on th'inventors' heads'. And to aid him in this, Horatio would produce a piece of written evidence: the letter to England signed by Claudius calling for Hamlet's execution, which Hamlet gave to him—'Here's the commission; read it at more leisure' (5.2.26).

If *Hamlet* ended like this, it would not be alone among Shakespeare's plays. The use of letters as clinching evidence is widespread. The identity of the abandoned child, Perdita, in *The Winter's Tale* is vouchsafed by 'the letters of Antigonus found with it, which they know to be his character' (5.2.35–6); while the identity of Pericles' wife, buried at sea, is revealed to the physician Cerimon by Pericles' signed letter accompanying the corpse. In *Twelfth Night*, Malvolio intends to use the letter he believes is from Olivia as evidence, as he tells her:

> You must not now deny it is your hand:
> Write from it, if you can, in hand, or phrase,
> Or say, 'tis not your seal, not your invention:
> You can say none of this.
>
> (5.1.330–3)

Ultimately, of course, it emerges that the letter is a forgery, but nevertheless the letter is still required as evidence for that forgery to be revealed: 'Alas, Malvolio', says Olivia, 'this is not my writing, | Though I confess much like the character: | But, out of question, 'tis Maria's hand' (5.1.344–6).

Other Shakespeare plays end with letters, in what seems to be a horribly untheatrical manner. In the closing moments of *Romeo and Juliet*, the Prince stands silent, scanning a letter from Romeo, brought by his boy Balthasar, concluding that 'This letter doth make good the Friar's words', filling the gaps of the story: 'Their course of love, the tidings of her death, | And here he writes that he did buy a poison | Of a poor pothecary, and therewithal | Came to this vault to die and lie with Juliet' (5.3.285–9). In the final scene of *The Merchant of Venice*, Portia produces letters that will explain to Bassanio the details that the audience already knows, and will confirm to Antonio that three of his argosies have come safely to harbour, ensuring his finances. Portia explicitly refuses to explain how this information came to her—'You shall not know by what strange accident | I chanced on this letter'—to which wonderful and unverifiable news Antonio replies (perhaps dutifully), 'I am dumb' (5.1.278–9). At the end of *Othello*, Lodovico finds no fewer than three letters in Roderigo's pockets—

> Sir, you shall understand what hath befallen . . .
> . . . Here is a letter
> Found in the pocket of the slain Roderigo,
> And here another: the one of them imports
> The death of Cassio, to be undertook
> By Roderigo . . .
> Now here's another discontented paper
> Found in his pocket too, and this, it seems,
> Roderigo meant t'have sent this damned villain
> But that, belike, Iago in the nick
> Came in, and satisfied him.
>
> (5.2.304–15)

We need these letters, since by this point Othello, Desdemona, Roderigo, and Emilia are dead, and Iago's not talking, but Thomas Rymer found the conceit ridiculous: 'Then for the *unraveling of the Plot*, as they call it, never was old deputy Recorder in a Country Town, with his spectacles in summoning up the evidence, at such a puzzle: so blunder'd, and be doultefied; as is our Poet, to have a good riddance: And get the *Catastrophe* off his hands.'[83] More recently, Ann Pasternak Slater has attacked as 'painful' Shakespeare's apparent 'readiness to pull explanatory letters out of the air in the hurried conclusions of both comedy and tragedy. No chronological development is evident here: Shakespeare is inveterately slipshod over narrative organisation.' Rymer, she feels, was 'justly incensed by the ending of *Othello*, where the dead Roderigo is pressed into

posthumous postal service'; faced with these last-minute explanatory letters, 'Like Antonio, we are dumb, and can only admire
Shakespeare's impertinence.'[84] Impertinent, perhaps, but in these
plays, the letters are not contradicted.

With *Hamlet*, however, the scene would be more complicated. For
when, in our hypothetical Act 5, Scene 3, Horatio produces Claudius'
letter to the English king, given to him by Hamlet, to prove the
case against Claudius, then the English ambassadors will produce
what they think is Claudius' letter to the English king, which they
received from the hands of Rosencrantz and Guilderstern. What
is there to say that the second letter is not in fact the original,
real letter? The seal that links Horatio's letter to Claudius is identical to the seal affixed to the Englishmen's letter. Ultimately, then,
the forensic evidence produced to validate Horatio's version of
events will be two letters, by all external signs the same letter,
folded in the same way, written in the same hand, signed by the
same man, sealed with the same seal, but containing two different
texts.[85]

If Horatio tells the truth, as Hamlet so persistently demands that
he should, then he could explain that one letter is from Claudius,
one forged by Hamlet. But in so doing, the material fact of the two
identical letters would, at best, insist on the moral equivalence of
the acts of the king and the prince—they both deceived men and
sent them to their deaths—and at worst, show Hamlet to be a thief
and a forger, stealing diplomatic letters and taking on him the name
and status of his king.

Once again, Hamlet's reliance on the supplemental technologies
of memory fails to deliver. The letter that should be the clinching
evidence for posterity, and for Hamlet's good name, turns instead
to bite him—truly an instance of 'purposes mistook | Fallen on
th'inventors' heads'. Horatio would not benefit Hamlet by producing the letter as evidence: better for the English ambassadors to
believe that Claudius really did order the execution of his ambassadors Rosencrantz and Guildenstern. But perhaps Horatio could

take comfort from the fact that, though a paper letter is difficult to erase, it's very easy to conceal and destroy. No one else need know that he has the letter, since Hamlet stole it from the envoys under cover of darkness, and passed it to him in private—there was no public delivery. What's etched on the tables of Horatio's memory need not survive anywhere else—except, of course, in the remembrance of the audience, who have heard all about these 'deaths put on by cunning'.

Postscript

On 16 March 1810, the Stratford-upon-Avon historian R. B. Wheler wrote to *The Gentleman's Magazine* with the familiar lament that 'it is a circumstance somewhat extraordinary, that so little should be known either of [Shakespeare's] theatrical or private epistolary correspondence'. He had a new plea for owners of ancient manuscripts:

I thus address their possessor, requesting the insertion of them in your extensively circulated Magazine, with fac-similes of the signatures, and of *any* seals (*whatever may be their device*) yet remaining upon them. For this latter acquisition I am particularly anxious; and, as it is reasonable to suppose that some Shakspearian MSS. are buried among other masses of antient papers distributed throughout this kingdom, or in the unexplored repositories of private individuals, should any of your numerous Correspondents possess Letters, or any other memoranda, written by, or bearing the Signature or *Seal* of the Poet, the communication of them would particularly oblige.[1]

One might wonder why Wheler would choose to flog this particular dead horse in 1810, only fourteen years after the Ireland debacle. But the emphatic italics in his letter betray the catalyst, as he admitted in a second letter to the *Magazine*, dated 10 September, where he revealed the cause of his renewed interest.

On 16 March, six days before Wheler wrote his first letter, a Stratford-upon-Avon labourer's wife made a chance discovery on the soil of the Mill Close, next to the churchyard. She came across an old ring with the initials W.S., linked by ornamental tassels, carved in reverse, showing that the ring had been designed for use as a 'ring seal' or signet (illustration 15).[2] Although the ring

15. A signet ring bearing the initials WS, *c.* 1600.

was black with age, the woman immersed it in aqua-fortis, and revealed its original colour as gold. Wheler claimed it as 'evidently a gentleman's ring of Elizabeth's age', noted its similarity to the 'T.L.' motif adorning the porch of Sir Thomas Lucy's Charlcote Hall, not far away, and triumphantly announced that there was no other significant local W.S. who could have worn the signet: 'I find no Stratfordian of that period so likely to own such a Ring.'[3] However, as he later conceded, 'I was equally aware that the only probability, perhaps at this distant period the only possibility, of authenticating it was to discover an impression of it upon a letter of Shakespeare's, or some other document bearing his signature.'[4] Wheler therefore immediately launched his campaign in *The Gentleman's Magazine* to find, not necessarily letters in Shakespeare's hand—the Ireland debacle had tarnished that holy grail—but letters showing Shakespeare's seal, which would authenticate the signet.[5]

The find certainly excited some. The artist Robert Haydon wrote to John Keats in a frenzy: 'I shall certainly go mad! In a field at

Stratford upon Avon, in a field that belonged to Shakespeare; they
have found a gold ring and seal, with initial thus—W.S. and a true
lover's knot!! As sure as you breathe, & he that was the first of beings
the Seal belonged to him—Oh Lord!'[6] But in terms of attracting new
archival finds, it was all to no avail. The plea prompted no response,
and a letter from Wheler to Edmond Malone, himself still intent
on tracking down Shakespeare's papers, produced a terse, exhausted
response: 'I have not in my possession, nor have I ever seen any letter
written by Shakspeare; nor have I an impression of any seal of his.
I am unable, therefore, to furnish any document that can throw a
light on the ancient seal-ring which you have lately acquired.'[7]

Shakespeare might well have found this shift in archival
priorities—from handwriting to seals—amusing. Throughout his
plays, he demonstrates a heightened awareness of the dual authentification offered by handwriting and seal. When the disguised Duke
in *Measure for Measure* is trying to persuade the Provost of the validity
of a letter, he demands 'Look you, sir, here is the hand and seal
of the Duke: you know the character, I doubt not, and the signet
is not strange to you?', to which the Provost replies, 'I know them
both' (*MM* 4.2.191–4). Flavius tells Timon of Athens that he has 'been
bold . . . to use your signet and your name', in his vain appeal to the
senators for funding (*Tim* 2.2.203–5). Malvolio thinks he recognizes
not only 'my lady's hand' but also 'the impressure her Lucrece, with
which she uses to seal', her personalized ring (*TN* 2.5.87–8, 95–6).
As these examples indicate, both character and seal can be used
equally to authenticate, or to falsify. And the two come together,
with predictably puzzling results, on the lengthiest Shakespearean
document to survive.

The Missing Seal

Two hundred years after Wheler made his plea, no letter has been
found bearing the imprint of the W. S. seal-ring. But Shakespeare
scholars are nothing if not imaginative, and that very absence has

come to tell its own story. The one document from Shakespeare's later life that does survive is his will and testament, an artefact that has occasioned a good deal of critical comment.[8] According to Henry Swinburne's 1591 treatise, wills, and testaments should ideally be in the testator's own hand. Failing that, the testator must at least subscribe the document in the presence of witnesses, or it should be 'sealed with the seale of the testator'.[9] Shakespeare's will, however, is drafted in the hand of a scribe, perhaps the clerk of his solicitor Francis Collins of Warwick.[10] The text of the document declares that a seal is to be appended, but no seal appears. Of course, say the biographers. Shakespeare lost his seal-ring shortly before he was due to seal his will—and it turned up in 1810 on the Mill Close next to the churchyard because he lost it in Stratford's churchyard perhaps on the occasion of his daughter's marriage to Thomas Quiney. It's as good an explanation as any other.[11]

But the seal-less will and testament has a better story to tell. Although the text says that the document is to be sealed, the word 'Seale' is crossed through and replaced with 'hand'.[12] It was by some optimistically believed that this one word, 'hand', might be in Shakespeare's own 'hand',[13] but since the early twentieth century, critical opinion has tilted towards recognizing the word as the scrivener's. So, with no seal, and no addition to the text in Shakespeare's hand, the only trace of the playwright is the signature. A signature—that great authenticating agent of the twentieth century—comes with its own problems, however. Swinburne is at pains to point out that, unless the act of signing is witnessed, it has no validity:

But it is not inough for the witnesses to say this is the testators owne hand, for we knowe his hand, neither is it sufficient (in the opinion of diuers) to bring forth other writings of the knowne hande of the testator, and so proue the will to bee written or subscribed by the testator, by comparing such writings with the testament: For the witnesses may be deceiued (the testators hand being easie to be counterfeited) and therefore proofe by similitude of handes is not a full proofe.[14]

'Similitude of handes' is not even possible here: the signature on Shakespeare's will is, notoriously, different from every other Shakespeare signature we have. After reading the letters of Shakespeare's plays, this final piece of slippery paperwork comes as no surprise. This document shows that in itself a carefully drafted signed and sealed will and testament could be worth nothing: what renders it authentic is not seal nor signature, but its witnesses. And ultimately it is this culture of witnessing that draws Shakespeare's letters away from our own into a different realm.

The letters that this book has examined operate in a bewildering variety of ways, but a theme emerges. As Mary Poovey and Barbara Shapiro have argued, the culture in which and for which Shakespeare wrote his plays had an increasing interest in and reliance on bureaucratic record-keeping, documentary evidence, and verifiable proofs.[15] Letters were part of this trend, not merely a means to maintain communication across distances, but increasingly taken as documentary evidence of transactions, of responsibility, and ultimately of guilt. This impulse is registered repeatedly throughout Shakespeare's plays: Octavius insisting on the story that can be told by his 'writings'; Shylock insisting on his 'bond'; Hamlet insisting that Horatio take Claudius's letter as evidence. To some extent, the plays themselves appear to buy into this documentary culture. Identity is vouchsafed by letters in *Pericles* and *The Winter's Tale*. In *King Lear* one letter exposes the adultery of Goneril and Edmund, while another is the clinching proof of Gloucester's alleged treachery; a letter proves the conspiracy of Aumerle in *Richard II*; a letter proves the cowardice and disloyalty of Parolles in *All's Well That Ends Well*. *Othello*, *Romeo and Juliet*, and *The Merchant of Venice* all end with the flamboyant production and reading of letters to explain their plots. Even on those occasions where letters are forged or mistaken—the letters from 'Edgar' to Gloucester, from 'Olivia' to her servant—it could be argued, the characters still subscribe to their power as evidentiary documents.

Indeed, an account focused on the sheer incidence of these letters in the plays might well conclude that Shakespeare was admitting the priority of written documents. But this verdict ignores the fact that these are plays performed in a theatre in front of an audience: the audience does not read the letters, but instead sees the transactions they produce. In performance, Octavius's writings do not trump Cleopatra's suicide pageant; there is much that the audience knows about the workings of *Romeo and Juliet* or *Othello*, *Hamlet* or *King Lear* that explanatory letters will never tell. In some instances, such as *The Merchant of Venice*, our faith in the letter documents, pulled out of thin air to provide a happy ending, is allowed to wilt even at the moment they are produced.

For all the attempts to imbue early modern letters with legally verifiable authenticity, there is a rooted suspicion of paperwork *per se* in early modern culture, a deep-seated belief that it cannot tell the whole story. That is why it is wrong, although understandable, that we should separate out Shakespeare's letters as transparent 'documents', or as proof of private acts of reading and writing. His letters rightly belong to a much wider realm, where they are transacted between individuals, vouched for by their bearers, literally *handed* over, from hand to hand, read and responded to in the gaze of others. They make their full sense only on the public stage—which is why Shakespeare's stage letters were not an embarrassment for their original audiences, not a crude 'plot device' to be derided. Instead, Shakespeare perceived the innate theatricality of letters—and recognized that they would only finally reach their full potential when they were realized on stage: written, folded, sealed, superscribed, delivered, received, read, and archived, with his audience as their witnesses.

NOTES

INTRODUCTION: SEARCHING FOR SHAKESPEARE'S LETTERS

1. For an example of the invitation letter, see Samuel Ireland to Eva Garrick, n.d. (1795). Folger Shakespeare Library, Washington DC (hereafter Folger) MS Y.c.1661: 'Mr. I hopes to have the honor of seeing Mrs. Garrick with Mrs Nicols & the rest of her party to morrow at 12 to view *the* Shakespeare Papers'.
2. Samuel Ireland, untitled advertisement, dated 4 March 1795 (Folger shelf-mark PR 2950 A22b Cage).
3. Samuel Ireland ed., *Miscellaneous Papers and Legal Instruments under the hand and seal of William Shakspeare* (London: Egerton *et al.*, 1796).
4. James Boaden, *A Letter to George Steevens, Esq. containing a critical examination of the papers of Shakespeare* (London: Martin and Bain, 1796).
5. Edmond Malone, *An Inquiry into the Authenticity of certain Miscellaneous Papers and Legal Instruments, published Dec. 24, M DCC XCV* (London: T. Cadell and W. Davies, 1796). Ireland accused Malone of deliberately delaying publication to ruin *Vortigern*'s chances. After advertising his *Inquiry* in December 1795, Malone announced on 16 February 1796 that his 'detection of this forgery has been unavoidably delayed by the engravings having taken more time than was expected', hoping for a late February publication date. Following the eventual publication on 31 March, the *Oracle* and *Morning Herald* reviewed the *Inquiry* on 1 April. Samuel Ireland, *Mr. Ireland's Vindication of his Conduct, respecting the publication of the Supposed Shakespeare MSS.* (London: Faulder and Robson; Egerton; White, 1796), 41–2.
6. Peter Thomson, 'Kemble, John Philip (1757–1823)', *ODNB*.
7. Ireland, *Mr. Ireland's Vindication*; idem., *An Investigation of Mr. Malone's Claim to the Character of Scholar, or Critic, Being an Examination of his Inquiry into the Authenticity of the Shakspeare Manuscripts, &c.* (London: Faulder; Egerton; Payne; Whites, (1798)).

8. W[illiam] H[enry] Ireland, *An authentic account of the Shaksperian manu-scripts, &c.* (London: J. Debrett, 1796).

9. John Mair, *The Fourth Forger: William Ireland and the Shakespeare Papers* (London: Cobden-Sanderson, 1938); Bernard Grebanier, *The Great Shakespeare Forgery* (New York: W.W. Norton, 1965); S. Schoenbaum, *Shakespeare's Lives*, 2nd edn (Oxford: Clarendon Press, 1991), chs. 7–11; Jeffrey Kahan, *Reforging Shakespeare: The Story of a Theatrical Scandal* (Bethlehem and London: Lehigh University Press/Associated University Presses, 1998); Michael Keevak, *Sexual Shakespeare: Forgery, Authorship, Portraiture* (Detroit: Wayne State University Press, 2001), esp. ch. 1; Patri-cia Pierce, *The Great Shakespeare Fraud: The Strange True Story of William-Henry Ireland* (Thrupp, Glos.: Sutton, 2004).

10. Jeffrey Kahan points out in his study of the Ireland scandal, 'the imitator and the forger respond to contemporary tastes. After all, to succeed, their works must be noticed, must be relevant'. Kahan, *Reforging Shakespeare*, 20.

11. I am grateful to Jeffrey Kahan for pointing this out to me.

12. Ireland ed., *Miscellaneous Papers*, unnumbered plate.

13. James Boaden to Samuel Ireland, 28 February 1796, as quoted in William-Henry Ireland, *The Confessions of William-Henry Ireland* (London: Thomas Goddard, 1805), 280.

14. Malone, *Inquiry*.

15. 'Mr Malones New Edition of Shakespeare', *Gentleman's Magazine* (February 1795), 120–1. Malone suggested searching for papers once belonging to Edward Bagley, executor to Shakespeare's granddaughter, Elizabeth Hall; those descending from the estates of her three step-daughters; and from the heirs of Ralph Hubaud and John Heminge, with whom Shakespeare had property dealings. For possible rest-ing places of these (entirely hypothetical) papers, see Peter Milward, 'Some Missing Shakespeare Letters', *Shakespeare Quarterly* 20 (1969), 84–7.

16. My figure here is based on Frances Teague's 'Appendix B: Property Cat-egories and Frequency' in her *Shakespeare's Speaking Properties* (Lewis-burg PA: Bucknell University Press, 1991), 195–7.

17. Montaigne writes of a nation with 'nulle cognoissance de lettres': pre-sumably he means 'letters' in a wider sense, but the double meaning of the word in English is often exploited by early modern English writ-ers. Michel de Montaigne, *The essayes or morall, politike and millitarie discourses*, trans. John Florio (London: Edward Blount, 1603), K3^v.

18. For Shakespeare and Euripides see James T. Svendsen, 'The Letter Device in Euripides and Shakespeare', in *Legacy of Thespis: Drama Past and Present, Volume IV: The University of Florida Department of Classics Comparative Drama Conference Papers* (Lanham, New York and London: University Press of America, 1984), 75–88.

19. For a useful and impressive survey of the field, see James Daybell's articles, 'Recent Studies in Sixteenth-Century Letters', *English Literary Renaissance* 35 (2005), 331–62, and 'Recent Studies in Seventeenth-Century Letters', *English Literary Renaissance* 36 (2006), 135–70.

20. Susan E. Whyman, *Sociability and Power in Late-Stuart England: The Cultural Worlds of the Verneys 1660–1720* (Oxford: Oxford University Press, 1999), esp. her discussion of the issues facing social historians working with a letter archive (3–12); Daybell, *Women Letter-Writers in Tudor England* (Oxford: Oxford University Press, 2006).

21. Roger Chartier *et al.*, *La Correspondance: les usages de la lettre au XIXe siècle* (Paris: Fayard, 1991), only partially translated as *Correspondence: Models of Letter-Writing from the Middle Ages to the nineteenth century*, trans. Christopher Woodall (Princeton: Princeton University Press, 1997); Gary Schneider, *The Culture of Epistolarity: Vernacular letters and letter writing in early modern England, 1500–1700* (Newark: University of Delaware Press, 2005).

22. Frank Whigham, 'The rhetoric of Elizabethan suitors' letters', *PMLA* 96 (1981), 864–82; Peter Mack, *Elizabethan Rhetoric: Theory and Practice* (Cambridge: Cambridge University Press, 2002), esp. 109–10, 114–24.

23. See Jonathan Goldberg, 'Colin to Hobbinol: Spenser's familiar letters', in *Displacing Homophobia: Gay Male Perspectives in Literature and Culture*, ed. Ronald R. Butters, John M. Clum and Michael Moon (Durham, NC: Duke University Press, 1989), 107–26; David M. Bergeron, *King James & Letters of Homoerotic Desire* (Iowa City: University of Iowa Press, 1999); Alan Bray, *The Friend* (Chicago: University of Chicago Press, 2003), esp. 67–70, 159–64; Jeffrey Masten. 'Toward a Queer Address: The Taste of Letters and Early Modern Male Friendship', *GLQ: A Journal of Lesbian and Gay Studies* 10 (2004), 367–84.

24. James Daybell ed., *Early Modern Women's Letter Writing, 1450–1700* (Basingstoke: Palgrave, 2001); Daybell, *Women Letter-Writers*.

25. Philip Beale, *A History of the Post in England from the Romans to the Stuarts* (Aldershot: Ashgate, 1998), revised as *England's Mail: Two Millennia of Letter Writing* (Stroud, Glos.: Tempus, 2005); Mark Brayshay, Philip Harrison, and Brian Chalkley, 'Knowledge, Nationhood and

Governance: The Speed of the Royal Post in Early-Modern England', *Journal of Historical Geography* 24 (1998), 265–88.

26. See for example, *Studies in the Cultural History of Letter Writing*, ed. Linda C. Mitchell and Susan Green, special issues of *Huntington Library Quarterly* 66: 3 and 4 (2003); *Letterwriting in Renaissance England*, ed. Alan Stewart and Heather Wolfe (Washington DC: Folger Shakespeare Library, 2004), the catalogue for the Folger exhibition of 2004–5.

27. Lynne Magnusson, *Shakespeare and Social Dialogue: Dramatic Language and Elizabethan Letter* (Cambridge: Cambridge University Press, 1999).

28. Frederick Kiefer, *Writing on the Renaissance Stage: Written Words, Printed Pages, Metaphoric Books* (Newark: University of Delaware Press, 1996), 14.

29. M. C. Bradbrook, *Shakespeare and Elizabethan Poetry: A Study of his Earlier Work in Relation to the Poetry of the Time* (London: Chatto and Windus, 1951), 153.

30. Ann Pasternak Slater, *Shakespeare the Director* (Brighton: Harvester, 1982), 179–80.

31. Stephen Orgel, 'Knowing the Character', *Zeitschrift für Anglistik und Amerikanistik* 40 (1992), 124–9 at 124, 125.

32. This list is based on Teague's 'Appendix B: Property Categories and Frequency' in her *Shakespeare's Speaking Properties*, 195–7. Teague classes together all these items as 'D' (document).

33. Jonas Barish, ' "Soft, here follows prose": Shakespeare's Stage Documents' in *The Arts of Performance in Elizabethan and Early Stuart Drama: Essays for G. K. Hunter* ed. Murray Biggs *et al.* (Edinburgh: Edinburgh University Press, 1991), 32–45 at 47. This essay was drawn to my attention by Kiefer, *Writing on the Renaissance Stage,* 13.

34. See for example Kiefer, *Writing on the Renaissance Stage*; and the essays in *Reading and Writing in Shakespeare* ed. David M. Bergeron (Newark: University of Delaware Press and London: Associated University Presses, 1996); Teague, *Shakespeare's Speaking Properties*.

35. But see Jonathan Goldberg, 'Shakespearean Characters: The Generation of Silva' in his *Voice Terminal Echo* (London: Methuen, 1986), 68–100 and 175–9, rpt in *Shakespeare's Hand* (Minneapolis: University of Minnesota Press, 2003), 10–47 and 310–15; Goldberg, 'Hamlet's Hand', *Shakespeare Quarterly* 39 (1988), 307–26, rpt in *Shakespeare's Hand*, 105–31 and 324–7; Goldberg, 'Rebel Letters: Postal Effects from *Richard II* to *Henry IV*', *Renaissance Drama*, n.s. 19 (1989), 3–28, rpt in *Shakespeare's Hand*, 189–211 and 336–40; Teague, *Shakespeare's Speaking Properties*, 20–2; Julian Hilton, 'Reading Letters in Plays: Short Courses in Practical Epistemology?' in *Reading Plays: Interpretation and Reception* ed. Hanna Scolnicov and Peter

Holland (Cambridge: Cambridge University Press, 1991), 140–60; Teague, 'Letters and Portents in *Julius Caesar* and *King Lear*', *Shakespeare Yearbook* 3 (1992), 97–104; Bergeron, 'Deadly Letters in *King Lear*', *Philological Quarterly* 72 (1993), 157–76; Lisa Jardine, 'Reading and the Technology of Textual Affect: Erasmus's Familiar Letters and Shakespeare's *King Lear*', in her *Reading Shakespeare Historically* (London: Routledge, 1996), 78–97 and notes at 184–9; Yukiko Takeoka, 'The "Letter" as a Device of Discommunication in *Twelfth Night*', *Shakespeare Studies* 34 (1996), 49–71; David Thatcher, 'Shakespeare's *All's Well*: The Case of Bertram's Letter', *Cahiers Elisabéthains* 53 (1998), 77–80; Eve Rachele Sanders, 'Interiority and the Letter in *Cymbeline*', *Critical Survey* 12 (2000), 49–70.

36. Jacques Derrida, *Post Card: From Socrates to Freud and Beyond*, trans. Alan Bass (Chicago: University of Chicago Press, 1987); Bernhard Siegert, *Relays: Literature as an Epoch of the Postal System*, trans. Kevin Repp (Stanford: Stanford University Press, 1999). Derrida's earlier work has been particularly influential on Jonathan Goldberg's studies of writing practices in early modern England: see Goldberg, *Writing Matter: From the Hands of the English Renaissance* (Stanford: Stanford University Press, 1990); and the essays collected in *Shakespeare's Hand*.

37. Goldberg, *Writing Matter*, ch. 5; Richard Rambuss, *Spenser's Secret Career* (Cambridge: Cambridge University Press, 1993), ch. 2; Alan Stewart, *Close Readers: Humanism and Sodomy in Early Modern England* (Princeton: Princeton University Press, 1997), ch. 5.

38. Harold Love, *Scribal Publication in Seventeenth-Century England* (Oxford: Clarendon Press, 1993); Peter Beal, *In Praise of Scribes: Manuscripts and their Makers in Seventeenth-Century England* (Oxford: Clarendon Press, 1998).

39. This is the suggestion of Daybell, *Women Letter-Writers*, esp. chs. 3 and 4, although a cross-gender comparison has not yet been attempted.

40. Siegert, *Relays*, 7–8.

41. This account is based on Stewart and Wolfe, *Letterwriting in Renaissance England*, 121–4.

42. Ian Watt, 'Private Experience and the Novel' in *The Rise of the Novel: Studies in Defoe, Richardson and Fielding* (Berkeley: University of California Press, 1957), 174–207 esp. 187–96, at 189.

43. Watt, *Rise of the Novel*, 189. See also Janet Gurkin Altman, *Epistolarity: Approaches to a Form* (Columbus OH: Ohio State University Press, 1982); Elizabeth Heckerdorn Cook, *Epistolary Bodies: Gender and Genre in the Eighteenth-Century Republic of Letters* (Stanford: Stanford University Press, 1996).

44. [George Gascoigne], *A hundreth sundry flowres* (London: Richard Smith, 1573), discussed in Alan Stewart, 'Gelding Gascoigne', in *Prose Fiction and Early Modern Sexualities, 1570–1640* ed. Constance C. Relihan and Goran V. Stanivukovic (New York: Palgrave Macmillan, 2003), 147–69.

45. Nicholas Breton. *A poste with a madde packet of letters* (London: Iohn Smethicke, 1602), with eleven other editions to 1678; idem, *Conceyted letters, newly layde open: or A most excellent bundle of new wit wherin is knit vp together all the perfections or arte of episteling* (London: Samuel Rand, 1618; other edns 1632, 1638); idem, *New conceited letters, newly laid open. Or, A most excellent bundle of new wit wherein is knit up together all the perfections, or art of epistoling* (London: John Stafford, 1662).

46. Judith Rice Henderson, 'Defining the Genre of the Letter: Juan Luis Vives' *De conscribendis epistolis*', *Renaissance and Reformation* 19 (1983), 89–105; Henderson, 'On Reading the Rhetoric of the Renaissance Letter', in *Renaissance-Rhetorik/Renaissance Rhetoric*, ed. Heinrich F. Plett (Berlin: De Gruyter 1993), 143–62. See also the essays in *Self-Presentation and Social Identification: The Rhetoric and Pragmatics of Letter Writing in Early Modern Times*, ed. Toon Van Houdt, Gilbert Tournoy and Constant Matheeussen (*Supplementa Humanistica Louvaniensa* 18 (Leuven: Leuven University Press, 2002)).

47. William Fulwood, *The Enimie of Idlenesse* (London: Leonard Maylard, 1568).

48. Abraham Fleming, *A Panoplie of Epistles* (London: Ralph Newberie, 1576).

49. Walter Darell, *A short discourse of the life of seruingmen . . . With certeine letters verie necessarie for seruingmen, and other persons to peruse* (London: Ralphe Newberrie, 1578).

50. Angel Day, *The English Secretarie* (London: Richard Jones, 1586). See also W. Phist[on], *The Welspring of wittie Conceites* (London: Richard Jones, 1584).

51. Thomas Gainsford, *The secretaries studie containing new familiar epistles* (London: Roger Iackson, 1616).

52. J[ohn] B[rowne], *The marchants avizo* (London: William Norton, 1589).

53. 'Philomusus', *The academy of complements* (London: H. Moseley, 1640); Hannah Wooley, *The gentlewomans companion* (London: Edward Thomas, 1682).

54. Magnusson, *Shakespeare and Social Dialogue*; Schneider, *Culture of Epistolarity*. For earlier surveys of letter-writing manuals, see Katherine Gee Hornbeak, 'The Complete Letter-Writer in English, 1568–1800', *Smith College Studies in Modern Languages* 15 (1934), 1–150; Jean Robertson, *The Art of Letter Writing: An Essay on the Handbooks Published in England during the*

Sixteenth and Seventeenth Centuries (Liverpool: Liverpool University Press and London: Hodder and Stoughton, 1942).

55. See A. Gerlo, 'The *Opus de conscribendis epistolis* of Erasmus and the tradition of the *ars epistolica*', in *Classical Influences on European Culture A.D. 500–1500: Proceedings of an international conference held at King's College, Cambridge April 1969*, ed. R. R. Bolgar (Cambridge: Cambridge University Press, 1971), 103–14; James J. Murphy, '*Ars dictaminis*: the art of letter-writing', in *Rhetoric in the Middle Ages: A History of Rhetorical Theory from Saint Augustine to the Renaissance* (Berkeley: University of California Press, 1974), 194–268; Les Perelman, 'The Medieval Art of Letter Writing: Rhetoric as Institutional Expression', in *Textual Dynamics of the Professions*, ed. Charles Bazerman and James Paradis (Madison: University of Wisconsin Press, 1991), 97–119.

56. Jardine, *Erasmus Man of Letters: The Construction of Charisma in Print* (Princeton: Princeton University Press, 1993).

57. Erasmus, *De conscribendis epistolis*, in *Collected Works of Erasmus* vol. 25, *Literary and Educational Writings 3: De conscribendis epistolis, Formula, De civilitate*, ed. J. K. Sowards (Toronto: Univeristy of Toronto Press, 1985), 1–254. See Judith Rice Henderson, 'Erasmus on the art of letter-writing', in *Renaissance Eloquence: Studies in the Theory and Practice of Renaissance Rhetoric*, ed. James J. Murphy (Berkeley: University of California Press, 1983), 331–55; Erika Rummel, 'Erasmus' Manual of Letter-Writing: Tradition and Innovation', *Renaissance and Reformation* n.s. 13 (1989), 299–312.

58. Erasmus, *Copia: Foundations of the Abundant Style (De duplici copia verborum ac rerum commentarii duo)* trans. / annot.. Betty I. Knott, in *Collected Works of Erasmus*, vol. 24, *Literary and Educational Writings 2: De copia / De ratione studii* (Toronto: University of Buffalo Press, 1978), 348–54.

59. Erasmus, *Conficiendarum epistolarum formula* in *Collected Works of Erasmus* 25:258. In *De conscribendis epistolis* he writes: 'For a letter, as the comic poet Turpilius skillfully put it, is a mutual conversation between absent friends' (*Collected Works of Erasmus* 25: 20).

60. See Anthony T. Grafton and Lisa Jardine, *From Humanism to the Humanities: Education and the Liberal Arts in Fifteenth- and Sixteenth-Century Europe* (London: Duckworth, 1986).

61. T. W. Baldwin, *William Shakspere's Small Latine & Lesse Greeke*, 2 vols. (Urbana: University of Illinois Press, 1944), 2:239–87.

62. Jardine, 'Reading and the technology of textual affect'.

63. Marvin Rosenberg, *The Masks of King Lear* (Berkeley: University of California Press, 1972), 257.

64. Jardine, 'Reading and the technology of textual affect', 79, 90–1.

65. Jardine, 'Reading and the technology of textual affect', 91.
66. Euripides, *Euripides*, trans. David Kovacs, 6 vols. (Cambridge, MA: Harvard University Press (Loeb Classical Library), 1994–2002). The extant passages are usefully collected in Patricia A. Rosenmeyer ed., *Ancient Greek Literary Letters: Selections in translation* (London and New York: Routledge, 2006), 11–13 (discussion), 15–18 (texts). See also Svendsen, 'Letter Device'; Patricia A. Rosenmeyer, *Ancient Epistolary Fictions: The letter in Greek literature* (Cambridge: Cambridge University Press, 2001), ch. 4.
67. Baldwin, *Shakspere's Small Latine & Lesse Greeke*, 1:422–3, prints a list of text and reference books bought for St Paul's School in 1582/1583 including 'Euripides graeco-lat. cum annotat. Stiblini et Brodaei'.
68. Svendsen, 'Letter Device', 75.
69. Euripides, *Iphigenia at Aulis*, 32–41, in *Euripides*, trans. Kovacs 6:171.
70. Euripides, *Hippolytus*, 862–5 in *Euripides*, trans. Kovacs, 2:209.
71. Euripides, *Iphigenia Among the Taurians*, 755–92 in *Euripides*, trans. Kovacs, 4: 229–33.
72. *Plautus*, trans. Paul Nixon, 5 vols. (Cambridge, MA: Harvard University Press (Loeb Classical Library), 1916–38). See A. Scafuro, 'The Rigmarole of the Parasite's Contract for a Prostitute in *Asinaria*: Legal Documents in Plautus and his Predecessors', *Leeds International Classical Studies* 3, 4 (2004), 1–21, appendix; Thomas E. Jenkins, 'At Play with Writing: Letters and Readers in Plautus', *Transactions of the American Philological Association* 135 (2005), 359–92.
73. Plautus, *Curculio* in *Plautus*, trans. Nixon, 2:185–269.
74. Plautus, *Pseudolus* in *Plautus*, trans. Nixon, 4:144–285, at 153.
75. Plautus, *Triummnus* in *Plautus*, trans. Nixon, 5:97–221, at 173–5.
76. 'The Conversion of Saint Paul', in Glynne Wickham ed., *English Moral Interludes* (London: Dent, 1976), 103–26, at 109.
77. Thomas Norton and Thomas Sackvile, *The Tragedie of Gorbodvc* (London: William Griffith, 1565).
78. Nicholas Udall, *Ralph Roister Doister* (London: Henry Denham, 1566/7?).
79. John Skelton, *Magnyfycence, a goodly interlude and a mery* (n.p: (J. Rastell, 1533)), B.i.^r, B.ii.^v, B.iii.^v. Fancy is again the go-between in a dubious epistolary transaction in Francis Merbury's 1570s play, *The Marriage between Wit and Wisdom*. Fancy declares 'I meant to counterfeit, and smoothly for to flatter, | And say I am a messenger from Lady Wisdom sent, | To see if that will be a mean to bring him to my bent'. Presenting the letter to Wit, Fancy persuades him to 'go with me | Unto a place, with her to meet;' but at the supposed rendezvous, Lady Wisdom is nowhere to

be seen, and Wit is instead confronted with a terrible vision (which we do not see): 'Alas, I am betrayed! this sight makes me aghast!' Francis Merbury, *The Marriage between Wit and Wisdom* in Glynne Wickham ed., *English Moral Interludes* (London: Dent, 1976), 163–94, at 186.

80. [Robert Wilson], *A right excellent and famous Comœdy, called the three Ladies of London* (London: Roger Warde, 1584). See also Kiefer, *Writing on the Renaissance Stage*, 124.

81. For this notion of prosthesis, see Will Fisher, *Materializing Gender in Early Modern English Literature and Culture* (Cambridge: Cambridge University Press, 2006).

82. See Felix Bosonnet, *The Function of Stage Properties in Christopher Marlowe's Plays* (Bern: Francke, 1978); Slater, *Shakespeare the Director*; David Bevington, *Action is Eloquence: Shakespeare's Language of Gesture* (Cambridge: Harvard University Press, 1984); Teague, *Shakespeare's Speaking Properties*; Alan C. Dessen, *Recovering Shakespeare's Theatrical Vocabulary* (Cambridge: Cambridge University Press, 1995); Andrew Sofer, *The Stage Life of Props* (Ann Arbor: University of Michigan Press, 2003); Natasha Korda, 'Conclusion: Household Property/Stage Property' in her *Shakespeare's Domestic Economies: Gender and Property in Early Modern England* (Philadelphia: University of Pennsylvania Press, 2002), 192–212; and the essays in *Staged Properties in Early Modern English Drama*, ed. Jonathan Gil Harris and Natasha Korda (Cambridge: Cambridge University Press, 2002).

83. For exceptions see Bosonnet, *The Function of Stage Properties*; Bevington, *Action is Eloquence*, 55–7 (on LLL); Teague, *Shakespeare's Speaking Properties*.

84. See for example, *Subject and Object in Renaissance Culture*, ed. Margreta de Grazia, Maureen Quilligan, and Peter Stallybrass (Cambridge: Cambridge University Press, 1996), and the essays in the 'Symposium: Material Culture', ed. Peter Stallybrass, *Shakespeare Studies* 28 (2000), 123–261.

85. Arjun Appardurai, 'Introduction: Commodities and the Politics of Value', *The Social Life of Things: Commodities in Cultural Perspective*, ed. Arjun Appardurai (Cambridge: Cambridge University Press, 1988), 3–63.

86. Igor Kopytoff, 'The Cultural Biography of Things: Commoditization of Process', in *Social Life of Things*, ed. Appardurai, 64–91.

87. Lena Cowen Orlin, 'The Performance of Things in *The Taming of the Shrew*', *Yearbook of English Studies* 23 (1993), 167–88 at 167–8. Orlin here draws on Pierre Bourdieu, *Distinction: A Social Critique of the Judgement of*

Taste, trans. Richard Nice (1979; Cambridge: Harvard University Press, 1984), 6.

88. Sofer, *The Stage Life of Props*, vi.

89. Shakespeare's authorship of *A Lover's Complaint* is not universally accepted: see Brian Vickers, *Shakespeare, A Lover's Complaint, and John Davies of Hereford* (Cambridge: Cambridge University Press, 2007). For my purposes here, the authorship is not crucial.

90. John Kerrigan, 'Introduction' to his edn, *Motives of Woe: Shakespeare and 'Female Complaint': A Critical Anthology* (Oxford: Clarendon Press, 1991), 1–83 at 46.

91. Colin Burrow, 'Life and Work in Shakespeare's Poems', *Proceedings of the British Academy* 97 (1998), 15–50 at 28.

92. Patrick Cheney, ' "Deep-brained Sonnets" and "Tragic Shows": Shakespeare's Late Ovidian Art in *A Lover's Complaint*', in *Critical Essays on Shakespeare's A Lover's Complaint*, ed. Shirley Sharon-Zisser (Aldershot, Hants and Burlington VT: Ashgate, 2006), 55–78 at 56.

93. The irrelevance of a letter's contents to its power to exert influence has been most famously explored by psychoanalytic readings of Edgar Allan Poe's story 'The Purloined Letter'. See Jacques Lacan, 'Seminar on "The Purloined Letter" ', trans. Jeffrey Melhman, *Yale French Studies* 48 (1972), 39–72; Barbara Johnson, 'The Frame of Reference: Poe, Lacan, Derrida', *Yale French Studies* 55/56 (1977), 457–505. While my interpretation here shares some common ground, my interest is in the letter's materiality, which Lacan *et al.* do not address.

94. David Scott Kastan, 'Shakespeare in Print' in *Shakespeare After Theory* (New York and London: Routledge, 1999), 71–92, provides an elegant summary of this position.

95. Most notably, Lukas Erne, *Shakespeare as literary dramatist* (Cambridge: Cambridge University Press, 2003).

96. The first English dedicatory epistle typeset as a manuscript letter appeared in 1545: Edward Walshe's *Office and duety of fightyng for our countrey* (London: John Herford, 1545). The phenomenon was earlier seen in the Aldine press in 1543 and by two other Venetian printers, Giovanni Giolito and Michele Tramezzino, in 1544. Cathy Shrank, ' "These fewe scribbled rules": Representing Scribal Intimacy in Early Modern Print', *Huntington Library Quarterly* 67 (2004), 295–314 at 309, 311 n. 48.

97. Leah S. Marcus, *Unediting the Renaissance: Shakespeare, Marlowe, Milton* (London and New York: Routledge, 1996), 168–72 at 169–70.

98. Goldberg, 'Hamlet's Hand', 324–6; rpt in *Shakespeare's Hand*, 125–9.

99. Goldberg, 'Hamlet's Hand' 324, rpt in *Shakespeare's Hand*, 127.

100. Dulwich College MS I, item 138 (fo. 261–71), first printed (with errors) in J. Payne Collier, 'Alleyn's Part in R. Greene's *Orlando Furioso*', appendix III of *Memoirs of Edward Alleyn* ((London?): Shakespeare Society, 1841), 198. Greg's edition is *Two Elizabethan Stage Abridgements: The Battle of Alcazar & Orlando Furioso*, ed. W. W. Greg (Oxford: Malone Society, 1923).

101. Robert Greene, *The Historie of Orlando Furioso One of the twelue Pieres of France* (London Cuthbert Burbie, 1594).

102. Greene, *Orlando Furioso*, D.ij.ᵛ–D.iiij.ʳ.

103. Greg, *Two Elizabethan Stage Abridgements*, 302–3. For responses to Greg's work, see B. A. P. van Dam, 'Alleyn's player's part of Greene's *Orlando Furioso*, and the text of the Q of 1594', *English Studies* 11 (1929), 182–203 and 209–20, esp. 213–14, 217–19; Alfred Hart, *Stolne and Surreptitious Copies: A comparative study of Shakespeare's bad quartos* (Melbourne and London: Melbourne University Press/Oxford University Press, 1942). Neither departs from Greg's rationale for the missing letters.

104. Tiffany Stern, *Making Shakespeare: From stage to page* (London and New York: Routledge, 2004), 113–14. Here Stern develops some ideas and material from her article 'Letters, verses and double speech-prefixes in *The Merchant of Venice*', *Notes and Queries* 46 (June 1999), 231–3.

105. Edward Cape Everard, *Memoirs of an Unfortunate Son of Thespis* (Edinburgh: James Ballatyne, 1818), 48–9.

106. '[Act: 1] writing out of the booke with a small peece of Siluer | for Mr Swantton: | .3. notes for Mr pollard: | Act: 2: A writing for Mr Taylor: | Act: 3: A letter. for Mr Robinson | .2. letters for Mr Lowin: | Act: 5: A letter for Mr Benfeild /' Philip Massinger, *Believe as You List*, manuscript playbook annotated by Edward King: BL Egerton MS 2828, these notes at f. 29ᵛ; reproduced in *Believe as You List by Philip Massinger 1631* ed. Charles J. Sisson (Oxford: Oxford University Press (Malone Society Reprints), 1927). E. K. Chambers first added this piece of evidence to his endorsement of Greg's views: *William Shakespeare: A Study of Facts and Problems*, 2 vols. (Oxford: Clarendon Press, 1930), I: 122–4. Although, as William B. Long reminds us, this playbook is unrepresentative, it is still helpful for capturing a sense of the care with which letters had to be treated. Long, ' "Precious Few": English Manuscript Playbooks', in *A Companion to Shakespeare*, ed. David Scott Kastan (Oxford: Blackwell, 1999), 414–33 at 429–30.

107. For the will and testament, see Kiefer, *Writing on the Renaissance Stage*, 124–5; for the confession, see *Mac* 5.1.6 n.

I THE MATERIALITY OF SHAKESPEARE'S LETTERS

1. Beyond the drama, Lucrece says, 'Go get me hither paper, ink, and pen; | Yet save that labour, for I have them here' (*Luc* 1289–90).
2. Lavinia's act of writing (*Tit* 4.1.77–8) is of course very different in kind.
3. Claude Holiband, *Campo di Fior or else The Flovrie Field of Fovre Langvages* (London: Thomas Vautroullier, 1583), Y vij^v–Z^r. See also Juan Luis Vives, *Lingvae Latinae Exercitatio* (Basel: Robert Winter, 1541), trans. Foster Watson as *Tudor School-Boy Life: The Dialogues of Juan Luis Vives* (London: J. M. Dent, 1907).
4. See Marc Drogin, *Anathema! Medieval Scribes and the History of Book Curses* (Towota, NJ and Montclair, NJ: Allanheld and Schram, 1983).
5. John Evans ed., 'XXVII. Extracts from the Private Account Book of Sir William More, of Loseley, in Surrey, in the Time of Queen Mary and of Queen Elizabeth', *Archaeologia* 36 (1855), 284–310 at 290.
6. John de Beau Chesne and John Baildon, *A Booke Containing Divers Sortes of Handes as well the English as French Secretarie with the Italian, Roman, Chancelry & Court Hands* (London: Thomas Vantrollier, 1571), 4th leaf verso.
7. Richard Mulcaster, *Positions Wherin Those Primitive Circvmstances be Examined, which are Necessarie for the Training Vp of Children* (London: Thomas Chare, 1581), E^v.
8. [Francis Clement], *The Petie Schole with an English Orthographie* (London: Thomas Vautrollier, 1587), D.ij.^{v}.
9. John Florio, *Florios Second Frvtes* (London: Thomas Woodcock, 1591), N^r.
10. Lena Cowen Orlin, 'Gertrude's Closet', *Shakespeare Jahrbuch* 134 (1998), 44–67 at 57.
11. Peter Bales, *The Writing Schoolemaster* (London: Thomas Orwin (1590)), Q4^r.
12. Clement, *Petie Schole*, D.ij.^{v}.
13. See D. C. Coleman, *The British Paper Industry 1495–1860: A Study in Industrial Growth* (Oxford: Oxford University Press, 1958); D. L. Gants, 'Identifying and Tracking Paper Stocks in Early Modern London', *PBSA* 94 (2000), 531–40; J. Bidwell, 'French Paper in English Books', in *The Cambridge History of the Book in Britain*, 7 vols. (Cambridge: Cambridge University Press, 2000–), 4:583–601; Mark Bland, 'Italian Paper in Early Seventeenth-Century England', in *Paper as a Medium of Cultural Heritage. Archaeology and Conservation*, ed. Rosella Graziaplena with Mark Livesey (Roma: Istitute centrale per la patologia del libro, 2004), 243–55.

14. Bales, *Writing Scholemaster*, Q4^v; Holibrand, *Campo di Fior*, Y vij^v–Z^r.

15. Bales, *Writing Schoolemaster*, Q4^v.

16. Florio, *Florios Second Frvtes*, N^r.

17. *OED* s.v. sink, verb 6b.

18. Hugh Platte, *The Jewell House of Art and Nature* (London: Peter Short, 1594), H3^v.

19. de Beau Chesne and Baildon, *Booke*, 3rd leaf verso.

20. de Beau Chesne and Baildon, *Booke* leaf 3^v. Clement concurs: 'Of quills, the fayrest, whitest, and roundest are best, the third and fourth of the wing of goose, or rauen: but where these are not, the pinnion quill hath no fellow.' Clement, *Petie Schole*, D ij^v.

21. de Beau Chesne and Baildon, *Booke*, 4th leaf recto.

22. Clement, *Petie Schole*, D.iii.$^{r-v}$.

23. Holibrand, *Campo di Fior*, X vij^r, based on Vives, *Lingvae Latinae Exercitatio*, d7^r; Watson, *Tudor School-Boy Life*, 71).

24. Bales, *Writing Schoolemaster*, Q2^r.

25. [Thomas Kyd], *The Spanish Tragedie* (London: Edward Allde, 1592), L^v.

26. Bales, *Writing Schoolemaster*, Q2^r.

27. de Beau Chesne and Baildon, *Booke*, 3rd leaf recto.

28. de Beau Chesne and Baildon, *Booke*, 3rd leaf recto, verso.

29. Clement, *Petie School*, D ij^v.

30. Thomas Lupton's *A Thousand Notable Things, of Sundry Sortes* (London: Hughe Spooner, (1595?)), E.ij.^{r}, for example, advises that 'If some droppes of Aqua vite, be myxt with wryting ynke, the same ynke wyl neuer be frozen.'

31. Folger MS V.a.340, p. 42; Stewart and Wolfe, *Letterwriting*, 35–53.

32. Holibrand, *Campo di Fior*, X viij^r.

33. Holibrand, *Campo di Fior*, X viij^r.

34. Florio, *Florios Second Frvtes*, N^r.

35. Thomas Middleton, *Michaelmas Terme* (London: A.I., 1607), D3^v–D4^r.

36. Vives, *Lingvae Latinae exercitatio*, d8^{r-v}; Watson, *Tudor School-Boy Life*, 73–4.

37. [Kyd], *The Spanish Tragedie*, E2^r; Christopher Marlowe, *The tragicall history of D. Faustus* (London: Thomas Bushell, 1604), B4^v–C^v.

38. A. R. Braunmuller, 'Accounting for absence: the transcription of space', in *New Ways of Looking at Old Texts: Papers of the Renaissance English Text Society, 1985–1991* ed. W. Speed Hill (Binghamton, NY: Medieval and Renaissance Texts and Studies (vol. 107) in conjunction with Renaissance English Text Society, 1993), 47–56; Jonathan Gibson, 'Significant Space

in Manuscript Letters', *The Seventeenth Century* 12 (1997), 1–9. Some of the following examples are drawn from Braunmuller's and Gibson's work; see also Sara Jayne Steen, 'Reading Beyond the Words: Material Letters and the Process of Interpretation', *Quidditas*, 22 (2001), 55–69; Sue Walker, 'The Manners on the Page: Prescription and Practice in the Visual Organisation of Correspondence', *Huntington Library Quarterly*, 66 (2003), 307–29; Stewart and Wolfe, 'The material letter and social signals', *Letterwriting*, 35–53; James Daybell, *Women Letter-Writers in Tudor England* (Oxford: Oxford University Press, 2006), ch. 2. For a cross-period survey see Sue Walker, 'Letter-writing', in *Typography and Language in Everyday Life: Prescriptions and Practices* (Harlow: Longman, 2001), 126–70.

39. Gibson, 'Significant space', 1.

40. Antoine de Courtin, *The Rules of Civility; or, Certain Ways of Deportment Observed in France*, 3rd edn (London: J. Martyn and John Starkey, 1675), 146–7.

41. See the examples in Stewart and Wolfe, *Letterwriting*, 51–2.

42. Quoted in David Cecil, *The Cecils of Hatfield House: An English Ruling Family* (Boston: Houghton Mifflin, 1973), 142. I am grateful to Rebecca Calcagno for this reference.

43. Florio, *Florios Second Frvtes*, N^r.

44. *The First Part of Ieronimo. With the Warres of Portugall, and the life and death of Don Andræa* (London: Thomas Pauyer, 1605), C1^v–C2^r.

45. 'I ever write my letters in post-haste, and so rashly-head-long, that howbeit I write intolerably ill, I had rather write with mine owne hand, than employ another: for I finde none that can followe me, and I never copie them over againe. I have accustomed those great persons that know mee, to endure blotts, blurres, dashes, and botches, in my letters, and a sheete without folding or margine.' Michel de Montaigne, *The Essayes or Morall, Politike and Millitarie Discourses*, trans. John Florio (London: Edward Blount, 1603), M3^v.

46. 'Solec nunc interstitium vacuum relinqui inter salutationem et ipsam epistolam pro dignitate eius ad quem scribitur vel amplius vel adstrictius. Vocetur id sane margo honorarium'. Juan Luis Vives, *De conscribendis epistolis*, trans./ed. Charles Fantazzi (Leiden: E. J. Brill, 1989), 112, trans. on 113.

47. Pierre Fabri, *En lhonneur / gloire / et exultation de tous amateurs de lettres et signamment de eloquence Cy ensuyt le grant et vray art de pleine Rhetorique* (Rouen: Thomas Rayer, 1521), M.iiij.^{r}. For a modern edition see *Le grand*

et vrai art de pleine rhétorique ed. A. Héron (Rouen: Espérance Cagniard, 1889–1890), 1:195–6.

48. William Fulwood, *The Enimie of Idlenesse* (London: Leonard Maylard, 1568), A.viij.^{r}.

49. Angel Day, *The English Secretorie* (London: Richard Jones, 1586), C2^{r-v}.

50. Braunmuller, 'Accounting for Absence', 54.

51. Gibson, 'Significant space', 2 and 8 n.16.

52. *First Part of Jeronimo*, C3^r.

53. Claire McEachern, *MA*, 168, note on 1.1.262–5.

54. Richard Day, *A booke of Christian prayers* (London: John Day, 1578), Mm.iij.^{v}.

55. Abraham Fleming, *A Panoplie of Epistles* (London: Ralph Newberie, 1576), B.iii.^{r}, B.iiii.^{r}.

56. Fleming, *Panoplie*, B.iiii.^{r}.

57. Fulwood, *Enimie of Idlenesse*, A.viij.$^{r-v}$.

58. Day, *English Secretorie*, C4^v.

59. Thomas Blount, *The Academie of Eloquence* (London: Humphrey Moseley, 1654), L4^r.

60. William Shakespeare, *Venus and Adonis* (London: Richard Field, 1593) A2^v; idem, *Lvcrece* (London: Richard Field, for Iohn Harrison, 1594), A2^r.

61. Johann Amos Comenius, *Opera didactica omnia* (Amsterdam: Laurentius de Geer, 1657), F5^v (col. 117); trans. and ed. M. W. Keatinge as *The Great Didactic of John Amos Comenius Now for the First Time Englished* (London: Adam and Charles Black, 1896), 340.

62. Eric Partridge, *Shakespeare's Bawdy*, 3rd edn (1968; London and New York: Routledge, 2001), 196, 208.

63. J. M. Lothian and T. W. Craik, for example, gloss the word as 'an exclamation of surprise or caution as he examines the seal'. *TN* 2.5.94 n.

64. For previous discussions of the letters in this play, see John A. Guinn, 'The Letter Device in the First Act of *The Two Gentlemen of Verona*', [*University of Texas*] *Studies in English* (1940) 72–81 at 72–3; Carroll, 'Introduction', *TGV*, 59–67; and especially Frederick Kiefer, 'Love Letters in *The Two Gentlemen of Verona*', *Shakespeare Studies* 18 (1986), 65–86.

65. M. C. Bradbrook, *Shakespeare and Elizabethan Poetry: A Study of his Earlier Work in Relation to the Poetry of the Time* (London: Chatto and Windus, 1951), 147–54.

66. Carroll, 'Introduction', *TGV*, 59–60.

67. Adrian Kiernander, '*The Two (?) Gentlemen (?) of Verona (?)*: Binarism, patriarchy and non-consensual sex somewhere in the vicinity of Milan',

Social Semiotics 4 (1994), 31–46; Peter J. Smith, 'Re(-)fusing the Sign: Linguistic ambiguity and the subversion of patriarchy in *Romeo and Juliet* and *The Two Gentlemen of Verona*', in *Social Shakespeare: Aspects of Renaissance Dramaturgy and Contemporary Society* (New York: St Martin's Press, 1995), 120–45.

68. Kiefer writes illuminatingly of this incident, but assumes it is Shakespeare's invention: 'By introducing the destruction, and then reconstruction of the letter (neither of which occurs in Montemayor), Shakespeare not only satisfies the audience's desire to see some engaging incident but also makes that incident comically surprising.' Kiefer, 'Love Letters', 68.

69. T. P. Harrison Jr, 'Shakespeare and Montemayor's *Diana*', *University of Texas Studies in English* 6 (1926), 76–8; Guinn, 'Letter Device', 72–5.

70. STC 19969.8–19974: I here quote from Piccolomini, *The M[ost] Excell[ent] Historie, of Euryalus and Lucresia* (London: William Barley, 1596). In 1940 John Guinn pointed out this derivation ('Letter Device', 72–3) but in 1973 William Leigh Godshalk deemed the connection inconclusive, and recent editors including Clifford Leech, June Schlueter, and Carroll do not mention Piccolomini in their surveys of sources. Godshalk, *Patterning in Shakespearean Drama: Essays in Criticism* (The Hague: Mouton, 1973), 45 n.6.

71. *Euryalus and Lucresia*, D^v–D2^r.

72. *Euryalus and Lucresia*, D2^v.

73. Albert Cohn ed., *Shakespeare in Germany in the Sixteenth and Seventeenth Centuries: An Account of English Actors in Germany and the Netherlands and of the Plays Performed by Them During the Same Period* (1865; rpt Wiesbaden: Dr. Martin Sändig OHG, 1967).

74. [Gascoigne], *A Hundreth Sundrie Flowres Bounde Vp in one Small Poesie* (London: Richard Smith, 1573), A.iiij.$^{r–v}$.

75. Robert Greene, *Philomela The Lady Fitzwaters Nightingale* (London: Edward White, 1592), D3^v.

76. Emanuel Forde, [*The Most Pleasant Historie of Ornatus and Artesia*] (London: Thomas Creede, 1599?), C2$^{r–v}$. I am grateful to Tiffany Werth for this reference.

77. Carroll, *TGV*, 4.4.121n.

78. Kiefer, 'Love Letters', 77.

79. Edward Hall, *The Vnion of the Two Noble and Illustre Famelies of Lancastre & Yorke* (London: Richard Grafton, 1548), X.iiii.^{v}.

80. Day, *English Secretorie*, C4^v.

81. Fulwood, *Enimie of Idlenesse*, B.iii.$^{r–v}$.

82. Frederick Kiefer, *Writing on the Renaissance Stage: Written Words, Printed Pages, Metaphoric Books* (Newark: University of Delaware Press, 1996), 285.
83. R[oger] C[otton], *An Armor of Proofe* (London: G. Simson and W. White, 1596), A3^v.
84. Edward Burns, *1H6*, 4.4.185 n.
85. Richard Hakluyt, *The Principall Navigations, Voiages, and Discoveries of the English Nation* (London: George Bishop and Ralph Newberie, 1589), O.vi.^{v} See S. A. Skilliter, *William Harborne and the Trade with Turkey 1578–1582: A Documentary Study of the First Anglo-Ottoman Relations* (London: Oxford University Press for the British Academy, 1977), ch. 4.
86. Hall, *Vnion*, X.iiii.^{r}
87. F has '*Poictiers*', which must be an error: Poitiers was a famous victory for the English under Edward III.
88. *Original Leters, &c. of Sir John Falstaff and his Friends* (London: G. G. and J. Robinson *et al.*, 1796).

2 SHAKESPEARE'S ROMAN LETTERS

1. Sigurd Burckhardt, *Shakespearean Meanings* (Princeton: Princeton University Press, 1968), 9; Clifford Ronan, *'Antike Roman': Power Symbology and the Roman Play in Early Modern England, 1585–1635* (Athens, GA: University of Georgia Press, 1995), esp. chs. 1 and 2; Coppélia Kahn, *Roman Shakespeare: Warriors, wounds, and women* (London: Routledge, 1997), 22–3 n. 6.
2. Phyllis Rackin, *Stages of History: Shakespeare's English Chronicles* (Ithaca: Cornell University Press, 1990), 94. See also Rackin, 'Temporality, Anachronism, and Presence in Shakespeare's English Histories', *Renaissance Drama* n.s. 17 (1986), 103–23.
3. *Epistolarvm M. T. Ciceronis libri tres* ed. Johann Sturm (Prague: Georg Melantrich, 1577).
4. T. W. Baldwin, *William Shakspere's Small Latine & Lesse Greeke*, 2 vols. (Urbana: University of Illinois Press, 1944), 2:239–87.
5. Antonio Schor, *De ratione discendæ docendæqve lingvæ Latinæ & Græcæ, Libri duo* (Strasbourg: Wendelin Rihel, 1549), I iij^r–I iiij^v.
6. William Kempe, *The Education of children in learning* (London: John Potter and Thomas Gubbin, 1588), G^r; John Brinsley, *Lvdvs Literarivs: or, The Grammar Schoole* (London: Thomas Man, 1612), Z^v–Z2^r.
7. Kempe, *Education of children*, G^r.
8. Brinsley, *Ludus literarivs*, Z^r.

9. Kempe, *Education of children*, G^{r-v}.

10. The Romans reckoned the days forward to the Kalends, Nones, or Ides next following. See *OED* s.vv. kalends, nones, ides.

11. Brinsley, *Lvdvs Literarivs*, Y3^{v}–Y4^{r}.

12. Desiderius Erasmus, *De conscribendis epstolis* in *Literary and Educational Writings 3: De conscribendis epistolis / Formvla / De civilitate* trans./ed. J. W. Sowards, *Collected Works of Erasmus* 25 (Toronto: University of Toronto Press, 1985), 50, 52, 64.

13. Erasmus, *De conscribendis epistolis*, 65.

14. See Alan Stewart and Heather Wolfe, *Letterwriting in Renaissance England* (Washington DC: Folger Shakespeare Library, 2004).

15. Anthony Grafton and Lisa Jardine, *From Humanism to the Humanities: Education and the Liberal Arts in Fifteenth- and Sixteenth-Century Europe* (London: Duckworth, 1986), 140.

16. Juan Luis Vives, *De conscribendis epistolis* [and others] (Cologne: Johannes Gymnicus, 1537).

17. George Macropedius, *Methodvs de conscribendis epistolis* [and others] (London: Richard Field 1592); further Field editions appeared in 1595, 1600, 1604, 1609, 1614 and 1621.

18. Brinsley, *Lvdvs Literarivs*, Y3^{v}–Y4^{r}.

19. On writing practices in antiquity see Colin H. Roberts and T. C. Skeat, *The Birth of the Codex* (London: Oxford University Press for the British Academy, 1983); Jocelyn Penny Small, *Wax Tablets of the Mind: Cognitive Studies of Memory and Literacy in Classical Antiquity* (London: Routledge, 1997); Tiziano Dorandi, *Le stylet et la tablette: Dans le secret des auteurs antiques* (Paris: Les belles lettres, 2000); Shane Butler, *The Hand of Cicero* (London: Routledge, 2002).

20. Juan Luis Vives, *De conscribendis epistolis: Critical Edition with Introduction, Translation and Annotation*, trans./ed. Charles Fantazzi (Leiden: E. J. Brill, 1989). On Vives' epistolography, see Judith Rice Henderson, 'Defining the Genre of the Letter: Juan Luis Vives' *De conscribendis epistolis*', *Renaissance and Reformation* n.s. 7 (1983), 89–105.

21. Vives, *De conscribendis epistolis*, 72–3.

22. Justus Lipsius, *Principles of Letter-writing: A Bilingual Text of Justi Lipsi Epistolica Institutio* ed./trans. R. V. Young and M. Thomas Hester (Carbondale and Edwardsville: Southern Illinois University Press (Library of Renaissance Humanism), 1995).

23. Ben Jonson, *Seianvs his fall* (London: Thomas Thorpe, 1605), M^{v}. I am grateful to Adam Hooks for this reference. See also Mark Bland, 'Ben

Jonson and the legacies of the past', *Huntington Library Quarterly* 67 (2004), 371–400 at 394.

24. Barnabé Brisson, *De formvlis et sollemnibvs Populi Romani verbis, Libri VIII* (Paris: Sebastian Nivell, 1583), B.ij.ʳ. Vives discusses this custom: see *De conscribendis epistolis*, 80–3.

25. Bate, *Tit*, 4.2.23 n.

26. Lipsius, *Principles*, 7.

27. Plutarch, *The lives of the noble Grecians and Romanes compared together*, trans. Thomas North (London: Thomas Vautrollier and Iohn Wight, 1579); Geoffrey Bullough ed., *Narrative and Dramatic Sources of Shakespeare* vol. 5, *The Roman Plays: Julius Cæsar, Antony and Cleopatra, Coriolanus* (London: Routledge and Kegan Paul, 1964) (hereafter Bullough 5), 66–7. Suetonius also remarked on Caesar's letters: *Suetonius* vol. 1, trans. J. C. Rolfe (Cambridge, MA: Harvard University Press (Loeb Classical Library), 1998), 106–07.

28. Plutarch, *Lives*, 4T6ᵛ; Bullough 5:91.

29. Plutarch, *Lives*, 3V6ᵛ; Bullough 5:82.

30. Plutarch, *Lives*, 4V2ʳ; Bullough 5:95.

31. Plutarch, *Lives*, 4V2ʳ; Bullough 5:96.

32. Andrew Gordon, 'The Act of Libel: Conscripting Civic Space in Early Modern England', *Journal of Medieval and Early Modern Studies* 32 (2002), 375–97.

33. 7 September 1586, Corporation of London Record Office, Rep. 21, f. 334ᵛ, cit. Gordon, 'Act of Libel', 376.

34. Sir John Spencer to Burghley, 26 June 1595, London. British Library, London (BL) Lansdowne MS 78, f.159ʳ (art. 78), cit. Gordon, 'Act of Libel', 376.

35. Plutarch, *Lives*, 3X1ʳ⁻ᵛ; Bullough 5:84–5.

36. Suetonius, *The historie of twelve Caesars emperours of Rome*, trans. Philemon Holland (London: Matthew Lownes, 1606), C5ʳ; Bullough 5:153–4.

37. John Higgins, *The Mirror for Magistrates* (London: Henry Marsh, 1587), L2ᵛ; Bullough 5:172.

38. See Roberts and Skeat, *Birth of the Codex*.

39. Vives, *De conscribendis epistolis*, 125. Seneca, epistle XLV, in *Seneca In Ten Volumes IV Ad Lucilium epistulae morales*, trans. Richard M. Gummere, 3 vols., vol. 1 (Cambridge, MA: Harvard University Press (Loeb Classical Library), 1979), 298–9.

40. Vives, *De conscribendis epistolis*, 127.

41. Lipsius, *Principles*, 6–7.

42. W. B. Worthen, 'The Weight of Antony: Staging "Character" in *Antony and Cleopatra*', *Studies in English Literature 1500–1900* 26 (1986), 295–308 at 297.

43. C. C. Barfoot, 'News from the Roman Empire: Hearsay, Soothsay, Myth and History in *Antony and Cleopatra*', in *Reclamations of Shakespeare*, ed. A. J. Hoenselaars (Amsterdam/Atlanta GA: Rodopi, 1994), 105–28 at 113. I am grateful to Garrett Sullivan for bringing this essay to my attention.

44. Garrett A. Sullivan, ' "My oblivion is a very Antony" ', in *Memory and Forgetting in English Renaissance Drama* (Cambridge: Cambridge University Press, 2005), 88–108 at 89.

45. Linda Charnes, 'Spies and Whispers: Exceeding Reputation in *Antony and Cleopatra*', in *Notorious Identity: Materializing the Subject in Shakespeare* (Cambridge MA: Harvard University Press, 1993), 103–47 at 106, 107.

46. See, for example, Ronald Syme, *The Roman Revolution* (Oxford: Clarendon Press, 1939), 459–75, esp. 460–1; Leo Braudy, *The Frenzy of Renown: Fame & Its History* (New York and Oxford: Oxford University Press, 1986), 90–111. Braudy would agree with Charnes that 'In both life and drama Octavian wins the conflict with Antony' (91).

47. P. A. Brunt and J. M. Moore, 'Introduction' to their edn, *Res gestae divi Augusti: The achievements of the divine Augustus* (Oxford: Oxford University Press, 1967), 1–16.

48. Simon Goulart, 'The Life of Octaius Cæsar Augustus', in *The Lives of Epaminondas, of Philip of Macedon, of Dionysivs the Elder, and of Octavivs Cæsar Avgvstvs . . .* , trans. Thomas North (London: Richard Field, 1603), e4^r–g4^r (51–75) at e4^v–e5^r (52–3).

49. Ronald Macdonald also argues that Shakespeare indulged in 'an historical questioning of classicism in general. . . . He came to see that the centrality of classicism was not a "natural" phenomenon at all, but a cultural and historical construct.' Ronald R. Macdonald, 'Playing Till Doomsday: Interpreting *Antony and Cleopatra*', *English Literary Renaissance* 15 (1985), 78–99 at 79.

50. Worthen similarly: 'Caesar relies on narrative . . . to characterize his general, means which enable Caesar more easily to assimilate Antony's actions to an interpretive text: Antony becomes the "abstract of all faults | That men follow" (I.iv.9–10). Caesar's characterization of Antony consistently privileges the absent "character" of history over the present "character" of performance'. Worthen, 'The Weight of Antony', 299.

51. Plutarch, *The Lives of the Noble Grecians and Romaines, compared together . . . Hereunto are affixed the liues of Epaminados . . . etc* [by Simon Goulart], trans.

Thomas North (London: Richard Field for Thomas Wight, 1603), 4L5^v (946).

52. See James Hirsh, 'Rome and Egypt in *Antony and Cleopatra* and in Criticism of the Play', in *Antony and Cleopatra: New Critical Essays* ed. Sara Munson Deats (New York: Routledge, 2005), 175–91.

53. John F. Danby, *Poets on Fortune's Hill: Studies in Sidney, Shakespeare, Beaumont and Fletcher* (London: Faber and Faber, 1952), 140.

54. Maurice Charney, *Shakespeare's Roman Plays: The Function of Imagery in the Drama* (Cambridge MA: Harvard University Press, 1961), 93.

55. See, for example, Charney, *Shakespeare's Roman Plays*, 93–112; Rosalie L. Colie, '*Antony and Cleopatra*: the Significance of Style' in *Shakespeare's Living Art* (Princeton: Princeton University Press, 1974), 168–207 at 168, 177, 179; Wilders, *AC*, 28.

56. Danby, *Poets on Fortune's Hill*, 151.

57. Jonathan Gil Harris, ' "Narcissus in thy face": Roman Desire and the Difference it Fakes in *Antony and Cleopatra*', *Shakespeare Quarterly* 45 (1994), 408–25; Carol Cook, 'The Fatal Cleopatra', in *Shakespearean Tragedy and Gender*, ed. Shirley Nelson Garner and Madelon Sprengnether (Bloomington: Indiana University Press, 1996), 241–67; Hirsh, 'Rome and Egypt'.

58. In 1958, Benjamin Spencer argued that the play 'shows ... an as yet undefined synthesis lying beyond both Rome and Egypt but partaking of the values of both'. Spencer, '*Antony and Cleopatra* and the Paradoxical Metaphor', *Shakespeare Quarterly* 9 (1958), 373–8.

59. 'No one gets far into *Antony and Cleopatra* without discovering that it is a play swarming with messengers': Macdonald, 'Playing Till Doomsday', 85.

60. 'Many important incidents ... occur largely in report, not on the stage.' Robert S. Miola, *Shakespeare's Rome* (Cambridge: Cambridge University Press, 1983), 117.

61. Janet Adelman, *The Common Liar: An Essay on Antony and Cleopatra* (New Haven: Yale University Press, 1973), esp. 34–9; Charnes, 'Spies and Whispers'; Barfoot, 'News from the Roman Empire'.

62. Barfoot comments similarly that 'Verbally, orally, the Roman Empire is observed articulating itself, giving conscious expression to itself through word of mouth, and through deliberate acts of writing; and defining itself spatially, geographically, through the need to conduct business by letter and messenger, and historically by the provision of documents and of witnesses'. Barfoot does not distinguish, however, between Roman and

Egyptian modes of communication. Barfoot, 'News from the Roman Empire', 108.

63. Miola notes that 'Unlike Antony, Caesar is eager for news, already in the process of receiving a message as he appears'. Miola, *Shakespeare's Rome*, 128.

64. Barfoot notes, 'Significantly, the main charge levelled against Lepidus when he is deposed is that he wrote letters to Pompey (3.5.8–10): clearly letter writing can be a contentious and dangerous occupation in the Roman Empire, and may be used in evidence against you'. 'News from the Roman Empire', 108–09.

65. John Michael Archer, *Old Worlds: Egypt, Southwest Asia, India, and Russia in Early Modern English Writing* (Stanford: Stanford University Press, 2001), 23–62.

66. Philemon Holland 'The Summarie' to his trans., Plutarch, 'Of Isis and Osiris' in *The Philosophie, commonlie called the Morals* (London: Arnold Hatfield, 1603), 5Q^v–5Q2^r (1286–7).

67. Plutarch, *Lives*, 4L^v (938).

68. Samuel Brandon, *The Tragicomoedi of the virtuous Octauia* (London: William Ponsonby, 1598), B3^r; for the letters see F8^r (argument), F8^v–H2^r (Octavia to Antony), and H2^r–H7^v (Antony to Octavia); Samuel Daniel, 'A Letter sent from Octauia to her husband Marcus Antonius into Egypt', in *Certaine Small Workes* rev. edn (London: Simon Waterson, 1607), F2^r–G2^v.

69. See Anton J. L. van Hooff, *From Autothanasia to Suicide: Self-killing in Classical Antiquity* (London: Routledge, 1990); Timothy D. Hill, *Ambitiosa Mors. Suicide and Self in Roman Thought and Literature* (New York: Routledge, 2004).

70. Leeds Barroll, *Politics, Plague, and Shakespeare's Theater: The Stuart Years* (Ithaca and London: Cornell University Press, 1991), 160–5.

71. Plutarch, *Lives*, 4L5^{r-v} (945–6).

72. Plutarch, *Les vies des hommes illvstres grecs et romains, compares l'vne avec l'avtre*, trans. Jacques Amyot [with additions by Charles de l'Écluse] (Paris: Pierre Cheuillot, 1579), EEE. iij.^{r}

73. Mary [Sidney Herbert], countess of Pembroke, *The Tragedie of Antonie. Doone into English* (London: William Ponsonby, 1595), F5^r.

74. Robert Garnier, *M. Antoine, Tragedie* (Paris: Mamert Patisson, 1578), I.j.^{r}

75. Richard Barckley, *A Discovrse of the Felicitie of Man: or his Summum bonum* (London: William Ponsonby, 1598), D6^v–D7^r.

76. Robert Allott, *Wits Theater of the little World* (London: N.L., 1599), K6^v–K7^r.

77. Brandon, *Tragicomoedi of the virtuous Octauia*, F4^v.

78. The 1607 revision of Daniel's closet drama *Cleopatra* also makes Eros 'his late infranchis'd seruant', suggesting he may have seen or read Shakespeare's play. Daniel, 'The Tragedie of Cleopatra' in *Certaine Small Workes*, G3^r–L^r, at G8^r. The scene (Dircetus' account to Caesar of Antony's demise) is not in earlier editions of the play.

79. A. M. Duff, *Freedmen in the Early Roman Empire* (Oxford: Clarendon Press, 1928), 90–1; Susan Treggiari, *Roman Freedmen during the Late Republic* (1969; rpt Oxford: Clarendon Press, 2000), 68–81, 145–9; Aaron Kirschenbaum, *Sons, Slaves and Freedmen in Roman Commerce* (Jerusalem: The Magnes Press/Washington DC: The Catholic University of America Press, 1987), 98, 127–40.

80. Plutarch, *Lives*, 4K5^r (933).

81. The Rhamnus moment had earlier been dramatized by Samuel Brandon who does not, however, confer any status on Rhamnus. *Tragicomoedi of the virtuous Octauia*, B6^r.

82. Barroll, *Politics, Plague, and Shakespeare's Theater*, 163.

83. Plutarch, *Lives*, 415^r (921).

84. Plutarch, *Lives*, 4R^v (1010).

85. Barroll, *Politics, Plague, and Shakespeare's* Theater, 163 n.14.

86. Again, the passage is taken from North's Plutarch, where the character is named Thyrsus: 'To be short, if this mislike thee (said he) thou hast *Hipparchus* one of my infranchised bondmen with thee: hang him if thou wilt, or whippe him at thy pleasure, that we may crie quittance.' Plutarch, *Lives*, 4L4^v (944).

87. Plutarch, *Lives*, 4L3^v (942).

88. Miola argues that among Roman suicides, 'Antony's suicide is unique. While testifying to Roman love of honor and aversion to shame, it expresses Antony's rejection of Rome and Roman values . . . The removal of armor emblematically repudiates all the demands of battlefield, Empire, and world.' Miola, *Shakespeare's Rome*, 149–50 at 149.

89. Wilders makes the general point, but misses the earliest introduction of the character: 'This is Plutarch's first reference to Eros, but Shakespeare introduces him as early as 3.11.24 [*sic*—it's in 3.5] and gives his name repeatedly in 4.4'. 258, note on 4.14.63–8.

90. Plutarch, *Lives*, 4L3^v (942).

91. Kirschenbaum, *Sons, Slaves and Freedmen*, 135–8.

92. Angel Day, *The English secretary, or Methode of writing of epistles and letters* (London: C. Burbie, 1599), Nn^v. On the figure of the secretary Jonathan

Goldberg, *Writing Matter: From the hands of the English Renaissance* (Stanford: Stanford University Press, 1990), ch. 5; Richard Rambuss, *Spenser's Secret Career* (Cambridge: Cambridge University Press, 1993), ch. 2; Alan Stewart, *Close Readers: Humanism and sodomy in early modern England* (Princeton: Princeton University Press, 1997), ch. 5.

93. Rambuss, *Spenser's Secret Career*, 43–6 at 46.

94. Plutarch, *Lives*, 4M^r (949).

95. Charnes, 'Spies and Whispers', 144–5.

96. *Res gestae divi Augusti*, ed. Brunt and Moore, 18–19.

97. Colie, '*Antony and Cleopatra*: the Significance of Style', 180.

98. See for example, Phyllis Rackin, 'Shakespeare's Boy Cleopatra, the Decorum of Nature, and the Golden World of Poetry', *PMLA* 87 (1972), 201–12; Jyotsna Singh, 'Renaissance Antitheatricality, Antifeminism, and Shakespeare's *Antony and Cleopatra*', *Renaissance Drama* n.s. 20 (1990), 99–121.

99. Rackin makes a similar argument for Cleopatra's supremacy: 'By admitting the reality of Rome, Shakespeare is able to celebrate the power of Egypt: by acknowledging the validity of the threat, he can demonstrate the special power that shows have to overcome the limitations of a reality that threatens to refute them.' Rackin, 'Shakespeare's Boy Cleopatra', 207.

3 SHAKESPEARE AND THE CARRIERS

1. Francis Gentleman, notes on *Bell's Edition of Shakespeare's Plays, As they are now performed at the Theatres Royal in London*, 9 vols. (London: John Bell, 1773–4), 4: I6^v (22 (2nd seq.)), cited in Kastan, *1H4*, 2.1n.

2. Folger Shakespeare Library, Washington DC, MS V.b.34; reproduced in William Shakespeare, *The History of King Henry the Fourth as revised by Sir Edward Dering, Bart.: A Facsimile Edition*, ed. George Walton Williams and Gwynne Blakemore Evans (Charlottesville VA: University of Virginia Press for the Folger Shakespeare Library, 1974).

3. British Library, London, Additional MS 64078: the notes on 2.1 are on fol. 47v (volume inverted). See Hilton Kelliher, 'Contemporary Manuscript Extracts from Shakespeare's *Henry IV, Part I*', *English Manuscript Studies 1100–1700*, I, ed. Peter Beal and Jeremy Griffiths (Oxford: Basil Blackwell, 1989), 144–71, at 156 (extracts) and 162–3 (commentary).

4. *K. Henry IV. With the humours of Sir John Falstaff. A Tragi-Comedy* rev. Thomas Betterton, (London: John Deere, 1700); see also, Kastan, *1H4*, 83–4.

5. *The first part of the true and honorable historie, of the life of Sir John Old-castle, the good Lord Cobham* (London: Thomas Pauier, 1600), 13ᵛ–14ʳ; for a modern edition, see *The Oldcastle controversy: Sir John Oldcastle, Part I and The Famous Victories of Henry V,* ed. Peter Corbin and Douglas Sedge (Manchester: Manchester University Press (The Revels Plays Companion Library), 1991).

6. Fredson Bowers, 'Theme and Structure in *King Henry IV, Part I*', in *The Drama of the Renaissance: Essays for Leicester Bradner* ed. Elmer B. Blistein (Providence, RI: Brown University Press, 1970), 42–68 at 53.

7. Kastan, *1H4*, 15.

8. Malone to Boswell, 1 September 1793. *The Correspondence of James Boswell with David Garrick, Edmund Burke, and Edmond Malone,* ed. Peter S. Baker *et al.* (New Haven: Yale University Press (The Yale Boswell, Correspondence vol. 4), 1986), quoted in Peter Martin, *Edmond Malone Shakespearean scholar: A literary biography* (Cambridge: Cambridge University Press, 1995), 179.

9. Malone to Charlemont, 15 November 1793, London. Historical Manuscripts Commission, *Thirteenth Report, Appendix, Part VIII: The Manuscripts and Correspondence of James, first earl of Charlemont,* vol. II, *1784–1799* (London: HMSO, 1894), 220–2 at 221.

10. Malone to Percy, September 21 1793, London. Bodleian Library, Oxford, MS Malone 26f. 21. *The Correspondence of Thomas Percy & Edmond Malone,* ed. Arthur Tillotson (Louisiana State University Press, 1944) (vol. 1 of *The Percy Letters*, general editors David Nichol Smith and Cleanth Brooks), 60–1.

11. Richard Quiney to Shakespeare, 25 October 1598, 'the Bell in Carter Lane' (London). Shakespeare Birthplace Trust Records Office (hereafter SBTRO) ER 27/4. Measurements are from Tarnya Cooper ed., *Searching for Shakespeare* (London: National Portrait Gallery, 2006), catalogue entry 58, p. 144.

12. *Acts of the Privy Council* n.s. 29 A.D. *1598–9,* ed. John Roche Dasent (London: HMSO, 1905), 232–4.

13. Edmond Malone and James Boswell, *The Life of William Shakespeare, by the Late Edmond Malone: And an Essay on the Phraseology and Metre of the Poet and His Contemporaries, by James Boswell* (London: privately printed, 1821), 485 (letter); 481–6 (discussion).

14. On Quiney see Edgar I. Fripp, *Master Richard Quyny Bailiff of Stratford-upon-Avon and Friend of William Shakespeare* (London: Humphrey Milford/Oxford University Press, 1924).

15. Fripp, *Master Richard Quyny*, 13, 30–1.

16. Fripp, *Master Richard Quyny*, 45, 83–4.

17. Mark Eccles, *Shakespeare in Warwickshire* (Madison WI: University of Wisconsin Press, 1961), 92–3.

18. Fripp, *Master Richard Quyny*, 201.

19. S. Schoenbaum, *Shakespeare's Lives* (Oxford: Clarendon Press, 1970), 13.

20. Quiney died intestate while in office in May 1602, his 'heade grevouselye brooken' during a scuffle with supporters of a local rival. His papers remained in the Stratford archives in a packet labelled 'A bundell of *lettres* and divers other matters concerninge suiets petitions and other matters concerninge the Corporation ... vnsorted, bound vp January 7 1603'. SBTRO BRU 15/1/137. Damage from flooding has rendered several of the letters in BRU 15/1 unreadable; here I rely on transcripts made in the early nineteenth century by Captain James Saunders (ER 1/97). I have provided references for both originals and transcripts. I am grateful for the guidance of Dr Robert Bearman and Mairi MacDonald at the Shakespeare Birthplace Trust Record Office.

21. Sturling to Quiney, n.d. SBTRO ER 1/97 f. 143v, transcript of SBTRO BRU 15/1/140, faded and now illegible; Fripp, 160.

22. Adrian Quiney to Richard Quiney, 20 October 1598. SBTRO BRU 15/1/130; Fripp, 135, 136.

23. Sturley to Quiney, 27 October 1598. SBTRO BRU 15/1/145; Fripp, 140.

24. Sturley to Quiney, 27 October 1598. SBTRO BRU 15/1/145; Fripp, 142.

25. Sturling to Quiney, 27 October 1598. SBTRO BRU 15/1/145; see also Sturley to Quiney, n.d. (1598). SBTRO BRU 15/1/140; Fripp, 159, 144.

26. On the various postal systems available in Elizabethan England, see Howard Robinson, *The British Post Office: A History* (Princeton: Princeton University Press, 1948), esp. chs. 2 and 3; J. Crofts, *Packhorse, Waggon and Post: Land Carriage and Communications under the Tudors and Stuarts* (London: Routledge and Kegan Paul/Toronto: University of Toronto Press, 1967); Philip Beale, *A History of the Post in England from the Romans to the Stuarts* (Aldershot: Ashgate, 1998), revised as *England's Mail: Two Millennia of Letter Writing* (Stroud, Glos: Tempus, 2005); Alan Stewart and Heather Wolfe, *Letterwriting in Renaissance England* (Washington DC: Folger Shakespeare Library, 2004), 121–44. On carriers, see also David Hey, *Packmen, Carriers and Packhorse Roads: Trade and Communications in North Derbyshire and South Yorkshire* (Leicester: Leicester University Press, 1980), ch. 9.

27. Sturley to Quiney, 4 November 1598. STBRO BRU 15/1/136; Fripp, 148.

28. John Earle, *Micro-cosmographie or, a peece of the world discovered; in essayes and characters* (London: Robert Allot, 1628), D4^v–D5^r.

29. Claude Holibrand, *Campo di Fior or else The Flovrie Field of fovre langvages* (London: Thomas Vautrollier, 1583), Q.iij.^{r}.

30. Earle, *Micro-cosmographie*, D4^v–D5^r.

31. Adrian Quiney to Richard Quiney, 20 October 1598 and 18 November 1598. SBTRO BRU 15/1/130 and BRU 15/1/129; Fripp, 135–6, 151.

32. Sturley to Quiney, 27 October 1598. SBTRO BRU 15/1/145. Fripp, 144; Eccles, *Shakespeare in Warwickshire*, 96.

33. Richard Quiney jr. to Richard Quiney, *c.* 5 October 1598. SBTRO ER 1/97 f. 106^r (transcript); the original is lost. Fripp, 133.

34. Daniel Baker to Quiney, 13 November 1598. SBTRO BRU 15/1/126 (postscript).

35. T. F. Thiselton-Dyer, *Old English Social Life as told by the Parish Registers* (London: Elliot Stock, 1898), 169, quoted in Crofts, *Packhorse, Waggon and Post*, 135, note 06.

36. James Shapiro, *1599: A Year in the Life of William Shakespeare* (London: Faber, 2005), 260–1.

37. Fynes Moryson, *An Itinerary* (London: John Beale, 1617), 318^v.

38. Thomas Dekker, *The Second Part of the Honest Whore* (London: Elizabeth All-de for Nathaniel Butter, 1630), F2^v, L^v, quoted in Crofts, *Packhorse, Waggon and Post*, 135, note 08.

39. *Robin Good-Fellow, His Mad Prankes, and merry Iests, Full of honest Mirth, and is a Medicine for Melancholy* (London: F. Groue, 1628), E^v, quoted in Crofts, *Packhorse, Waggon, and Post*, 135–6, n. 08.

40. *Robin Good-Fellow*, E^r.

41. *The Life of Long Meg of Westminster* (London: Robert Bird, 1635).

42. *Life of Long Meg*, B^r.

43. On the alehouse see Peter Clark, 'Migration in the city: the process of social adaptation in English towns, 1500–1800', in *Migration and Society in Early Modern England*, ed. Peter Clark and David Souden (London: Hutchinson, 1987), 267–91 at 280–1; also Peter Clark, *The English Alehouse: A Social History 1200–1830* (London and New York: Longman, 1983), 47–50, chs. 4, 6.

44. *Life of Long Meg*, B^v.

45. *Life of Long Meg*, D^r–D2^r.

46. John Taylor, *The Carriers Cosmographie* (London: A. G. 1637), A^r (titlepage).

47. Taylor, *Carriers Cosmographie*, A4^v.

48. For attempts to reconstruct the journey, see John W. Hales, 'From Stratford to London', *Notes and Essays on Shakespeare* (London: George Bell, 1884), 1–24; Russell Fraser, *Young Shakespeare* (New York: Columbia University Press, 1988), 79–86; Shapiro, *1599*, 260. The Oxford—London route is listed in [Richard Grafton], *A briefe treatise conteyning many proper Tables and easie rules* (London: John Walley, 1582), H.iiij.ʳ.

49. *Barlow's Journal of his life at sea in King's ships, East and West Indiamen & other merchantmen from 1659 to 1703* ed. Basil Lubbock, 2 vols. (London: Hurst and Blackett, 1934), 17, 21–4. Barlow's journal is at the centre of Patricia Fumerton's important recent study, *Unsettled: The Culture of Mobility and the Working Poor in Early Modern England* (Chicago: University of Chicago Press, 2006).

50. *Barlow's Journal*, 26.

51. The Sign of the Axe is named as a Manchester carriers' inn in 1637: Taylor, *Carriers Cosmographie*, B4ʳ.

52. Thomas Heywood, *The second part of, If you know not me, you know no bodie* (London: Nathaniell Butter, 1606), A4ᵛ.

53. John Donne, *Letters to Severall Persons of Honour*, ed. John Donne (London: Richard Marriot, 1651). For Goodere and Polesworth Hall, see John Considine, 'Goodere, Sir Henry (*bap.* 1571, *d.* 1627),' *ODNB*.

54. Donne, *Letters*, G4ᵛ, Kᵛ, Ffʳ⁻ᵛ, H3ʳ.

55. Donne, *Letters*, Q2ᵛ.

56. Taylor, *Carriers Cosmographie*, Bᵛ.

57. Shapiro, *1599*, 232–3.

58. Sturley to Quiney, 14 November 1598. SBTRO ER 1/97 f. 138 (transcript of SBTRO BRU 15/1/144, now illegible); Fripp, 150–1.

59. Sturley to Quiney, 20 November. SBTRO ER 1/97 f. 141 (transcript of SBTRO BRU 15/1/141, now illegible); Fripp, 152–3.

60. Taylor, *Carriers Cosmographie*, A2ᵛ.

61. Sturley to Quiney, 20 November. SBTRO ER 1/97 f. 141r (transcript of SBTRO BRU 15/1/141, now illegible); Fripp, 153.

62. Baker to Quiney, 26 October 1598. SBTRO BRU 15/1/128.

63. See for example, letters from Adrian Quiney on 20 October 1598 (SBTRO BRU 15/1/130), 29 October 1598 (BRU 15/1/133), and undated (BRU 15/1/131); Sturley wrote 'To his moste his lovinge brother master Richard Quinej at the Belle in Charter Lane att London geve these' on 23 November (1598) (ER 3/676); see also letters from Sturley on 4 November 1598 (ER 1/97 f. 145, transcript of BRU 15/1/136); 14 November 1598 (ER 1/97 f. 138, transcript of BRU 15/1/144). On 16 November 1598, William Walford wrote the superscription 'To his aprooved and very good frend master

Rychard Quyney at the bell in Carter Lane geve thes wythe speed' (BRU 15/1/117).

64. Edward H. Sugden, *A Topographical Dictionary to the Works of Shakespeare and his Fellow Dramatists* (Manchester: Manchester University Press, 1925), 102. See John Stow, *A Survay of London* (London: John Wolfe, 1598), U4ᵛ (p. 296); and *The London Encyclopædia*, ed. Ben Weinreb and Christopher Hibbert (London: Macmillan, 1983), 54, 126.

65. John Eliot, *Ortho-Epia Gallica. Eliots Frvits for the French* (London: John Wolfe, 1593), dʳ.

66. A. L. Beier and Roger Finlay, 'Introduction: The significance of the metropolis', in *London 1500–1700: The making of the metropolis* (London: Longman, 1986), 1–33 at 21; Clark, 'Migration in the city', 274.

67. Clark, 'Migration in the city', 274.

68. William Parsons to Quiney, (25 October 1598). SBTRO BRU 15/1/114; Fripp, 140.

69. David Kathman points out to me that the leaseholders of the Bell Inn were William and Mary Haughton. But Mary Haughton's maiden name was Griffin, so it is possible that 'Misteries Greffine' refers to her mother. Personal communication, 28 December 2007; see also his 'Citizens, Innholders, and Playhouse Builders, 1543–1622', *Research Opportunities in Medieval and Renaissance Drama* 44 (2005), 38–64 at 45–6.

70. Halliwell-Phillipps affirms, 'It may be concluded that the great dramatist forwarded the letter to his solicitor with instructions to prepare the requisite security, for otherwise it would be all but impossible to account for its having been preserved, with other papers of {Thomas} Greene, {town clerk, Shakespeare's solicitor}, amongst the records of the Corporation'. J. O. Halliwell-Phillipps, *Outlines of the Life of Shakespeare* (London: Longmans, Green, and Co., 1882), 104–5. See also René Weiss, *Shakespeare Revealed: A Biography* (London: John Murray, 2007), 239–44, who speculates that Quiney 'either never left for Whitehall at all, or else returned early to find Shakespeare waiting for him' (243).

71. Sturley to Quiney, 4 November 1598. SBTRO ER 1/97, ff. 144ᵛ–145ʳ (transcript of SBTRO BRU 15/1/136, now faded and illegible); Fripp, 146; Eccles, 95.

72. *The Famous Victories of Henry the Fifth containing the honourable battell of Agin-court* (London: Thomas Creede, 1598). For a modern edition, see *The Oldcastle controversy*, ed. Corbin and Sedge.

73. Peter Thomson, 'Tarlton, Richard (d. 1588)', *ODNB*.

74. John Davies, 'On Tarlton', in *Wits Bedlam. Where is had, Whipping-cheer, to cure the Mad* (London: James Davies, 1617), K6ʳ⁻ᵛ at K6ᵛ.

75. Richard Helgerson, *Forms of Nationhood: The Elizabethan Writing of England* (Chicago: University of Chicago Press, 1992), 217.

76. David Wiles, *Shakespeare's Clown: Actor and Text in the Elizabethan Playhouse* (Cambridge: Cambridge University Press, 1987), 23 and ch. 2 *passim*.

77. Thomson, 'Tarlton, Richard'.

78. Beier and Finlay, 'Introduction', 9–1 0.

79. Antimo Galli to Andrea Cioli, 12/22 August 1613, relating the visit of ambassador Antonio Foscarini in disguise to the Curtain. E. K. Chambers, 'Elizabethan Stage Gleanings', *Review of English Studies* 1 (1925), 182–6 at 186; John Orrell, 'The London Stage in the Florentine Correspondence, 1604–18', *Theatre Research International* 3 (1977–8), 157–7 6 at 171. For Florio's translation see John Florio, *Queen Anna's new world of words, or dictionarie of the Italian and English tongues* (London: Edw. Blount and William Barret, 1611), G3^v s.v. canaglia.

80. *OED* s.v. cutter 3.a 'One over-ready to resort to weapons; a bully, bravo; also, a cutthroat, highway-robber. *Obs*'.

81. An episode based on, but departing from a sequence in Thomas Eliot's *Boke named the Gouernour* (1531), recently retold in John Stow's 1592 *Annales*. See John Stow, *The Annales of England* (London: Ralph Newbery, 1592), Nn.2.$^{r-v}$.

82. Although, as David Bevington rightly notes, Rochester is not named as the location of the inn during the scene, there is nothing to contradict the information, given earlier, that Gadshill will spend the night at Rochester. Bevington ed., *Henry IV, Part 1* (Oxford: Oxford University Press, 1994), 2.1 n.

83. George Chapman, *The Conspiracie, and Tragedie of Charles Duke of Byron Marshall of France* (London: Thomas Thorpe, 1608), F3^r.

84. [William Shakespeare], *The history of Henrie the Fourth with the battell at Shrewsburie, betweene the King and Lord Henry Percy* (London: Andrew Wise, 1598), C2^{r-v}.

85. The turkey was quite anachronistic for the early fifteenth century, since it was only later introduced to Europe from America by the Spanish (*1H4*, 2.1.26n).

86. See for example [Richard Rowlands (i.e., Richard Verstegan)], *The Post for diuers partes of the world* (London: Thomas East, 1576), H.ij.^{v}, and [Grafton], *Briefe treatise*, H.iiij.^{r}.

87. Crofts, *Packhorse, Waggon and Post*, 61–2, 64–5.

88. *1H4* 2.1.5–6n.

89. Harrison, 'Description of England', P.ij.^{v}.

90. Drayton *et al.*, *Sir John Old-castle*, 13^v–14^r.

91. Harrison, 'Description of England', Pij^v.

92. [Francis Beaumont and John Fletcher?], *The Knight of the Burning Pestle* (London: Walter Burre, 1613), E2^r.

93. Robert Wilson, *A right excellent and famous comoedy called the three ladies of London* (London: Roger Warde, 1584), A.iii.$^{r-v}$.

94. Christopher Marlowe, *The famous tragedy of the rich Iew of Malta* (London: Nicholas Vavasour, 1633), B2^v.

95. Kastan, *1H4*, 64.

96. Croft also makes this point: *Packhorse, Waggon and Post*, 43.

97. At 1.2.154–5, both Q and F have Poins suggest that will be '*Falstaffe, Haruey, Rossill,* and *Gads-hill*, shall robbe those men that wee haue already way-layde'. Harvey and Rossill seem to disappear from the play; editors replace them with Peto and Bardoll.

98. Drayton *et al.*, *Sir John Old-castle*, F4^r. Barham is six miles SE of Canterbury; Cobham six miles SE of Gravesend; Wrotham or Wrootham eleven miles NW of Maidstone; Blackheath the open common between Eltham and Greenwich, five miles from London; Coxheath is near Maidstone. Sugden, *Topographical Dictionary*, 47, 122, 572, 64, 123. Sugden suggests Birchen Wood is 'Probably Bircholt, which lies in E. Kent near Ashford' (61); Birchwood Park near Dartford remains a possibility.

99. Henry Smith, *The Poore-Mans Teares, opened in a Sermon* (London: William Wright, 1592), A7^{r-v}.

100. *The Lamentable and Trve Tragedie of M. Arden of Feversham in Kent* (London: Edward White, 1592), I4^v.

101. B[en] J[onson], *The Comicall Satyre of Every Man ovt of his Hvmor* (London: William Holme, 1600), A.iiij^r, M.iij.$^{r-v}$.

102. Thomas Dekker and John Webster, *West-ward Hoe* (London: John Hodges, 1607) D^v.

103. Harrison, 'Description of England', P.ij.^{v}–P.iij.^{r}.

104. Harrison, 'Description of England', P.ij.^{v}.

105. Schøyen Collection MS 1627, reproduced, transcribed and discussed in Arthur Freeman, 'The "Tapster Manuscript": An Analogue of Shakespeare's *Henry the Fourth Part One*', in *English Manuscript Studies 1100–1700*, vol. 6 (London: The British Library, 1997), 93–105, transcript here at 97. Freeman claims that 'the robbery at Gads Hill is set up in exactly the same way', and 'we have here the same sum (three hundred marks), the same sort of carrier, and the same destination' (94). However the robbery in *Henry IV Part One* is very different, precisely because this is

not 'the same sort of carrier': this man is explicitly travelling alone, and no carrier is involved.

106. *OED* s.v. hue and cry. In *Arden of Faversham*, Will complains 'I am so pursued with hues and cryes, | For petty robberies that I haue done,| That I can come vnto no Sanctuary . . . the Constable had 20 warrands to apprehend me, | Besides that, I robbed him and his Man once at Gades hill'. *Arden of Feversham*, I4$^\mathrm{v}$.

107. For an intriguing assessment of these four words, however, see Anthony B. Dawson, *Watching Shakespeare: A Playgoers' Guide* (Basingstoke: Macmillan, 1988), 91–2.

108. [Beaumont and Fletcher?], *Knight of the Burning Pestle*, E2$^\mathrm{r}$.

109. John Milton, 'On the University Carrier', *Poems &c. upon Severall Occasions* (London: Tho. Dring, 1673), B8$^\mathrm{v}$–C$^\mathrm{r}$ at C$^\mathrm{r}$.

110. See Oliver Wendell Holmes, Jr., *The Common Law* (Boston: Little, Brown, and Company, 1881), lecture 5, 'The Bailee at Common Law', 164–205. For a critique of Holmes, see Joseph H. Beale, Jr., 'The Carrier's Liability: Its History', *Harvard Law Review* 11 (1897–1898), 158–68. More recently, see J. H. Baker, *An Introduction to English Legal History*, 4th edn (London: Butterworths, 2002), 407–08, and the documents in *Sources of English Legal History: Private Law to 1750*, ed. J. H. Baker and S. F. C. Milsom (London: Butterworths, 1986), 522–7.

111. Baker, *Introduction to English Legal History*, 407–8.

112. Harrison, 'Description of England', P.ij.$^\mathrm{v}$.

113. Drayton *et al.*, *Sir John Old-castle*, I2$^\mathrm{v}$.

114. Drayton *et al.*, *Sir John Old-castle*, I2$^\mathrm{v}$.

115. Earle, *Micro-cosmographie*, D5$^\mathrm{v}$.

116. Harrison, 'Description of England', P.ij.$^\mathrm{v}$.

117. Crofts, *Packhorse, Waggon and Post*, 29.

118. *The Dialoges in English, betwene a Docter of Diuinity, and a Student in the lawes of England*, rev edn (London: Richard Tottell, 1580), R.$^\mathrm{v}$–R.ij.$^\mathrm{r}$.

119. Edward Coke, *Le qvart part des reportes* (London: Companie of Stationers, 1610), X.iii.$^\mathrm{v}$. (83b). 'Nota Lecteur, est bone policie a cestuy que prist ascun biens a garder, a prendre eux in speciall maner, s. a garder eux sicome il garde ses biens demesne, ou a garder eux le melieux q' il poit al peril del pl', ou q' sils happ' destre emblee ou purloigne, que il ne respondera pur eux, car couient a cesty q' accept eux a prendr eux in tiel ou semblable maner, ou auterment il poit ester charge per son generall acceptance'. Translation from Crofts, *Packhorse, Waggon, and Post*, 30

120. *Life of Long Meg*, D2$^\mathrm{r}$.

121. Earle, *Micro-cosmographie*, D5^{r-v}.

122. Suit of Edward Bromley vs Nicholas Jevens, 1600–1601. SBTRO BRU 15/6/72. For a summary see James O. Halliwell, *A descriptive calendar of the ancient manuscripts and records in the possession of the Corporation of Stratford-upon-Avon* (London: James Evan Adlard, 1863), 338.

123. Edward Bromley, a common carrier, attached to answer Daniel Baker, 1602–03. SBTRO BRU 12/6/162. For a summary see Halliwell, *Descriptive calendar*, 205.

124. John Stow, *The Chronicles of England, from Brute vnto this present yeare of Christ. 1580* (London: Henrie Bynneman, 1580), Oo.iij.^{v}–Oo.iiij.^{r} (582–3).

125. In both Qq and F, Bardolph has these lines, but it is not clear why he would have this information; editors have reassigned the speech to Gadshill. See Bevington, ed., *King Henry IV Part 1*, 2.2.49n; and Kastan, *1H4*, 2.2.52n.

126. See *OED* s.v. derrick *n.* and *v.*

127. Grafton's *Briefe Treatise* details a route from London through Barnet, St Albans, Dunstable, Brickhill, Stony Stratford, Towcester, and Daventry to Coventry (H.iij.^{v}); Falstaff intends to march through Coventry to reach 'Sutton-cop-hill' (Sutton Coldfield) that night.

4 SHYLOCK IS SHAKESPEARE: LETTERS OF CREDIT IN *THE MERCHANT OF VENICE*

1. Edmond Malone, *An Inquiry into the Authenticity of certain Miscellaneous Papers and Legal Instruments, published Dec. 24, M DCC XCV* (London: T. Cadell and W. Davies, 1796).

2. See *The Correspondence of Edmond Malone... with the Rev. James Davenport...* ed. J. O. Halliwell (London: Thomas Richards, 1864); *Original Letters from Edmund Malone... to John Jordan, the Poet...* ed. J. O. Halliwell (London: Thomas Richards, 1864).

3. For Stratford's attempts to retrieve the papers in 1799, see *Correspondence of Malone with Davenport*, 49–50; Peter Martin, *Edmond Malone Shakespearean scholar: A literary biography* (Cambridge: Cambridge University Press, 1995), 182–3 quotes from an unpublished letter in Photostat in the Boswell Papers at Yale University, dated December 1805: 'Mr Hunt [the town clerk] has himself, and several others have called upon you repeatedly from these papers, and you have as repeatedly promised they should be carefully returned, and the Corporation do conceive they are by no means well treated... we must inform you that in case they [the

books covering 1563–1650] are not . . . delivered, that we shall be under the necessity of applying to the Court of King's Bench in order to get them restored'.

4. Edmond Malone and James Boswell, *The Life of William Shakespeare, by the late Edmond Malone: and An Essay on the Phraseology and Metre of the Poet and his Contemporaries, by James Boswell. With portraits* (London: privately printed, 1821), 484–5 with discussion 481–6.

5. Richard Quiney to Shakespeare, 25 October 1598. SBTRO ER 27. See also Edgar I. Fripp, *Master Richard Quyny Bailiff of Stratford-upon-Avon and Friend of William Shakespeare* (London: Humphrey Milford/Oxford University Press, 1924), 93–5.

6. Malone and Boswell, *Life,* 484.

7. James Orchard Halliwell, *The Life of William Shakespeare* (London: John Russell Smith, 1848), 177.

8. E. A. J. Honigmann, 'Shakespeare's life', in *The Cambridge Companion to Shakespeare,* ed. Margreta de Grazia and Stanley Wells (Cambridge: Cambridge University Press, 2001), 1–12 at 7. See also idem, ' "There is a World Elsewhere": William Shakespeare, Businessman', in *Images of Shakespeare: Proceedings of the Third Congress of the International Shakespeare Association, 1986,* ed. Werner Habicht, D. J. Palmer and Roger Pringle (Newark: University of Delaware Press, 1988), 40–6.

9. Stephen Greenblatt, 'Laugher at the scaffold', in *Will in the World: How Shakespeare became Shakespeare* (New York: Norton, 2004), 256–87; Kenneth Gross, *Shylock is Shakespeare* (Chicago: University of Chicago, 2006).

10. Richard Quiney to Shakespeare, 25 October 1598. SBTRO MS ER 27/4.

11. William Walford to Quiney, 16 October 1598 and 16 November 1598. SBTRO ER 1/97 ff. 111^v–112^r, 110^v–111^r (transcriptions of lost originals); Fripp 134–5, 151.

12. Sturley to Quiney, 20 November 1598 (with postscript 21 November 1598). SBTRO ER 1/97 f. 142v (postscript), transcript of SBTRO BRU 15/1/141, now illegible; Fripp 153–4.

13. Abraham Sturley to Quiney, 20 November, 1598. SBTRO BRU 15/1/141. faded; SBTRO ER 1/97 f. 141^r.

14. Isabell Bardel to Quiney, n.d. SBTRO BRU 15/1/116.

15. Robert Allen to Raffe Allen, 8 October 1598. SBTRO BRU 15/12 art. 51.

16. Daniel Baker to Quiney, 26 October 1598. SBTRO BRU 15/1/128; Baker to Leonard Benet, 27 October 1598: SBTRO BRU 15/1/127; Baker to Quiney, 13 November 1598. SBTRO BRU 15/1/126; Baker to Quiney. 24 November 1598. SBTRO BRU 15/1/124.

17. Baker to Quiney, 26 October 1598. SBTRO BRU 15/1/128.

18. Baker to Quiney, 13 November 1598. SBTRO BRU 15/1/126.

19. Sturley to Quiney, n.d. SBTRO BRU 15/1/140. Fripp 159.

20. Adrian Quiney to Richard Quiney, 20 October 1598. SBTRO ER 1/97 f.155, transcription of SBTRO BRU 15/1/130; Fripp 135–6.

21. William Parsons to Quiney, 25 October 1598. SBTRO BRU 15/1/114; Fripp 140.

22. Baker to Quiney, 24 November 1598. SBTRO BRU 15/1/124; Fripp 157.

23. Adrian Quiney to Richard Quiney, [29 or 30 October] 1598. SBTRO BRU 15/1/131. Fripp 145–6; Eccles, Mark Eccles, *Shakespeare in Warwickshire* (Madison WI: University of Wisconson Press, 1961), 96.

24. Sturley to Quiney, 4 November 1598. SBTRO ERI/97 ff. 144^v–145^r, transcript of SBTRO BRU 15/1/136, now faded and illegible; Fripp 146; Eccles, *Shakespeare in Warwickshire*, 95.

25. Robert Bearman, *Shakespeare in the Stratford Records* (For Thrupp, Stroud: Shakespeare Birthplace Trust/Alan Sutton Publishing, 1994), 35–6.

26. Craig Muldrew, 'Interpreting the market: the ethics of credit and community relations in early modern England', *Social History* 18 (1993), 163–8; idem., *The Economy of Obligation: The Culture of Credit and Social Relations in Early Modern England* (Basingstoke: Macmillan, 1998); idem., ' "Hard food for Midas": Cash and its social value in early modern England', *Past and Present* 170 (Feb. 2001), 78–120. For related work in later periods, see Julian Hoppit, 'The use and abuse of credit in eighteenth-century England', in *Business Life and Public Policy: Essays in honour of D.C. Coleman* ed. Neil McKendrick and R. B. Outhwaite (Cambridge: Cambridge University Press, 1986), 64–78; Margot C. Finn, *The Character of Credit: Personal Debt in English Culture, 1740–1914* (Cambridge: Cambridge University Press, 2003); Deborah Valenze, *The Social Life of Money in the English Past* (Cambridge: Cambridge University Press, 2006). For previous literary critical work building on Muldrew's researches see Theodore B. Leinwand, *Theatre, finance and society in early modern England* (Cambridge: Cambridge University Press, 1999); and Jean Howard, *Theater of a City* (Philadelphia: University of Pennsylvania Press, 2007) ch. 2. Lorna Hutson's *The Usurer's Daughter: Male friendship and fictions of women in sixteenth-century England* (London: Routledge, 1994), ch. 4, made a similar case ahead of Muldrew's work being published.

27. Valenze, *Social Life of Money*, 17.

28. *The Merchant of Venice* ed. Arthur Quiller-Couch and J. Dover Wilson (Cambridge: Cambridge University Press (New Cambridge edition), 1926), cix. *MV*, 5.1.278–9 n.

29. *The Comedy of the Merchant of Venice*, ed. Isaac-Ambrose Eccles (Dublin, 1805) quoted in *A New Variorum Edition of Shakespeare*, ed. Horace Howard Furness, *The Merchant of Venice* (Philadephia: J. B. Lippincott, 1871). 5.1.298 n.

30. Christopher Marlo[we], *The Famous Tragedy of the Rich Iew of Malta* (London: Nicholas Vavasour, 1633), B^{v}.

31. John Weddington, *A Briefe Instruction, and manner, howe to kepe, merchantes bokes, of accomptes* (Antwerp: Peter van Keerberghen, 1567) quoted in B. S. Yamey, H. C. Edey and Hugh W. Thomson, *Accounting in England and Scotland: 1543–1800: Double Entry in Exposition and Practice* (London: Sweet and Maxwell, 1963), 48.

32. Hans Holbein the Younger, *Portrait of the merchant George Gisze*, 1532, Gemaldegalerie, Berlin; Jan Gossaert, *Portrait of a Merchant*, c. 1530, oil on panel, National Gallery of Art, Washington DC.

33. The tables were noted in the Folger Shakespeare Library exhibition (28 September 2006–17 February 2007) on *Technologies of Writing in the Age of Print*, curated by Peter Stallybrass, Michael Mendle, and Heather Wolfe.

34. Mary Poovey, *A History of the Modern Fact: Problems of Knowledge in the Sciences of Wealth and Society* (Chicago: University of Chicago Press, 1998), ch. 2; Ceri Sullivan, *The Rhetoric of Credit: Merchants in Early Modern Writing* (Madison NJ, Cranbury NJ and London: Fairleigh Dickinson University Press / Associated University Presses, 2002); Rebecca Elisabeth Connor, *Women, Accounting, and Narrative: Keeping Books in Eighteenth-Century England* (New York: Routledge, 2004).

35. Luca Pacioli, *Summa de arithmetica geometria proportioni et proportionalita* (Venice, 1494). The sixteenth-century English tracts are as follows: Hugh Oldcastle, *A Profitable Treatyce called the Instrument or Boke to learne to knowe the good order of the kepyng of the famouse reconynge called in Latyn, Dare and Habere, and in Englyshe, Debitor and Creditor* (London: John Gough, 1543), no longer extant; Jan Ympyn Christoffels, *A Notable and very excellente woorke, expressyng and declaring the maner and forme how to kepe a boke of accomptes or reconynges* (London: Richard Grafton, 1547); James Peele, *The maner and fourme how to kepe a perfecte reconyng, after the order of the moste worthie and notable accompte, of debitour and creditour* (London: Richard Grafton, 1553); Weddington, *A Briefe Instruction, and manner*; James Peele, *The Pathwaye to perfectnes, in th' accomptes of Debitour and Creditour* (London: T. Purfoot, 1569); Hugh Oldcastle, *A Briefe Instruction, and maner, how to keepe bookes of Accompts after the order of debitor and creditor*, ed. John Mellis (London: John Windet, 1588); John Browne,

*The Marchants Avizo very necessarie for their sonnes and servants, when they
first send them . . . to Spaine and Portingale* (London: William Norton, 1589);
[Nicolaus Petri], *The Pathway to Knowledge . . . of keeping a marchants booke,
after the Italian manner . . . written in Dutch, and translated into English*, trans.
W.P. (London: William Barley, 1596). For a survey and extracts, see Yamey,
Edey and Thomson, *Accounting in England and Scotland*.

36. Peele, *Manor and fourme*, A.iii.^{v}. Peele later increased the number of books
    required: 'there be other bookes necessarie, as the booke for copies of
    letters, and enuoyces of goodes shipped from your handes, and the booke
    of acquittaunces taken for money paid out daylye'. Peele, *Pathe waye to
    perfectnes* (1569), A.vi.^{r}.

37. [Oldcastle], *Briefe Instruction and Maner*, ed. Mellis.

38. References in the text are to the 1589 edition. For a modern edition,
    see *The Marchants Avizo (1589)*, ed. Patrick McGrath (Boston, MA: Baker
    Library, Harvard Graduate School of Business Adminstration, 1957). For
    the context of Browne's activities see David Harris Sacks, *Trade, Society
    and Politics in Bristol 1500–1640*, 2 vols. (New York: Garland Publishing,
    1985); see also Lynne Magnusson, *Shakespeare and Social Dialogue: Dra-
    matic Language and Elizabethan Letters* (Cambridge: Cambridge University
    Press, 1999), 114–37.

39. On merchant's marks see F. A. Girling, *English Merchants' Marks: A field
    survey of marks made by Merchants and Tradesmen in England between 1400
    and 1700* (London: Oxford University Press, 1964), esp. 9–27.

40. Thomas S. Holman, 'Holbein's Portraits of the Steelyard Merchants:
    An Investigation', *Metropolitan Museum Journal* 14 (1979), 139–58 at
    143.

41. As several critics have noted, this is an unlikely combination for a
    Venetian merchant, but might correspond to Elizabethan mercantile
    aspirations. John Gillies, *Shakespeare and the Geography of Difference* (Cam-
    bridge: Cambridge University Press, 1994), 65–6; Leinward, *Theatre,
    Finance and Society*, 114.

42. William Haughton, *English-men for my money: or, a pleasant comedy, called,
    A woman will haue her will* (London: W. White, 1616); all references in the
    text are to this edition. The only critical edition is *William Haughton's
    Englishmen For My Money Or A Woman Will Have Her Will* ed. Albert Croll
    Baugh (PhD dissertation, University of Pennsylvania, 1917); an edition by
    Lloyd Kermode is forthcoming.

43. Howard, *Theater of a City*, 38–49, esp. 41.

44. [John Eliot], *Ortho-Epia Gallica. Eliots Frvits for the French* (London: Iohn
    Wolfe, 1593), d2^{r}.

45. Thomas Bell, *Speculation of Usury* (London: Valentine Simmes, 1596), B3^v cit. John Russell Brown, *MV* 1.3.48–53 n.

46. *The Merchant of Venice*, ed. M. M. Mahood (Cambridge: Cambridge University Press, 1987), 1.3.49 n.

47. Maxine MacKay, '*The Merchant of Venice*: A reflection of the early conflict between courts of law and courts of equity', *Shakespeare Quarterly* 15 (1964), 371–5; Mark Edwin Andrews, *Law versus Equity in 'The Merchant of Venice'* (Boulder: University of Colarado Press, 1965); W. Nicholas Knight, 'Equity, *The Merchant of Venice*, and William Lambarde', *Shakespeare Survey* 27 (1974), 93–104; E. F. J. Tucker, 'The letter of the law in *The Merchant of Venice*', *Shakespeare Survey* 29 (1976), 93–101.

48. Charles Spinosa, 'The Transformation of Intentionality: Debt and Contract in *The Merchant of Venice*', *ELR* 24 (1994), 370–409. Spinosa is indebted to J. H. Baker's groundbreaking article, 'New light on *Slade's Case*', *The Cambridge Law Journal* 29 (1971), 51–67, 213–36. Others have rejected the notion of any specific contemporary relevance, pointing instead to long-standing stories about flesh-bearing bonds: see William Chester Jordan, 'Approaches to the court scene in the bond story: equity or mercy or reason and nature', *Shakespeare Quarterly* 33 (1982), 49–59.

49. Muldrew, *Economy of Obligation*, 109.

50. C. W. Brooks, *Pettyfoggers and Vipers of the Commonwealth: the 'Lower Branch' of the Legal Profession in Early Modern England* (Cambridge: Cambridge University Press, 1986), 68.

51. Muldrew, *Economy of Obligation*, 109.

52. Muldrew, *Economy of Obligation*, 110. On obligations, see also Samuel E. Thorne, 'Tudor social transformation and legal change', *New York University Law Review* 26 (1951), 10–23 at 19; A. W. B. Simpson, 'The Penal Bond with Conditional Defeasance', *Law Quarterly Review* 82 (1966), 392–422; S. F. C. Milsom, *Historical Foundations of the Common Law* (London: Butterworths, 1969), 215–17; Brooks, *Pettyfoggers and Vipers*, 67–70, 93–7; J. H. Baker, *An Introduction to English Legal History*, 4th edn (London: Butterworths, 2002), 323–5.

53. Milsom, *Historical Foundations*, 215.

54. Baker, *Introduction*, 324–5.

55. *Waberley v. Cockerel* (1542), in J. H. Baker and S. F. C. Milsom, *Sources of English Legal History: Private Law to 1950* (London: Butterworths, 1999), 257–8 at 258, cit. in Baker, *Introduction*, 325.

56. Lorna Hutson has scrutinized the importance of this dilemma to theorizations of equity. Hutson, *Usurer's Daughter*, 145–7.

57. Baker, *Introduction*, 323.

58. G. Norburie, 'The Abuses and Remedies of Chancery' in F. Hargrave ed., *A Collection of Tracts Relative to the Laws of England, from Manuscripts* vol. 1 (London: E. Brooke, 1787), 433.

59. *OED* s.v. obligatory 2.

60. See for example SBTRO BRU 15/12 arts. 43, 47, 48.

61. F reads 'steale loues bonds'; 'seale', clearly the correct reading, is supplied from Q.

62. 'Et quando u il tempo d'andare, essendo per mouere, M. Ansaldo disse a Giannetto, Figliuol mio, tu uai, & uedi nell'obligo ch'io rimango, d'una gratiati prego, che se pure tu arriuassi male, che ti piaccia uenire à uedermi, si ch'io possa uedere te innanzi ch'io mouia, e andronne contento. Giannetto gli rispose, M. Ansaldo, io faro tutte quelle cose ch'io creda piacer ui'. *Il Pecorone di ser Giovanni Fiorentino, nel qvale si contengono cinqvanta novella antiche, belle d'inventione et di stile* (Vinegia: Domenico Farri, 1565), D7^v–F4^v at E5^v–E6^r; translation by Bullough, 1: 463–76 at 469.

63. 'Ora auuenne che compiuto il termine, il Giudeo fe pigliare messer' Ansaldo, & uoleuagli leuare una libra di carne d'addosso, onde messer Ansaldo lo pregaua, che gli piacesse d'indugiargli quel la morte qualche dì, accioche se il suo Gianetto uenisse almeno, e' lo potesse uedere. Disse il Giudeo, Io son contento di dare ciò uoi uolete quanto all'ondugio, ma s'egli uenisse cento uolte, io intendo di leuarui una libri di carne d'adosso, come diconno le carte'. Giovanni, *Pecorone*, E8^r; Bullough 1:471.

64. See Jonathan Woolfson, *Padua and the Tudors: English students in Italy, 1485–1603* (Toronto: University of Toronto Press, 1998).

5 THE MATTER OF MESSENGERS IN *KING LEAR*

1. Stanley Wells, 'Introduction', to William Shakespeare, *The History of King Lear*, ed. Wells, text prepared by Gary Taylor (Oxford: Oxford University Press (The Oxford Shakespeare), 2000), 1–93 at 31.

2. See A. C. Bradley, *Shakespearean Tragedy: Lectures on 'Hamlet', 'Othello', 'King Lear', 'Macbeth'*, 2nd edn (London: Macmillan, 1905), 256–7, 448–50, 463–4; Jonathan Goldberg, 'Shakespeare Writing Matter Again: Objects and Their Detachments', *Shakespeare Studies* 28 (2000), 248–51 at 249, reprinted in *Shakespeare's Hand* (Minneapolis: University of Minnesota Press, 2003), 149–51 at 150; Henry Schwarz, ' "He is no unlettered man": *King Lear*, "The Courier's Tragedy", and the historical agency of postage', *Shakespeare Jahrbuch* 127 (1991), 63–76; Frances Teague, 'Letters and

Portents in *Julius Caesar* and *King Lear*', *Shakespeare Yearbook* 3 (1992), 97–104; David M. Bergeron, 'Deadly Letters in *King Lear*', *Philological Quarterly* 72 (1993), 157–76; Lisa Jardine, 'Reading and the technology of textual affect: Erasmus's familiar letters and Shakespeare's *King Lear*', in *Reading Shakespeare Historically* (London: Routledge, 1996), 78–97 and notes at 184–9.

3. 'Est enim (quod scite scriptum est Turpilio comico) epistola absentium amicorum quasi mutuus sermo'. Desiderius Erasmus, *De conscribendis epistolis*; in *Opera omnia Desiderii Erasmi Roterodami, Ordinis primi, tomus secundus*, ed. Jean-Claude Margolin and Pierre Mesnard (Amsterdam: North-Holland Publishing Company, 1971), 225.

4. Miles Coverdale, *Certain most goldy, fruitful, and comfortable letters of such true Saintes and holy Martyrs of God* ... (London: John Day, 1564), A.ii.^{v}.

5. Abraham Fleming, *A Panoplie of Epistles* (London: Ralph Newberie, 1576), A.i.^{r}.

6. Angel Day, *The English secretorie* (London: Richard Jones, 1586), A^r.

7. Day later writes that 'Letters are onely messengers of each mans intendments'. Day, *English secretorie*, [A]3^r.

8. Day, *English Secretorie*, M2^v–M3^r, N^v–N2^r, N2^v–N3^r, N3^v–N4^r.

9. Day, *Englsh Secretorie*, N4^{r-v}.

10. British Library, London, Additional MS 33271 fo. 46^v.

11. BL Additional MS 33271 fo. 46^v.

12. G. Wilson Knight, 'The Lear Universe', in *The Wheel of Fire: Essays in Interpretation of Shakespeare's Sombre Tragedies* (London: Oxford University Press, 1930), 194–226 at 194.

13. Bradley, *Shakespearean Tragedy*, 263.

14. John Danby, *Shakespeare's Doctrine of Nature: A Study of 'King Lear'* (London: Faber and Faber, 1951), 52, 138, 45–6; see also Marshall McLuhan, *The Gutenberg Galaxy: The Making of Typographic Man* (London: Routledge and Kegan Paul, 1962), 11–17; Marvin Rosenberg, *The Masks of King Lear* (Berkeley: University of California Press, 1972), 34; Rosalie L. Colie, 'Reason and Need: *King Lear* and the "Crisis" of the Aristocracy', in *Some Facets of King Lear: Essays in Prismatic Criticism* ed. Rosalie L. Colie and F. T. Flahiff (Toronto and Buffalo: University of Toronto Press, 1974), 185–219; Paul Delany, '*King Lear* and the Decline of Feudalism', *PMLA* 92 (1977), 429–40.

15. Margreta de Grazia, 'The ideology of superfluous things: *King Lear* as period piece', in *Subject and object in Renaissance culture*, ed. Margreta de Grazia, Maureen Quilligan, and Peter Stallybrass (Cambridge: Cambridge University Press, 1996), 17–42 at 20.

16. John Turner, 'The Tragic Romances of Feudalism', in Graham Holderness, Nick Potter and John Turner, *Shakespeare: The Play of History* (Basingstoke: Macmillan, 1988), 83–154 at 101.

17. Richard Halpern, *The Poetics of Primitive Accumulation: English Renaissance Culture and the Genealogy of Capital* (Ithaca: Cornell University Press, 1991), 243. To some extent, Rosalie Colie prefigures Halpern's argument, seeing Edmund as having 'a parallel at a lower rank' in 'the opportunist Oswald, a clothes rack, a mock-man, a braggart-soldier, a go-between'. Colie, '*King Lear* and the 'Crisis' of the Aristocracy', 206. In a very different analysis, Richard Strier agrees that 'In the structure of the play, Kent and Oswald are *systematically* contrasted'. Strier, *Resistant Structures: Particularity, Radicalism, and Renaissance Texts* (Berkeley: University of California Press, 1995), 186.

18. Jonas A. Barish and Marshall Waingrow, 'Service in *King Lear*' *Shakespeare Quarterly* 9 (1958), 347–55 at 349.

19. Strier, *Resistant Structures*, 186. He convincingly rejects Jonathan Dollimore's claim that 'Kent insults Oswald ... almost entirely in terms of the latter's lack of material wealth, his mean estate and consequent dependence upon service'. Jonathan Dollimore, *Radical Tragedy: Religion, Ideology and Power in the Drama of Shakespeare and his Contemporaries*, 3rd edn (Houndmills: Palgrave Macmillan, 2004), 201.

20. D. R. Hainsworth, *Stewards, Lords and People: The estate steward and his world in later Stuart England* (Cambridge: Cambridge University Press, 1992), 112, 7 and *passim*.

21. Sibbald David Scott ed., 'A Booke of Orders and Rules' of Anthony Viscount Montague in 1595', *Sussex Archaeological Collections, relating to the history and antiquities of the county* 7 (1854), 173–212 at 185–6.

22. Scott ed., 'Booke', 186.

23. Hainsworth, *Stewards, Lords and People*, 112 and *passim*.

24. R. W. Dent, *Shakespeare's Proverbial Language: An Index* (Berkeley: University of California Press, 1981), T38, cited in R. A. Foakes, *KL* 1.4.32 n.

25. Walter Darell, *A Short discourse of the life of Seruingmen* (London: Ralph Newberry, 1578), A.iij^r.

26. [Incipit:] *Here in thys boke afore ar contenyt the bokys of haukyng and huntyng* ([St Albans, 1486]) f vj^v.

27. Kent Cartwright, *Shakespearean Tragedy and Its Double: The Rhythms of Audience Response* (University Park, PA: The Pennsylvania State University Press, 1991), 185.

28. Samuel Johnson ed., *The Plays of William Shakespeare*, 8 vols. (London: J. and R. Tonson *et al.*, 1765), 6:121 n.*.

29. Bradley, *Shakespearean Tragedy*, 298. Bradley also cites the Johnson quotation: 'He now refuses the letter, and afterwards, when he is dying, thinks only how it may be safely delivered'. Johnson, *Plays*, 6:121 n.*.

30. Bradley, *Shakespearean Tragedy*, 448; see also Strier, *Resistant Structures*, 195 n. 83.

31. Mark Thornton Burnett, *Masters and Servants in English Renaissance Drama and Culture* (Basingstoke: Macmillan, 1997), 166–7, lists Gunwater, steward to Sir Bounteous Progress in Middleton's *A Mad World, My Masters*; Mallfort in Fletcher's *The Lovers' Progress*; and the usher Bassiolo in Chapman's *The Gentleman Usher*.

32. *The True Chronicle Historie of King Leir, and his three daughters, Gonorill, Ragan, and Cordella* (London: John Wright, 1605). See Martin Mueller, 'From Leir to Lear', *Philological Quarterly* 73 (1994), 195–218.

33. 'him' is supplied from Q.

34. Robert Greene, *The honorable historie of frier Bacon, and frier Bongay* (London: Edward White, 1594). I am grateful to Rebecca Calcagno for pushing me towards this play.

35. Francis Beaumont and John Fletcher, *The Custome of the Countrey*, in *Comedies and Tragedies* (London: Humphrey Robinson and Humphrey Moseley, 1647), C3^r. Once again, I owe this reference to Rebecca Calcagno.

36. See *infra*, Introduction.

37. Bradley, *Shakespearean Tragedy*, 257. In a footnote, Bradley adds, 'It is vain to suggest that Edmund has only just come home, and that the letter is supposed to have been sent to him when he was "out" ' (257 n.1).

38. When Claudius receives a letter from Hamlet, for example, Laertes asks 'Know you the hand?' and the King replies ' 'Tis Hamlet's character' (*Ham* 4.7.49). When the disguised Duke offers a letter, he says, 'Look you, sir, here is the hand . . . of the duke: you know the character, I doubt not' (*MM* 4.2.191–2). But 'character' and 'hand' need not be identical: Olivia has to tell Malvolio that the letter he has received 'this is not my writing, | Though I confess much like the character: | But, out of question, 'tis Maria's hand' (*TN* 5.1.344–6).

39. See Alan Stewart, 'The Early Modern Closet Discovered', *Representations* 50 (1995), 76–100.

40. Colie, 'Reason and Need', 192.

41. Bradley, *Shakespearean Tragedy*, 257–8.

42. In 1770, Charles Jennens raised the possibility in his edition: '— 'Tis from *Cordelia*, [*Opening the letter*] | Who hath most fortunately been inform'd | Of my obscured course—*and shall find time* [*Reading parts of the*

letter]. | *From this enormous state—seeking to give* | *Losses their remedies.*—
All weary and o'erwatched...' While Jennens gives the quoted lines as
two separate extracts, most modern editors give the words 'And shall
finde time | From this enormous State, seeking to giue | Losses their
remedies' as a single quoted line. Against this reading, the lines are
not italicized in F. Charles Jennens ed., *King Lear. A Tragedy... Collated
with the old and modern editions* (London: W. and J. Richardson, 1770),
72.

43. Richard Knowles, 'Cordelia's Return', *Shakespeare Quarterly* 50 (1999), 33–
50 at 35.

44. Foakes changes the speech prefixes to 'Knight', assuming this identification. *KL* 3.1.0.1n.

45. Jodi Mikalachki, *The Legacy of Boadicea: Gender and Nation in Early Modern
England* (London and New York: Routledge, 1998), 91–5 at 91.

46. Stephen Orgel, 'Shakespeare Imagines a Theater', *Poetics Today* 5 (1984),
549–61 at 556–7.

47. Jonathan Goldberg, 'Perspectives: Dover Cliff and the Conditions of Representation', in *Shakespeare and Deconstruction*, ed. David M. Bergeron
and G. Douglas Atkins (New York: Peter Lang, 1988), 245–65; rpt in
Shakespeare's Hand, 132–48 at 134.

48. Goldberg, 'Shakespeare Writing Matter Again', 249, rpt in *Shakespeare's
Hand*, 150.

49. Bradley, *Shakespearean Tragedy*, note U: 'Movements of the dramatis per-
sonæ in act II. of *King Lear*', 448–50 at 449.

50. Nowhere does 'Goneril tell her that she is about to arrive'—'if they come
to sojourn' clearly refers not to Goneril, but to Lear's retinue.

51. Thomas Heywood, *The first and second partes of King Edward the Fourth*
(London: Humfrey Lownes and Iohn Oxenbridge, 1600), C6ᵛ.

52. Orgel suggests that Gloucester is 'apparently not the earl but the town,
which would therefore be the location of Regan and Cornwall'. *King
Lear: A Conflated Text*, ed. Stephen Orgel (New York: Penguin (Pelican
Shakespeare), 1999), 1.5.1n.

53. F has the stage direction '*Reads the Letter*'.

54. Mary I to the City of London, 9 January 1557/8. City of London Records
Office Journal 17, f. 56, as cited in Reginald R. Sharpe, *London and the
Kingdom: A History*, 3 vols. (London: Longmans, Green and Co., 1894)
1:480. See also Burghley to Charles Howard, 2nd lord Howard of Eff-
ingham, August 26, 1588, Folger MS X.d.494, with the message 'post
hast/hast/hast/post hast for lief'. Alan Stewart and Heather Wolfe,

Letterwriting in Renaissance England (Washington DC: Folger Shakespeare Library, 2004), 139–40.

55. Day, *English secretorie*, A^r.

6 LOVERS' LINES: LETTERS TO OPHELIA

1. Simon Palfrey, *Doing Shakespeare* (London: Thomson Learning (Arden Shakespeare), 2005), 250–1.

2. On contested marriage contracts, see R. H. Helmholz, *Marriage Litigation in Medieval England* (Cambridge: Cambridge University Press, 1974), ch. 2; Ralph Houlbrooke, *Church Courts and the People during the English Reformation 1520–1570* (Oxford: Oxford University Press, 1979), ch. 3; Martin Ingram, 'Spousals Litigation in the English Ecclesiastical Courts, *c.* 1350–1640', in *Marriage and Society: Studies in the Social History of Marriage*, ed. R. B. Outhwaite (New York: St Martin's Press, 1982), 35–57; Houlbrooke, 'The Making of Marriage in Mid-Tudor England: Evidence from the Records of Matrimonial Contract Litigation', *Journal of Family History* 10 (1985), 339–52; Ingram, *Church Courts, Sex and Marriage in England 1570–1640* (Cambridge: Cambridge University Press, 1987), ch. 2; Eric Josef Carlson, *Marriage and the English Reformation* (Oxford: Blackwell, 1994), esp. ch. 6; R. B. Outhwaite, *Clandestine Marriage in England, 1500–1850* (London and Rio Grande: Hambledon Press, 1995); Laura Gowing, *Domestic Dangers: Women, Words, and Sex in Early Modern London* (Oxford: Clarendon Press, 1996), ch. 5; Richard Adair, *Courtship, Illegitimacy and Marriage in early modern England* (Manchester: Manchester University Press, 1996); Diana O'Hara, *Courtship and Constraint: Rethinking the making of marriage in Tudor England* (Manchester: Manchester University Press, 2000). On the relevance of clandestine marriage to Tudor literature, see Lorna Hutson, *The Usurer's Daughter: Male Friendship and Fictions of Women in Sixteenth-Century England* (London: Routledge, 1994).

3. Adair, *Courtship, Illegitimacy and Marriage*, 143–4.

4. See William G. Meader, *Courtship in Shakespeare: Its Relation to the Tradition of Courtly Love* (New York: Columbia University Press, 1954), 165–203; Margaret Loftus Ranald, ' "As marriage binds and blood breaks": English Marriage and Shakespeare', *Shakespeare Quarterly* 30 (1979), 68–81; Carol Thomas Neely, *Broken Nuptials in Shakespeare's Plays* (New Haven: Yale University Press, 1985); Ranald, *Shakespeare and his Social Context: Essays in Osmotic Knowledge and Literary Interpretation* (New York: AMS

Press, 1987), 1–49; Ann Jenalie Cook, *Making a Match: Courtship in Shakespeare and his Society* (Princeton: Princeton University Press, 1991); Anne Barton, ' "Wrying but a little": marriage, law and sexuality in the plays of Shakespeare', in *Essays, Mainly Shakespearean* (Cambridge: Cambridge University Press, 1994), 3–30; B. J. Sokol and Mary Sokol, *Shakespeare, Law, and Marriage* (Cambridge: Cambridge University Press, 2003).

5. Barton, "Wrying but a little", 11.

6. On clandestine marriage in Shakespeare see Cook, *Making a Match*, ch. 8; Sokol and Sokol, *Shakespeare, Law, and Marriage*, ch. 6.

7. See also Karl Wentersdorf, 'The marriage contracts in *Measure for Measure*: a reconsideration', *Shakespeare Survey* 32 (1979), 129–44.

8. Neely, *Broken Nuptials*: see her brief treatment of Ophelia (103).

9. Cook, *Making a Match*, 203 n. 77.

10. 'It is simple to explain . . . that the return of Hamlet's gifts by Ophelia is important because the act denotes the breaking of a betrothal': Meader, *Courtship in Shakespeare*, 207; see also Lisa Jardine, *Still Harping on Daughters: Women and Drama in the Age of Shakespeare* (Brighton: Harvester, 1983), 72–3.

11. Adair, *Courtship, Illegitimacy and Marriage*, 143–4.

12. Holbrooke, 'Making of Marriage', 344.

13. Norfolk and Norwich Record Office, Act Books of the Consistory Court, 4A:48, quoted in Houlbrooke, 'Making of Marriage', 343.

14. Gowing, *Domestic Dangers*, 160.

15. John Marston, *What you Will* (London: Thomas Thorpe, 1607), A4^{r-v}.

16. A. C. Bradley, *Shakespearean Tragedy: Lectures on 'Hamlet', 'Othello', 'King Lear', 'Macbeth'*, 2nd edn. (London: Macmillan, 1905), 150 n. 1: 'This letter, of course, was written before the time when the action of the drama begins, for we know that Ophelia, after her father's commands in I.iii., received no more letters (II.i.109)'.

17. H[enry] C[onsett], *The Practice of the Spiritual or Ecclesiastical Courts* (London: Will. Hensman, 1685), K2^r.

18. O'Hara, *Courtship and Constraint*, 70.

19. O'Hara, *Courtship and Constraint*, 70, citing Henry Swinburne, *A Treatise of Spousals, or Matrimonial Contracts* (London: Robert Clavell, 1686).

20. Nicholas Udall, *Ralph Roister Doister* (London: Henry Denham, 1566/7?).

21. Edmund Tilney, *A Brief and Pleasant Discourse of Duties in Mariage* (London: Henry Denham, 1568), E.ij^v.

22. Peter Stallybrass, 'Patriarchal Territories: The Body Enclosed', in *Rewriting the Renaissance: The Discourses of Sexual Difference in Early Modern*

Europe, ed. Margaret W. Ferguson, Maureen Quilligan and Nancy J. Vickers (Chicago: University of Chicago Press, 1986), 123–42 at 127, 128 and *passim*; see also Georgianna Ziegler, 'My lady's chamber: female space, female chastity in Shakespeare', *Textual Practice* 4 (1990), 73–100.

23. Svetlana Alpers suggested the importance of the letter as an object of visual attention in these paintings in her *The Art of Describing: Dutch Art in the Seventeenth Century* (Chicago: University of Chicago Press, 1983), 192–207. Many of these paintings were brought together in the 2003 exhibition *Love Letters: Dutch Genre Paintings in the Age of Vermeer*: see Peter C. Sutton, Lisa Vergara, Ann Jensen Adams, with Jennifer Kilian and Marjorie E. Wieseman, *Love Letters: Dutch Genre Paintings in the Age of Vermeer* (London: Frances Lincoln / Bruce Museum of Arts and Science / National Gallery of Ireland, 2003).

24. See, for example, Pieter de Hooch, *A Woman Reading a Letter by a Window* (1664), *Love Letters*, cat. 34, pp. 172–3; de Hooch, *A Woman Reading a Letter with a Messenger by a Window* (n.d.), *Love Letters*, cat. 35, pp. 174–5.

25. For example, Gerard ter Borch, *Officer reading a letter with a trumpeter* (c. 1657–8), *Love Letters*, cat. 6, pp. 94–5; idem, *An Officer writing a Letter*, n.d., *Love Letters*, cat. 7, pp. 96–8; idem, *An Officer writing a Letter with a Trumpeter* (1658–9), *Love Letters*, cat. 8, pp. 99–100, 102. The *Love Letters* curators identify the waiting men as 'trumpeters', but the post, associated with the horn, seems far more likely.

26. Gabriel Metsu's *A Young Woman Receiving a Letter* (c. 1658); *Love Letters*, cat. 17, p. 127.

27. Metsu, *Woman Reading a Letter*; *Love Letters*, cat. 19, pp. 132–3.

28. Johannes Vermeer, *The Love Letter* (c. 1667–70); *Love Letters*, cat. 37, pp. 185–6.

29. Vermeer, *Lady Writing a Letter with her Maidservant*; *Love Letters*, cat. 39, pp. 186–9.

30. Jan Steen, *Bathsheba with King David's Letter* (1659–60); *Love Letters*, cat. 31, pp. 162–3.

31. James Knowles, unpublished paper.

32. Lena Cowen Orlin, 'Three Ways to be Invisible in the Renaissance: Sex, Reputation, and Stitchery' in *Renaissance Culture and the Everyday*, ed. Patricia Fumerton and Simon Hunt (Philadelphia: University of Pennsylvania Press, 1999), 183–203, at 199, 185–7.

33. Richard Brathwait, *The English Gentlewoman, drawne out to the full Body* (London: B. Alsop and T. Fawcett, 1631), G4^v, H^r, also quoted in Ziegler, 'My lady's chamber', 86.

34. As Lena Cowen Orlin has rightly warned, documents of the period 'give us at least nine permutations of the closet, all simultaneously possible', namely a prayer closet, a study, a counting-house, a store-house, a private pantry, a jewel house, a pharmaceutical closet, a parlour, and a bed-chamber. Significantly, however, Orlin's evidence for this last definition comes directly from the variant texts of *Hamlet*, with Ophelia sewing either in her chamber or closet: this slippage, argues Orlin, would make it appear 'as if these terms, too, were loosely interchangeable'. I would argue instead that the revision marks a distinct change. Lena Cowen Orlin, 'Gertrude's Closet', *Shakespeare Jahrbuch* 134 (1998), 44–65 at 53, 63–4.

35. See Roger Chartier and Peter Stallybrass, 'Reading and Authorship: The Circulation of Shakespeare 1590–1619' in *A Concise Companion to Shakespeare and the Text*, ed. Andrew Murphy (Oxford: Blackwell, 2007), 35–56, esp. 52–3.

36. In both Q2 and F, the typography is confused. In Q2, the entire passage is given in italic (implying it is all quoted from the letter) including Polonius's commentary; in F, a heading ('*The Letter*') and the phrase '*To the Celestiall . . . Ophelia*' are given in italic, but the closing phrase of the superscription 'these, in her . . . these' is given as if part of Polonius's commentary on the letter. The final '&c.', a common touch in superscriptions, is only in Q2.

37. *Hamlet*, ed. Harold Jenkins (London: Methuen (Arden Shakespeare, 2nd ser.), 1982), 2.2.117 n.

38. Gowing, *Domestic Dangers*, 161.

39. Gowing, *Domestic Dangers*, 161.

40. O'Hara, *Courtship and Constraint*, 65; Houlbrooke, 'Making of Marriage', 344.

41. Canterbury Cathedral Archives and Library MS X/10/12 f. 287^v, *Longley v. Marchant* (1566), as quoted in O'Hara, *Courtship and Constraint*, 66. O'Hara comments, 'Although, at one level, this seeming lack of curiosity would appear unconvincing, it may be assumed that in her eyes, the very act of revelation and making public would be considered indiscreet.'

42. Ann Jenalie Cook sees Polonius as more protective of Ophelia: 'an experienced courtier portrays his daughter as dutiful, himself as prudent, diligent, virtuous, above all faithful to the crown'. *Making a Match*, 256.

43. John Jones, *Shakespeare at Work* (Oxford: Clarendon Press, 1995), 113.

44. David Bevington argues along similar lines, but does not note the importance of witnessing: 'The "nunnery" scene in *Hamlet* is a savage parody

of a wedding ritual: the bride's father is present only as a spy, Ophelia gives back Hamlet's gifts to her rather than receiving a ring, and Hamlet's dowry to her is a curse of sterility.' Bevington, *Action is Eloquence: Shakespeare's language of gesture* (Cambridge MA: Harvard University Press, 1984), p. 145.

45. Although the line sequence is different in Q1, it follows Q2 in stressing 'you know right well what you did'.

46. Jardine, *Still Harping on Daughters*, 72–3.

47. Maurice Charney, *Shakespeare on Love and Lust* (New York: Columbia University Press, 2000), 78.

48. 'Tragœdia der Bestrafte Brudermord oder: Prinz Hamlet aus Dænnemark (Fratricide Punished or Hamlet Prince of Denmark)', trans. in *A New Variorum Edition of Shakespeare*, ed. Horace Howard Furness, vol. 4, *Hamlet vol. II, appendix*, 4th edn (London and Philadelphia: J. B. Lippincott, 1871), 121–42.

7 REWRITING HAMLET

1. References in this chapter are to Q1: *The tragicall historie of Hamlet Prince of Denmarke* (London: N[icholas] L[ing] and Iohn Trundell, 1603); Q2: *The tragicall historie of Hamlet, Prince of Denmarke* (London: N[icholas] L[ing], 1604); F: *Mr. William Shakespeares comedies, histories, & tragedies Published according to the true originall copies* (London: Isaac Iaggard, and Ed. Blount, 1623).

2. The notable exception is Jonathan Goldberg: see his 'Hamlet's Hand', *Shakespeare Quarterly* 39 (1988), 307–26; rpt in *Shakespeare's Hand* (Minneapolis: University of Minnesota Press, 2003), 105–31 and 324–7. See also P. K. Ayers, 'Reading, writing, and *Hamlet*,' *Shakespeare Quarterly* 44 (1993), 423–39. Despite its title, Margaret W. Ferguson's '*Hamlet*: Letters and Spirits' does not deal with the correspondence in the play: in *Shakespeare and the Question of Theory*, ed. Patricia Parker and Geoffrey Hartman (New York and London: Methuen, 1985), 292–309.

3. Homer, *The Iliad*, trans. A. T. Murray, rev. William F. Wyatt, 1999), 2 vols. (Cambridge MA: Harvard University Press (Loeb Classical Library, 1999), 1:286–7.

4. *The Iliads of Homer Prince of Poets. Neuer before in any language truely translated*, trans. George Chapman (London: Nathaniell Butter, (1611)), I2^r.

5. *Ten Bookes of Homers Iliades, translated out of French*, trans. Arthur Hall (London: Ralph Newberie, 1581), P.iij.^{r}.

6. *Iliads of Homer*, trans. Chapman, I^v–I2^r, marginal note on I2^r.

7. 'Itaque quisquis imprudens aut nunciat, aut facit quippiam, quo se prodit, in eum recte dicetur: Βελλεροφοντυσ τᾳ γραμματα aut quamcunque sub officij prætextu læditur.' Erasmus, *Adagia qvaecvmqve ad hanc diem exiervnt* (Venice: Dominicus de Farris, 1591), Gg2ᵛ–3ʳ; trans. in *Collected Works of Erasmus*, vol. 33, *Adages II i 1 to II vi 100*, trans./ed. R. A. B. Mynors (Toronto: University of Toronto Press, 1991), 330–1 (II.vi.82).

8. Homer, *Iliad*, 1:286–9 (vi.171–95).

9. Samuel Taylor Coleridge, *S.T. Coleridge's Treatise on Method*, ed. Alice D. Snyder (London: Constable, 1934), 27–30; see the recent discussion in Margreta de Grazia, *'Hamlet' without Hamlet* (Cambridge: Cambridge University Press, 2007), 15–16.

10. 'sed huic præcepto non paret uulgus nostæ nobilitatis, quæ pulchrum & decorum sibi esse ducit nescire literas formare: dicas scarificationem esse gallinarum & nisi præmonitus sis cuius sit manus, nunquam diuinaris.' Juan Luis Vives, *Linguae latinae exercitatio* (Basel: Robert Winter, 1541), d 5ʳ⁻ᵛ, trans. Foster Watson as *Tudor School-Boy Life: The Dialogues of Juan Luis Vives* (London: J. M. Dent, 1907), 67.

11. Michel de Montaigne, *The Essayes Or Morall, Politike and Millitarie Discourses*, trans. John Florio (London: Edward Blount, 1603), M3ʳ.

12. Goldberg, 'Hamlet's Hand', 123.

13. See Edward Maunde Thompson, 'Handwriting', in *Shakespeare's England: An Account of his Life & Manners of his Age*, ed. Sidney Lee, 2 vols. (Oxford: Clarendon Press, 1916), 1:284–310 at 287.

14. My reading. *Ham* gives 'as, sir', but F reads 'Assis', which I take to be supposed plural of 'as', with a pun on 'asses'.

15. Coleridge also interprets this question as crucial, alerting us to the fact that Hamlet's discourse has wandered into 'the wayward or fantastical'. In de Grazia's gloss, 'Hamlet's omission of an important detail about the forged commission suggests too casual a response to the outside world. He must be prompted to provide it by a direct question from Horatio'. Coleridge, *Treatise*, 29; de Grazia, *'Hamlet' without Hamlet*, 16.

16. For a survey of critical opinion, see Laurie E. Maguire, *Shakespearean Suspect Texts: The Bad Quartos and their Contexts* (Cambridge: Cambridge University Press, 1996), 256.

17. The scene also allows us to rethink what is going on in the final act of *Hamlet* as given to us in Q2 and F. Although Horatio does not meet Gertrude, there is a letter in these versions that remains unexplained. In 4.7, a messenger enters *'with letters'* and gives them 'These to your majesty, this to the Queen' (4.7.37–8) (in F, he specifies that these are

'Letters my Lord from *Hamlet*'). Dismissing the messenger, the King opens his letter and reads it out to Laertes. But what becomes of the letter to the Queen? Gertrude appears ninety-five lines later with tragic news of Ophelia's drowning, and the letter is not mentioned again. Does Hamlet use this letter to communicate to his mother what he has discovered about Claudius, as Horatio relays the news in Q1? Does Claudius take the letter, or does the messenger's 'this to the Queen' imply that he keeps hold of it because it must be delivered personally? Is the letter taken offstage by the messenger to be delivered to Gertrude? Does he succeed in doing this?

18. Garrett Mattingly, *Renaissance Diplomacy* (1955; rpt. Baltimore MD: Penguin, 1964), 32. Bernard du Rosier's manuscript treatise *Ambaxiator brevilogus prosaico moralique dogmate pro felice et prospero ducato circa ambaxiatus insistencium excerptus* (1436) is printed in Vladimir E. Grabar, *De Legatis et Legationibus Tractatus Varii* (Dorpati Livonorum: e typographeo Mattienseniano, 1905), 1–28.

19. Jean Hotman, *The Ambassador* (London: James Shawe, 1603), F1^{r-v}.

20. Robert Parry, *Moderatus, the most delectable & famous historie of the blacke knight* (London: Richard Jones, 1595), K^{r-v}. G. Blakemore-Evans argues that this is similar to the scene in *Hamlet*, and suggests that Parry 'was recalling a moment he had witnessed in the *Ur-Hamlet*'. Blakemore-Evans, 'An Echo of the Ur-*Hamlet*?', *Notes and Queries* 246 (September 2001), 266.

21. In Thomas Middleton's *Your Five Gallants*, Bungler displays 'my Grandfathers seale ring', containing 'an antient armes': 'The great codpeice with nothing int', encircled by the motto '*parturiunt montes*, which he helpfully mistranslates as 'You promise to mount vs'. Middleton, *Your fiue gallants* (London: Richard Bonlan, (1608)), D3^{v}.

22. Thomas Hanmer, *Some remarks on the tragedy of Hamlet, Prince of Denmark* (London: W. Wilkins, 1736), 46.

23. As Ayers notes, 'Hamlet here becomes another type of serpent in the scribal garden—the forger'. Ayers, 'Reading, Writing, and *Hamlet*', 433.

24. For 25 E. 3, Statute of Purveyors, cap. 2 see *The whole volume of statutes at large* (London: Christopher Barker, 1587), H2^{r}, p. 115; Edward Coke, *The Third Part of the Institutes Of the Laws of England* (London: W. Lee and D. Pakeman, 1644), B3^{r}, D2^{r-v}. For the later statute, see 1 Mary (1st Parliament, 2nd session) *c.* 6 'An act against counterfeiting of strange coins being currant within this realme, or of the queenes highnesse signe manuall, signet, or priuie seale' (*Whole volume of statutes*, N7^{v}; p. 206).

25. The point is made three times in [Francis Bacon], A *declaration of the practises & treasons attempted and committed by Robert late Earle of Essex and his complices* (London: Robert Barker, 1601): H^v, O4^{r-v}, P^v–P2^r.

26. For Somerset's trial, see T. B. Howell, ed., *Cobbett's Complete Collection of State Trials and Proceedings for High Treason and Other Crimes and Misdemeanors*, vol. 2, *1603–1627* (London, 1809), 911–1022 at 990. This incident is discussed at further length in Alan Stewart, 'The Body Archival: Re-reading the Trial of the Earl of Somerset', in *The Body in Late Medieval and Early Modern Culture* ed. Darryll Grantley and Nina Taunton (Aldershot: Ashgate, 2000), 65–82, esp. 78–9.

27. Juliet Fleming, 'Whitewash', in *Graffiti and the Writing Arts of Early Modern English* (London: Reaktion, 2001), 73–8, at 75–6.

28. Vives, *Tudor School-boy Life*, 77.

29. Jehan Palsgraue, *Lesclarissement de la langue Francoyse* (n.p.: n.pub, 1530), B.ij.^{v}, SS vi^v.

30. John Weddington, *A Briefe Instruction, and manner, howe to kepe, merchantes bokes, of accomptes* (Antwerp: Peter van Keerberghen, 1567), quoted in B. S. Yamey, H. C. Edey and Hugh W. Thomson, *Accounting in England and Scotland: 1543–1800: Double Entry in Exposition and Practice* (London: Sweet and Maxwell, 1963), 28.

31. Gerard Malynes, *Consuetudo, vel lex mercatoria, or The ancient law-merchant* (London: Adam Islip, 1622), Ii 2^r.

32. See the letter from William Boswell to the Privy Council, n.d. (1630?). National Archives, Kew, State Papers 63/250, art. 79. On Boswell, see Alan Stewart, 'Boswell, Sir William (d. 1650)', *ODNB*.

33. The first edition, which survives in a single copy in the National Library of Scotland, is entitled *Discovrs memorables de plvsieurs histories tragiqves* (Paris: Jean Hulpeau, 1570); I quote from the 1576 edition, *Le cinqviesme livre des histories tragiques* (Lyon: Benoist Rigaud, 1576). On the complex publication history, see Michel Simonin, *Vivre de sa plume au XVIe siècle ou la carrière de François de Belleforest* (Geneva: Droz, 1992), 233–307, 311. I am grateful to András Kiséry for advice on this volume. The relevant passages from Belleforest and a partial English translation, *The Hystorie of Hamblet* (London: Thomas Pauier, 1608), are printed in Robert Gericke, *Shakespeare's Hamlet-Quellen: Saxo Grammaticus (Lateinisch und Deutsch) Belleforest und The Hystorie of Hamlet* (Leipzig: Johann Ambrosius Barth, 1881) and Israel Gollancz, *The Sources of Hamlet: With essay on the legend* (London: Humphrey Milford/Oxford University Press, 1926).

34. For a modern edition see Saxo Grammaticus, *The History of the Danes*, Books I–IX, ed. Hilda Ellis Davidson, trans. Peter Fisher, 2 vols. (Cambridge and Towota NJ: DS Brewer/Rowman and Littlefield, 1979–80). For discussions of Shakespeare's use of Saxo, see Hans Sperber, 'The Conundrums in Saxo's Hamlet Episode', *PMLA* 64 (1949), 864–70; William F. Hansen, *Saxo Grammaticus and the Life of Hamlet: A Translation, History and Commentary* (Lincoln: University of Nebraska Press, 1983).

35. Saxo Grammaticus, *Danorum Regum . . . Historiæ,* ed. Christiern Pedersen (Paris: Jodocus Badius Ascensius, 1514), episode at d v^r.

36. Saxo Grammaticus, *Danica historia libris XVI* (Frankfurt: Andreas Wechel, 1576), episode at D.v.^{r} (p. 47).

37. *Hystorie of Hamblet*, rpt in Gericke, *Shakespeare's Hamlet-Quellen*, LXV. Belleforest has: 'Auquel auec luy furent envuoyez deux des fideles ministres de Fengon, portans des letters, grauees dans du boys, qui portoyent la mort de Amleth, ainsi qu'il la commandoit à l'Anglois: mais le rusé Prince Danois, tandis que ses compaignons dormoyent ayant visité le pacquet, & cogneu la grande trahison de son oncle, & la meschanceté des courtisans qui le conduisoient à la boucherie, rasa les lettres mentionnans sa mort, & au lieu y graua & cisa vn commandement à l'Anglois de faire pendre & estrangler ses compaignons: & non content de tourner sur eux la mort ordonnee pour sa teste, il y adiousta que Fengon commandoit au Roy Insulaire de donner au nepueu du Roy sa fille en mariage. Arriuez qu'ils sont en la grand Bretaigne, les messagers se presentent au Roy, et luy donnent les lettres de leur seigneur, lequel voiant le contenu d'icelles, dissimula le tout attendant son opportunité, de mettre en effect la volonté de Fengon . . .' Belleforest, *Le conqviesme livre* (1576), P7^v–P8^r (pp. 238–9).

38. *Saxonis Grammatici historiae Danicæ libri XVI,* ed. Stephanvs Iohannis Stephanivs (Copenhagen: Joachim Moltken, 1644), I2^r (p. 99).

39. A. C. Bradley, 'Note D. "My Tables—Meet it is I Set it Down"', in *Shakespearean Tragedy*, 2nd edn (London: Macmillan, 1905), 409–12.

40. Bradley, 'Note D.', 410. Garrett Sullivan notes: 'Interestingly, the forgetting that is to precede Hamlet's inscription would destroy the contents of his memory. Hamlet understands the contents of his memoria and the Ghost's demand that Hamlet remember him as mutually exclusive . . . Hamlet's keeping his word is concomitant with his wiping away all (memory) traces of his past.' Sullivan, *Memory and Forgetting in English Renaissance Drama: Shakespeare, Marlowe, Webster* (Cambridge: Cambridge University Press, 2005), 13.

41. For a similar reading, see Ann Pasternak Slater, *Shakespeare the Director* (Brighton: Harvester Press, 1982), 23: 'Again, it is ironic that Hamlet's first resolve, after meeting his father's ghost, is metaphorically to wipe away all trivial observations from the tables of his memory, and to remember only the ghost's injunction to revenge. Yet his first impulse, following hot on this resolve, is to note down just such an observation...But his word...has already been broken...Theoretically, Hamlet is ready to act; in actuality, he is a theoretician, as the rest of the play bears out.'

42. See especially Frances A. Yates, *The Art of Memory* (London: Routledge and Kegan Paul, 1966); Mary Carruthers, *The Book of Memory: A Study of Memory in Medieval Culture* (Cambridge: Cambridge University Press, 1990); Lina Bolzoni, *The Gallery of Memory: Literary and Iconographic Models in the Age of the Printing Press*, trans. Jeremy Parzen (Toronto: University of Toronto Press, 2001); Douwe Draaisma, *Metaphors of Memory: A History of Ideas about the Mind*, trans. Paul Vincent (Cambridge: Cambridge University Press, 2000).

43. See Carruthers, *Book of Memory*, 21–2; Draaisma, *Metaphors of Memory*, 3 and *passim*.

44. Plato, *Theaetetus*, 191D–E, in Plato, vol. VII, *Theaetetus; Sophist*, trans. Harold North Fowler (Cambridge, MA: Harvard University Press (Loeb Classical Library), 1977), 184–7.

45. Carruthers, *Book of Memory*, 21–2.

46. M. T. Clanchy, *From Memory to Written Record: England 1066–1307*, 2nd edn (Oxford: Blackwell, 1993), 118.

47. Juan Luis Vives, *De conscribendis epistolis* [and others] (Cologne: Johannes Gymnicus, 1537), D7^r; *De conscribendis epistolis: Critical Edition with Introduction, Translation and Annotation*, trans./ed. Charles Fantazzi (Leiden: E. J. Brill, 1989), 107.

48. Richard Taverner, *On Saynt Andrewes day the Gospels with brief sermons vpon them for al the holy dayes in th[e] yere* (London): Rycharde Bankes, 1542), cc.iiij.^{r}.

49. For the Hebrew tradition of memory residing in the heart see Proverbs 3: 1–3 ('let thine heart keep my commandments...bind them about thy neck; write them upon the table of thine heart') and Jeremiah 17:1 ('The sin of Judah is written with a pen of iron, and with the point of a diamond: it is graven upon the table of their heart...'). Draaisma, *Metaphors of Memory*, 46 n. 11.

50. Bolzoni cites the Franciscan friar Filippo Gesualdo whose *Plutosofia*, (Padua: Paolo Megietti, 1592), contains 'a medicine for memory that takes

literally the idea that the *phantasmata* and *simulacra* of memory have an actual physical consistency and are located in a specific area of the brain' (f. 9ᵛ). Bolzoni, *Gallery of Memory*, 137.

51. Bacon rejected the analogy: admitting to his 'son', the addressee of *The Masculine Birth of Time*, that he would not be able to purge his mind of its idols, he notes: 'In tabulis nisi priora deleveris, non alia inscripseris. In mento contra: nisi alia inscripseris, non priora deleveris' ('On waxen tablets you cannot write anything new until you rub out the old. With the mind it is not so; there you cannot rub out the old till you have written in the new'). Trans. Benjamin Farrington as 'The Masculine Birth of Time', in *The Philosophy of Francis Bacon: An Essay on its Development from 1603 to 1609 with New Translations of Fundamental Texts* (Chicago: University of Chicago Press/Phoenix Books, 1964), 59–72 at 72. I am grateful to Jerry Passannante for directing me to this passage.

52. H. R. Woudhuysen, 'Writing-Tables and Table Books', *eBLJ* 2004, article 3; Peter Stallybrass, Roger Chartier, Franklin Mowery Jr. and Heather Wolfe, 'Hamlet's tables and the technologies of writing in Renaissance England', *Shakespeare Quarterly* 55 (2004), 379–419; Roger Chartier, 'Writing and Memory: Cardenio's *Librillo*', in *Inscription and Erasure: Literature and Written Culture from the Eleventh to the Eighteenth Century,* trans. Arthur Goldhammer (Philadelphia: University of Pennsylvania Press, 2007), 13–27.

53. Stallybrass *et al.*, 'Hamlet's Tables', 381.

54. Joseph Hall depicts a 'Hypocrite' using tables: 'At Church hee will euer sit where hee may bee seene best, and in the midst of the Sermon pulles out his Tables in haste, as if he feared to leese that note; when hee writes either his forgotten errand, or nothing.' Joseph Hall, *Characters of vertues and vices in two bookes* (London: Eleazar Edgar and Samuel Macham, 1608), F5ʳ.

55. Francis Goyet, 'Hamlet, étudiant du XVIᵉ siècle', *Poétique* 113 (1998), 3–15, at 3, 15 n.3, quoting Philip Melanchthon, *Rhetorica* (Paris: Robert Estienne, 1527), 4ʳ: 'in hic locos communes, uitiorum, uirtutum, fortunae, mortis, diuitiarum, literarum, & similes exerceat ... Ad hoc plurimum conducet, formas locorum communium diligenter notates in manibus habere, ut si quam sententiam, si quod adagium, si quod apophthegma dignum, quod in tabulas referatur, exceperis, suo recondas loco.'

56. Goyet, 'Hamlet, étudiant du XVIᵉ siècle', 5.

57. See Alan C. Dessen and Leslie Thomson, *A Dictionary of Stage Directions in English Drama 1580–1642* (Cambridge: Cambridge University Press, 1999),

s.v. 'book' (34–5) and 'tables' (225). The essays by Woudhuysen and Stally-brass *et al.* survey many examples.

58. B[en] J[onson], *The Comicall Satyre of Every Man Ovt of His Hvmor* (London: William Holme, 1600), 12ʳ, when Fung sees a suit he desires and starts to dictate instructions to the tailor, saying 'Haue you a pair of Tables? . . . For Gods sake do, note all'.

59. Anon., *The Cuck-Queanes and Cuckolds Errants* in *The Cuck-Queanes and Cuckolds Errants or The Bearing Down the Inne. A Comœdye. The Faery Pas-torall or Forrest of Elues. By W—— P—— Esq. From a manuscript, in the library, of Joseph Haslewood, Esq.*, ed. William Nicol (London: Shakspeare Press, 1824), 12. The goldsmith Wright tells the Latin-spouting civil lawyer Pearle, 'Nay, Mr. Pearle, if your worship be so Tropicall [figurative] with mee, I must needes haue a paire of Tables for you' (SD: 'He drewe furth his writing Tables').

60. If Gabriel Harvey held forth in Paul's, 'O we should haue the Proctors and Registers as busie with their Table-books as might bee, to gather phrases.' Thomas Nashe, *Haue with you to Saffron-walden* (London: John Danter, 1596), G4ᵛ–Hʳ.

61. John Marston, *Antonios Reuenge. The second part* (London: Thomas Fisher, 1602), B2ʳ.

62. Robert Greene, *The Scottish Historie of Iames the Fourth, slaine at Flodden* (London: Thomas Creede, 1598), C2ᵛ.

63. Anonymous, *Everie Woman in her Humor* (London: Thomas Archer, 1609), B1ʳ.

64. Jonson, *Every Man Ovt of His Hvmor*, H2ʳ.

65. Thomas Dekker, *Blvrt Master-Constable. Or The Spaniards Night-walke* (London: Henry Rockyett, 1602). The scene is at E3ʳ–Fᵛ, quoted at E3ʳ, E3ᵛ. I am grateful to Rebecca Calcagno for this reference.

66. One nineteenth-century critic denied that Hamlet actually writes the phrase: 'This jotting down by Hamlet, upon a real substantial, of one of those "generalised truths" which he had just excluded from the table of his memory, would be such a *literalising of the metaphor,* that it is a great relief to me to feel convinced that Shakespeare never intended it.' A. E. B[rae], 'Readings in Shakespeare no. III', *Notes and Queries* vol. 5, no. 124 (13 March 1852), 241–2 at 241.

67. Ferguson, '*Hamlet*: letters and spirits', 292. Ferguson sees this phenom-enon as operative 'in dialogues with others, though not in his soliloquies', but I would argue in this instance we can forward her claim in under-standing this soliloquy at least.

68. Woudhuysen, 'Writing-Tables', e7.

69. Chartier, *Inscription and Erasure*, 23.

70. Francis Bacon, 'New Atlantis' in *Sylua syluarum: or A naturall historie In ten centuries* (London: William Lee, 1627), a3ᵛ: the travellers encounter a man who 'drew forth a little Scroule of Parchment, (somewhat yellower then our Parchment, and shining like the Leaues of Writing Tables, but otherwise soft and flexible).'

71. John Florio, *Qveen Anna's New World of Words, or Dictionarie of the Italian and English Tongues* (London: Edw. Blount and William Baret, 1611), Hᵛ. Florio glosses the Italian *cartella* as 'a kind of sleeked pasteboord to write vpon and may bee blotted out againe. Also leaues of writing tables.'

72. See the instructions in Francis Adams, *Writing Tables with a Kalender for xxiiii. yeeres* (London: Francis Adams, 1594), cit. Stallybrass *et al.*, 'Hamlet's tables,' p. 382. Although, as Woudhuysen argues, 'writing-tables which combined print and a set of reusable writing surfaces were relatively rare', they provide valuable information about how all tables might have been used. Woudhuysen, 'Writing Tables', e8.

73. *OED* s.v. tabula 1. b. *tabula rasa* (L. = scraped tablet), a tablet from which the writing has been erased, and which is therefore ready to be written upon again; a blank tablet: usually *fig.*

74. *OED* s.v. slate n.¹ 2.b. *fig.* A record of any kind concerning or against a person; esp. in phr. *a clean slate*. Also in phrs. *to wipe (off) the slate*, *to wipe the slate clean*: to obliterate or cancel a record, usu. of a debt, misdemeanour, etc.; hence *loosely*, to make a fresh start. The phrase has no recorded uses before 1868, but the use of 'slate' to mean 'A tablet of slate, usually framed in wood, used for writing on' (slate n.¹ 2. a.) dates back to Chaucer.

75. Plato, *Theaetetus*, 191E (p. 187).

76. 'To Sir Nicholas Smyth', *The Poems of John Donne*, ed. Herbert J. C. Grierson, 2 vols. (Oxford: Oxford University Press, 1912), 1:401–7 at 404, cit. Woudhuysen, 'Writing-Tables', e9.

77. An alternative reading has been offered by Katherine Rowe, who points out that 'Ancient wax tablets were reusable but somewhat challenging to erase, and they never entirely lost impressions... In the context of Hamlet's pun on matter, it is tempting to associate this form of storage with the weaknesses of a humoral memory: not easily wiped of impressions in a way that permits reordered priorities of recall. In response, Hamlet reaches for the latest technology to redress the failures of an earlier one. He looks to a portable repository, invitingly separable from the mater of an embodied mind, and more easily wiped. If [*pace* Stallybrass et al.]...

we resist the temptation to collapse "table", "book", "volume", and writing into a single kind of technology, Hamlet seems to be groping through a variety of storage forms here, seeking the one that best serves the functions of sorting and reordering the matter of the past.' As Rowe points out, however, 'Judging by the force of the spontaneous recollections that follow...the attempt is at best a partial success'. Rowe, ' "Remember me": technologies of memory in Michael Almereyda's *Hamlet*', in *Shakespeare, The Movie, II: Popularizing the Plays on Film, TV, Video, and DVD*, ed. Richard Burt and Lynda E. Boose (New York and London: Routledge, 2003), 37–55 at 43. For Cicero on the failure of wax tablets to lose their impression, see Shane Butler's important study, *The Hand of Cicero* (London and New York: Routledge, 2002), 66–7.

78. Sigmund Freud, 'Notiz über den "Wunderblock" ' (1925), trans. James Strachey as 'A Note upon the "Mystic Writing-Pad" ' (1940), rpt. in *Collected Papers*, vol. V, *Miscellaneous Papers, 1888–1938* (New York: Basic, 1959), 175–80. For an interesting application relevant to this discussion see Juliet Fleming, 'Whitewash', 73–8. Fleming works through Jacques Derrida's discussion in *Writing and Difference*, trans. Alan Bass (Chicago: University of Chicago Press, 1978), 222.

79. Iachimo's model of memory as riveted and screwed is mechanical, notably unlike the Polonius family model discussed below.

80. Thomas Playfere, *Ten sermons* ((Cambridge): Cantrell Legge, 1610), M7$^\text{v}$.

81. J[ohn] G[ough], *The Academy of Complements* (London, 1639), 13$^\text{r–v}$. cit. Stallybrass *et al.*, 'Hamlet's Tables', 411–12.

82. 'And then, sir, does 'a this, 'a does—| What was I about to say? By the mass, I was about to say something! Where did I leave?' (*Ham* 2.1.48–50).

83. Thomas Rymer, *A Short View of Tragedy; It's [sic] Original, Excellency, and Corruption* (London: Richard Baldwin, 1693), L$^\text{r–v}$ (145–6).

84. Pasternak Slater, *Shakespeare the Director*, 179–80.

85. David E. Johnson sees the two letters ultimately as 'only one letter, but with a difference...self-identical but nonself-same.' Johnson, 'Addressing the Letter', in *Reading and Writing in Shakespeare*, ed. David M. Bergeron (Newark: University of Delaware Press and London: Associated University Presses, 1996), 194–219, 208–11 at 209–10.

POSTSCRIPT

1. Letter from R. B. W[heler], *The Gentleman's Magazine*, 80 (January–June 1810), 221–2. Wheler's emphases.

2. Shakespeare Birthplace Trust Records Office SBT 1868–3/274.

3. Letter from R. B.W[heler], *The Gentleman's Magazine* 80 (July–December 1810), 322–3.

4. Wheler, *Guide to Stratford-upon-Avon* (Stratford-upon-Avon: J. Ward, 1814), 154–5.

5. Wheler continued to advertise his discovery in his *Guide to Stratford-upon-Avon*, 153–60.

6. Robert Haydon to John Keats, quoted in *Searching for Shakespeare*, ed. Tarnya Cooper (London: National Portrait Gallery, 2006), 143.

7. Malone to Wheler, 13 June 1810, quoted in Wheler, *Guide to Stratford-upon-Avon*, 155.

8. For the will, see NA Prerogative Court of Canterbury, Prob 1/4, most recently reproduced in *Searching for Shakespeare*, ed. Cooper, 193–5. See also S. Schoenbaum, *Shakespeare's Lives*, rev. edn (Oxford: Clarendon Press, 1991), 19–22.

9. Henry Swinburne, *A briefe treatise of testaments and last willes* (London: John Windet, 1590 (i.e. 1591)), Cc3^r–Cc4^r.

10. Schoenbaum, *Shakespeare's Lives*, 19–20.

11. Even the *Searching for Shakespeare* catalogue suggests that 'One piece of circumstantial evidence that might point towards it having been owned, but then lost, by Shakespeare, is to be found in his will . . .' *Searching for Shakespeare*, ed. Cooper, 143.

12. Samuel A. Tannenbaum, *Problems in Shakspere's Penmanship: including a study of The Poet's Will* (New York: The Century Co. for the MLA, 1927).

13. See Mr [Howard] Staunton, *Memorials of Shakespeare. Comprising the poet's will . . . letter-press copy of same and record of the will in the register book* (London, n.d.).

14. Swinburne, *Briefe treatise*, Cc3^r.

15. Mary Poovey, *History of the Modern Fact: Problems of Knowledge in the Sciences of Wealth and Society* (Chicago: University of Chicago Press, 1998); Barbara Shapiro, *A Culture of Fact: England 1550–1720* (Ithaca: Cornell University Press, 2000).

BIBLIOGRAPHY

SHAKESPEARE—STANDARD EDITIONS USED

All's Well That Ends Well, ed. G. K. Hunter (London: Methuen (Arden, 2nd ser.), 1959)

Antony and Cleopatra, ed. John Wilders (London: Routledge (Arden, 3rd ser.), 1995)

As You Like It, ed. Agnes Latham (London: Methuen (Arden, 2nd ser.), 1975)

The Comedy of Errors, ed. R. A. Foakes (London: Methuen (Arden, 2nd ser.), 1962)

Coriolanus, ed. Philip Brockbank (London: Methuen (Arden, 2nd ser.), 1976)

Cymbeline, ed. J. M. Nosworthy (London: Methuen (Arden, 2nd ser.), 1955)

Hamlet, ed. Ann Thompson and Neil Taylor (London: Thomson (Arden, 3rd ser.), 2006)

Julius Caesar, ed. David Daniell (London: Thomas Nelson (Arden, 3rd ser.), 1998)

King Henry IV Part 1, ed. David Scott Kastan (London: Thomson (Arden, 3rd ser.), 2002)

King Henry IV Part 2, ed. A. R. Humphreys (London: Methuen (Arden, 2nd ser.), 1966)

King Henry V, ed. T. W. Craik (London: Routledge (Arden, 3rd ser.), 1995)

King Henry VI Part 1, ed. Edward Burns (London: Thomson (Arden, 3rd ser.), 2000)

King Henry VI Part 2, ed. Ronald Knowles (London: Thomas Nelson (Arden, 3rd ser.), 1999)

King Henry VI Part 3, ed. John D. Cox and Eric Rasmussen (London: Thomson (Arden, 3rd ser.), 2001)

King Henry VIII (All is True), ed. Gordon McMullan (London: Thomson (Arden, 3rd ser.), 2000)

King John, ed. E. A. J. Honigmann (London: Methuen (Arden, 2nd ser.), 1954)

King Lear, ed. R. A. Foakes (London: Thomas Nelson (Arden, 3rd ser.), 1997)

King Richard II, ed. Peter Ure (London: Methuen (Arden, 2nd ser.), 1956)

King Richard III, ed. Anthony Hammond (London: Methuen (Arden, 2nd ser.), 1981)

Love's Labour's Lost, ed. H. R. Woudhuysen (London: Thomson (Arden, 3rd ser.), 1998)

Macbeth, ed. Kenneth Muir (London: Methuen (Arden, 2nd ser.), 1962)

Measure for Measure, ed. J. W. Lever (London: Methuen (Arden, 2nd ser.), 1965)

The Merchant of Venice, ed. John Russell Brown (London: Methuen (Arden, 2nd ser.), 1964)

The Merry Wives of Windsor, ed. H. J. Oliver (London: Methuen (Arden, 2nd ser.), 1971)

A Midsummer Night's Dream, ed. Harold F. Brooks (London: Methuen (Arden, 2nd ser.), 1979)

Much Ado About Nothing, ed. Claire McEachern (London: Thomson (Arden, 3rd ser.), 2006)

Othello, ed. E. A. J. Honigmann (London: Thomson (Arden, 3rd ser.), 1997)

Pericles, ed. Suzanne Gossett (London: Thomson (Arden, 3rd ser.), 2004)

The Poems, ed. F. T. Prince (London: Methuen (Arden, 2nd ser.), 1960)

Romeo and Juliet, ed. Brian Gibbons (London: Methuen (Arden, 2nd ser.), 1980)

Shakespeare's Sonnets, ed. Katherine Duncan-Jones (London: Thomas Nelson (Arden, 3rd ser.), 1997)

The Taming of the Shrew, ed. Brian Morris (London: Methuen (Arden, 2nd ser.), 1981)

The Tempest, ed. Virginia Mason Vaughan and Alden T. Vaughan (London: Thomas Nelson (Arden, 3rd ser.), 1999)

Timon of Athens, ed. H. J. Oliver (London: Methuen (Arden, 2nd ser.), 1959)

Titus Andronicus, ed. Jonathan Bate (London: Routledge (Arden, 3rd ser.), 1995)

Troilus and Cressida, ed. David Bevington (London: Thomas Nelson (Arden, 3rd ser.), 1998)

Twelfth Night, ed. J. M. Lothian and T. W. Craik (London: Methuen (Arden, 2nd ser.), 1975)

The Two Gentlemen of Verona, ed. William C. Carroll (London: Thomson (Arden, 3rd ser.), 2004)

The Two Noble Kinsmen, ed. Lois Potter (London: Thomas Nelson (Arden, 3rd ser.), 1997)

The Winter's Tale, ed. J. H. P. Pafford (London: Methuen (Arden, 2nd ser.), corrected edn, 1965)

SHAKESPEARE—OTHER EDITIONS (IN CHRONOLOGICAL ORDER)

Venus and Adonis (London: Richard Field, 1593)

Lvcrece (London: Richard Field, for Iohn Harrison, 1594)

The history of Henrie the Fourth vvith the battell at Shrewsburie, betweene the King and Lord Henry Percy (London: Andrew Wise, 1598)

The tragicall historie of Hamlet Prince of Denmarke (London: N[icholas] L[ing] and Iohn Trundell, 1603)

The tragicall historie of Hamlet, Prince of Denmarke (London: N[icholas] L[ing], 1604)

Mr. William Shakespeares comedies, histories, & tragedies Published according to the true originall copies (London: Isaac Iaggard, and Ed. Blount, 1623)

The Plays of William Shakespeare, ed. Samuel Johnson, 8 vols. (London: J. and R. Tonson *et al.*, 1765)

K. Henry IV. With the humours of Sir John Falstaff. A Tragi-Comedy, rev. Thomas Betterton (London: John Deere, 1700)

King Lear. A Tragedy . . . Collated with the old and modern editions, ed. Charles Jennens (London: W. and J. Richardson, 1770)

Bell's Edition of Shakespeare's Plays, As they are now performed at the Theatres Royal in London, ed. Francis Gentleman, 9 vols. (London: John Bell, 1773–4)

The Comedy of the Merchant of Venice, ed. Isaac-Ambrose Eccles (Dublin, 1805)

A New Variorum Edition of Shakespeare, ed. Horace Howard Furness, vol. IV, *Hamlet vol. II, appendix*, 4th edn. (London and Philadelphia: J. B. Lippincott, 1871)

The Merchant of Venice, ed. Arthur Quiller-Couch and J. Dover Wilson (Cambridge: Cambridge University Press (New Cambridge edition), 1926)

The History of King Henry the Fourth as revised by Sir Edward Dering, Bart.: A Facsimile Edition, ed. George Walton Williams and Gwynne Blakemore Evans (Charlottesville VA: University of Virginia Press for the Folger Shakespeare Library, 1974)

Hamlet, ed. Harold Jenkins (London: Methuen (Arden Shakespeare, 2nd ser.), 1982)

The Merchant of Venice, ed. M. M. Mahood (Cambridge: Cambridge University Press, 1987)

Henry IV Part 1, ed. David Bevington (Oxford: Oxford University Press, 1994)

King Lear: A Conflated Text, ed. Stephen Orgel (New York: Penguin (Pelican Shakespeare), 1999)

The History of King Lear, ed. Stanley Wells, text prepared by Gary Taylor (Oxford: Oxford University Press (The Oxford Shakespeare), 2000)

MANUSCRIPT SOURCES

National Archives, Kew

State Papers 63/250, art. 79

British Library, London

Additional MS 33271

Folger Shakespeare Library, Washington DC

V.a.340
X.d.494
Y.c.1661

Shakespeare Birthplace Trust Records Office, Stratford-upon-Avon

ER 1/97
ER 3/676
ER 27/4
BRU 12/6
BRU 15/1
BRU 15/6
BRU 15/12

Editions and Calendars of Manuscripts

ANON. 'The Conversion of Saint Paul', in Glynne Wickham, ed., *English Moral Interludes* (London: Dent, 1976), 103–26

BARLOW, WILLIAM. *Barlow's Journal of his life at sea in King's ships, East and West Indiamen & other merchantmen from 1659 to 1703* ed. Basil Lubbock, 2 vols. (London: Hurst and Blackett, 1934)

DASENT, JOHN ROCHE. ed. *Acts of the Privy Council* n.s. 29 A.D. 1598–9 (London: HMSO, 1905)

EVANS, JOHN. ed. 'XXVII. Extracts from the Private Account Book of Sir William More, of Loseley, in Surrey, in the time of Queen Mary and of Queen Elizabeth', *Archaeologia* 36 (1855), 284–310

GRABAR, VLADIMIR E. ed. *De Legatis et Legationibus Tractatus Varii* (Dorpati Livonorum: e typographeo Mattienseniano, 1905)

HALLIWELL, JAMES O. *A descriptive calendar of the ancient manuscripts and records in the possession of the Corporation of Stratford-upon-Avon* (London: James Evan Adlard, 1863)

HARGRAVE, F., ed. *A Collection of Tracts Relative to the Laws of England, from Manuscripts* vol. I (London: E. Brooke, 1787)

HISTORICAL MANUSCRIPTS COMMISSION. *Thirteenth Report, Appendix, Part VIII: The Manuscripts and Correspondence of James, first earl of Charlemont*, vol II, *1784–1799* (London: HMSO, 1894)

HOWELL, T. B. ed. *Cobbett's Complete Collection of State Trials and Proceedings for High Treason and Other Crimes and Misdemeanors*, vol. 2, *1603–1627* (London, 1809)

MASSINGER, PHILIP. *Believe as you List by Philip Massenger 1631* ed. Charles J. Sisson (Oxford: Oxford University Press Malone Society Reprints 1927) Malcone.

MERBURY, FRANCIS. *The marriage between Wit and Wisdom*, in Glynne Wickham ed., *English Moral Interudes* (London: Dent, 1976), 163–94.

NICOL, WILLIAM ed. *The Cuck-Queanes and Cuckolds Errants or The Bearing Down the Inne. A Comædye. The Faery Pastorall or Forrest of Elues. By W—— P—— Esq. From a manuscript, in the library, of Joseph Haslewood, Esq.* (London: Shakspeare Press, 1824)

SCOTT, SIBBALD DAVID ed. '"A Booke of Orders and Rules" of Anthony Viscount Montague in 1595', *Sussex Archaeological Collections, relating to the history and antiquities of the county* 7 (1854), 173–212

CLASSICAL AND EARLY MODERN SOURCES TO 1700 (INCLUDING LATER EDITIONS)

ADAMS, FRANCIS. *Writing Tables with a Kalender for xxiiii. yeeres* (London: Francis Adams, 1594)

ALLOTT, ROBERT. *Wits Theater of the little World* (London: N.L., 1599)

ANON. *Everie Woman in her Humor* (London: Thomas Archer, 1609)

—— *Here in thys boke afore ar contenyt the bokys of haukyng and huntyng* (St Albans, 1486)

—— *Robin Good-Fellow, His Mad Prankes, and merry Iests, Full of honest Mirth, and is a Medicine for Melancholy* (London: F. Groue, 1628)

—— *The Famous Victories of Henry the Fifth containing the honourable battell of Agin-court* (London: Thomas Creede, 1598)

—— *The First Part of Ieronimo. With the Warres of Portugall, and the life and death of Don Andræa* (London: Thomas Pauyer, 1605)

ANON. *The Hystorie of Hamblet* (London: Thomas Pauier, 1608)

—— *The Lamentable and Trve Tragedie of M. Arden of Feversham in Kent* (London: Edward White, 1592)

—— *The Life of Long Meg of Westminster* (London: Robert Bird, 1635)

—— *The True Chronicle Historie of King Leir, and his three daughters, Gonorill, Ragan, and Cordella* (London: John Wright, 1605)

—— *The whole volume of statutes at large* (London: Christopher Barker, 1587)

AUGUSTUS. *Res gestae divi Augusti: The achievements of the divine Augustus*, ed. P. A. Brunt and J. M. Moore (Oxford: Oxford University Press, 1967)

BACON, FRANCIS. *A declaration of the practises & treasons attempted and committed by Robert late Earle of Essex and his complices* (London: Robert Barker, 1601)

—— *Sylua syluarum: or A naturall historie In ten centuries* (London: William Lee, 1627)

—— *The Philosophy of Francis Bacon: An essay on its development from 1603 to 1609 with new translations of fundamental texts*, ed./trans. Benjamin Farrington (Chicago: University of Chicago Press/Phoenix Books, 1964)

BALES, PETER. *The writing schoolemaster* (London: Thomas Orwin, [1590])

BARCKLEY, RICHARD. *A Discovrse of the Felicitie of Man: or his Summum bonum* (London: William Ponsonby, 1598)

BEAUMONT, FRANCIS, and JOHN FLETCHER. *The Custome of the Countrey*, in *Comedies and Tragedies* (London: Humphrey Robinson and Humphrey Moseley, 1647)

(BEAUMONT, FRANCIS, and JOHN FLETCHER?). *The Knight of the Burning Pestle* (London: Walter Burre, 1613)

BELL, THOMAS. *Speculation of Usury* (London: Valentine Simmes, 1596)

BELLEFOREST, FRANCOIS DE. *Le cinqvisme livre des histories tragiques* (Lyon: Benoist Rigaud, 1576)

—— *Discovrs memorables de plvsieurs histories tragiqves* (Paris: Jean Hulpeau, 1570)

BLOUNT, THOMAS. *The Academie of Eloquence* (London: Humphrey Moseley, 1654)

BRANDON, SAMUEL. *The Tragicomoedi of the virtuous Octauia* (London: William Ponsonby, 1598)

BRATHWAIT, RICHARD. *The English Gentlewoman, drawne out to the full Body* (London: B. Alsop and T. Fawcett, 1631)

BRETON, NICHOLAS. *Conceyted letters, newly layde open* (London: Samuel Rand, 1618)

—— *New conceited letters, newly laid open* (London: John Stafford, 1662)

—— *A poste with a madde packet of letters* (London: Iohn Smethicke, 1602)

BRINSLEY, JOHN. *Lvdvs Literarivs: or, The Grammar Schoole* (London: Thomas Man, 1612)

BRISSON, BARNABÉ. *De formvlis et sollemnibvs Populi Romani verbis, Libri VIII* (Paris: Sebastian Nivell, 1583)

BROWNE, JOHN. *The marchants avizo* (London: William Norton, 1589)

—— *The Marchants Avizo (1589)*, ed. Patrick McGrath (Boston, MA: Baker Library, Harvard Graduate School of Business Administration, 1957)

BULLOUGH, GEOFFREY, ed. *Narrative and Dramatic Sources of Shakespeare*, 8 vols. (London: Routledge and Paul, 1957–75)

CHAPMAN, GEORGE. *The Conspiracie, and Tragedie of Charles Duke of Byron Marshall of France* (London: Thomas Thorpe, 1608)

CHRISTOFFELS, JAN YMPYN. *A Notable and very excellente woorke, expressyng and declaring the maner and forme how to kepe a boke of accomptes or reconynges* (London: Richard Grafton, 1547)

CICERO, MARCUS TULLIUS. *Epistolarvm M. T. Ciceronis libri tres*, ed. Johann Sturm (Prague: Georg Melantrich, 1577)

CLEMENT, FRANCIS. *The Petie Schole with an English orthographie* (London: Thomas Vautrollier, 1587)

COKE, EDWARD. *The Third Part of the Institutes Of the Laws of England* (London: W. Lee and D. Pakeman, 1644)

—— *Le quart part des reportes* (London: Companie of Stationers, 1610)

COMENIUS, JOHANN AMOS. *Opera didactica omnia* (Amsterdam: Laurentius de Geer, 1657)

—— *The Great Didactic of John Amos Comenius now for the first time englished* ed./trans. M. W. Keatinge (London: Adam and Charles Black, 1896)

CONSETT, HENRY. *The Practice of the Spiritual or Ecclesiastical Courts* (London: Will. Hensman, 1685)

CORBIN, PETER and DOUGLAS SEDGE, eds. *The Oldcastle controversy: Sir John Oldcastle, Part I and The Famous Victories of Henry V* (Manchester: Manchester University Press (The Revels Plays Companion Library), 1991)

COTTON, ROGER. *An Armor of Proofe* (London: G. Simson and W. White, 1596)

COVERDALE, MILES. *Certain most goldy, fruitful, and comfortable letters of such true Saintes and holy Martyrs of God* (London: John Day, 1564)

DANIEL, SAMUEL. *Certaine Small Workes*, rev. edn. (London: Simon Waterson, 1607)

DARELL, WALTER. *A Short discourse of the life of Seruingmen* (London: Ralph Newberry, 1578)

DAVIES, JOHN. *Wits Bedlam. Where is had, Whipping-cheer, to cure the Mad* (London: James Davies, 1617)

DAY, ANGEL. *The English Secretorie* (London: Richard Jones, 1586)

—— *The English secretary, or Methode of writing of epistles and letters* (London: C. Burbie, 1599)

DAY, RICHARD. *A booke of Christian prayers* (London: John Day, 1578)

DE BEAU CHESNE. JOHN and JOHN BAILDON, *A Booke Containing divers sortes of handes as well the English as French secretarie with the Italian, Roman, Chancelry & court hands* (London: Thomas Vautrouillier, 1571)

DE COURTIN, ANTOINE. *The rules of civility; or, Certain ways of deportment observed in France*, 3rd edn. (London: J. Martyn and John Starkey, 1675)

DEKKER, THOMAS and JOHN WEBSTER. *West-ward Hoe* (London: John Hodges, 1607)

—— *Blvrt Master-Constable. Or The Spaniards Night-walke* (London: Henry Rockyett, 1602)

—— *The Second Part of the Honest Whore* (London: Nathaniel Butter, 1630)

DONNE, JOHN. *Letters to Severall Persons of Honour* ed. John Donne (London: Richard Marriot, 1651)

—— *The Poems of John Donne*, ed. Herbert J. C. Grierson, 2 vols. (Oxford: Oxford University Press, 1912)

DRAYTON, MICHAEL, RICHARD HATHWAY, ANTONY MUNDAY, and ROBERT WILSON. *The first part Of the true and honorable historie, of the life of Sir John Old-castle, the good Lord Cobham* (London: Thomas Pauier, 1600)

EARLE, JOHN. *Micro-cosmographie or, a peece of the world discovered; in essayes and characters* (London: Robert Allot, 1628)

ELIOT, JOHN. *Ortho-Epia Gallica. Eliots Frvits for the French* (London: Iohn Wolfe, 1593)

ERASMUS, DESIDERIUS. *Adages II i 1 to II vi 100*, ed./trans. R. A. B. Mynors, *Collected Works of Erasmus 33* (Toronto: University of Toronto Press, 1991)

—— *Adagia qvaecvmqve ad hanc diem exiervnt* (Venice: Dominicus de Farris, 1591)

—— *Literary and Educational Writings 2: De copia/De ratione studii*, ed./trans. Betty I. Knott, *Collected Works of Erasmus 24* (Toronto: University of Toronto Press, 1978)

—— *Literary and Educational Writings 3: De conscribendis epistolis/Formvla/De civilitate*, ed./trans. J. W. Sowards, *Collected Works of Erasmus 25* (Toronto: University of Toronto Press, 1985)

——*Opera omnia Desiderii Erasmi Roterodami, Ordinis primi, tomus secundus* ed. Jean-Claude Margolin and Pierre Mesnard (Amsterdam: North-Holland Publishing Company, 1971)

EURIPIDES. *Euripides* vol. 2, ed./trans. David Kovacs (Cambridge MA: Harvard University Press (Loeb Classical Library), 1995)

——*Euripides* vol. 4, ed./trans. David Kovacs (Cambridge MA: Harvard University Press (Loeb Classical Library), 1999)

——*Euripides*, vol. 6, ed./trans. David Kovacs (Cambridge, MA: Harvard University Press (Loeb Classical Library, 2002)

FABRI, PIERRE. *En lhonneur/gloire/et exultation de tous amateurs de lettres et signamment de eloquence Cy ensuyt le grant et vray art de pleine Rhetorique* (Rouen: Thomas Rayer, 1521)

——*Le grand et vrai art de pleine rhétorique*, ed. A. Héron (Rouen: Espérance Cagniard, 1889–1890)

FLEMING, ABRAHAM. *A Panoplie of Epistles* (London: Ralph Newberie, 1576)

FLORIO, JOHN. *Florios Second Frvtes* (London: Thomas Woodcock, 1591)

——*Queen Anna's nevv vvorld of words, or dictionarie of the Italian and English tongues* (London: Edw. Blount and William Barret, 1611)

FORD, EMANUAL. *The most pleasant historie of Ornatus and Artesia* (London: Thomas Creede, 1599?)

FULWOOD, WILLIAM. *The Enimie of Idlenesse* (London: Leonard Maylard, 1568)

GAINSFORD, THOMAS. *The secretaries studie containing new familiar epistles* (London: Roger Jackson, 1616)

GARNIER, ROBERT. *M. Antoine, Tragedie* (Paris: Mamert Patisson, 1578)

GASCOIGNE, GEORGE. *A hundreth sundry flowres* (London: Richard Smith, 1573)

GIOVANNI, SER, FIORENTINO. *Il Pecorone* (Vinegia: Domenico Farri, 1565)

GOUGH, JOHN. *The Academy of Complements* (London, 1639)

GOULART, SIMON. 'The Life of Octaius Cæsar Augustus', in *The Lives of Epaminondas, of Philip of Macedon, of Dionysivs the Elder, and of Octavivs Cæsar Avgvstvs . . . Also the liues of nine excellent Chieftaines of warre, taken out of Latine from Emylivs Probvs*, trans. Thomas North (London: Richard Field, 1603)

GRAFTON, RICHARD. *A briefe treatise conteyning many proper Tables and easie rules* (London: John Walley, 1582)

GREENE, ROBERT. *Philomela The Lady Fitzvvaters nightingale* (London: Edward White, 1592)

GREENE, ROBERT. *The Historie of Orlando Furioso One of the twelue Pieres of France* (London: Cuthbert Burbie, 1594)

—— *The honorable historie of frier Bacon, and frier Bongay* (London: Edward White, 1594)

—— *The Scottish Historie of Iames the Fourth, slaine at Flodden* (London: Thomas Creede, 1598)

—— *Two Elizabethan Stage Abridgements: The Battle of Alcazar & Orlando Furioso*, ed. W. W. Greg (Oxford: Malone Society, 1923)

HAKLUYT, RICHARD. *The Principall Navigations, voiages, and discoveries of the English nation* (London: George Bishop and Ralph Newberie, 1589)

HALL, JOSEPH. *Characters of Vertues and Vices* (London: Eleazar Edgar and Samuel Macham, 1608)

HALLE, EDWARD. *The Vnion of the two noble and illustrate famelies of Lancastre & Yorke* (London: Richard Grafton, 1548)

HAUGHTON, WILLIAM. *English-men for my money: or, a pleasant comedy, called, A woman will haue her will* (London: W. White, 1616)

—— *William Haughton's Englishmen For My Money Or A Woman Will Have Her Will*, ed. Albert Croll Baugh (PhD dissertation, University of Pennsylvania, 1917)

HERBERT, MARY (Sidney), countess of Pembroke, *The Tragedie of Antonie. Doone into English* (London: William Ponsonby, 1595)

HEYWOOD, THOMAS. *The first and second partes of King Edward the Fourth* (London: Humfrey Lownes and Iohn Oxenbridge, 1600)

—— *The second part of, If you know not me, you know no bodie* (London: Nathaniell Butter, 1606)

HIGGINS, JOHN. *The Mirror for Magistrates* (London: Henry Marsh, 1587)

HOLIBAND, CLAUDE. *Campo di Fior or else The Flovrie Field of Fovre Langvages* (London: Thomas Vautrollier, 1583)

HOLINSHED, RAPHAEL. *et al. The Third volume of Chronicles* rev. edn (London: Henry Denham, 1587)

HOLLAND, PHILEMON. 'The Summarie' to his trans., Plutarch, 'Of Isis and Osiris', in *The Philosophie, commonlie called the Morals* (London: Arnold Hatfield, 1603)

HOMER. *Ten Bookes of Homers Iliades, translated out of French*, trans. Arthur Hall (London: Ralph Newberie, 1581)

—— *The Iliads of Homer Prince of Poets*, trans. George Chapman (London: Nathaniell Butter, [1611])

—— *The Iliad*, trans. A. T. Murray, rev. William F. Wyatt 2 vols. (Cambridge MA: Harvard University Press (Loeb Classical Library), 1999)

HOTMAN, JEAN. *The Ambassador* (London: James Shawe, 1603)

JONSON, BEN. *Seianvs his fall* (London: Thomas Thorpe, 1605)

—— *The Comicall Satyre of Every Man Ovt of His Hvmor* (London: William Holme, 1600)

KEMPE, WILLIAM. *The Education of children in learning* (London: John Potter and Thomas Gubbin, 1588)

KYD, THOMAS. *The Spanish tragedie* (London: Edward White, 1592)

LIPSIUS, JUSTUS. *Principles of Letter-writing: A Bilingual Text of Justi Lipsi Epistolica Institutio*, ed./trans. R. V. Young and M. Thomas Hester (Carbondale and Edwardsville: Southern Illinois University Press (Library of Renaissance Humanism), 1995)

LUPTON, THOMAS. *A Thousand Notable things, of sundry sortes* (London: Hughe Spooner, [1595?])

MACROPEDIUS, GEORGE. *Methodvs de conscribendis epistolis* [and others] (London: Richard Field, 1592)

MALYNES, GERARD. *Consuetudo, vel lex mercatoria, or The ancient law-merchant* (London: Adam Islip, 1622)

MARLOWE, CHRISTOPHER. *The Famous Tragedy of the Rich Iew of Malta* (London: Nicholas Vavasour, 1633)

—— *The tragicall history of D. Faustus* (London: Thomas Bushell, 1604)

MARSTON, JOHN. *Antonios Reuenge. The second part* (London: Thomas Fisher, 1602)

—— *The Malcontent* (London: William Aspley, 1604)

—— *What you Will* (London: Thomas Thorpe, 1607)

MELANCHTHON, PHILIP. *Rhetorica* (Paris: Robert Estienne, 1527)

MIDDLETON, THOMAS. *Michaelmas Terme* (London: A.I., 1607)

—— *Your fiue gallants* (London: Richard Bonlan, [1608])

MILTON, JOHN. *Poems &c. upon Severall Occasions* (London: Tho. Dring, 1673)

MONTAIGNE, MICHEL DE. *The Essayes Or Morall, Politike and Millitarie Discourses*, trans. John Florio (London: Edward Blount, 1603)

MORYSON, FYNES. *An Itinerary* (London: John Beale, 1617)

MULCASTER, RICHARD. *Positions wherin those primitive circvmstances be examined, which are necessarie for the training vp of children* (London: Thomas Chare, 1581)

NASHE, THOMAS. *Haue with you to Saffron-walden* (London: John Danter, 1596)

NORTON, THOMAS and THOMAS SACKVILE. *The Tragedie of Gorbodvc* (London: William Griffith, 1565)

OLDCASTLE, HUGH. *A briefe instruction and maner how to keepe bookes of accompts after the order of debitor and creditor*, ed. John Mellis (London: John Windet, 1588)

PACIOLI, LUCA. *Summa de arithmetica geometria proportioni et proportionalita* (Venice, 1494)

PALSGRAUE, JEHAN. *Lesclarissement de la langue Francoyse* (n.p., 1530).

PARRY, ROBERT. *Moderatus, the most delectable & famous historie of the blacke knight* (London: Richard Jones, 1595)

PEELE, JAMES. *The maner and fourme how to kepe a perfecte reconyng after the order of the moste worthie and notable accompte, of debitour and creditour* (London: Richard Grafton, 1553)

—— *The pathe waye to perfectnes, in th'accomptes of debitour, and creditour* (London: Thomas Purfoote, 1569)

PETRI, NICOLAUS. *The Pathway to Knowledge . . . of keeping a marchants booke, after the Italian manner . . . written in Dutch, and translated into English*, trans. W.P. (London: William Barley, 1596)

'PHILOMUSUS'. *The academy of complements* (London: H. Moseley, 1640)

PHIST[ON], W. *The Welspring of wittie Conceites* (London: Richard Jones, 1584).

PICCOLOMINI, ENEA SILVIO. *The m[ost] excell[ent] historie, of Euryalus and Lucresia* (London: William Barley, 1596)

PLATO. *Plato*, vol. VII, *Theaetetus; Sophist*, trans. Harold North Fowler (Cambridge, MA: Harvard University Press (Loeb Classical Library), 1977)

PLATTE, HUGH. *The Jewell House of Art and Nature* (London: Peter Short, 1594)

PLAYFERE, THOMAS. *Ten sermons* ([Cambridge]: Cantrell Legge, 1610)

PLUTARCH. *Les vies des hommes illvstres grecs et romains, compares l'vne avec l'avtre*, trans. Jacques Amyot [with additions by Charles de l'Écluse] (Paris: Pierre Cheuillot, 1579)

—— *The Lives of the Noble Grecians and Romaines, compared together . . . Hereunto are affixed the liues of Epaminados. etc.* [by Simon Goulart], trans. Thomas North (London: Thomas Wight, 1603)

—— *The lives of the noble Grecians and Romanes compared together*, trans. Thomas North (London: Thomas Vautroullier and John Wight, 1579)

ROSENMEYER, PATRICIA A., ed. *Ancient Greek Literary Letters: Selections in Translation* (London and New York: Routledge, 2006)

ROWLANDS, RICHARD. [i.e., Richard Verstegan], *The Post for diuers partes of the world* (London: Thomas East, 1576)

RYMER, THOMAS. *A Short View of Tragedy; It's [sic] Original, Excellency, and Corruption* (London: Richard Baldwin, 1693)

SACKVILLE, THOMAS and THOMAS NORTON. *The Tragedie of Gorbodvc* (London: William Griffith, 1565)

ST GERMAN, CHRISTOPHER. *The Dialoges in English, betwene a Docter of Diuinity, and a Student in the lawes of England*, rev. edn. (London: Richard Tottell, 1580)

SAXO GRAMMATICUS. *Danica historia libris XVI* (Frankfurt: Andreas Wechel, 1576)

—— *Danorum Regum...Historiæ* ed. Christiern Pedersen (Paris: Jodocus Badius Ascensius, 1514)

—— *Historiae Danicæ libri XVI*, ed. Stephanvs Iohannis Stephanivs (Copenhagen: Joachim Moltken, 1644)

—— *The History of the Danes*, Books I-IX, ed. Hilda Ellis Davidson, trans. Peter Fisher, 2 vols. (Cambridge and Towota NJ: DS Brewer/Rowman and Littlefield, 1979–80)

SCHOR, ANTONIO. *De ratione discendæ docendæqve lingvæ Latinæ & Græcæ, Libri duo.* (Strasbourg: Wendelin Rihel, 1549)

SENECA. *Seneca In Ten Volumes IV Ad Lucilium epistulae morales*, trans. Richard M. Gummere, 3 vols., vol. 1 (Cambridge, MA: Harvard University Press (Loeb Classical Library), 1979)

SKELTON, JOHN. *Magnyfycence, a goodly interlude and a mery* (n.p: J. Rastell, 1533)

SMITH, HENRY. *The Poore-Mans Teares, opened in a Sermon* (London: William Wright, 1592)

STOW, JOHN. *A Survay of London* (London: John Wolfe, 1598)

—— *The Annales of England* (London: Ralph Newbery, 1592)

—— *The Chronicles of England, from Brute vnto this present yeare of Christ. 1580* (London: Henrie Bynneman, 1580)

Suetonius vol. 1, trans. J. C. Rolfe (Cambridge, MA: Harvard University Press (Loeb Classical Library), 1998)

SUETONIUS. *The historie of twelve Caesars emperours of Rome*, trans. Philemon Holland (London: Matthew Lownes, 1606)

SWINBURNE, HENRY. *A briefe treatise of testaments and last willes* (London: John Windet, 1590 [i.e. 1591])

—— *A treatise of spousals, or matrimonial contracts* (London: Robert Clavell, 1686)

TAVERNER, RICHARD. *On Saynt Andrewes day the Gospels with brief sermo[n]s vpon them for al the holy dayes in y[e] yere.* ([London]: Rycharde Bankes, 1542)

TAYLOR, JOHN. *The Carriers Cosmographie* (London: A. G., 1637)

TILNEY, EDMUND. *A Brief and Pleasant Discourse of Duties in Mariage* (London: Henry Denham, 1568)

UDALL, NICHOLAS. *Ralph Roister Doister* (London: Henry Denham, 1566/7?)

VIVES, JUAN LUIS. *De conscribendis epistolis* [and others] (Cologne: Johannes Gymnicus, 1537)

—— *De conscribendis epistolis: Critical Edition with Introduction, Translation and Annotation*, ed./trans. Charles Fantazzi (Leiden: E. J. Brill, 1989)

—— *Lingvae Latinae exercitatio* (Basel: Robert Winter, 1541)

—— *Tudor School-Boy Life: The Dialogues of Juan Luis Vives*, trans. Foster Watson (London: J. M. Dent, 1907)

WALSHE, EDWARD. *Office and duety of fightyng for our countrey* (London: John Herwood, 1546)

WEDDINGTON, JOHN. *A Briefe Instruction, and manner, howe to kepe, merchantes bokes, of accomptes* (Antwerp: Peter van Keerberghen, 1567)

WILSON, ROBERT. *A right excellent and famous Comœdy, called the three Ladies of London* (London: Roger Warde, 1584)

WOOLEY, HANNAH. *The gentlewomans companion* (London: Edward Thomas, 1682)

SECONDARY SOURCES

ADAIR, RICHARD. *Courtship, Illegitimacy and Marriage in Early Modern England* (Manchester University Press, 1996)

ADELMAN, JANET. *The Common Liar: An Essay on Antony and Cleopatra* (New Haven: Yale University Press, 1973)

ALLEN, E. JOHN B. *Post and Courier Service in the Diplomacy of Early Modern Europe* (The Hague: Martinus Nijhoff, 1972)

ALPERS, SVETLANA. *The Art of Describing: Dutch Art in the Seventeenth Century* (Chicago: University of Chicago Press, 1983)

ALTMAN, JANET GURKIN. *Epistolarity: Approaches to a Form* (Columbus OH: Ohio State University Press, 1982)

ANDREWS, MARK EDWIN. *Law versus Equity in 'The Merchant of Venice'* (Boulder, 1965)

ANON. *Original Leters, &c. of Sir John Falstaff and his friends* (London: G. G. and J. Robinson *et al.*, 1796)

APPARDURAI, ARJUN. 'Introduction: Commodities and the Politics of Value', *The Social Life of Things: Commodities in Cultural Perspective*, ed. Arjun Appardurai (Cambridge: Cambridge University Press, 1988), 3–63

ARCHER, JOHN MICHAEL. *Old Worlds: Egypt, Southwest Asia, India, and Russia in Early Modern English Writing* (Stanford: Stanford University Press, 2001), 23–62

AYERS, P. K. 'Reading, writing, and *Hamlet*', *Shakespeare Quarterly* 44 (1993), 423–39

BAKER, J. H. 'New light on *Slade's Case*', *The Cambridge Law Journal* 29 (1971), 51–67, 213–36

—— *An Introduction to English Legal History*, 4th. edn. (London: Butterworths, 2002)

BAKER, J. H. and S. F. C. MILSON, eds. *Sources of English Legal History: Private Law to 1750* (London: Butterworths, 1986)

BALDWIN, T. W. *William Shakspere's small Latine & lesse Greeke*, 2 vols. (Urbana: University of Illinois Press, 1944)

BARFOOT, C. C. 'News from the Roman Empire: Hearsay, Soothsay, Myth and History in *Antony and Cleopatra*', in *Reclamations of Shakespeare*, ed. A. J. Hoenselaars (Amsterdam/Atlanta GA: Rodopi, 1994), 105–28

BARISH, JONAS A. ' "Soft, here follows prose": Shakespeare's Stage Documents', in *The Arts of Performance in Elizabethan and Early Stuart Drama: Essays for G. K. Hunter*, ed. Murray Biggs *et al.* (Edinburgh: Edinburgh University Press, 1991), 32–49

—— and MARSHALL WAINGROW. 'Service in *King Lear*', *Shakespeare Quarterly* 9 (1958), 347–55

BARROLL, LEEDS. *Politics, Plague, and Shakespeare's Theater: The Stuart Years* (Ithaca: Cornell University Press, 1991)

BARTON, ANNE. ' "Wrying but a little": Marriage, Law and Sexuality in the Plays of Shakespeare', in *Essays, Mainly Shakespearean* (Cambridge: Cambridge University Press, 1994), 3–30

BEAL, PETER. *In Praise of Scribes: Manuscripts and their Makers in Seventeenth-Century England* (Oxford: Clarendon Press, 1998)

BEALE, JOSEPH H., JR. 'The Carrier's Liability: Its History', *Harvard Law Review* 11 (1897–8), 158–68

BEALE, PHILIP. *A History of the Post in England from the Romans to the Stuarts* (Aldershot: Ashgate, 1998)

—— *England's Mail: Two Millennia of Letter Writing* (Stroud, Glos: Tempus, 2005)

BEARMAN, ROBERT. *Shakespeare in the Stratford Records* (Far Thrupp, Stroud: Shakespeare Birthplace Trust/Alan Sutton Publishing, 1994)

BEIER, A. L., and ROGER FINLAY. 'Introduction: The Significance of the Metropolis', in *London 1500–1700: The Making of the Metropolis* (London and New York: Longman, 1986), 1–33

BERGERON, DAVID M. *King James & Letters of Homoerotic Desire* (Iowa City: University of Iowa Press, 1999)

—— 'Deadly Letters in *King Lear*', *Philological Quarterly* 72 (1993), 157–76

BERGERON, DAVID M. ed. *Reading and Writing in Shakespeare* (Newark: University of Delaware Press and London: Associated University Presses, 1996)

BEVINGTON, DAVID. *Action is Eloquence: Shakespeare's Language of Gesture* (Cambridge: Harvard University Press, 1984)

BIDWELL, J. 'French Paper in English Books', in *The Cambridge History of the Book in Britain*, 7 vols. (Cambridge: Cambridge University Press, 2000–), 4:583–601

BLAKEMORE-EVANS, G. 'An Echo of the Ur-*Hamlet*?' *Notes and Queries* 246 (September 2001), 266

BLAND, MARK. 'Ben Jonson and the legacies of the past', *Huntington Library Quarterly* 67 (2004), 371–400

—— 'Italian Paper in Early Seventeenth-Century England', in *Paper as a Medium of Cultural Heritage. Archaeology and Conservation*, ed. Rosella Graziaplena with Mark Livesey (Roma: Istitute centrale per la patologia del libro, 2004), 243–55

BOADEN, JAMES. *A Letter to George Steevens, Esq. containing a critical examination of the papers of Shakespeare* (London: Martin and Bain, 1796)

BOLZONI, LINA. *The Gallery of Memory: Literary and Iconographic Models in the Age of the Printing Press*, trans. Jeremy Parzen (Toronto: University of Toronto Press, 2001)

BOSONNET, FELIX. *The Function of Stage Properties in Christopher Marlowe's Plays* (Bern: Francke, 1978)

BOSWELL, JAMES. *The Correspondence of James Boswell with David Garrick, Edmund Burke, and Edmond Malone*, ed. Peter S. Baker *et al.* (New Haven: Yale University Press (The Yale Boswell, Correspondence vol. 4), 1986)

BOURDIEU, PIERRE. *Distinction: A Social Critique of the Judgement of Taste*, trans. Richard Nice (1979; Cambridge: Harvard University Press, 1984)

BOWERS, FREDSON. 'Theme and Structure in *King Henry IV, Part I*', in *The Drama of the Renaissance: Essays for Leicester Bradner*, ed. Elmer B. Blistein (Providence, RI: Brown University Press, 1970), 42–68

BRADBROOK, M. C. *Shakespeare and Elizabethan Poetry: A Study of his Earlier Work in Relation to the Poetry of the Time* (London: Chatto and Windus, 1951)

BRADLEY, A. C. *Shakespearean Tragedy: Lectures on 'Hamlet', 'Othello', 'King Lear', 'Macbeth'*, 2nd edn. (London: Macmillan, 1905)

BRAE, A. E. 'Readings in Shakespeare, no. III', *Notes and Queries*, vol. 5, no. 124 (13 March 1852), 241–2

BRAUDY, LEO. *The Frenzy of Renown: Fame & its History* (New York and Oxford: Oxford University Press, 1986)

BRAUNMULLER, A. R. 'Accounting for absence: the transcription of space', in *New Ways of Looking at Old Texts: Papers of the Renaissance English Text Society, 1985–1991*, ed. W. Speed Hill (Binghamton, NY: Medieval and Renaissance Texts and Studies (vol. 107) in conjunction with Renaissance English Text Society, 1993), 47–56

BRAY, ALAN. *The Friend* (Chicago: University of Chicago Press, 2003)

BRAYSHAY, MARK, PHILIP HARRISON, and BRIAN CHALKLEY. 'Knowledge, Nationhood and Governance: The Speed of the Royal Post in Early-Modern England', *Journal of Historical Geography* 24 (1998), 265–88

BROOKS, C. W. *Pettyfoggers and Vipers of the Commonwealth: the 'Lower Branch' of the Legal Profession in Early Modern England* (Cambridge: Cambridge University Press, 1986)

BURCKHARDT, SIGURD. *Shakespearean Meanings* (Princeton: Princeton University Press, 1968)

BURNETT, MARK THORNTON. *Masters and Servants in English Renaissance Drama and Culture* (Basingstoke: Macmillan, 1997)

BURROW, COLIN. 'Life and Work in Shakespeare's Poems'. *Proceedings of the British Academy 97* (1998), 15–50

BUTLER, SHANE. *The Hand of Cicero* (London: Routledge, 2002)

CARLSON, ERIC JOSEF. *Marriage and the English Reformation* (Oxford: Blackwell, 1994)

CARRUTHERS, MARY. *The Book of Memory: A Study of Memory in Medieval Culture* (Cambridge: Cambridge University Press, 1990)

CARTWRIGHT, KENT. *Shakespearean Tragedy and Its Double: The Rhythms of Audience Response* (University Park, PA: The Pennsylvania State University Press, 1991)

CECIL, DAVID. *The Cecils of Hatfield House: An English Ruling Family* (Boston: Houghton Mifflin, 1973)

CHAMBERS, E. K. 'Elizabethan Stage Gleanings', *Review of English Studies* 1 (1925), 182–6

—— *William Shakespeare: A Study of Facts and Problems*, 2 vols. (Oxford: Clarendon Press, 1930)

CHARNES, LINDA. *Notorious Identity: Materializing the Subject in Shakespeare* (Cambridge MA: Harvard University Press, 1993)

CHARNEY, MAURICE. *Shakespeare on Love and Lust* (New York: Columbia University Press, 2000)

—— *Shakespeare's Roman Plays: The Function of Imagery in the Drama* (Cambridge MA: Harvard University Press, 1961)

CHARTIER, ROGER. *Inscription and Erasure: Literature and Written Culture from the Eleventh to the Eighteenth Century*, trans. Arthur Goldhammer (Philadelphia: University of Pennsylvania Press, 2007)

CHARTIER, ROGER et al., *Correspondence: models of letter-writing from the Middle Ages to the nineteenth century*, trans. Christopher Woodall (Princeton: Princeton University Press, 1997)

—— *La Correspondance: les usages de la lettre au XIXe siècle* (Paris: Fayard, 1991)

CHARTIER, ROGER, and PETER STALLYBRASS. 'Reading and Authorship: The Circulation of Shakespeare 1590–1619', in *A Concise Companion to Shakespeare and the Text*, ed. Andrew Murphy (Oxford: Blackwell, 2007), 35–56

CHENEY, PATRICK. ' "Deep-brained Sonnets" and "Tragic Shows": Shakespeare's Late Ovidian Art in *A Lover's Complaint,*' in *Critical Essays on Shakespeare's* A Lover's Complaint, ed. Shirley Sharon-Zisser (Aldershot, Hants and Burlington VT: Ashgate, 2006), 55–78

CLANCHY, M. T. *From Memory to Written Record: England 1066–1307*, 2nd edn (Oxford: Blackwell, 1993)

CLARK, PETER. 'Migration in the City: The Process of Social Adaptation in English Towns, 1500–1800', in *Migration and Society in Early Modern England*, ed. Peter Clark and David Souden (London: Hutchinson, 1987), 267–91

—— *The English Alehouse: A Social History 1200–1830* (London: Longman, 1983)

COHN, ALBERT ed. *Shakespeare in Germany in the Sixteenth and Seventeenth Centuries* (1865; rpt Wiesbaden: Dr. Martin Sändig oHG, 1967).

COLEMAN, D. C. *The British Paper Industry 1495–1860: A Study in Industrial Growth* (Oxford: Oxford University Press, 1958)

COLERIDGE, SAMUEL TAYLOR. *S. T. Coleridge's Treatise on Method*, ed. Alice D. Snyder (London: Constable, 1934)

COLIE, ROSALIE L. 'Antony and Cleopatra: the Significance of Style', in *Shakespeare's Living Art* (Princeton: Princeton University Press, 1974), 168–207

—— 'Reason and Need: *King Lear* and the "Crisis" of the Aristocracy', in *Some Facets of King Lear: Essays in Prismatic Criticism*, ed. Rosalie L. Colie and F. T. Flahiff (Toronto and Buffalo: University of Toronto Press, 1974), 185–219

COLLIER, J. PAYNE. 'Alleyn's Part in R. Greene's *Orlando Furioso*', appendix III of *Memoirs of Edward Alleyn* [London?]: Shakespeare Society, 1841

CONNOR, REBECCA ELISABETH. *Women, Accounting, and Narrative: Keeping Books in Eighteenth-Century England* (New York: Routledge, 2004)

CONSIDINE, JOHN. 'Goodere, Sir Henry (bap. 1571, d. 1627)', *ODNB*

COOK, ANN JENALIE. *Making a Match: Courtship in Shakespeare and his Society* (Princeton: Princeton University Press, 1991)

COOK, CAROL. 'The Fatal Cleopatra', in *Shakespearean Tragedy and Gender*, ed. Shirley Nelson Garner and Madelon Sprengnether (Bloomington: Indiana University Press, 1996), 241–67

COOK, ELIZABETH HECKERDORN. *Epistolary Bodies: Gender and Genre in the Eighteenth-Century Republic of Letters* (Stanford: Stanford University Press, 1996)

COOPER, TARNYA, ed. *Searching for Shakespeare* (London: National Portrait Gallery, 2006)

CROFTS, J. *Packhorse, Waggon and Post: Land Carriage and Communications under the Tudors and Stuarts* (London: Routledge and Kegan Paul / Toronto: University of Toronto Press, 1967)

DANBY, JOHN F. *Poets on Fortune's Hill: Studies in Sidney, Shakespeare, Beaumont and Fletcher* (London: Faber and Faber, 1952)

—— *Shakespeare's Doctrine of Nature: A Study of 'King Lear'* (London: Faber and Faber, 1951)

DAWSON, ANTHONY B. *Watching Shakespeare: A Playgoers' Guide* (Basingstoke: Macmillan, 1988)

DAYBELL, JAMES. 'Recent Studies in Seventeenth-Century Letters', *English Literary Renaissance* 36 (2006), 135–70

—— 'Recent Studies in Sixteenth-Century Letters', *English Literary Renaissance* 35 (2005), 331–62

—— *Women Letter-Writers in Tudor England* (Oxford: Oxford University Press, 2006)

—— ed. *Early Modern Women's Letter Writing, 1450–1700* (Basingstoke: Palgrave, 2001)

DE GRAZIA, MARGRETA. *'Hamlet' without Hamlet* (Cambridge: Cambridge University Press, 2007)

—— 'The Ideology of Superfluous Things: *King* Lear as Period Piece', in *Subject and Object in Renaissance Culture*, ed. de Grazia, Quilligan, and Stallybrass, 17–42

DE GRAZIA, MARGRETA, MAUREEN QUILLIGAN, and PETER STALLYBRASS, eds. *Subject and Object in Renaissance Culture* (Cambridge: Cambridge University Press, 1996)

DELANY, PAUL. '*King Lear* and the Decline of Feudalism', *PMLA* 92 (1977), 429–40

DENT, R. W. *Shakespeare's Proverbial Language: An Index* (Berkeley: University of California Press, 1981)

DERRIDA, JACQUES. *Post Card: From Socrates to Freud and beyond*, trans. Alan Bass (Chicago: University of Chicago Press, 1987)

—— *Writing and Difference*, trans. Alan Bass (Chicago, IL, 1978)

DESSEN, ALAN C. *Recovering Shakespeare's Theatrical Vocabulary* (Cambridge: Cambridge University Press, 1995)

DESSEN, ALAN C. and LESLIE THOMSON. *A Dictionary of Stage Directions in English Drama 1580–1642* (Cambridge: Cambridge University Press, 1999)

DOLLIMORE, JONATHAN. *Radical Tragedy: Religion, Ideology and Power in the Drama of Shakespeare and his Contemporaries*, 3rd edn. (Houndmills: Palgrave Macmillan, 2004)

DORANDI, TIZIANO. *Le stylet et la tablette: Dans le secret des auteurs antiques* (Paris: Les belles lettres, 2000)

DRAAISMA, DOUWE. *Metaphors of Memory: A History of Ideas about the Mind*, trans. Paul Vincent (Cambridge: Cambridge University Press, 2000)

DROGIN, MARC. *Anathema! Medieval scribes and the History of Book Curses* (Towota, NJ and Montclair, NJ: Allanheld and Schram, 1983)

DUFF, A. M. *Freedmen in the Early Roman Empire* (Oxford: Clarendon Press, 1928)

ECCLES, MARK. *Shakespeare in Warwickshire* (Madison, WI: University of Wisconsin Press, 1961)

ERNE, LUKAS. *Shakespeare as literary dramatist* (Cambridge: Cambridge University Press, 2003)

EVERARD, EDWARD CAPE. *Memoirs of an Unfortunate Son of Thespis* (Edinburgh: James Ballatyne, 1818)

FERGUSON, MARGARET W. '*Hamlet*: Letters and Spirits' in *Shakespeare and the Question of Theory*, ed. Patricia Parker and Geoffrey Hartman (New York and London: Methuen, 1985), 292–309

FINN, MARGOT C. *The Character of Credit: Personal Debt in English Culture, 1740–1914* (Cambridge: Cambridge University Press, 2003)

FISHER, WILL. *Materializing Gender in Early Modern English Literature and Culture* (Cambridge: Cambridge University Press, 2006)

FLEMING, JULIET. *Graffiti and the Writing Arts of Early Modern England* (London: Reaktion, 2001)

FRASER, RUSSELL. *Young Shakespeare* (New York: Columbia University Press, 1988)

FREEMAN, ARTHUR. 'The 'Tapster Manuscript': An Analogue of Shakespeare's *Henry the Fourth Part One*', in *English Manuscript Studies 1100–1700*, vol. 6 (London: The British Library, 1997), 93–105

FREUD, SIGMUND. 'Notiz über den "Wunderblock"' (1925), trans. James Strachey as 'A Note upon the "Mystic Writing-Pad"' (1940), in Freud, *Collected Papers*, vol. V, *Miscellaneous Papers, 1888–1938* (New York: Basic, 1959), 175–80

FRIPP, EDGAR I. *Master Richard Quyny Bailiff of Stratford-upon-Avon and Friend of William Shakespeare* (London: Humphrey Milford/Oxford University Press, 1924)

FUMERTON, PATRICIA. *Unsettled: The Culture of Mobility and the Working Poor in Early Modern England* (Chicago: University of Chicago Press, 2006)

GANTS, D. L. 'Identifying and Tracking Paper Stocks in Early Modern London', *PBSA* 94 (2000), 531–40

GERICKE, ROBERT. *Shakespeare's Hamlet-Quellen: Saxo Grammaticus (Lateinisch und Deutsch) Belleforest und The Hystorie of Hamlet* (Leipzig: Johann Ambrosius Barth, 1881)

GERLO, A. 'The *Opus de conscribendis epistolis* of Erasmus and the tradition of the *ars epistolica*', in *Classical Influences on European Culture A.D. 500–1500: Proceedings of an international conference held at King's College, Cambridge April 1969*, ed. R. R. Bolgar (Cambridge: Cambridge University Press, 1971), 103–14

GIBSON, JONATHAN. 'Significant Space in Manuscript Letters', *The Seventeenth Century* 12 (1997), 1–9

GILLIES, JOHN. *Shakespeare and the Geography of Difference* (Cambridge: Cambridge University Press, 1994)

GIRLING, F. A. *English Merchants' Marks: A Field Survey of Marks made by Merchants and Tradesmen in England between 1400 and 1700* (London: Oxford University Press, 1964)

GODSHALK, WILLIAM LEIGH. *Patterning in Shakespearean Drama: Essays in Criticism* (The Hague: Mouton, 1973)

GOLDBERG, JONATHAN. 'Colin to Hobbinol: Spenser's Familiar Letters', in *Displacing Homophobia: Gay Male Perspectives in Literature and Culture*, ed. Ronald R. Butters, John M. Clum and Michael Moon (Durham, NC: Duke University Press, 1989), 107–26

—— 'Hamlet's Hand', *Shakespeare Quarterly* 39 (1988), 307–26

GOLDBERG, JONATHAN. 'Perspectives: Dover Cliff and the Conditions of Representation', in *Shakespeare and Deconstruction*, ed. David M. Bergeron and G. Douglas Atkins (New York: Peter Lang, 1988), 245–65

—— 'Rebel Letters: Postal Effects from *Richard II* to *Henry IV*', *Renaissance Drama* n.s. 19 (1989), 3–28

—— 'Shakespeare Writing Matter Again: Objects and Their Detachments', *Shakespeare Studies* 28 (2000), 248–51

—— 'Shakespearean Characters: The Generation of Silva', in his *Voice Terminal Echo* (London: Methuen, 1986), 68–100 and 175–9

—— *Shakespeare's Hand* (Minneapolis: University of Minnesota Press, 2003)

—— *Writing Matter: From the hands of the English Renaissance* (Stanford: Stanford University Press, 1990)

GOLLANCZ, ISRAEL. *The Sources of* Hamlet: *With Essay on the Legend* (London: Humphrey Milford/Oxford University Press, 1926)

GORDON, ANDREW. 'The Act of Libel: Conscripting Civic Space in Early Modern England', *Journal of Medieval and Early Modern Studies* 32 (2002), 375–97

GOWING, LAURA. *Domestic Dangers: Women, Words, and Sex in Early Modern London* (Oxford: Clarendon Press, 1996)

GOYET, FRANCIS. 'Hamlet, étudiant du XVIe siècle', *Poétique* 113 (1998) 3–15

—— *Le Sublime du 'lieu commun': L'invention rhétorique dans l'Antiquité et à la Renaissance* (Paris: Champion, 1996)

GRAFTON, ANTHONY T. and LISA JARDINE. *From Humanism to the Humanities: Education and the Liberal Arts in Fifteenth- and Sixteenth-Century Europe* (London: Duckworth, 1986)

GREBANIER, BERNARD. *The Great Shakespeare Forgery* (New York: W.W. Norton, 1965)

GREENBLATT, STEPHEN. *Will in the World: How Shakespeare became Shakespeare* (New York: Norton, 2004)

GROSS, KENNETH. *Shylock is Shakespeare* (Chicago: University of Chicago, 2006)

GUINN, JOHN A. 'The Letter Device in the First Act of *The Two Gentlemen of Verona*', *[University of Texas] Studies in English* (1940), 72–81

HAINSWORTH, D. R. *Stewards, Lords and People: The Estate Steward and his World in later Stuart England* (Cambridge: Cambridge University Press, 1992)

HALES, JOHN W. *Notes and Essays on Shakespeare* (London: George Bell, 1884)

HALLIWELL, JAMES ORCHARD. *The Life of William Shakespeare* (London: John Russell Smith, 1848)

HALLIWELL-PHILLIPPS, J. O. *Outlines of the Life of Shakespeare* (Lonodn: Longmans, Green, and Co., 1882)

HALPERN, RICHARD. *The Poetics of Primitive Accumulation: English Renaissance Culture and the Genealogy of Capital* (Ithaca: Cornell University Press, 1991)

HANMER, THOMAS. *Some remarks on the tragedy of Hamlet, Prince of Denmark* (London: W. Wilkins, 1736)

HANSEN, WILLIAM F. *Saxo Grammaticus and the Life of Hamlet: A Translation, History and Commentary* (Lincoln: University of Nebraska Press, 1983)

HARRIS, JONATHAN GIL. ' "Narcissus in thy face": Roman Desire and the Difference it Fakes in *Antony and Cleopatra*', *Shakespeare Quarterly* 45 (1994), 408–25

HARRIS, JONATHAN GIL and NATASHA KORDA, eds. *Staged Properties in Early Modern English Drama* (Cambridge: Cambridge University Press, 2002)

HARRISON, T. P., JR. 'Shakespeare and Montemayor's *Diana*', *University of Texas Studies in English* 6 (1926), 76–8

HART, ALFRED. *Stolne and Surreptitious Copies: A Comparative Study of Shakespeare's Bad Quartos* (Melbourne and London: Melbourne University Press/Oxford University Press, 1942)

HAY, DAVID. *Packmen, Carriers and Packhorse Roads: Trade and Communications in North Derbyshire and South Yorkshire* (Leicester: Leicester University Press, 1980)

HELGERSON, RICHARD. *Forms of Nationhood: The Elizabethan Writing of England* (Chicago: University of Chicago Press, 1992)

HELMHOLZ, R. H. *Marriage Litigation in Medieval England* (Cambridge: Cambridge University Press, 1974)

HENDERSON, JUDITH RICE. 'Defining the Genre of the Letter: Juan Luis Vives', *De conscribendis epistolis*', *Renaissance and Reformation* n.s. 7 (1983), 89–105

—— 'Erasmus on the art of letter-writing', in *Renaissance Eloquence: Studies in the Theory and Practice of Renaissance Rhetoric*, ed. James J. Murphy (Berkeley: University of California Press, 1983), 331–55

—— 'On Reading the Rhetoric of the Renaissance Letter', in *Renaissance-Rhetorik/Renaissance Rhetoric*, ed. Heinrich F. Plett (Berlin: De Gruyter, 1993), 143–62

HILL, TIMOTHY D. *Ambitiosa Mors. Suicide and Self in Roman Thought and Literature* (New York: Routledge, 2004)

HILTON, JULIAN. 'Reading Letters in Plays: Short Courses in Practical Epistemology?' in *Reading Plays: Interpretation and Reception*, ed. Hanna Scolnicov and Peter Holland (Cambridge: Cambridge University Press, 1991), 140–60

HIRSH, JAMES. 'Rome and Egypt in *Antony and Cleopatra* and in Criticism of the Play', in *Antony and Cleopatra: New Critical Essays*, ed. Sara Munson Deats (New York and London: Routledge, 2005), 175–91

HOLMAN, THOMAS S. 'Holbein's Portraits of the Steelyard Merchants: An Investigation', *Metropolitan Museum Journal* 14 (1979), 139–158

HOLMES, OLIVER WENDELL, JR. *The Common Law* (Boston: Little, Brown, and Company, 1881)

HONIGMANN, E. A. J. ' "There is a World Elsewhere": William Shakespeare, Businessman', in *Images of Shakespeare: Proceedings of the Third Congress of the International Shakespeare Association, 1986*, ed. Werner Habicht, D. J. Palmer and Roger Pringle (Newark: University of Delaware Press, 1988), 40–6

—— 'Shakespeare's life', in *The Cambridge Companion to Shakespeare*, ed. Margreta de Grazia and Stanley Wells (Cambridge: Cambridge University Press, 2001), 1–12

HOPPIT, JULIAN. 'The Use and Abuse of Credit in Eighteenth-Century England', in *Business Life and Public Policy: Essays in Honour of D.C. Coleman*, ed. Neil McKendrick and R. B. Outhwaite (Cambridge: Cambridge University Press, 1986), 64–78

HORNBEAK, KATHERINE GEE. 'The Complete Letter-Writer in English, 1568–1800', *Smith College Studies in Modern Languages* 15 (1934), 1–150

HOULBROOKE, RALPH. 'The Making of Marriage in Mid-Tudor England: Evidence from the Records of Matrimonial Contract Litigation', *Journal of Family History* 10 (1985), 339–52

—— *Church Courts and the People during the English Reformation 1520–1570* (Oxford: Oxford University Press, 1979)

HOWARD, JEAN. *Theater of a City* (Philadelphia: University of Pennsylvania Press, 2007)

HUTSON, LORNA. *The Usurer's Daughter: Male Friendship and Fictions of Women in Sixteenth-Century England* (London: Routledge, 1994)

INGRAM, MARTIN. 'Spousals Litigation in the English Ecclesiastical Courts, c. 1350–1640', in *Marriage and Society: Studies in the Social History of Marriage*, ed. R. B. Outhwaite (New York: St Martin's Press, 1982), 35–57

—— *Church Courts, Sex and Marriage in England 1570–1640* (Cambridge: Cambridge University Press, 1987)

IRELAND, SAMUEL. *An Investigation of Mr. Malone's Claim to the Character of Scholar, or Critic, Being an Examination of his Inquiry into the Authenticity of the Shakspeare Manuscripts, &c.* (London: Faulder; Egerton; Payne; Whites, [1798])

——— Mr. *Ireland's Vindication of his Conduct, respecting the publication of the Supposed Shakespeare MSS.* (London: Faulder and Robson; Egerton; White, 1796)

——— untitled advertisement, dated 4 March 1795

——— ed. *Miscellaneous Papers and Legal Instruments under the hand and seal of William Shakspeare* (London: Egerton *et al.*, 1796)

IRELAND, WILLIAM HENRY. *The Confessions of William-Henry Ireland* (London: Thomas Goddard, 1805)

——— *An authentic account of the Shaksperian manuscripts, &c.* (London: J. Debrett, 1796)

JARDINE, LISA. 'Reading and the Technology of Textual Affect: Erasmus's Familiar Letters and Shakespeare's *King Lear*', in *Reading Shakespeare Historically* (London: Routledge, 1996), 78–97 and 184–9

——— *Erasmus Man of Letters: The Construction of Charisma in Print* (Princeton: Princeton University Press, 1993)

——— *Still Harping on Daughters: Women and Drama in the Age of Shakespeare* (Brighton: Harvester, 1983)

JENKINS, THOMAS E. 'At Play with Writing: Letters and Readers in Plautus', *Transactions of the American Philological Association* 135 (2005), 359–92

JOHNSON, BARBARA. 'The Frame of Reference: Poe, Lacan, Derrida', *Yale French Studies* 55/56 (1977), 457–505

JOHNSON, DAVID E. 'Addressing the Letter', in *Reading and Writing in Shakespeare*, ed. David M. Bergeron (Newark: University of Delaware Press and London: Associated University Presses, 1996), 194–219, 208–11

JONES, JOHN. *Shakespeare at Work* (Oxford: Clarendon Press, 1995)

JORDAN, WILLIAM CHESTER. 'Approaches to the Court Scene in the Bond Story: Equity or Mercy or Reason and Nature', *Shakespeare Quarterly* 33 (1982), 49–59

KAHAN, JEFFREY. *Reforging Shakespeare: The Story of a Theatrical Scandal* (Bethlehem and London: Lehigh University Press/Associated University Presses, 1998)

KAHN, COPPÉLIA. *Roman Shakespeare: Warriors, Wounds, and Women* (London: Routledge, 1997)

KASTAN, DAVID SCOTT. *Shakespeare After Theory* (New York and London: Routledge, 1999)

KATHMAN, DAVID. 'Citizens, Innholders, and Playhouse Builders, 1543–1622', *Research Opportunities in Medieval and Renaissance Drama* 44 (2005), 38–64

KEEVAK, MICHAEL. *Sexual Shakespeare: Forgery, Authorship, Portraiture* (Detroit: Wayne State University Press, 2001)

KELLIHER, HILTON. 'Contemporary Manuscript Extracts from Shakespeare's *Henry IV, Part I*', *English Manuscript Studies 1100–1700*, 1, ed. Peter Beal and Jeremy Griffiths (Oxford: Basil Blackwell, 1989), 144–71

KERRIGAN, JOHN. *Motives of Woe: Shakespeare and 'Female Complaint': A Critical Anthology* (Oxford: Clarendon Press, 1991)

KIEFER, FREDERICK. 'Love Letters in *The Two Gentlemen of Verona*', *Shakespeare Studies* 18 (1986), 65–86

—— *Writing on the Renaissance Stage: Written Words, Printed Pages, Metaphoric Books* (Newark: University of Delaware Press, 1996)

KIERNANDER, ADRIAN. '*The Two (?) Gentlemen (?) of Verona (?)*: Binarism, Patriarchy and Non-Consensual Sex Somewhere in the Vicinity of Milan', *Social Semiotics* 4 (1994), 31–46

KIRSCHENBAUM, AARON. *Sons, Slaves and Freedmen in Roman Commerce* (Jerusalem: The Magnes Press / Washington DC: The Catholic University of America Press, 1987)

KNIGHT, G. WILSON. 'The Lear Universe', in *The Wheel of Fire: Essays in Interpretation of Shakespeare's Sombre Tragedies* (London: Oxford University Press, 1930), 194–226

KNIGHT, W. NICHOLAS. 'Equity, *The Merchant of Venice*, and William Lambarde', *Shakespeare Survey* 27 (1974)

KNOWLES, RICHARD. 'Cordelia's Return', *Shakespeare Quarterly* 50 (1999), 33–50

KOPYTOFF, IGOR. 'The Cultural Biography of Things: Commoditization of Process', in *Social Life of Things: Commodities in Cultural Perspective*, ed. Arjun Appardurai (Cambridge: Cambridge University Press, 1988), 64–91

KORDA, NATASHA. *Shakespeare's Domestic Economies: Gender and Property in Early Modern England* (Philadelphia: University of Pennsylvania Press, 2002)

LACAN, JACQUES. 'Seminar on "The Purloined Letter" ', trans. Jeffrey Melhman, *Yale French Studies* 48 (1972), 39–72

LEINWAND, THEODORE B. *Theatre, Finance and Society in Early Modern England* (Cambridge: Cambridge University Press, 1999)

LONG, WILLIAM B. ' "Precious Few": English Manuscript Playbooks', in *A Companion to Shakespeare*, ed. David Scott Kastan (Oxford: Blackwell, 1999), 414–33

LOVE, HAROLD. *Scribal Publication in Seventeenth-Century England* (Oxford: Clarendon Press, 1993)

MACDONALD, RONALD R. 'Playing Till Doomsday: Interpreting *Antony and Cleopatra*', *English Literary Renaissance* 15 (1985), 78–99

MACKAY, MAXINE. '*The Merchant of Venice*: A Reflection of the Early Conflict between Courts of Law and Courts of Equity', *Shakespeare Quarterly* 15 (1964), 371–5

MACK, PETER. *Elizabethan Rhetoric: Theory and Practice* (Cambridge: Cambridge University Press, 2002)

MAGNUSSON, LYNNE. *Shakespeare and Social Dialogue: Dramatic Language and Elizabethan Letter* (Cambridge: Cambridge University Press, 1999)

MAGUIRE, LAURIE E. *Shakespearean Suspect Texts: The Bad Quartos and their Contexts* (Cambridge: Cambridge University Press, 1996)

MAIR, JOHN. *The Fourth Forger: William Ireland and the Shakespeare Papers* (London: Cobden-Sanderson, 1938)

MALONE, EDMOND. 'Mr Malones New Edition of Shakespeare', *Gentleman's Magazine* (February 1795), 120–1

——— *An Inquiry into the Authenticity of certain Miscellaneous Papers and Legal Instruments, published Dec. 24, M DCC XCV* (London: T. Cadell and W. Davies, 1796)

——— *Original Letters from Edmund Malone . . . to John Jordan, the Poet . . .* ed. J. O. Halliwell (London: Thomas Richards, 1864)

——— *The Correspondence of Edmond Malone . . . with the Rev. James Davenport . . .* ed. J. O. Halliwell (London: Thomas Richards, 1864)

MALONE, EDMOND, and JAMES BOSWELL. *The Life of William Shakespeare, by the Late Edmond Malone: and An Essay on the Phraseology and Metre of the Poet and his Contemporaries, by James Boswell* (London: privately printed, 1821)

MARCUS, LEAH S. *Unediting the Renaissance: Shakespeare, Marlowe, Milton* (London and New York: Routledge, 1996)

MARTIN, PETER. *Edmond Malone Shakespearean Scholar: A Literary Biography* (Cambridge: Cambridge University Press, 1995)

MASTEN, JEFFREY. 'Toward a Queer Address: The Taste of Letters and Early Modern Male Friendship', *GLQ: A Journal of Lesbian and Gay Studies* 10 (2004), 367–384

MATTINGLY, GARRETT. *Renaissance Diplomacy* (1955; rpt. Baltimore MD: Penguin, 1964)

McLUHAN, MARSHALL. *The Gutenberg Galaxy: The Making of Typographic Man* (London: Routledge and Kegan Paul, 1962)

MEADER, WILLIAM G. *Courtship in Shakespeare: Its Relation to the Tradition of Courtly Love* (New York: Columbia University Press, 1954)

MIKALACHKI, JODI. *The Legacy of Boadicea: Gender and Nation in Early Modern England* (London and New York: Routledge, 1998)

MILSOM, S. F. C. *Historical Foundations of the Common Law* (London: Butterworths, 1969)

MILWARD, PETER. 'Some Missing Shakespeare Letters', *Shakespeare Quarterly* 20 (1969), 84–7

MIOLA, ROBERT S. *Shakespeare's Rome* (Cambridge: Cambridge University Press, 1983)

MITCHELL, LINDA C., and SUSAN GREEN, eds. *Studies in the Cultural History of Letter Writing*, special issues of *Huntington Library Quarterly* 66: 3 and 4 (2003)

MUELLER, MARTIN. 'From Leir to Lear', *Philological Quarterly* 73 (1994), 195–218

MULDREW, CRAIG. ' "Hard Food for Midas": Cash and its Social Value in Early Modern England', *Past and Present* 170 (Feb. 2001), 78–120

—— 'Interpreting the Market: The Ethics of Credit and Community Relations in Early Modern England', *Social History* 18 (1993), 163–8

—— *The Economy of Obligation: The Culture of Credit and Social Relations in Early Modern England* (Basingstoke: Macmillan, 1998)

MURPHY, JAMES J. '*Ars dictaminis*: The Art of Letter-Writing', in *Rhetoric in the Middle Ages: a History of Rhetorical Theory from Saint Augustine to the Renaissance* (Berkeley: University of California Press, 1974), 194–268

NEELY, CAROL THOMAS. *Broken Nuptials in Shakespeare's Plays* (New Haven: Yale University Press, 1985)

O'HARA, DIANA. *Courtship and Constraint: Rethinking the Making of Marriage in Tudor England* (Manchester: Manchester University Press, 2000)

ORGEL, STEPHEN. 'Shakespeare Imagines a Theater', *Poetics Today* 5 (1984), 549–61

—— 'Knowing the Character', *Zeitschrift für Anglistik und Amerikanistik* 40 (1992), 124–9

ORLIN, LENA COWEN. 'Gertrude's Closet', *Shakespeare Jahrbuch* 134 (1998), 44–65

—— 'The Performance of Things in *The Taming of the Shrew*', *Yearbook of English Studies* 23 (1993), 167–88

—— 'Three Ways to be Invisible in the Renaissance: Sex, Reputation, and Stitchery', in *Renaissance Culture and the Everyday*, ed. Patricia Fumerton and Simon Hunt (Philadelphia: University of Pennsylvania Press, 1999), 183–203

ORRELL, JOHN. 'The London Stage in the Florentine Correspondence, 1604–1618', *Theatre Research International* 3 (1977–78), 157–76

OUTHWAITE, R. B. *Clandestine Marriage in England, 1500–1850* (London and Rio Grande: Hambledon Press, 1995)

Oxford Dictionary of National Biography (Oxford: Oxford University Press, 2004)

Oxford English Dictionary 2nd edn (Oxford: Clarendon Press, 1989)

PALFREY, SIMON. *Doing Shakespeare* (London: Thomson Learning (Arden Shakespeare), 2005)

PARTRIDGE, ERIC. *Shakespeare's Bawdy*, 3rd edn. (1968; London and New York: Routledge, 2001)

PERCY, THOMAS. *The Correspondence of Thomas Percy & Edmond Malone*, ed. Arthur Tillotson (Baton Rouge: Louisiana State University Press, 1944) (vol. 1 of *The Percy Letters*, general editors David Nichol Smith and Cleanth Brooks)

PERELMAN, LES. 'The medieval art of letter writing: rhetoric as institutional expression', in *Textual Dynamics of the Professions*, ed. Charles Bazerman and James Paradis (Madison: University of Wisconsin Press, 1991), 97–119

PIERCE, PATRICIA. *The Great Shakespeare Fraud: The Strange True Story of William-Henry Ireland* (Thrupp, Glos.: Sutton, 2004)

POOVEY, MARY. *A History of the Modern Fact: Problems of Knowledge in the Sciences of Wealth and Society* (Chicago: University of Chicago Press, 1998)

RACKIN, PHYLLIS. 'Shakespeare's Boy Cleopatra, the Decorum of Nature, and the Golden World of Poetry', *PMLA* 87 (1972), 201–12

—— 'Temporality, Anachronism, and Presence in Shakespeare's English Histories', *Renaissance Drama* n.s. 17 (1986), 103–23

—— *Stages of History: Shakespeare's English Chronicles* (Ithaca: Cornell University Press, 1990)

RAMBUSS, RICHARD. *Spenser's Secret Career* (Cambridge: Cambridge University Press, 1993)

RANALD, MARGARET LOFTUS. ' "As marriage binds and blood breaks": English Marriage and Shakespeare', *Shakespeare Quarterly* 30 (1979), 68–81

—— *Shakespeare and his Social Context: Essays in Osmotic Knowledge and Literary Interpretation* (New York: AMS Press, 1987)

ROBERTS, COLIN H. and T. C. SKEAT. *The Birth of the Codex* (London: Oxford University Press for the British Academy, 1983)

ROBERTSON, JEAN. *The Art of Letter Writing: An Essay on the Handbooks Published in England During the Sixteenth and Seventeenth Centuries* (Liverpool: Liverpool University Press and London: Hodder and Stoughton, 1942)

ROBINSON, HOWARD. *The British Post Office: A History* (Princeton: Princeton University Press, 1948)

RONAN, CLIFFORD. *'Antike Roman': Power Symbology and the Roman Play in Early Modern England, 1585–1635* (Athens, GA: University of Georgia Press, 1995)

ROSENBERG, MARVIN. *The Masks of King Lear* (Berkeley: University of California Press, 1972)

ROSENMEYER, PATRICIA A. *Ancient Epistolary Fictions: The Letter in Greek Literature* (Cambridge: Cambridge University Press, 2001)

ROWE, KATHERINE. ' "Remember me": Technologies of Memory in Michael Almereyda's *Hamlet*', in *Shakespeare, The Movie, II: Popularizing the Plays on Film, TV, Video, and DVD*, ed. Richard Burt and Lynda E. Boose (New York and London: Routledge, 2003), 37–55

RUMMEL, ERIKA. 'Erasmus' manual of letter-writing: tradition and innovation', *Renaissance and Reformation*, n.s. 13 (1989), 299–312

SACKS, DAVID HARRIS. *Trade, Society and Politics in Bristol 1500–1640*, 2 vols. (New York: Garland Publishing, 1985)

SANDERS, EVE RACHELE. 'Interiority and the Letter in *Cymbeline*', *Critical Survey* 12 (2000), 49–70

SCAFURO, A. 'The Rigmarole of the Parasite's Contract for a Prostitute in *Asinaria*: Legal Documents in Plautus and his Predecessors', *Leeds International Classical Studies* 3, 4 (2004), 1–21

SCHNEIDER, GARY. *The Culture of Epistolarity: Vernacular Letters and Letter Writing in Early Modern England, 1500–1700* (Newark: University of Delaware Press, 2005)

SCHOENBAUM, S. *Shakespeare's Lives* (Oxford: Clarendon Press, 1970)

—— *Shakespeare's Lives*, 2nd edn (Oxford: Clarendon Press, 1991)

SCHWARZ, HENRY. ' "He is no unlettered man": *King Lear*, "The Courier's Tragedy", and the historical agency of postage', *Shakespeare Jahrbuch* 127 (1991), 63–76

SHAPIRO, BARBARA. *A Culture of Fact: England 1550–1720* (Ithaca: Cornell University Press, 2000)

SHAPIRO, JAMES. *1599: A Year in the Life of William Shakespeare* (London: Faber, 2005)

SHARPE, REGINALD R. *London and the Kingdom: A History*, 3 vols. (London: Longmans, Green, 1894)

SHRANK, CATHY. ' "These fewe scribbled rules": Representing Scribal Intimacy in Early Modern Print', *Huntington Library Quarterly* 67 (2004), 295–314

SIEGERT, BERNARD. *Relays: Literature as an Epoch of the Postal System*, trans. Kevin Repp (Stanford: Stanford University Press, 1999)

SIMONIN, MICHEL. *Vivre de sa plume au XVIe siècle ou la carrière de François de Belleforest* (Geneva: Droz, 1992)

SIMPSON, A. W. B. 'The Penal Bond with Conditional Defeasance', *Law Quarterly Review* 82 (1966), 392–422

SINGH, JYOTSNA. 'Renaissance Antitheatricality, Antifeminism, and Shakespeare's *Antony and Cleopatra*', *Renaissance Drama* n.s. 20 (1990), 99–121

SKILLITER, S. A. *William Harborne and the Trade with Turkey 1578–1582: A Documentary Study of the First Anglo-Ottoman Relations* (London: Oxford University Press for the British Academy, 1977)

SLATER, ANN PASTERNAK. *Shakespeare the Director* (Brighton: Harvester Press, 1982)

SMALL, JOCELYN PENNY. *Wax Tablets of the Mind: Cognitive Studies of Memory and Literacy in Classical Antiquity* (London: Routledge, 1997)

SMITH, PETER J. 'Re(-)fusing the Sign: Linguistic Ambiguity and the Subversion of Patriarchy in *Romeo and Juliet* and *The Two Gentlemen of Verona*', in *Social Shakespeare: Aspects of Renaissance dramaturgy and contemporary society* (1995), 120–45

SOFER, ANDREW. *The Stage Life of Props* (Ann Arbor: University of Michigan Press, 2003)

SOKOL, B. J., and MARY SOKOL. *Shakespeare, Law, and Marriage* (Cambridge: Cambridge University Press, 2003)

SPENCER, BENJAMIN. '*Antony and Cleopatra* and the Paradoxical Metaphor', *Shakespeare Quarterly* 9 (1958), 373–8

SPERBER, HANS. 'The Conundrums in Saxo's Hamlet episode', *PMLA* 64 (1949), 864–70

SPINOSA, CHARLES. 'The Transformation of Intentionality: Debt and Contract in *The Merchant of Venice*', *ELR* 24 (1994), 370–409

STALLYBRASS, PETER. 'Patriarchal Territories: The Body Enclosed', in *Rewriting the Renaissance: The Discourses of Sexual Difference in Early Modern Europe*, ed. Margaret W. Ferguson, Maureen Quilligan, and Nancy J. Vickers (Chicago: University of Chicago Press, 1986), 123–42

—— ed. 'Symposium: Material Culture', special issue of *Shakespeare Studies* 28 (2000), 123–261

—— ROGER CHARTIER, FRANKLIN MOWERY JR, and HEATHER WOLFE. 'Hamlet's Tables and the Technologies of Writing in Renaissance England', *Shakespeare Quarterly* 55 (2004), 379–419

STAUNTON, [HOWARD]. *Memorials of Shakespeare. Comprising the poet's will … letter-press copy of same and record of the will in the register book* (London, n.d)

STEEN, SARA JAYNE. 'Reading Beyond the Words: Material Letters and the Process of Interpretation', *Quidditas*, 22 (2001), 55–69

STERN, TIFFANY. 'Letters, Verses and Double Speech-Prefixes in *The Merchant of Venice*', *Notes and Queries* 46 (June 1999), 231–3

—— *Making Shakespeare: From Stage to Page* (London and New York: Routledge, 2004)

STEWART, ALAN. 'Boswell, Sir William (d. 1650)', *ODNB*

—— 'Gelding Gascoigne', in *Prose Fiction and Early Modern Sexualities, 1570–1640*, ed. Constance C. Relihan and Goran V. Stanivukovic (New York and Houndmills: Palgrave Macmillan, 2003), 147–69

—— 'The Body Archival: Re-Reading the Trial of the Earl of Somerset', in *The Body in Late Medieval and Early Modern Culture*, ed. Darryll Grantley and Nina Taunton (Aldershot: Ashgate, 2000), 65–82

—— 'The Early Modern Closet Discovered', *Representations* 50 (1995), 76–100

—— *Close Readers: Humanism and Sodomy in Early Modern England* (Princeton: Princeton University Press, 1997)

—— and HEATHER WOLFE, eds. *Letterwriting in Renaissance England* (Washington DC: Folger Shakespeare Library, 2004)

STRIER, RICHARD. *Resistant Structures: Particularity, Radicalism, and Renaissance Texts* (Berkeley: University of California Press, 1995)

SUGDEN, EDWARD H. *A Topographical Dictionary to the Works of Shakespeare and his Fellow Dramatists* (Manchester: Manchester University Press, 1925)

SULLIVAN, CERI. *The Rhetoric of Credit: Merchants in Early Modern Writing* (Madison NJ, Cranbury NJ and London: Fairleigh Dickinson University Press/Associated University Presses, 2002)

SULLIVAN, ERNEST W. II, 'The problem of text in familiar letters', *Papers of the Bibliographical Society of America* 75 (1981), 115–26, at 122–3

SULLIVAN, GARRETT. *Memory and Forgetting in English Renaissance Drama: Shakespeare, Marlowe, Webster* (Cambridge: Cambridge University Press, 2005)

SUTTON, PETER C., LISA VERGARA, ANN JENSEN ADAMS, with JENNIFER KILIAN and MARJORIE E. WIESEMAN. *Love Letters: Dutch Genre Paintings in the Age of Vermeer* (London: Frances Lincoln/Bruce Museum of Arts and Science/National Gallery of Ireland, 2003)

SVENDSEN, JAMES T. 'The Letter Device in Euripides and Shakespeare', in *Legacy of Thespis: Drama Past and Present, Volume IV: The University of Florida Department of Classics Comparative Drama Conference Papers* (Lanham, New York and London: University Press of America, 1984), 75–88

SYME, RONALD. *The Roman Revolution* (Oxford: Clarendon Press, 1939)

TAKEOKA, YUKIKO. 'The "Letter" as a Device of Discommunication in *Twelfth Night*', *Shakespeare Studies* 34 (1996), 49–71

TANNENBAUM, SAMUEL A. *Problems in Shakspere's Penmanship: Including a Study of The Poet's Will* (New York: The Century Co. for the MLA, 1927).

TEAGUE, FRANCES. 'Letters and Portents in *Julius Caesar* and *King Lear*', *Shakespeare Yearbook* 3 (1992), 97–104

—— *Shakespeare's Speaking Properties* (Lewisburg PA: Bucknell University Press, 1991)

THATCHER, DAVID. 'Shakespeare's *All's Well*: The Case of Bertram's Letter', *Cahiers Elisabéthains* 53 (1998), 77–80

THISLETON-DYER, T. F. *Old English Social Life as told by the Parish Registers* (London: Elliot Stock, 1898)

THOMPSON, EDWARD MAUND. 'Handwriting', in *Shakespeare's England: An Account of his Life & Manners of his Age*, ed. Sidney Lee, 2 vols. (Oxford: Clarendon Press, 1916), 1:284–310

THOMSON, PETER. 'Kemble, John Philip (1757–1823)', *ODNB*

—— 'Tarlton, Richard (*d*. 1588)', *ODNB*

THORNE, SAMUEL E. 'Tudor Social Transformation and Legal Change', *New York University Law Review* 26 (1951), 10–23

TREGGIARI, SUSAN. *Roman Freedmen during the Late Republic* (1969; rpt Oxford: Clarendon Press, 2000)

TUCKER, E. F. J. 'The Letter of the Law in *The Merchant of Venice*', *Shakespeare Survey* 29 (1976), 93–101

TURNER, JOHN. 'The Tragic Romances of Feudalism', in Graham Holderness, Nick Potter, and John Turner, *Shakespeare: The Play of History* (Basingstoke: Macmillan, 1988), 83–154

VALENZE, DEBORAH. *The Social Life of Money in the English Past* (Cambridge: Cambridge University Press, 2006)

VAN DAM, B. A. P. 'Alleyn's player's part of Greene's *Orlando Furioso*, and the text of the Q of 1594', *English Studies* 11 (1929), 182–203 and 209–20

VAN HOOFF, ANTON J. L. *From Autothanasia to Suicide: Self-Killing in Classical Antiquity* (London: Routledge, 1990)

VAN HOUDT, TOON, GILBERT TOURNOY, and CONSTANT MATHEEUSSEN, eds. *Self-Presentation and Social Identification: The Rhetoric and Pragmatics of Letter Writing in Early Modern Times* (Leuven: Leuven University Press (*Supplementa Humanistica Louvaniensa* 18) (2002))

VICKERS, BRIAN. *Shakespeare, A Lover's Complaint, and John Davies of Hereford* (Cambridge: Cambridge University Press, 2007)

WALKER, SUE. 'Letter-Writing', in *Typography and Language in Everyday Life: Prescriptions and Practices* (Harlow: Longman, 2001), 126–70

—— 'The Manners on the Page: Prescription and Practice in the Visual Organisation of Correspondence', *Huntington Library Quarterly*, 66 (2003), 307–29

WATT, IAN. *Rise of the Novel: Studies in Defoe, Richardson and Fielding* (Berkeley: University of California Press, 1957)

WEISS, RENÉ. *Shakespeare Revealed: A Biography* (London: John Murray, 2007)

WEINREB, BEN and CHRISTOPHER HIBBERT, eds. *The London Encyclopædia* (London: Macmillan, 1983)

WENTERSDORF, KARL. 'The Marriage Contracts in *Measure for Measure*: A Reconsideration', *Shakespeare Survey* 32 (1979), 129–44

W[HELER], R. B. letter in *The Gentleman's Magazine*, 80 (January–June 1810), 221–2

—— letter in *The Gentleman's Magazine* 80 (July–December 1810), 322–3

—— *Guide to Stratford-upon-Avon* (Stratford-upon-Avon: J. Ward, 1814)

WHIGHAM, FRANK. 'The Rhetoric of Elizabethan Suitors' Letters,' *PMLA* 96 (1981), 864–92

WHYMAN, SUSAN E. *Sociability and Power in Late-Stuart England: The Cultural Worlds of the Verneys 1660–1720* (Oxford: Oxford University Press, 1999)

WILES, DAVID. *Shakespeare's Clown: Actor and Text in the Elizabethan Playhouse* (Cambridge: Cambridge University Press, 1987)

WOOLFSON, JONATHAN. *Padua and the Tudors: English Students in Italy, 1485–1603* (Toronto: University of Toronto Press, 1998)

WORTHEN, W. B. 'The Weight of Antony: Staging "Character" in *Antony and Cleopatra*', *Studies in English Literature 1500–1900* 26 (1986), 295–308

WOUDHUYSEN, H. R. 'Writing-Tables and Table Books', *eBLJ (electronic British Library Journal)* (2004), article 3

YAMEY, B. S., H. C. EDEY, and HUGH W. THOMSON. *Accounting in England and Scotland: 1543–1800: Double Entry in Exposition and Practice* (London: Sweet and Maxwell, 1963)

YATES, FRANCES A. *The Art of Memory* (London: Routledge and Kegan Paul, 1966)

ZIEGLER, GEORGIANNA. 'My Lady's Chamber: Female Space, Female Chastity in Shakespeare', *Textual Practice* 4 (1990), 73–100

INDEX